DUAL LANGUAGE INSTRUCTION

A Handbook
for
Enriched Education

DUAL LANGUAGE INSTRUCTION

A Handbook
for
Enriched Education

NANCY CLOUD

FRED GENESEE

ELSE HAMAYAN

HEINLE & HEINLE

THOMSON LEARNING

United States • Australia • Canada • Mexico • Singapore • Spain • United Kingdom

Vice President, Editorial Director ESL/EFL: Nancy Leonhardt
Acquisition Editor: Erik Bredenberg
Director, Global ESL Training and Development: Evelyn Nelson
Developmental Editor: Thomas Healy
Production Editor: Michael Burggren
Senior Marketing Manager: Charlotte Sturdy
Manufacturing Coordinator: Mary Beth Hennebury
Composition: PageMasters & Company
Text Design: PageMasters & Company
Cover Design: Linda Dana Willis

For permission to use material from this text, contact us:
    web   www.thomsonrights.com
    fax   1-800-730-2215
    phone 1-800-730-2214

Heinle & Heinle Publishers
20 Park Plaza
Boston, MA 02116

UK/EUROPE/MIDDLE EAST:
Thomson Learning
Berkshire House
168-173 High Holborn
London, WC1V 7AA, United Kingdom

AUSTRALIA/NEW ZEALAND:
Nelson/Thomson Learning
102 Dodds Street
South Melbourne
Victoria 3205 Australia

CANADA:
Nelson/Thomson Learning
1120 Birchmount Road
Scarborough, Ontario
Canada M1K 5G4

LATIN AMERICA:
Thomson Learning
Seneca, 53
Colonia Polanco
11560 México D.F. México

ASIA (excluding Japan):
Thomson Learning
60 Albert Street #15-01
Albert Complex
Singapore 189969

JAPAN:
Thomson Learning
Palaceside Building, 5F
1-1-1 Hitotsubashi, Chiyoda-ku
Tokyo 100 0003, Japan

SPAIN:
Thomson Learning
Calle Magallanes, 25
28015-Madrid
Espana

ISBN: 0-8384-8801-3

This book is printed on acid-free recycled paper.

Printed in the United States of America
3 4 5 6 7 8 9 04 03 02 01 00

*To all the students and parents who value
bilingualism and cultural diversity
and to those teachers who enrich
our children's lives
in dual language programs.*

Table of Contents

Expanded Table of Contents

Part I: Foundations
Chapter One
Introduction
This chapter explains the purpose of the handbook, defining characteristics of Enriched Education (EE) Programs, and the educational, cognitive, socio-cultural, and economic benefits of knowing two or more languages. It also introduces three models of Enriched Education in two languages: 1) second/foreign language immersion programs, 2) developmental bilingual education programs, and 3) two-way immersion programs.

Chapter Two
Critical Features of Enriched Education
Chapter two presents nine critical features of effective Enriched Education Programs. The critical features include programmatic, administrative, and instructional characteristics common to all enriched programs. Subsequent chapters use these features to discuss, in practical terms, the design and implementation of effective programs as it relates to particular program components.

Chapter Three
Program Development and Implementation
Organized around frequently asked questions of teachers, administrators, and parents, this chapter describes how Enriched Education programs are developed and maintained. It identifies and discusses seven areas to take into account when starting up a program, from gaining support for the program to staffing and student selection. It then dicusses important areas related to program maintenance, including the role of parents, staff development and teacher competence, time allocation by language, program coordination and material selection.

Part II: The Instructional Process
Chapter Four
Oral Language Development
Chapter four describes the characteristics of successful language learners, expectations that have been set for oral language development, and the interdependency between first and second language development. Organized around common instructional questions, it describes ways of developing oral language proficiency in four learning contexts: 1) the native language arts class, 2) the second language class, 3) content area classes, and 4) social interactions with peers and adults.

Chapter Five
Teaching Literacy in Two Languages
Chapter five considers the foundations of dual literacy development, including how to introduce literacy in two languages and how to plan for transfer of skills among the two languages. It presents a framework for teaching which includes the selection of materials, development of vocabulary and background knowledge, and the teaching of skills and strategies. The chapter suggests a range of teaching strategies for learners of different stages of development and background characteristics.

Chapter Six
Teaching Content
Chapter six outlines the goals of integrated language and content instruction, as well as how to plan for integrated instruction and select or modify curriculum materials. A step-by-step planning guide to integrated language and content instruction follows which presents specific teaching strategies, organized around phase of instruction (preview, focused learning, extension). A final section lists teaching ideas and grouping arrangements for beginning, intermediate and advanced learners as well as those with special learning characteristics.

Chapter Seven
Assessment
Chapter seven describes practical ways to design assessment to guide instruction and improve learning. It discusses major goals of assessment (accountability, monitoring progress, understanding student needs, and helping students accept responsibility for their own learning). The chapter lists seven characteristics of effective assessment as well as the distinctive features of assessment in EE programs. It suggests methods of assessment, in many cases with illustrative samples provided. The chapter also places special emphasis on student and parent participation in the assessment process.

Part III: Applications and Resources
Chapter Eight
Model Lessons and Assessment Procedures
This chapter provides sample second language lessons. The first lesson is an early grade literature-based, thematic unit for second language learners of Spanish. The lesson specifies the content, language, general skills and cross-cultural objectives, describes grouping arrangements to be used, and

presents teaching activities by phase of instruction. Recommended curriculum materials and assessment strategies are also detailed and the adaptations that would be needed if delivered in a dual language or developmental bilingual education program are provided. The second lesson is a middle school ESL content-based unit on the theme of forces of nature (weather). The detailed plan lists the essential concepts, vocabulary and skills and strategies to be taught along with the teaching activities and resources to be used in delivering the lesson. A five-step lesson cycle is followed, including an experiential phase, conceptual preview phase, focused learning phase, transfer and expansion phase and learner action phase. A companion literature unit is attached.

Chapter Nine
Advocacy

Chapter nine explains the purpose of advocacy in relation to the development and delivery of EE programs. It defines and discusses the concept in relation to the different audiences toward whom advocacy efforts can be directed, from students and parents to administrators and policy makers. Helpful suggestions and resources are included in each section.

Appendices:

Reference and Resource Materials

Foreword

It is a privilege to write the Foreword to this unique volume. Nancy Cloud, Fred Genesee, and Else Hamayan have brought together in a lucid and stimulating manner the essence of what is known about promoting bilingual proficiency through school programs. I have been immersed in the area of bilingualism and second language learning for more than 25 years and yet I learned an enormous amount from this book. It is rare to find a book that balances equally the knowledge gained from academic research and theory with the insights that educators generate from their teaching practice. The perspectives of teachers, students, parents, and administrators are woven throughout the chapters in such a way that the reader gains a sense of both the complexities and excitement of implementing innovative Enriched Education programs.

As the authors emphasize throughout the volume, Enriched Education programs have been pioneering from both sociopolitical and pedagogical perspectives. At a sociopolitical level, these programs are unapologetic about the validity and educational importance of promoting additive forms of bilingualism. The authors have done the field a major service by grouping second language immersion programs for language majority students, developmental bilingual programs for language minority students, and two-way bilingual immersion programs for both groups, under the inclusive label of *Enriched Education* (EE). In doing so, they clearly articulate that bilingualism and biliteracy are feasible goals for *all* students and each of these three programs have extremely strong empirical evidence of success in attaining these goals. With just these two words (*Enriched Education*), they communicate that the dividing line between successful and non-successful programs is not whether a program is called "bilingual" or "English-only," but rather whether the program adopts instructional approaches that will result in strong bilingual and biliteracy development among its students. Programs that take effective steps to ensure that students develop full bilingualism and biliteracy succeed; by contrast, programs that adopt a remedial approach and encourage bilingual students to forget their home languages are much less likely to produce strong academic results in English, despite the often exclusive emphasis on that language in the program.

For educators planning to implement Enriched Education programs, or those already in the process of doing so, this volume represents a "one-stop" source of information, insight, and ideas for innovation. The authors explicitly address virtually all the practical questions that

teachers have asked regarding the most effective ways of stimulating oral language development in the second language, teaching literacy and academic content in two languages, and appropriate ways of assessing dual language development. For example, they point out that in order to promote language learning, the teacher must attempt to increase both the amount of oral language use by students in the classroom and also the likelihood of students conversing with each other through the second language. Rather than providing only vague suggestions, the volume explains explicitly how to maximize the oral language development potential of an activity.

Similarly, explicit guidelines are provided for modifying instructional materials to make them appropriate for second language learners. Content area teaching strategies are grouped according to three phases: 1) Preview, 2) Focused Learning and 3) Extension. For teachers in dual language programs attempting to cover a curriculum developed for a monolingual program and with only native speakers of English in mind, the strategies which the authors articulate for teaching content according to these three phases are invaluable.

In discussing literacy, the authors note that many two-way programs have chosen to introduce reading to students in their home language although the research indicates that under certain conditions, reading can be taught successfully through a second language or simultaneously through both languages. They recommend teaching literacy in the two languages in a sequential rather than simultaneous manner so that teachers can insure that their students have a firm foundation in reading/writing one language before beginning formal literacy instruction in the other. They point out that sociopolitical rather than linguistic or cognitive considerations are primary in the choice of which language to begin reading instruction. I would concur with the authors that social rather than cognitive or linguistic considerations should be primary in this decision-making process (i.e. strong initial emphasis should be placed on the language that has less status in the wider society).

A wealth of information and useful suggestions are provided regarding involving parents in the literacy development process, selecting linguistically and culturally appropriate literacy materials, and teaching students at different levels of literacy (e.g. preliterate, emergent literate, late emergent, and intermediate literate students). The authors also address the strategies most likely to be effective in teaching students with limited formal schooling or special education needs.

In an era when policy-makers and the general public are demanding greater accountability, and imposing increased standardized testing in order to insure this, the authors highlight that a major goal of assessment is to engage students in the assessment process through *self-assessment* so that they can take active responsibility for their own learning. They point out the distinctive features of assessment in EE classes as compared to more conventional settings and highlight a variety of authentic assessment strategies that have proved useful in EE classrooms. They also note that the beneficial outcomes of EE programs are cumulative and, therefore, grade-appropriate levels of English proficiency may not be achieved until students have participated in the program for 5 or 6 years. The interpretation of standardized assessment measures must take this into account in order to judge the program's effectiveness appropriately.

Although this is an extremely comprehensive volume, the authors do not pretend to provide all the answers, recognizing that each context of implementation is unique in important respects. They are clear in what they recommend based on their experience and observations; however, they also acknowledge that alternative approaches have also been successful under some circumstances. For example, they suggest that the more intensive forms of program (90/10 minority/majority language in the early grades) is more effective than less intensive forms (50/50 minority/majority language) in developing strong bilingual skills; however, they acknowledge that many 50/50 programs have also been successful (e.g. the Oyster Bilingual School in Washington D.C. (Freeman, 1998)) and a variety of considerations (e.g. parental concerns, teacher availability) must be taken into account in program planning.

One of the well-established findings in the research literature on bilingualism is the greater metalinguistic awareness that bilingual children tend to develop as a result of their access to two languages and continued development of literacy in both languages throughout elementary school. In their evaluation of the original French immersion program in Canadian public schools, Wallace Lambert and Richard Tucker (1972) spoke of an "incipient contrastive linguistics" that students engaged in as they compared and contrasted their two languages. I believe that teachers in Enriched Education programs could do more to foster this awareness of language. Students could be encouraged to become "linguistic detectives" inquiring into cross-lingual relationships (e.g. cognates), language structures, lexicon and community use.

In conclusion, I very much welcome this book as an important contribution both to the societal debate on bilingual education and to the implementation of truly effective dual language programs. The book demonstrates clearly that there is no educational reason why every child should not be given the opportunity to graduate from high school fluent and literate in two or more languages.

Jim Cummins
University of Toronto

References

Freeman, R. D. (1998). *Bilingual education and social change. Clevedon, England: Multilingual Matters.*

Lambert, W. E., & Tucker, G. R. (1972). *Bilingual education of children: The St. Lambert Experiment. Rowley, MA: Newbury House.*

Part I
Foundations

1 INTRODUCTION

This book is for K–12 teachers, other educational professionals, and policy makers in the U.S., Canada, and other countries who are teaching students in two (or more) languages. We focus specifically on: foreign/second language immersion programs for language majority students, two-way immersion programs, and developmental bilingual programs (see Glossary). We refer to these programs collectively as enriched education programs (see Glossary), or EE for short, because they promote bilingualism (see Glossary) and biculturalism (see Glossary) along with the other objectives of a regular school program. These programs share the same challenging academic and language development standards as basic K–12 education. At the same time, they aim for advanced levels of functional proficiency in two languages (the students' primary language (see Glossary) and another language). They also promote understanding of and appreciation for the cultures of the languages they are studying. They achieve these additional goals by using the majority language along with another language as media of academic instruction for significant portions of the school day during the elementary school years. We describe these programs in more detail later in this chapter. We focus on education in the U.S. and Canada because we are most familiar with education in these countries. Thus, English is the majority language of the communities that we shall be talking about.

More about Enriched Education

Language is a central theme of this book. Indeed, language is a critical component of all sound education. A focus on language is critical because language plays a dual role in education. It is both a prerequisite to successful education, and it is an important outcome of successful education. Because language is the primary medium through which education is delivered, students must acquire the language skills they need to do academic work. We all know of individual students who struggle in school because they have not had the opportunity to develop the kinds of language skills that schooling calls for. It is our job to teach them those skills so that they can get on with their other school work. At the same time, a primary objective of education is to teach students language and literacy skills that will permit them to function effectively in their personal and professional lives. Our primary focus here is literacy development—as educators, we have responsibility to teach students the reading and writing skills they need to go on to do advanced studies, to get good jobs, or to read and write for personal pleasure. These are skills students will probably not acquire without our assistance.

Schooling plays a critical role in language development because it promotes the development of language skills that go beyond what students normally learn in their day-to-day lives. Schooling sets high standards with respect to language learning and, thus, advances students' levels of language proficiency (see Glossary) beyond what they normally need in their day-to-day lives. Every teacher understands that one of their responsibilities is to expand their students' language skills. Schooling teaches students new kinds of language skills—language for presenting oral reports, language for explaining procedures in a coherent and sensible manner, language for critical analysis of other's explanations and reports. These are language skills that students need if they are to be successful in the world of work and to be responsible and involved in a democratic society.

We believe that strong language skills are becoming increasingly important as we enter the new millennium. We are entering the age of information where international communication is commonplace and access to information worldwide is easy because of advances in electronic technology. New technologies facilitate and expand communication, but they do not diminish the need for individuals who are language competent. To the contrary, computers, the Internet, and communication technologies that we cannot yet imagine will demand individuals who are competent in multiple aspects of language use, such as computer literacy, that are only now emerging. Language competent individuals will have the greatest access to the information and the other advantages that are available through these new technologies. Individuals who are competent in multiple languages will be able to benefit the most from new technologies that give access to information in all the languages of the world.

At the same time, language competence, in its diverse forms, is fundamental to personal growth and fulfillment and to full and active participation in a democratic society. The ability to shape one's community and one's place and role within it requires access to information, decision-makers, and community resources. Language is the primary gateway to information, decision-makers, and community resources. Language competence leads to personal empowerment because effective use of language for engagement in society commands respect and attention. Language competence gives voice to individual's social, political, and economic concerns.

The enriched educational programs we discuss in this book stress communicative competence (see Glossary) in second and even third languages as well as in students' primary languages—for some students, English is their primary language; for others, it will be another language, such as Korean, Spanish, or Hmong. English is undoubtedly the common currency of most communication in political, economic, social, and academic spheres in North America and other English speaking countries. However, many of the local communities in which students in these regions live are populated by people from different language and cultural backgrounds. Proficiency in additional languages can enrich and benefit members of these communities. Moreover, with the increased used of advanced technology for worldwide communication, impediments to communication among people who speak different languages are diminishing every day. Proficiency in additional languages permits individuals to take full advantage of advances in communication and information technology to communicate with others around the world.

Effective communication requires more than simply knowing a linguistic code. It requires knowing how to use the code in socially and culturally appropriate and meaningful ways; that is to say, it requires cultural competence as well. Children normally acquire the cultural underpinnings of their primary language naturally and at the same time as they learn their primary language. This is not always the case when children acquire second languages (see Glossary)

in school settings. There has been a pedagogical tradition of disconnecting second language learning (see Glossary) from culture learning. It is now recognized that this is undesirable and that culture learning is an integral part of language learning (Heath, 1983).

Educational professionals also accept now that the development of advanced levels of language competence, in a primary or second language, is most successful when it occurs in conjunction with meaningful, important, and authentic communication. In school settings, this can be communication about academic subjects. Thus, including second languages not only as subjects of study but also as vehicles for teaching and learning other academic subjects is a logical and effective way of extending students' language competence. This is an approach that we endorse and consider in depth in this handbook.

We endorse competence in multiple languages for *all* students. We talk about students who come to school speaking the majority group language (English in North America) and seek to extend their linguistic repertoire by learning a second language. We refer to these students as language majority students (see Glossary). We also talk about language minority students (see Glossary) who grow up speaking other languages and must acquire English, the majority group language, in order to adapt to the majority culture. While some programs, such an immersion and bilingual education are designed for each of these groups separately, two-way immersion programs are designed for these two groups in the same classes. We will be discussing all three of these program models in the chapters ahead.

The Benefits of Knowing Two Languages

There are educational, cognitive, socio-cultural, and economic benefits to individuals as well as society at large that result from intensive study of second and even third languages in enriched educational programs. We talk about these benefits in the next section.

Educational Benefits

English-speaking students from the majority language group are capable of achieving high levels of functional proficiency in a second language in school without detrimental effects to their primary language development or their academic achievement. Evidence for this comes from research on the effectiveness of second language immersion programs for English-speaking students in Canada and the U.S. (Genesee, 1985, 1987; Lambert & Tucker, 1972; Swain & Lapkin, 1982). In second language immersion programs, students and teachers use the second language as the primary medium of communication for studying a major portion of the curriculum, either during the elementary or secondary grades. For example, in early total French immersion programs, English-speaking Canadian students do all of their school work from kindergarten to grade 2 or 3 entirely in French. Their teachers use only French with them at all times. English is used to teach language arts or other school subjects starting in grade 2, or even later in some school districts. The students learn the language naturally as they hear and use it during their academic and language arts classes.

Immersion programs in Canada and elsewhere are probably the most extensively evaluated educational programs in the world. The findings are clear and consistent. Students in immersion programs acquire the same proficiency in English and achieve the same levels of competence in their academic subjects (e.g., mathematics, science, and social studies) as comparable English-speaking students who attend regular all-English programs. At the same time, immersion students acquire advanced levels of functional proficiency in French. They are able to do all of their school work, communicate with their friends and teachers in school and with others outside school comfortably, effortlessly, and effectively. These results have been reported even in communities where there are few, if any, speakers of the target language; for example, French immersion in Cincinnati, Ohio. Thus, this form of enriched language education is feasible and effective in a variety of community settings. In addition, research has shown that immersion programs are effective for students who often struggle in school because they come from low socio-economic backgrounds or they have low levels of academic achievement. Thus, immersion need not be reserved only for the academic elite in our schools; they work for a wide variety of English-speaking students.

Research has also shown that students who come to school in the U.S. (or other English-speaking countries) with no or limited proficiency in English make better progress in acquiring English and in academic development if they receive some schooling in their primary language at the same time as they are introduced to English as a second language (Cummins, 1991; Ramirez, et al., 1991; Thomas & Collier, 1998). Providing English language learners instruction in their primary languages, especially in literacy, establishes a solid foundation on which they can acquire English. Students from language minority backgrounds who acquire strong literacy skills in their primary language are able to apply these skills to the acquisition of English literacy. Literacy in their primary language facilitates the acquisition of English literacy skills. Students who do not receive primary language support in school are faced with the double challenge of acquiring proficiency in both oral and written

forms of a new language at the same time that they try to stay at grade level in their academic subjects.

The point we want to make here is that enriched educational programs that provide opportunities for students to develop their primary language along with a second language, or even a third language (see Genesee & Lambert, 1983), are feasible and effective. Students benefit from these programs because they acquire high levels of proficiency in languages that they would not otherwise have—for English-speaking students, they acquire proficiency in second/foreign languages; and for language minority students, they develop their primary languages fully while adding proficiency in English.

Cognitive Benefits

Research has shown that students who acquire advanced levels of proficiency in second languages often experience certain cognitive and linguistic advantages when compared to monolingual students (Cummins, 1981; Lambert, Genesee, Holobow & Chartrand, 1993). Such benefits have been found in Montreal, for example, among English-speaking students in programs where virtually all their instruction in Kindergarten to grade 6 is in French. Students in these programs outperform control students in all-English schools on a variety of English language tests—reading, writing, listening, etc. (Lambert, et al., 1993). These findings seem counterintuitive to some people. However, when we think about it for a few moments, it is easy to imagine how one could gain insights about one's primary language as a result of learning another language. Students who know another language understand that different languages use different word orders to express the same ideas, and that some languages mark gender on nouns, pronouns, and verbs, while others, such as English, do not. These insights help students understand and use their own language better.

Fully proficient bilinguals also often demonstrate certain cognitive advantages. Research has shown that bilingual students perform better than monolingual students on tasks that call for divergent thinking, pattern recognition, and problem solving. Divergent thinking is involved in creativity—for example, discovering hidden or obscure meanings in familiar objects and arrays of information, finding novel or alternative solutions to problems, and exploring new ways of using familiar objects. Of most importance, bilingual children have been shown to have enhanced levels of metalinguistic awareness. Metalinguistic awareness is the knowledge we have about the structural properties of language, including the sounds, words, and grammar of language. Important metalinguistic knowledge that is related to reading is the awareness that words are made up of sounds—the word "cat" consists of three sounds: [c] [a] [t]. This knowledge is useful for understanding that the letters that make up written words in English correspond to the individual sounds of words. Metalinguistic awareness is very important in the acquisition of reading because it facilitates decoding (Adams, 1990). Explicit awareness of the grammatical conventions of language and how to use them to express meaning clearly and precisely is a hallmark of language use in academic and cognitively-demanding tasks that make up much of schooling.

These research findings dispel fears that acquiring a second language during the early school years is detrimental to students' primary language and cognitive development. We believe that learning more than one language is just as normal as learning only one, and that learning a second language in school teaches students additional language skills and advanced cognitive abilities. Indeed, research has shown that acquisition of more than one language during the pre-school or early school years is not problematic for children if they are provided with supportive, language-rich learning environments (Nicoladis & Genesee, 1997). Bilingual and multilingual individuals often demonstrate enhanced levels of language and cognitive functioning (Cenoz & Genesee, 1998). In this book, we talk about how to create enriched educational programs that lead to additive forms of bilingualism (see Glossary) and the enriched language and cognitive development that has been noted by researchers.

Socio-Cultural Benefits

There are also important socio-cultural advantages to knowing more than one language. Proficiency in multiple languages permits individuals to expand their world because it permits them to communicate with members of other cultural groups, be they members of cultural groups in one's own neighborhood, or groups in other countries or regions of the world. While English is useful for many purposes in many communities and countries, other languages are also useful. Individuals who know other languages can tap into and take advantage of opportunities that are available only in those languages. Knowing other languages can expand one's understanding of other cultural groups—their values, social customs, and ways of viewing the world. Knowing additional languages can be personally very beneficial because it allows one to travel, to read magazines in other languages, to listen to radio or television broadcasts in other languages. Knowing other languages can also be socially beneficial because it can lead to greater intercultural understanding and tolerance and, even, appreciation and respect. The global village is here, and it confronts us with linguistic and cultural differences that can be a source of conflict and misunderstanding or of celebration and enjoyment. Profic-iency in other languages is one step in understanding and enjoying difference.

Economic Benefits

A primary reason why English-speaking parents send their children to second language immersion programs is because they believe that it will enhance their employment opportunities when they complete school. This is true even for parents who live in communities, such as Washington D.C., that are clearly English dominant. Parents in these communities know that proficiency in another language will open up job prospects in business, the diplomatic corps, tourism, or communications, for example. In the global marketplace, there are plenty of jobs that call for bilingual proficiency. The European Union is now one of the world's largest economic zones—it is made up of countries that speak different languages and it does business multilingually. Similar economic zones are under development in Asia and in the Americas, and they will also do business multilingually. Thus, there are clear and powerful incentives for learning French, Spanish, Japanese, Chinese, or other languages that are linked to economic hot spots around the world. Individuals who know English along with these other languages will clearly be at an advantage in the global marketplace. Communities with large numbers of qualified multilingual professionals will also be at an advantage in the twenty-first century because they will be prepared to do business worldwide, no matter what the language being spoken. Increasingly, business, cultural, political, and social activities around the world call for people with different language and cultural backgrounds. Individuals with multilingual competence are able to take professional roles that cross linguistic boundaries. Cultural and national boundaries around the world are coming down in increasing numbers, and this trend will continue even more rapidly in the twenty-first century.

Enriched educational programs that stress knowledge of multiple languages and cultures provide responses to these global opportunities. Business and community leaders in Indianapolis, Indiana, for example, have come together to promote the creation of schools that will give English-speaking students opportunities to become bilingual and, thus, enhance their community's economic competitiveness in the twenty-first century. Immersion programs are the model of choice in this case. Language minority students who come to school proficient in other languages, such as Spanish, Korean, or Russian, are also an important linguistic resource that can contribute to the nation's future success because they already know major world languages. If these students are given opportunities to develop their existing language skills while they learn English as a second language, they will have an advantage that will benefit themselves personally and their communities because they will have the language and culture skills that will be demanded in the global market-place. Developmental bilingual programs or dual language immersion programs are the models of choice that can develop these human resources.

We discuss these program models now in more detail.

Models of Enriched Education in Two Languages

During the last three decades, educators have experimented with a variety of enriched forms of education that promote acquisition of English along with additional languages and cultures. We focus on three of these programs in this book:

1. second/foreign language immersion programs for English-speaking language majority students.

2. developmental bilingual programs for language minority students.

3. two-way immersion programs for language minority and language majority students.

Second foreign language immersion programs serve language majority students and they use a second or foreign language (e.g., Japanese or Spanish) to teach at least 50% of the curriculum during the elementary or secondary grades. Detailed examples of immersion in Canada can be found in Lambert & Tucker (1972), Swain & Lapkin (1982), and Genesee (1983); a detailed example of immersion in the U.S. is found in Cohen (1976). *Immersion Education: International Perspectives* by Keith Johnson and Merrill Swain (1997) is a useful collection of examples of immersion programs from around the world.

Immersion programs vary with respect to the amount of the second language that is used for instruction and the grade level during which immersion in the second language is offered (Genesee, 1983; 1987; Johnson & Swain, 1997). In *early* immersion programs, the second/foreign language is used for academic instruction beginning in kindergarten or grade 1, whereas in *late* immersion programs use of the second language as a medium of instruction does not begin until the end of elementary school or the beginning of secondary school. In *middle* or *delayed* immersion, use of the second language for academic instruction begins in the middle elementary grades, usually grade 4. Some early immersion programs present all curriculum instruction through the second language for one, two, or three years before English begins to be used for instructional purposes. These are called *early total immersion*. In other early immersion programs, English and the additional language are each used 50% of the time to teach academic content. These are called *early partial immersion*.

Despite some differences in program design and delivery, most immersion programs share the following objectives:

- grade-appropriate levels of primary language development.

- grade-appropriate levels of academic achievement.

- functional proficiency in the second/foreign language.

- an understanding of and appreciation for the culture of the target language group.

Developmental bilingual education programs serve language minority students—students who come to school in North America who are proficient in a language other than English. There are two general models of bilingual education: *early exit,* or *transitional bilingual* (see Glossary) programs and *late-exit,* or *developmental bilingual* programs. In *developmental bilingual programs,* language minority students receive at least 50% of curriculum instruction through the medium of their primary language, and they continue to receive instruction in and through this language throughout the elementary grades, and in rare cases high school, so as to ensure full proficiency in their primary language. In *transitional bilingual programs,* the students' primary language is used only during the first two or three grades, until such time as the students can make a full transition into all-English instruction. We focus on developmental bilingual programs because they aim for bilingual proficiency, a central theme of this book (see Ramirez, et al., 1991; and Thomas & Collier, 1998).

The primary goals of developmental bilingual programs are:

- maintenance and full development of the students' primary language.

- full proficiency in all aspects of English.

- grade-appropriate levels of achievement in all domains of academic study.

- integration into all-English language classrooms.

- positive identity with the culture of the primary language group and with the culture of the majority language group.

Two-way immersion programs (sometimes referred to as "dual language") are an amalgam of immersion and developmental bilingual programs. They serve both language minority and language majority students in the same classrooms. Generally, 50% of the students come from each language group. These programs embrace the goals of both immersion for language majority students and developmental bilingual programs for language minority students (Lindholm, 1992). The primary difference between two-way immersion programs and the other two is the incorporation of both groups of students in the same classrooms and the active use of instructional strategies that promote cross-cultural cooperation and learning. Useful examples of two-way immersion programs are given in Christian, Montone, Lindholm, & Carranza (1997).

In the chapters that follow, we focus on two forms of two-way immersion: 90/10 programs and 50/50 programs. In 90/10 programs, 90% of the curriculum in the early elementary grades is taught to both groups of students using the minority language and 10% (usually language arts) is taught using English. In 50/50 programs, English and the other language are each used 50% of the time to teach the curriculum; different languages are used to teach different subjects. The general rationale behind the 90/10 model is to promote the minority language as much as possible among both language groups on the assumption that this is the language that needs the most support. The 50/50 model is based on the belief that both languages need to be acquired from the beginning and the best way to do this is to split instructional time between the two. Schools may introduce variations of these two models according to their resources, priorities, or goals.

While two-way immersion programs in different school districts may serve somewhat different groups of learners and have somewhat different objectives, they share the following important goals:

- attainment of challenging, age-appropriate academic skills and knowledge.
- advanced levels of functional proficiency in English along with an additional language.
- understanding and appreciation of cross-cultural differences.

These forms of education have been undergoing a steady growth in numbers during the last several years. The aim of this book is to provide practical guidance to those developing new programs and those engaged in existing programs. We are not prescriptive in our guidance because each program must be developed and implemented so that it reflects and respects the unique characteristics of the community, parents, and students it serves.

Before proceeding, we want to point out that our discussion focuses on programs in the U.S. and Canada because we are most familiar with education in these two countries. Together, these two countries offer imaginative and extensive programs of enriched education. The examples of developmental bilingual and two-way immersion education all come from the U.S. because this is where these programs have been developed most extensively. Many of the "Voices from the Field" that we include in the remainder of this book refer to programs where Spanish is the other language because this is by far the most common other language in such programs. Similarly, we give many examples of Spanish and French immersion because these are the most common in the U.S. and Canada, respectively. It is important to know, however, that bilingual and immersion programs are available in many different languages, including Korean, German, Japanese, Chinese, and Portuguese. A directory of immersion and dual language/two-way immersion programs in the U.S. is available from the Center for Applied Linguistics in Washington, D.C. (see Appendix D). The directories provide brief descriptions and contact information for each program listed. Our focus is on the kindergarten to grade 8 years since these are the grades where the vast majority of such programs are presently available. However, what we have to say is equally true for high school grades as well.

Organization of the Book

Next, in Chapter 2, we discuss *Critical Features of Enriched Education*. You will notice that most of these features are also characteristic of effective general education. We use these features as critical reference points to make suggestions to those planning new programs and for those taking stock of existing programs. In the chapters that follow, we discuss practical issues related to *Program Development and Implementation* (Chapter 3), *Oral Language Development* (Chapter 4), *Teaching Literacy in Two Languages* (Chapter 5), *Teaching Content* (Chapter 6), and *Assessment* (Chapter 7). We summarize each of these chapters by returning to the critical features identified in Chapter 2. We use these critical features to create checklists of recommended best practices in each domain of concern—oral language development, literacy, content, and so on. Application of the suggestions we make in Chapters 2 to 7 is presented in Chapter 8, *Model Lessons and Assessment Procedures*. Chapter 9 discusses *Advocacy* and presents useful suggestions for working with parents, school administrators, community leaders, and others whose support is needed for EE programs.

In addition to the customary end-of-chapter reference lists of articles we have consulted in preparing each chapter, we provide other useful references in a series of appendices at the end of the book. Appendix A is *A Glossary of Terms for EE Teachers*. Appendix B is a list of *Publishers of Curriculum Materials*. Appendix C is a list of *Useful Organizations, Resource Centers, and Professional Periodicals and Journals*. Appendix D identifies some *Informational Videotapes/Directories of Programs*. Finally, Appendix E is an *Index to Title of Tables and Figures* that appear in the book. We hope these resource lists will encourage more in-depth examination of each topic so that the suggestions made here can be applied appropriately in particular school and community settings.

References

Adams, M. (1990). *Beginning to Read*. Cambridge, MA: MIT Press.

Cenoz, J., & Genesee, F. (1998). Psycholinguistic Perspectives on Multilingualism and Multilingual Education. In J. Cenoz & F. Genesee (Eds) *Beyond Bilingualism: Multilingualism and Multilingual Education*. Clevedon, Eng.: Multilingual Matters, 16–34.

Christian, D., Montone, C.L., Lindholm, K.J., & Carranza, I. (1997). *Profiles in Two-Way Immersion Education*. Washington, D.C.: Center for Applied Linguistics.

Cohen, A. (1976). The Acquisition of Spanish Grammar Through Immersion: Some Findings after Four Years. *Canadian Modern Language Review*, 32, 562–574.

Cummins, J. (1976). The Influence of Bilingualism on Cognitive Growth: A Synthesis of Research Findings and an Explanatory Hypothesis. *Workingpapers on Bilingualism*, 9: 1–43.

Cummins, J. (1981). The Role of Primary Language Development in Promoting Educational Success for Language Minority Students. In *Schooling and Language Minority Students: A Theoretical Framework*. Los Angeles, CA: Evaluation, Dissemination, and Assessment Center, 1–50.

Genesee, F. (1983). Bilingual Education of Majority-Language Children: The Immersion Experiments in Review. *Applied Psycholinguistics*, 4, 1–46.

Genesee, F. (1985). Second Language Learning through Immersion: A Review of U.S. Programs. *Review of Educational Research*, 55: 541–561.

Genesee, F. (1987). *Learning Through Two Languages: Studies of Immersion and Bilingual Education*. Rowley, MA: Newbury House.

Genesee, F., & Lambert, W.E. (1983). Trilingual Education for Majority Language Children. *Child Development*, 54: 105–114.

Heath, S.B. (1983). *Ways with Words*. Cambridge, MA: Cambridge University Press.

Johnson, R.K., & Swain, M. (1997). *Immersion Education: International Perspectives*. Cambridge, Eng.: Cambridge University Press.

Lambert, W.E., Genesee, F., Holobow, N., & Chartrand, L. (1993). Bilingual Education for Majority English-Speaking Children. *European Journal of Psychology of Education*, 8: 3–22.

Lambert, W.E., & Tucker, G.R. (1972). *The Bilingual Education of Children: The St. Lambert Experiment*. Rowley, MA: Newbury House.

Lindholm, K. (1992). Two-way Bilingual/Immersion Education: Theory, Conceptual Issues, and Pedagogical Implications. In R. Padilla & A. Benavides (Eds), *Critical Perspectives on Bilingual Education Research*. Tucson, AZ: Bilingual Review/Press.

Nicoladis, E. & Genesee, F. (1997). Language Development in Preschool Bilingual Children, *Journal of Speech-Language Pathology and Audiology*, 21, 258–270.

Ramirez, D.J., Yuen, S. D., Ramey, D.R., & Pasta, D.J. (1991). *Final Report: National Longitudinal Study of Structured-English Immersion Strategy, Early-Exit, and Late-Exit Transitional Bilingual Education Programs for Language-Minority Children*, Vol. I and II. San Mateo, CA: Aguirre International.

Swain, M., & Lapkin, S. (1982). *Evaluating Bilingual Education: A Canadian Case Study*. Clevedon, Eng.: Multilingual Matters.

Thomas, W., & Collier, V. (1998). *School Effectiveness for Language Minority Students*. Alexandria, VA: National Clearinghouse for Bilingual Education.

2 CRITICAL FEATURES OF ENRICHED EDUCATION

In this chapter, we discuss nine features that we believe are critical for effective EE programs—they are listed in Table 2.1. We identified these features from our reading of relevant research reports and professional literature related to EE programs (August & Hakuta, 1997; Collier, 1992). Our own professional experiences also influenced our thinking. Seven of these nine features apply to all educational programs, even programs that do not included enriched language and culture instruction. Thus, we regard them as the foundation of effective general education. They are relevant in their most general form to EE programs. At the same time, they take on special meaning when applied to EE programs. Take Feature 1, while parental involvement is important in the success of general education, parental involvement in EE programs is even more important. EE parents have to fight for a program that many school districts resist because it calls for the reallocation of resources; it calls for change and most school districts resist change.

The significance of these critical features is even more specific when you consider the particular learner groups participating in EE programs. Again, let's consider Feature 1. In order to involve parents in developmental bilingual or two-way immersion programs, it is often necessary to make special arrangements for translators or other parents who speak the parents' home language as well as English to attend parent-school meetings because the parents may not know English fluently. It is also important to distribute notices about such meetings in the parents' language for the same reason. It may even be necessary to telephone language minority parents to tell them about meetings at the school because many parents may not be able to read English well.

You can think about the application of each of these critical features like a periscope—they provide increasingly more fine-grained insights about what constitutes effective education as you think about the population of students being served in increasingly specific ways—first with respect to principles of effective general education, then with respect to effective enriched education, and, most specifically, with respect to EE programs for students from different language and cultural backgrounds. Feature 8 (integration with other school programs and schools) and Feature 9 (additive bilingualism) are specific to EE programs. In the sections that follow, we start with the features that are general and then consider those that are unique to EE programs.

Table 2.1   Critical Features of Effective EE Programs

1. PARENT INVOLVEMENT IS INTEGRAL TO PROGRAM SUCCESS
2. EFFECTIVE PROGRAMS HAVE HIGH STANDARDS
3. STRONG LEADERSHIP IS CRITICAL FOR EFFECTIVE PROGRAMS
4. EFFECTIVE EE PROGRAMS ARE DEVELOPMENTAL
5. EFFECTIVE INSTRUCTION IS STUDENT-CENTERED
6. LANGUAGE INSTRUCTION IS INTEGRATED WITH CHALLENGING ACADEMIC INSTRUCTION
7. TEACHERS IN EFFECTIVE EE PROGRAMS ARE REFLECTIVE
8. EFFECTIVE EE PROGRAMS ARE INTEGRATED WITH OTHER SCHOOL PROGRAMS AND SCHOOLS
9. EFFECTIVE EE PROGRAMS AIM FOR ADDITIVE BILINGUALISM

These features are useful for thinking about both new programs and established programs. Using these features when planning a new program helps to ensure adequate program resources and design. Using them when monitoring established programs helps to determine the effectiveness of the program and areas that need attention in the case of programs that are not functioning satisfactorily. We suggest that you use them like a checklist against which new and established programs can be assessed. In fact, we return to these features at the end of each chapter to create a checklist linked to the topic of each chapter. We discuss these features in very general terms in this chapter. They are discussed in more concrete, specific terms in subsequent chapters as we talk about how to design and implement each component of EE programs—content instruction, first language instruction, second language instruction, and so on.

Feature 1: Parent Involvement Is Integral to Program Success

As in general education, parents play critical roles in both establishing and maintaining EE programs. Some of the most successful EE programs were initially established because of strong parental interest in giving their children enriched language and culture education. The most well-documented case of this is the Canadian French immersion programs. They were started in 1965 in Montreal in response to the demands of a group of English-speaking parents who wanted a school program that would give their children the bilingual proficiency they needed to fit into a community that was predominantly French-speaking (see Lambert & Tucker, 1972, for a history of this program). We know that parent involvement is key in initiating new EE programs even now. School authorities are often reluctant to develop new programs on the grounds that resources are scarce and/or such programs are elitist because they do not serve all students. Parent advocacy is essential to overcome such resistance. In Canada, a volunteer parent group called *Canadian Parents for French* was created to provide ongoing support to parents and communities who wanted to start French language programs in their schools. *Advocates for Language Learning* is a U.S. equivalent of this group. Both of these groups are an important resource to those interested in starting up new programs (see Appendix C for contact information).

It is important to include parents in programs from the very beginning so that they are fully aware of the structure and goals of the program and they are prepared to make the long-term commitments of time and involvement that successful participation requires. English-speaking parents contemplating sending their children to two-way immersion or single-language immersion programs must understand that their children will be receiving significant portions of instruction, including reading and writing, in a second language. Likewise, language minority parents thinking about developmental bilingual or two-way immersion programs must understand that their children will be receiving instruction in the primary (home) language while they are introduced to English as second language. It is also important to inform parents of what to expect with respect to their children's language and academic achievement during the early and later grades of the program so that they are not surprised by the outcomes. This is critical if parents are to fully understand the importance of keeping their child in the program throughout its duration.

Feature 2: Effective Programs Have High Standards

Effective general education has clearly defined, well articulated, and challenging standards in all curricular areas, including language and academic subjects. EE programs do too. In addition, EE programs have clearly defined, well articulated, and challenging standards for second language learning and cultural domains. Most major national professional organizations concerned with K–12 education in the content areas of mathematics, social studies, history, and science, have developed standards that identify what students should know and be able to do at each grade level. Likewise, many state, regional, and local educational organizations, including many state departments of education, have developed subject matter standards and frameworks that identify benchmarks for planning instruction. These benchmarks are also useful for assessing K–12 student progress toward the attainment of specified objectives. The standards that are recommended in these various documents are really learning objectives or goals. The development and promulgation of these standards has been motivated by the recognition that standards are essential if K–12 students are to achieve the level and kinds of competence in the academic disciplines that is considered desirable and appropriate. Teaching in programs without standards is like traveling without a road map and a clearly identified destination—you have no way of knowing where you are going and you certainly do not know when you have reached your destination (or if you are lost).

It is not enough that standards be clearly defined and challenging, they must also be (a) understood, (b) accepted, and (c) implemented in a coherent fashion by all educational and support personnel in the program. This means that the school principal, *all* teachers, other educational professionals, and even support staff working in the school must understand and share the same standards. They must all work together to insure that the standards are implemented

Voices from the Field

Building Equitable Two-Way Bilingual Programs

Rosa Molina
Bilingual Director, San Jose Unified School District, and
President, CABE Two-Way Bilingual Immersion State Affiliate
San Jose, California

One of the most difficult aspects of starting two-way bilingual immersion schools for teachers and administrators is knowing how to develop programs that are additive and equitable for both language minority (English language learners) and language majority (English dominant) students. I have found that the most successful programs in the country started out with an impressive track record in providing programs for English language learners. This allowed the teaching staff to successfully include English dominant students in the language learning mix. This shift, however natural it might seem, requires extensive training in and understanding of the principles of second language acquisition, even among experienced practitioners. Language use and instruction have to be planned carefully as teachers face the challenge of using more than their language to convey meaning. Teachers in two-way programs have to draw from different bodies of research—foreign language and immersion education for English dominant students and second language acquisition and bilingual education for English language learners—to plan effective instruction. Most importantly, each teacher must strive to provide a program of academic and language study that adheres to classroom practices that are equitable and, thus, raise the status of the minority language and, in turn, the status of the students who are models of that language. A program that is equitable for all students raises all students' motivation to learn both languages! The fear of bilingual educators in the field is that, if equity is not kept in the forefront, two-way teachers will unconsciously skew the program to the language needs of the English dominant students at the expense of the academic success of minority language students.

Two-way teachers often complain to me that finding the correct level of difficulty for each student in their classroom is the greatest challenge they face. The most successful teachers have found that if they focus their instruction on the needs of the minority language students, they can be much more successful in ensuring academic and linguistic success for both groups. If they slow down development in the minority language so that English dominant students can "catch up", then the minority language students are adversely affected since academic and linguistic rigor have been reduced. Although it seems counterintuitive, teachers who work to make themselves language teachers and use "sheltering strategies" to make their content comprehensible, can be successful in maintaining the ever important instructional balance in the classroom. Teachers also report that self-monitoring and coaching are important ways in which they support their use of appropriate instructional, motivational, and linguistic strategies that result in overall stronger language comprehension and use from both groups of students. Program developers from two-way schools have had a "wake-up call" as they analyze the patterns of achievement of both language minority and language majority students. For many years, Dr. Kathyrn Lindholm, the leading researcher in two-way bilingual immersion programs in California, cautioned us to work diligently to "reduce the gap" between the two groups of students in our programs. She strongly urged all two-way programs to gather the data they needed to inform their decisions about program development, language use, scheduling, the introduction of English, and the development of curriculum for each grade level. She has conferred with programs that began to demonstrate a considerable academic and linguistic gap between the two student populations. She urged programs to focus on finding solutions that would ensure success for the language minority students and those that did found that they had higher patterns of achievement for both groups of students than they had ever seen before. Therein lies the success of schools like River Glen Elementary School in San Jose, California, whose success qualified them for

(continued)

the national Title VII Academic Excellence nomination in the years of 1992–1996. This award was based on the academic and linguistic success of the language minority children in the program. Another excellent example of high student achievement is Alicia Chacon Multilingual School in El Paso, Texas, whose students are not only involved in a two-way effort but also in learning a third language; and they are showing great results in their students' achievement rates. The primary goal in two-way programs is to narrow the gap between language minority and language majority students, not by slowing down the program so that English language learners can catch up, but by raising the achievement patterns of the students, thus providing an academically and linguistically rigorous program for all students. No language group is expendable in this program! The administration, teaching staff, and parents must share a commitment to the vision of equity and academic success for all of the children in their program. Without a watchful approach to the quality of their two-way programs, schools will find themselves tragically exploiting the language minority group they had hoped to help for the benefit of the language majority students.

in a systematic fashion across grade levels. For example, in addition to the instructional staff, employing bilingual clerical and janitorial assistants and encouraging them to use their other language skills with students in the program provides additional opportunities for students to practice their developing language skills everywhere in the school.

Student success in achieving challenging standards also calls for educators who believe that *all* students are capable of high levels of achievement. This attitude is especially important in the case of students who might be at-risk for academic failure. Those who are at-risk of failure in school include students from low socio-economic backgrounds, students from families with no or little formal education, and students who come to school with no or limited proficiency in English. These are all characteristics of many students from language minority backgrounds who participate in developmental or dual language immersion programs. Educators sometimes justify low expectations for these students on the misguided grounds that expecting high levels of achievement from them only sets them up for failure and poor self-esteem. We know that not all students achieve to the same level. However, we also know that students who are held to lower standards and are not given the opportunity to learn to high standards of achievement cannot realize their full learning capabilities. When this happens, students often come to view themselves as less capable than they actually are. High standards are critical to insure that EE provides enriched and not remedial schooling for language minority students. As we noted earlier, a variety of academic and language-related standards are now available. They provide a very useful starting point for those who want to develop standards that reflect the specific educational goals and public expectations of their communities and school districts.

Feature 3: Strong Leadership Is Critical for Effective Programs

Well-informed and committed principals provide the critical leadership that is necessary for the adoption and rigorous implementation of challenging standards in all curricular domains. Supportive, well informed, and proactive principals are also critical for creating the professional climate in schools that fosters and sustains the belief that all students can learn to high levels. Many decisions are made every school day that influence the success of EE programs. Strong leadership from principals is essential to insure sound coherent decision making that promotes the objectives of EE programs.

There are individuals both in the education profession and in the population at large who believe that EE programs are not practical or feasible and that they impede students' mastery of English and academic subjects. These individuals hold subtractive views of bilingualism (see "subtractive bilingualism" in Glossary). They are skeptical about the advantages of bilingualism and they are prone to openly oppose EE programs that support the development of bilingualism and biculturalism. Well-informed principals with strong leadership skills can actively defend EE programs in the face of such opposition.

Teachers and other educational professionals working in EE programs and/or in the district can also provide leadership in support of EE programs. Committed teachers can support the program by emphasizing the importance of challenging language and content standards (see Glossary) so that parents and others are reassured that nothing is sacrificed by the program. Teachers who have a solid understanding of the critical features of effective EE and are confident in its effectiveness make sound day-to-day decisions that support the program. EE teachers are often called on by worried parents and others to defend the program. They must be confident and well informed if they are to reassure others of the program's effectiveness. Educators who lack complete understanding of the goals and methods of effective EE cannot support it adequately. EE teachers who lack confidence in what they are doing can undermine the program by making decisions that run counter to the programs goals. For example, we have met teachers in immersion programs in the U.S. who believe that they should provide translations in English of instruction in the other language to make sure the students get it. However, by doing this, these teachers are impeding students' chances of acquiring functional proficiency in the second language. A vicious circle is created that blocks students from acquiring sufficient proficiency in the second language to function comfortably during classes taught in that language. As a result, teachers may be compelled to use more and more English for academic instruction in the higher grades when content becomes complex and demanding. It is important that educators in EE programs be familiar with the research and professional literature on EE so that they are confident about it and what they are doing.

Feature 4: Effective EE Programs Are Developmental

Effective EE programs are developmentally appropriate; they plan for continuous student development; and are based on the belief that the benefits of EE are cumulative and require long-term commitment. Let us discuss each of these aspects of development in turn.

First, to be effective, instruction in any education program must be developmentally appropriate. Effective teachers recognize and build on the skills, knowledge, and experiences that students acquire outside school and while they are in school. They extend and broaden their students' skills and knowledge in developmentally meaningful ways throughout the school years. Developmentally appropriate instruction is especially important for young students, as they begin their schooling. From the teacher's point of view, instruction that is linked to students' existing competencies, knowledge, and experiences provides a solid foundation for

extending their skills and knowledge in new directions. From the students' point of view, instruction that is linked to established skills and familiar experiences provides a reassuring context in which to acquire new skills, knowledge, and experiences.

The curriculum in general education reflects the knowledge and assumptions held by educators about the development of students from the majority group. In some cases, recommended instructional practices are based on systematic research on the development of mainstream children. For example, arguments for the inclusion of phonics (or phonological awareness—see Glossary) as a component of initial reading instruction is based on extensive research on children's awareness of speech and its relationship to emergent literacy (Adams, 1990; Snow et al. 1998). General education is developmentally sensitive to and culturally appropriate for students from the majority group. The skills,

Table 2.2 Effective EE Programs Are Developmental

1. Effective teachers recognize and build on the skills, knowledge, and experiences that students acquire outside school and while they are in school. They extend and broaden their students' skills and knowledge in developmentally meaningful ways throughout the school years.

2. Effective instruction plans for continuous student development in language and academic domains. EE teachers systematically plan instruction that advances students' language proficiency across grade levels. Systematic and careful articulation of instruction across grades is critically important to ensure that EE students acquire the second language skills they need for mastering progressively more complex academic skills and knowledge.

3. The benefits of education are cumulative and are only evident over the long term. Parents must commit to long term participation and schools must commit to long term program development.

knowledge, and experience that students from minority group backgrounds bring to school differ considerably from those of students from majority group backgrounds. Students who come to school with no or limited proficiency in English, for example, have language skills but not in English, and they will have acquired those skills in cultural settings that differ significantly from the majority culture. These developmental facts should shape curriculum and instruction for these students in significant ways. If they are to be effective, teachers working in programs that serve both minority and majority students must understand the developmental backgrounds of all their students and take any differences among their students into account when planning instruction. This does not mean that the overall *goals* of instruction are not the same for all students; they are. However, teachers must provide alternative educational means of achieving these goals if all of their students are to achieve to their maximum potential. Equal treatment does not lead to success for all.

Second, effective instruction plans for continuous student development in language and academic domains. This is evident in curriculum and instructional plans within and across grades. We take this for granted. It is obvious—of course we expect students to know more and be able to do more advanced work the longer they are in school. We believe that it is important to emphasize the importance of growth when talking about educational programs when instruction is presented in a second language because research suggests that development in such programs is not always continuous. To be more specific, research from immersion programs for English-speaking students indicates that their second language competence does not correlate directly with their length of participation in the program or with the amount of exposure they have in school to the second language. We do not know for sure why this is true, but it may be due to the fact that the primary focus of instruction and learning in immersion is on academic development; language skills are expected to develop in tandem. Immersion researchers and educators now believe that in order to insure continuous language development, *teachers must systematically plan instruction that advances students' language proficiency across grade levels.* This can be achieved through careful selection of instructional materials and activities that incorporate progressively advanced language skills and/or through appropriate modeling of progressively more sophisticated language usage.

Systematic and careful articulation of instruction across grades is critically important to ensure that EE students acquire the second language skills they need for mastering progressively more complex academic skills and

knowledge. For example, grade 2 teachers in a two-way immersion program can develop the language skills their students will need in their grade 3 science or mathematics classes so that they comprehend math and science instruction in the second language in grade 3. Students who have not acquired the language skills that are associated with the grade 3 science or mathematics curriculum will be slowed down in those curricular areas. Teachers who do not build their students' competencies in academic language (see Glossary) in the lower grades are not preparing them adequately for later learning. Their students will lack the language skills they need for studying academic subjects in higher grades. The same is also true within a given grade—effective teachers identify the language skills their students need later in the year and they begin to develop those language skills before they are actually required. Scheduling common times when teachers at the same grade level or teachers at different grade levels can plan together is essential to achieve such coordination.

Third, and related to the preceding point, the effects of education are cumulative and the full benefits of enriched education are only evident over the long term. This follows from a fact that all educators know—complete development takes time. Take the example of second language immersion programs again. Evaluations of students in early immersion programs in Canada and the U.S. indicate that they usually score significantly lower than control students in all-English programs on standardized English language tests if they are examined during the first two or three years of the program when instruction in English is lacking or minimal (Genesee, 1987). However, the same immersion students score as well as, or in some cases better than, comparable students in all-English programs when they are examined in grades 5 or 6. There is also evidence that immersion students outperform non-immersion students on English language tests; but this has been found only in the later elementary grades. Similarly, language minority students in developmental bilingual programs score better in English than comparable students in non-bilingual programs—but this is evident only at the end of the elementary grades (Cummins, 1981; Thomas & Collier, 1997). If the effectiveness of these EE programs had been judged at the end of kindergarten, grade 1 or grade 2, they would have been declared ineffective and maybe even terminated. It was only by examining the long term results that researchers were able to determine the true effectiveness of these programs. This should not surprise us as educators—we all know that the real fruits of education are evident only in the long term.

There are important implications associated with these developmental facts:

- Program planners must make long term commitments with respect to curriculum, materials, and professional development, staffing, space, and the allocation of other resources and services.

- Parents should be committed to keeping their children in EE programs from the early grades to the end.

- School principals and teachers should encourage students and their parents to stay in the program and to not abandon it at the faintest sign of possible difficulty.

- Decisions that permit students to enter the program after one or two years of the starting grade should be discouraged, unless the students can demonstrate that they have already acquired some proficiency in the second language. Students entering late have difficulty catching up to the students who have been in the program from the beginning and they often struggle and seldom realize the full benefits that result from sustained participation.

Feature 5: Effective Instruction Is Student-Centered

While effective instruction is built on patterns of development that most students exhibit, the individual differences that naturally distinguish one student from another must also be considered. In other words, an important starting point for planning instruction is the individual student. Students are different from one another because of differences in both constitutional and experiential background. Such diverse factors as social, cultural, linguistic, nutritional, psychomotor, interests, and personality can all influence students' learning styles (see Glossary) and aptitudes in school. Differences among students from minority backgrounds are likely to be extensive since they can differ with respect to their first languages (see Glossary), their levels of first and second language proficiency, previous educational experiences (especially with respect to literacy), preferred learning styles, and even medical and general socio-economic conditions. Thus, it is critical that EE teachers pay attention to individual differences among these students.

Such differences are likely to be unfamiliar to teachers from mainstream backgrounds who know only English and, thus, they pose a formidable challenge in planning appropriate instruction. (Educators working in urban settings are increasingly faced with some of the same challenges.) Teachers who come from language and cultural backgrounds that differ from those of their students must actively discover characteristics of their students that might influence their learning in school. Let us briefly consider a cognitive factor that can be linked to individual and group differences in learning. When planning instruction, teachers should consider individual students' *cognitive capacity* and the *cognitive demands* (see Glossary) of alternative instructional tasks. Generally speaking, older students have more cognitive capacity than younger students and, thus, can be expected to undertake more cognitively demanding tasks. It is important to recognize when EE students are working in their second language, they will find most tasks more cognitively demanding than when they are working in their primary language. Of course, this will also depend on individual students' relative proficiency in the second language. In addition, students' prior educational experiences, their familiarity with classroom activities, and their general physical and psychological well-being will influence the cognitive load imposed by particular tasks.

Student performance in class can also be influenced by a variety of *cultural factors*, including grouping and interactional patterns during instruction, reinforcers and motivational techniques, and the content of instructional activities. Certain instructional content, activities, goals, or interaction patterns can impede learning because they are unfamiliar to students. Students might appear to be indifferent during classroom activities when, in fact, they are conflicted by what is expected of them in class and how they have learned to behave at home. For example, students from some cultural groups have been taught that they should not show off or stand out in the company of others; that they should not look adults in the eye because it is a sign of disrespect; and that they should not speak out but rather should learn by watching others. When these students behave in these ways in class, they are doing what is culturally appropriate in their community. Schooling in Anglo-American settings calls for a different set of behaviors that they will eventually learn. But, it will take them time to become comfortable with these new ways of behaving.

Teachers in EE programs must be careful not to assume that all students who speak English share the same cultural background simply because they all speak English. Even English-speaking students come from different cultural groups that have different social norms and ways of behaving. For example, English-speaking American versus British students, or Anglo-American versus African-American students; or English-speaking Native Americans versus English-speaking Anglo-Americans. Alternatively, students from minority backgrounds may speak English well but identify strongly with a minority culture because that is the culture in which they grew up. While we all agree that all students should acquire and be proficient in the cultural norms and orientations of the main-stream culture, we should not assume that our students share these cultural norms and orientations in the beginning. Most teachers are familiar with and proficient in the cultural orientations of the mainstream cultural group, but they may be unfamiliar with the cultural norms of their students. Teachers who familiarize themselves with the cultural characteristics of their students can enhance the effectiveness of their instruction and, ultimately, their students' success.

Feature 6: Language Instruction Is Integrated with Challenging Academic Instruction

It is widely recognized by language development specialists that primary language acquisition occurs in conjunction with other aspects of children's development. Language acquisition contributes to the child's cognitive and social development and is, in turn, influenced by these aspects of development. Take the case of language and cognition, for

Voices from the Field

The Benefits of a Shared Philosophy

Conchita Medina
Program Coordinator
Alicia R. Chacón International School
El Paso, TX

Four years ago we were presented with the challenge of creating a two-way dual language school that incorporated instruction of a third language; Chinese, Japanese, German, and Russian. For many of us this was a far departure from our traditional way of thinking and teaching. Immersion, to us at that time, represented a negative method of learning a second language—one in which students were thrown in an educational setting without much help or support. Yet drawing upon the experiences of River Glen Elementary in San Jose, California, we slowly began to create some features that we believed to be critical for success of native and non-native speakers of both Spanish and English. Over the course of the summer of 1995 the first sixteen teachers chosen to participate in this endeavor, along with principal Bob Schulte, began to chip away at old beliefs about bilingual education, immersion, and high

expectations for minority students. And after much personal and professional soul searching, a new set of values emerged and quickly began to take shape. As a result, our new school's philosophy was one based on a common belief system that was shared by administrators, teachers, staff, and parents. This shared philosophy was probably the most critical factor attributed to the success of our school.

As a new staff with various degrees of experience in the teaching field, we were also aware of the fact that our traditional way of teaching might not be effective in a classroom of mixed language proficiencies. We had to develop an approach that would allow us to deliver quality lessons to students of both languages. Our approach was simple and complex at the same time. We did whatever we had to do to make our lessons understood. Cooperative learning, class presentations, singing, drawing,

sharing, and dancing, just to name a few, became the norm in the classroom. Teachers who once stood in front of the chalkboard while giving lessons were now found on the floor using a giant world map and unifix cubes in various colors to reenact historical invasions.

Along with the above features of our program, I must add that we were a staff dedicated to the success of all students regardless of their educational, socio-economic and/or cultural background. We as teachers worked hard against the belief that in order for our children to experience success they must have had all the "appropriate" experiences. Since our inception, we have never and continue not to screen students into our program. Our students come to us from all over the city. They represent the general make up of our community. We include all levels of learning as well as inclusion.

A common belief system, a change in the delivery of instruction, as well as high academic expectations makes for a truly successful school for all students.

example. Children's early language skills reflect their cognitive abilities so that their first words and utterances refer to concrete objects and to events that are physically present in their lives because these are meaningful and accessible to them. Children's first use of language consists of one, two, or three words, probably because of their short-term memory limitations. As children's cognitive capacities develop, they become increasingly able to use longer utterances and to refer to abstract concepts and to events that are remote in time and place. At the same time, language development contributes to the developing child's ability to think in abstract terms because language gives the child the means for referring to abstract and remote events and objects. School plays a particularly important role in helping students use language as a tool of cognitive development.

Effective educators recognize and understand these important relationships and they use them to promote language development and academic achievement in school. They see all school activities as opportunities to teach language, even when the explicit focus is not on language. This approach is known variously as *language-across-the-curriculum, whole language,* or *integrative language teaching.* The important point here is that effective education seeks to establish the same relationship between language and other aspects of development in school that characterizes normal language acquisition outside school. When this is accomplished, students can use their natural language learning abilities to develop more advanced language skills and ways of thinking. It is particularly important that educators working in programs that aim for second language proficiency fully understand this developmental interdependence. Some educators believe that language proficiency is a prerequisite to academic development and, therefore, that students being educated through the medium of a second language must first acquire proficiency in the language of instruction before they are provided full instruction in academic subjects. This perspective all too often results in English language learners being pulled out of class to receive ESL instruction. Such practices reduce English language learners' access to the academic curriculum. In fact, we now know that integrative second language instruction is much more effective than approaches that teach second languages in isolation—see, for example, the extensive evidence from evaluations of second language immersion programs (Genesee, 1987). At the same time, content instruction through the medium of a second language must accommodate the students' limited but developing second language proficiency; this will be discussed in greater detail in Chapter 6.

A number of national professional associations endorse the integration of academic instruction as a means of achieving high levels of proficiency in second or foreign languages. For example, TESOL (Teachers of English to Speakers of Other Languages, 1997) has made the learning of English for academic purposes a major goal for ESL instruction—Goal 2 in TESOL's *ESL Standards for Pre-K–12 Students* (1997) stipulates that students should be able to use their second language (1) to interact in the classroom, (2) to obtain, process, construct, and provide subject matter information in spoken and written form, and (3) to use appropriate learning strategies (see Glossary) to construct and apply academic knowledge. Likewise, ACTFL (The American Council on the Teaching of Foreign Languages), together with the American Association of Teachers of French, The American Association of Teachers of German, and the American Association of Teachers of Spanish and Portuguese, have identified the use of the second/foreign language for learning other content areas as one of five major standards of foreign language education (American Council on the Teaching of Foreign Languages, 1996).

Language proficiency is not monolithic. It varies as a function of the context, purpose, and content of communication. The language skills we use when talking with peers differ from those we use when talking with someone who has a position of authority; the language we use to present an oral report in school is different from the language we use when describing the day's events at home. Relevant to our discussion about schooling, there are obvious differences between the kind of language skills used in school when talking about academic subject matter and those that are used in every day informal conversations about grocery shopping or personal relationships. The differences can be found not only in the vocabulary we use, but also in our sentence and discourse structure. Generally speaking, language for academic purposes is more careful, includes explicit and coherent references to the topic of discussion, and provides considerable detail to insure that the discourse is comprehensible. In contrast, everyday language is abbreviated (or elliptical), generally lacks explicit reference, and often includes terms that are highly idiosyncratic to the speakers participating in the conversation.

Language proficiency also differs for different academic domains—the language skills that are required to talk or write proficiently about mathematics is different from the skills required to talk and write proficiently about science or social studies, and so on. This is recognized by a number of national professional associations, such as the National Council of Teachers of Mathematics (1989), that identify the importance of acquiring the ability to communicate using the language of mathematics, science, etc. Again, the differences are not only in vocabulary, but also in sentence structures and discourse patterns associated with different academic domains. Being competent in science and mathematics requires that students not only know the content associated with these subjects, but also know how to express what they know proficiently in oral and written language. Teachers face the dual task of teaching specialized subject matter and the specialized language skills associated with each domain. Educational programs that integrate language and content instruction are better able to teach the language skills that are essential for academic success than programs that teach language in isolation because the specialized language associated with each academic domain is presented along with the content itself. This is true whether instruction is through the students' primary language or their second language. It is particularly important in the case of instruction through the medium of a second language when students do not have extensive exposure to the language outside school.

Learning language to communicate about important, meaningful, and authentic subjects is motivating for most students. In contrast, few students are motivated to learn language in isolation, for its own sake. Integrating language instruction with meaningful academic instruction provides students with real reasons for learning language, embedding language acquisition in authentic communication provides students authentic contexts for acquiring the communication skills that are relevant to their needs in school. For an integrative approach to work effectively, students must find instruction meaningful, interesting, and appropriate. Instruction must also be focused on those language skills that are important for academic success.

We have worked in very diverse regions of the world where successful school programs integrate second language instruction with challenging academic content. Japanese students in Numazu, Japan study the national curriculum for all Japanese students through English with teachers who are native English-speakers. These students' parents want them to know English because it is an international language. Spanish-speaking students living in the Basque region of Northern Spain go to schools where only Basque is used to teach the curriculum. Basque is the predominant language in this region of Spain and Spanish-speaking parents want their children to know Basque and Spanish. Some of these parents are Basque but speak Spanish at home and want their children to acquire their ancestral language. The Estonian Ministry of Education is developing immersion programs in Estonian for Russian-speaking students. These students' parents have chosen to stay in Estonia following the break up of the USSR. The communities in which they live spoke only Russian during the Soviet regime, but now they need to know Estonian. English-speaking children of Hawaiian descent attend K–12 schools where the majority of their instruction is in Hawaiian. These children and their parents want to learn Hawaiian in this way because it is an important part of their cultural heritage and they want to preserve their language for future generations of Hawaiians.

Feature 7: Teachers in Effective EE Programs are Reflective

Effective general education as well as enriched education depends on teachers who are reflective about curriculum and instruction. Effective instruction occurs when teaching is modified in response to the results of formal and informal assessment of student progress, to feedback from students during instructional activities, and to teachers' observations of the appropriateness of curriculum materials and activities. Effective teachers have a repertoire of assessment techniques they use to obtain feedback about the effectiveness of their teaching and about student learning. Useful and versatile assessment methods include observation, conferencing, portfolios, dialogue journals, as well as teacher-made tests. We discuss these techniques in greater detail in Chapter 7. Effective teachers are familiar with and know how to devise reliable and valid classroom assessments to assess student progress in achieving curricular goals. They are also familiar with the uses and limitations of standardized tests. Their assessment activities are tightly linked to instructional planning and delivery and, more specifically, provide valuable information for tailoring instruction to meet the individualized and changing needs of students. Effective teachers are systematic in planning assessment and in reporting the results of assessment to parents and other educators involved in the education of these students.

Effective teachers working with students who are learning through the medium of a second language are able to devise assessments that distinguish between academic and language development so that the academic achievement of students in the early stages of second language acquisition can be assessed accurately. They are also able to assess students' ability to use language appropriately in communicating about specific academic subjects. Effective teachers can devise and use assessment activities, such as portfolios and dialogue journals, that have instructional value, so that assessment contributes to student learning and involves students in planning their own learning. They know how to include students in assessment so that they can take an active part in assessing their own progress.

Teachers who work effectively with students from minority and majority groups understand important cultural differences among their students. They can devise and use alternative assessment methods in ways that respect students' cultural orientations and sensitivities—for example, teachers working with students from cultural backgrounds that frown on assertive, individualistic displays of knowledge know how to elicit what students have learned using non-threatening and appropriate techniques. Teachers working with students from diverse cultural and linguistic groups

Voices from the Field

Reflective Teaching

Margarita P. Pinkos
Principal
Gove Elementary School
Belle Glade, Florida

Gove Elementary exemplifies in many ways the challenges that today's educators must face. It is located in a rural area, isolated from the coastal urban area by fields of sugar cane. Most of our students come from poor homes and represent a great diversity of ethnic and language groups. Most teachers travel from far to teach in our school. And yet there is a sense of community at the school, there is a sense of family.

I became principal at Gove Elementary five years ago. The school had gone through many changes, test scores were low and teachers taught in isolation. The school was divided in many subgroups and each felt the need to "defend their turf."

We decided that we needed to get together and clarify the mission of our school. Faculty and community members collaborated to define what was the purpose the school served in the community. The groups identified the values shared and how each group perceived their role in fulfilling the mission of the school. As expected, the groups had a great deal in common.

From then on the set of core values created a common language that was used to reflect on the efficacy of instructional strategies and procedures. All members of the school family decided that collaboration was how decisions were to be made and programs evaluated. Soon we realized that "the group" was all of us and that the common denominator was the best interest of our children.

That summer we held our first retreat. Teachers were paid a stipend and they volunteered to come before school started to reflect on past practices and to identify best practices. We looked back at the previous year, month by month, and reflected on instructional practices and the curriculum. We analyzed data, looked for patterns, and celebrated successful practices. We then planned for the following year school-wide themes. We created concept maps for each theme and later planned the content to be taught in each grade. There were many heated discussions to identify the appropriate curricular sequence and even questioning whether the concepts were significant.

Today Gove Elementary has developed the first dual language program in our district. Our retreat has become more focused each year. Although our test scores have gone up, we still have to improve, but now we have a mechanism to reflect on what we have done and to critically analyze where we must go next.

reflect on and monitor their own knowledge about and understanding of their students' backgrounds to ascertain whether they are sufficiently informed to plan effective instruction.

Feature 8: Effective EE Programs Are Integrated with Other School Programs and Schools

Descriptions of successful school programs, whether they include language and cultural enrichment or not, point to the importance of *coordination* with other programs and schools. EE programs that are integrated with the whole school or with schools elsewhere in the district create opportunities for language minority students to interact with native English-speaking students so that they can use English with native speakers of the same age. Integrating EE programs with the whole school also insures that EE students feel part of the whole school or district. EE students can lose their enthusiasm for staying in the program if they feel apart from other students. This is especially important as students become teenagers and the desire to "fit in" becomes strong. This is also particularly important for programs that serve language minority students who can feel stigmatized and marginal if the program is isolated. EE programs that are well integrated also give students throughout the school and district a greater appreciation of other languages and cultures.

Integration of EE programs with other programs in the school is important to ensure that their respective goals and plans are mutually compatible and that resources and expertise are shared to the benefit of all students in the school. We discuss critical resources for setting up programs in Chapter 3. When resources are in short supply, sharing resources is advantageous. In contrast, when school personnel are not familiar with EE, there is the risk that they will make decisions that interfere with or are incompatible with the EE program. Worse, personnel in the rest of the school may be threatened because of misconceptions about the program (believing, for example, that it will replace the all-English program). In such cases, the suspicions or misunderstandings that can result from such a situation can undermine EE programs. Programs that function in isolation can be targets of cutbacks or criticism if it is felt, correctly or incorrectly, that they are using additional resources that are not available to the "regular" program and students. Or, school personnel may misinterpret the incomplete English language development of minority or majority students in EE programs as evidence that they are not working. This can lead to calls for increased use of English, long before this is necessary.

Effective EE programs are well integrated with district-wide programs and activities such as during discussions about standardized testing or planning sessions for curriculum revision. Coordination is important to insure that EE programs are not neglected and that they are held to the same high standards as others. Programs that function in isolation can be vulnerable because decisions can be made that do not take them into consideration or, worse, that are contrary to their best interests. Resources may not be forthcoming because decision-makers are oblivious to the program's needs or simply do not care about the program. Involving EE programs in district activities insures visibility of the program, instills district-wide pride in the program, and demonstrates to everyone the advantages of learning other languages and knowing about other cultures.

Feature 9: Effective EE Programs Aim for Additive Bilingualism

This feature is unique to EE programs. As we noted in Chapter 1, the programs we discuss in this book are enriched because they aim for advanced levels of functional proficiency in a second language while fully developing students' primary languages. By functional proficiency in language, we mean the ability to use language accurately and appropriately in its oral and written forms in a variety of settings, including school and out-of-school settings. EE programs also aim to develop students' understanding and appreciation of the culture(s) of the second language group while affirming and building on students' home culture. Because these programs seek to *add* new language and culture skills while continuing to develop the students' existing language and culture skills, they are "additive bilingual programs." This term was first used by Wallace Lambert of McGill University in Montreal in 1972. He coined it to distinguish enriched language and culture programs of the type we review in this book from programs that by design, or unintentionally, result in students giving up or losing their home language and culture. Students from language minority backgrounds who acquire a language other than English at home prior to entering school are often encouraged to learn English as quickly as possible and to give up their home language. They are also encouraged to assimilate to the dominant American culture as quickly as possible, forsaking their cultural heritage. This approach, sometimes referred to as *submersion* or *sink-or-swim* education (see Glossary), is promoted on the assumptions that children are burdened by acquiring two languages, the fastest route to full proficiency in English is to concentrate on English only, and learning two languages early in development is not normal or natural.

Research has demonstrated clearly that these assumptions are inaccurate. Moreover, education that is based on these assumptions creates an unfavorable learning environment because it compels young learners to give up something that is an essential part of themselves in order to fit in. Regardless of all the research to the contrary, such beliefs persist and often form the basis for educational planning. It is important for those working in EE programs for language minority students to understand that such beliefs are diametrically opposed to the enriched language and cultural goals sought in these programs. These beliefs underestimate and, indeed undermine, children's natural ability to learn two languages and accommodate different cultural perspectives. Viewed differently, those who maintain such beliefs set low standards for schooling—they are satisfied with monolingualism and monoculturalism when we know that children's education can be enriched through bilingualism and biculturalism. An *additive bilingual* approach is fundamental to the success of EE programs because it confirms the belief that all children are capable of acquiring proficiency in more than one language if given appropriate learning environments. A belief in additive bilingualism supports high expectations and standards for what children can and should learn. Children who do not succeed in school often fail because educators have unacceptably low expectations for them.

Educators who understand the notion of additive bilingualism are better able than others to identify and establish the learning conditions that are necessary for the positive cognitive and linguistic consequences that we discussed in Chapter 1. Take the example of language transfer—English-speaking students who acquire advanced levels of functional proficiency in a second language are likely to experience superior levels of first language competence. Likewise, children who come to school speaking a language other than English develop proficiency in English more readily the more advanced their primary language skills. Both of these well-documented effects occur when learners have *advanced* levels of skills in one of their developing languages. This makes a great deal of sense—skills that are well developed can provide the basis for learning related skills, whereas skills that are not well developed provide a weak foundation for learning new skills. While this seems obvious, it is often forgotten. Educators who promote additive bilingualism organize the curriculum to give adequate exposure to both languages; they provide the kinds of extended and enriched learning experiences in both languages that are essential for their full mastery. To achieve additive benefits of bilingualism, it is necessary to promote language acquisition; to promote language acquisition it is necessary to promote active language use; to promote active language use, it is necessary to insist that students' use their second language in as many school domains as possible.

The status of the two languages being learned and of the cultures associated with those languages is important for creating additive bilingual environments in EE programs. In North America, for example, the high status language is English and the high status culture is Anglo-European. In comparison, other languages and cultures are likely to have lower status, although not low in any absolute sense. Even though the other languages in the program may be valued by school personnel, they may have low status in the community at large. Community attitudes can adversely influence students' and teachers' attitudes toward other languages and cultures. If educators behave, explicitly or implicitly, in ways that favor English and Anglo-European culture, they undermine students' motivation to learn the other language which, in turn, reduces program effectiveness. The same is true for cultural aspects of the program. If both languages and their related cultures are to be promoted equally, they must enjoy equal status and treatment within the school and the program.

Equalizing the status of the two languages and cultures is not always easy. It may actually be best achieved by giving more attention, time, and interest to the non-English language and its associated culture, at least in the beginning. There is no question that all students value English and the majority group culture. Giving some preference to the otherwise less supported language will not undermine English, but will serve to enhance the value of the other language and of learning the other language. A general rule-of-thumb is *provide extended and varied opportunities for all students to actively use the language and become familiar with the culture that are otherwise unused or given low status in the community at large*. This makes sense if one is guided by the notion of additive bilingualism.

In a related vein, it is important to distinguish between a program's goals and its structure. Some EE programs are structured so that both languages are represented equally and they are promoted at all grade levels and in all subject areas under the belief that a program that aims for bilingualism should itself be bilingual at all times. For example, some programs switch from one language to the other during the same lessons, from day to day, or from week to week. In contrast, the concept of additive bilingualism focuses our attention on the development of the learner, not the structure of the program. Language learning in school is often most effective when students focus on one language for an extended period of time. Dividing students' time and attention between two languages can interfere with learning.

Translated into program design, it is often best to devote instruction to one language for an extended period of time, rather than switching between the languages, so that skills in the language of concentration develop fully. Once developed, those language skills provide a solid foundation for the development of skills in the other language. Interrupting the use of the target language can interrupt learning. The disruption to learning can be significant since students come to rely on their already dominant language and avoid use of the second, non-dominant language. We consider what these developmental relationships mean more concretely in the following chapters as we examine specific aspects of the curriculum.

Summary

In this chapter, we discussed nine critical features of effective EE. We pointed out how these features apply to general education as well as to EE programs. We often focused on programs that serve language minority students because these programs require special consideration if we are to build really strong programs for all students. In the chapters that follow, we discuss program development and implementation (Chapter 3), oral language development (Chapter 4), developing literacy in two languages (Chapter 5), teaching content (Chapter 6), and assessment (Chapter 7). These chapters are followed by model lessons and assessment procedures (Chapter 8), and a discussion of advocacy (Chapter 9). We have discussed these nine critical features in somewhat general terms here. We discuss them in more concrete terms as we go along. At the end of each chapter, we summarize our discussions in a checklist that is organized around these critical features.

References

Adams, M.J. (1990). *Beginning to Read*. Cambridge, MA: MIT Press.

American Council on the Teaching of Foreign Languages (1996). *Standards for Foreign Language Learning: Preparing for the 21st Century*. Yonkers, NY: ACTFL.

August, D., & Hakuta, K. (1997). *Improving Schooling for Language-Minority Students*. Washington, D.C.: National Academy Press.

Collier, V. (1992). A Synthesis of Studies Examining Long-Term Language Minority Student Data on Academic Achievement. *Bilingual Research Journal,* 16: 187–212.

Cummins, J. (1981). The Role of Primary Language Development in Promoting Educational Success for Language Minority Students. In *Schooling and Language Minority Students: A Theoretical Framework*. Los Angeles, CA: Evaluation, Dissemination, and Assessment Center, 1–50.

Genesee, F. (1987). *Learning Through Two Languages: Studies of Immersion and Bilingual Education*. Rowley, MA: Newbury House.

Lambert, W.E., & Tucker, G.R. (1972). *The Bilingual Education of Children*. Rowley, MA: Newbury House.

National Council of Teachers of Mathematics (1989). *Curriculum and Evaluation Standards for School Mathematics*. Reston, VA: NCTM.

Snow, C.E., Burns, M.S., & Griffin, P. (1998). *Preventing Reading Difficulties in Young Children*. Washington, D.C.: National Academy Press.

Teachers of English to Speakers of Other Languages. (1997). *ESL Standards for Pre-K–12 Students*. Alexandria, VA: TESOL.

Thomas, W., & Collier, V. (1998). *School Effectiveness for Language Minority Students*. Alexandria, VA: National Clearinghouse for Bilingual Education.

3 PROGRAM DEVELOPMENT AND IMPLEMENTATION

In this chapter, we look at the way in which enriched education (EE) programs are developed and maintained. We address seven areas that must be taken into account when an EE program is started. These include initiating the program, the roles that parents and the larger community play in starting a program, the relationship of the program to the rest of the school, staff selection and preparation, and student selection. We then address ten areas for maintaining an EE program. These include issues for parents and the larger community, required teacher competencies, allocation of time to the two languages, coordination and student grouping, locating materials, and ensuring program effectiveness. This chapter, as some others following it, is organized around questions that are frequently asked by teachers, administrators, and parents as they get ready to develop an EE program.

Starting up an EE Program

Who initiates the idea of an EE program?

The idea of an EE program can be initiated at any level within a school district. Parents may decide that they would like for their children to be fully bilingual by the time they graduate from school. They may form a coalition and request that the school or district establish an EE program. Sometimes, district coordinators who are involved in language education first conceive the idea of an EE program. They may come from a foreign language background or have a responsibility for the education of language minority students in the district. In either case, their idea is based on a quest for a more effective instructional model. We know that the success of EE programs does not depend on the particular person or group that initiates it. However, most programs are initiated from within the educational community rather than being imposed from the top down. Regardless of who initiates the idea of an EE program, the next step of introducing it to key people is fundamental to the subsequent success of the program.

To whom is the idea of establishing a program introduced and how?

Despite the tremendous benefits that research has shown for students in EE programs, many people in the U.S. do not see language and culture enrichment as an asset or even a need. Whoever initiates the idea of an EE program usually needs to convince "the others" of its value. Regardless of whether the initiator is a parent or a staff member (such as a district coordinator or a principal), the superintendent and subsequently,

school board members have to be approached early on in the process. This way, they can be well informed from the beginning of the planning and they can be persuaded systematically of its value for the district and the larger community. In financially lean times, this may be an arduous task and will necessitate extensive planning. Teachers at the school where the EE program is to be housed also need to be informed as early as possible about the design and characteristics of the program, and some may also have to be persuaded of its worth. Teachers, specifically those who are monolingual, need to be reassured that the establishment of the program in their school does not mean the loss of a position for them. Finally, parents who are not part of the initial supportive core group also need to be presented with some facts regarding the program. They need to be reassured that their children's education will not suffer in any way as a result of the establishment of the program in their children's school. Parents whose children enroll in the program also need to be given a set of expectations and bilingual developmental landmarks through which their children are bound to pass.

The following steps may be taken by either parents or school staff to begin the process of establishing an EE program in their community. The order in which these steps are taken may differ according to the specific situation in the district or the community:

- A group that can spearhead the project and officially represent the interests of the program.

- Contact a higher educational organization (university or educational resource center) and, with their help, put together an information packet (see suggested list in Appendix C) that can be given to the superintendent, school board members, principal(s), and other parents and community members.

- Contact other schools in the area that have a successful EE program and enlist their help as well. The directory of two-way bilingual programs in the United States published biannually by the Center for Applied Linguistics can be useful for locating the program that is nearest to your school (Montone, Christian & Whitcher, 1997).

- Set up meetings with the superintendent, principal(s), and school board members. You may invite outside "experts" to give talks or answer questions at some of these meetings.

- Begin talking to neighbors and other community members about the project.

- Talk to school board members individually.

- Set up meetings with community members and parents of potential students. If you invite outside "experts" to talk or to answer questions, make sure they do so in lay terms that non-educators can understand.

- Involve the person who is responsible for foreign language education in the district. Regardless of whether the foreign language department will take part in the program, teachers who identify themselves with foreign language instruction (see Glossary) must be somewhat invested in it.

- Involve the person who is responsible for coordinating instructional programs for minority students—such as the bilingual program director. If the EE program is to involve minority students, that person must take a leading role in the project.

Voices from the Field

The Contrasting Stories of Two District Coordinators, One Who Succeeded to Have an EE Program Established Quickly, and One Whose Plans Took a Longer Time

Melissa Wolf, Bilingual Program Coordinator, Highland Park School District, Highland Park, Illinois

The summer of 1996, our superintendent, Dr. JoAnn Desmond, called for a study of models of bilingual education that would benefit all children. Although the self-contained model of bilingual education at the primary level was benefiting Spanish-dominant children academically, it did not provide social interactions with English-speaking children and it did not benefit English-speaking children. Dr. Desmond suggested contacting the AMIGOS program in Cambridge, which she had learned about while attending a conference in Boston. It was encouraging that the superintendent was committed to language minority students and

acknowledged the benefits of bilingualism for all students. Dual Language Instruction seemed to answer the need.

I started a thorough investigation of Dual Language programming. The Illinois Resource Center (IRC), the statewide resource center for bilingual education, provided a variety of resources for our district and community. We contacted and visited districts around the country with established dual language programs.

The proposal to investigate the possibility of dual language instruction was presented to the Board of Education in January of 1996, and the board asked for a report at its May

meeting. We sent out an invitation immediately for people to serve on the Dual Language Program Development Team. Over 40 people responded.

Five informational meetings for interested community members were scheduled. The meetings were carried on local cable TV. These meetings, which were well attended by English and Spanish speaking parents included theoretical information and presentations by parents, staff, and students from area dual language programs. Presentations were also given to the PTA Presidents' Council, the District Administrative Team, and area community organizations such as the Rotary Club. The program team, administrators, and principals from the host school visited area dual language sites.

A document entitled: "The Case For Dual Language Instruction" was finished. Many of the issues addressed in the document had to do with neighborhood versus mag-

(continued)

Voices from the Field (continued)

net site considerations, the host school's financial obligation to the program, and curricular issues concerned with student achievement in English if 80% of the instructional day was delivered in Spanish.

We then began to collect applications for interested students: 170 families responded, half of whom were Spanish-dominant. By the end of the summer, we had enough families for two kindergarten classes and one first grade.

The May school board meeting proved to be a challenge. The day started with phone calls to the superintendent and to board members who were skeptical, cautious, and concerned about our proposal. Newspaper reporters were eager to write about the program and the board decision. The discussion among the board members lasted well over a half an hour, but the board unanimously voted for the pilot magnet program to be implemented for the fall of 1996. My responses to their questions and concerns were detailed and decisive: The program would benefit a large group of children and families, and the district already employed excellent bilingual teachers who could adapt to the new program model.

That summer we worked on the curriculum, worked with the staff members in the schools housing the program, and introduced the program to the school community. Teachers attended IRC-sponsored workshops on dual language instruction. Media Center coordinators from host schools catalogued Spanish language books and coor-

dinated with the librarians at the new site. Parents and staff who were going to be part of the pioneering classes came together at the *Feria del Niño*. Families brought food, the music teacher prepared songs, and parents and staff shared their feelings about the program and spoke about how they became interested. Friendships were made and bridges were formed out of the vision to educate children together.

During the first year, the Dual Language Parent Teacher Group set short- and long-term goals for the program. Successful continuation of the program including marketing and recruiting new students became both a short- and a long-term priority. A group of parents volunteered to find friends who would produce a video about the program, which was released in January in both English and Spanish. The video, along with an informational brochure that was also produced, have been very useful in community meetings. The video was also shown regularly on the local cable station.

* * *

Elyze G. Minzer
Director of Curriculum and Instruction
Diamond Lake School,
Mundelein, Illinois*

Dual Language was an exciting concept I discovered in the Spring of 1995. As a Foreign Language Director, I had wondered why the acquisition of a second language was so difficult for so many English-speaking stu-

dents. After much research, discussions with experts, and visits to Dual Language schools, it was clear that this model would be ideal for our district that had a large population of language minority students. My first step was to make an appointment with our superintendent and share with him this cutting edge program, called Dual Language. Since our superintendent was always looking for innovative programs to better meet the needs of the community, I was given the green light to present the Dual Language concept to all the principals and coordinators of the district. My presentation included the following topics:

- What is Dual Language and who can participate in it?

- What are the outcomes of the program?

- Research supporting second language acquisition.

- What are the benefits of a Dual Language program to our school district?

- What is the cost of implementing and maintaining a Dual Language program?

- A timeline for implementation.

By the end of the presentation, the administrators unanimously supported the concept. Now it was time to educate the Board of Education, and they were given the same presentation. They questioned whether the community would embrace the concept and asked me to see if there was any interest. I hoped that interest would be high and that we would be able to begin a Dual Language pro-

(continued)

Voices from the Field (continued)

gram in Kindergarten and/or first grade in the 1997–1998 school year.

I began by selecting a primary building that would best accommodate the program and where the community that attended that school would be supportive. Once the site was selected, the building staff was inserviced in detail on how a Dual Language program would function in their school. A team of Spanish-speaking teachers from the district formed the team that helped create the program. The principal and the team of teachers visited schools with Dual Language programs. They also attended many workshops on Dual Language programs provided by the Illinois Resource Center.

While the district personnel were being inserviced, the community was receiving weekly flyers in both Spanish and English on different aspects of dual language education. Flyers were also distributed in area preschools. Three community meetings were set up in both English and Spanish to provide interested parents with more information. Coordinators, teachers, and consultants from dual language programs presented at these meetings. English- and Spanish-speaking parents who had children in dual language programs also presented at these meetings and gave a sense of what it was like to have a child in a dual language program. We showed videos on dual language instruction and gave participants a Dual Language English/Spanish Informational Booklet. The booklet addressed the following topics:

- the importance of dual language programs.
- benefits of being bilingual.
- the dual language philosophy.
- components of a dual language program.
- methods of dual language instruction.
- the elementary dual language curriculum.
- evaluation and student progress.
- the dual language staff.
- student enrollment.
- sample kindergarten and first grade schedules.

- common questions and concerns.

At the end of each meeting, parents were asked to fill out a questionnaire and indicate if they were interested in enrolling their child in a dual language program if one was offered. Despite the overwhelming interest by parents, the Board of Education and the district administration got cold feet. They felt that the year-long process needed to be put on the shelf for a year because they were not ready to implement the program just yet. Many families were upset at being offered the possibility and then watching it disappear before their very own eyes. Their children would miss the opportunity of ever participating in a dual language program since it starts only in kindergarten or first grade. This story, however, does have a happy ending: In the 1998–1999 school year, a dual language program was implemented in a half-day kindergarten class, and we hope it will continue to grow every year.

*This essay is about a district other than the one Ms. Minzer is currently with.

What is the role of parents in starting an EE program?

As is the case with educational programs in general, parents can exert tremendous influence in establishing an EE program within their school district. In fact, they are the only force within a school district that has the power to demand certain goals for their children. Many programs were created when parents wanted their children to have the advantage of being bilingual. As described briefly in Chapter 2, one of the earliest models of EE programs in North America was the highly successful Canadian Immersion programs that were established as a result of parental pressure on the local school board. Although parents can wield significant power over a school board or a superintendent, unfortunately, their wishes are not always heeded.

It is important to include parents in planning a new program to ensure that they are fully aware of the structure and goals of the program and are prepared to make the long-term commitments of time and involvement that successful participation in such a program entails. For example, English-speaking parents contemplating sending their children to dual language programs or single language immersion programs must understand that their children will be receiving significant portions of instruction, including reading and writing, through the medium of a second language. Likewise, language minority parents must understand that their children will be receiving primary instruction through the medium of the home language along with or prior to instruction in English. Parents must also be informed of what to expect with respect to their children's language and academic achievement during the early and later grades of the program so that they are not surprised by the outcomes. Such information is vital if parents are to fully understand that they should commit to keeping their child in the program throughout its duration. (See the suggestions for informational sessions to be held for parents in the question regarding teacher preparation in a later section of this chapter.)

While school districts have an unconditional responsibility to respond to parents' aspirations with respect to the educational goals for their children, it is unfair, for both educators and parents, to expect parents to play the role of educational advisors. Parents who are not educators themselves should not be placed in a position where they are asked to make pedagogical decisions. However, the parents' wishes for their children must be honored and parents must be kept fully informed. Open communication must be established, and this can only happen if a high level of trust exists between educators and parents.

What role does the larger community play in developing and maintaining an EE program?

Support from the larger community is very important. Community members can either be catalysts or hurdles to the establishment of an EE program. In communities with a large representation of the mainstream population, members of the mainstream are usually quite influential. It is important to get them on your side, and to do so, members of the mainstream must see the program as an asset to the whole community. Parents in the U.S. may not automatically see bilingualism as an asset for their children, and may have strong misgivings about their own lack of proficiency in the other language of instruction. As suggested in an earlier section of this chapter, other parents and students who are successfully completing an EE program can help alleviate some of these fears and begin to change community members' attitudes. It is also important to get the local business community involved in the program. Supportive local businesses can play the role of sponsors of different facets of the program by providing financial support for special projects that the school undertakes. They, in turn, might benefit from the language resources that the school has to offer (see Table 3.1).

Table 3.1   Suggestions for Getting Community Support

- Feature students' achievements, such as written work and correspondence with native-speaking peers from other countries or communities in community centers or at community events.
- Contact the local newspaper or other media to feature the program.
- Offer language resources to local businesses that have international connections or that serve speakers of the other language.
- Offer courses in English as a second language and in the language other than English to parents and community members.
- Prepare an information packet consisting of one-page summaries of program accomplishments, including any news stories that have appeared in the local newspaper.
- Prepare a very short video (or use one that another district has prepared; see suggested list of resources in Appendix D) that shows parents and community members talking about their experiences with the program and the benefits they have personally seen from bilingualism and cross-cultural proficiency.

What is the relationship of the EE program to the rest of the school?

Administrative support at all levels is crucial for an EE program to succeed. When an EE program is started, superintendents and school board members must be informed and their support must be cultivated. The entire teaching staff must be informed and reassured as to what the new program will mean for them. Regardless of how extensive the EE program is within a school, the involvement of the whole school is crucial. The EE program should not be seen as an isolated segment of the school. If the EE program extends over the entire school, then that school should not be seen as an isolated entity within the district. In either case, the program must be a conceptually and physically integral part of the larger school or district (McLeod, 1996). The program must be carefully planned so that it is closely integrated with the school's general curriculum and other offerings. This is especially true for programs that include minority students. In fact, in truly integrated programs, it is often difficult to point to the program for minority students. One model of such a tight-knit relationship between a program for minority students and the rest of the school is the two-way immersion school where the program for minority students is the program for all students. All students in the school regardless of their proficiency in English are instructed in both English and Spanish and are expected to become fully bilingual by the time they leave school, at grade eight.

Even if a school does not have a full-fledged two-way immersion program, the program for minority students must be fully integrated with the general educational program designed for the majority population. Many schools organize students in larger-than-class groups that include non-minority students. Within these units, students are grouped in various ways for different instructional purposes. In that way, minority students are integrated with other students in a variety of contexts. When minority students are fully integrated into the school, the whole staff also begins to take responsibility for their education, and the whole staff becomes familiar with the special program designed for the minority students. All teachers, regardless of whether they are part of the EE program, can participate in staff development sessions designed for EE teachers. All teachers can also participate in language classes that the program may be offering for adults in the community. The ideal is that all individuals associated with the school or district should take pride in the program, and must see it as an asset not just to the school but to the community at large (see Table 3.2).

How is staff located and prepared?

The first choice for hiring program staff should be teachers who are specialized in the area of language and culture education. Specialized staff for EE programs may come from the fields of foreign language education, bilingual education, or English as a second language. Teachers from these fields are likely to have the preparation that would help them develop students' proficiency in English and the language other than English, to advance students' knowledge in important subject matter, and to assist students in becoming active members of a culturally diverse commu-

nity. Since most EE programs become established in already existing schools, the program often has to absorb some of the teachers who have been part of the existing school or school district. Many of these teachers may be monolingual English speakers and may not have the qualifications to teach all aspects of a given grade in an EE program. However, if they are accomplished teachers, they will be able to provide students with the English portion of the curriculum and team up with a bilingual teacher who can teach the non-English portion of the curriculum.

Depending on their level of expertise in the area of enriched language and culture education, teachers need to have some training prior to the start of an EE program as well as some ongoing professional development. At a mini-

---

Table 3.2　Suggestions for Increasing Awareness and Improving Attitudes among School Staff

- Prepare a brief informational packet for administrators, board members, and teachers that includes the following: a description of the basic features of the program, a summary of the research showing the effectiveness of EE programs, and quotes from parents and students regarding the qualities of the program (see the suggested list of resources in Appendix C).

- Arrange for teachers and administrators to visit other schools in the area that have successful EE programs.

- Include sessions on EE programs in the district or school staff development plan.

- Offer courses in the language other than English to all the staff in the school or district.

- Allow all teachers the opportunity to team-teach with EE teachers or to participate as observers or language learners in EE classrooms.

mum, all teachers in a school where the EE program is to be housed need a general informational session on the purpose, design, and goals of the program. Other school staff also needs to be informed about the coming program and to be given the opportunity to voice any concerns they may have. The role that a school receptionist or a lunchroom employee plays in determining the success of a program cannot be

ignored. Monolingual English-speaking teachers, and teachers who do not have much training or experience with second language or bilingual education, who are going to take part in the EE program need additional staff development prior to the start of the program. Table 3.3 shows a suggested staff development plan for teachers with varying levels of expertise.

Table 3.3 Sample Staff Development Plan: Critical Topics to Address Prior to Program Startup

For all school staff, and separately, for parents and community members:
- What the EE program is all about.
- Why have this program in our school?
- Who is the program for?
- Basic principles of the program.
- Design of the program.
- Who will be teaching in the program?
- How is the program being funded?
- What opportunities does this program offer to members of the school community?
- What does having the program in our school mean for me?

In addition, for parents of participating students:
- What can I expect from my child in the first year and in subsequent years?
- What can I do at home to help my child?
- What resources will I have in the language that I am not proficient in?

In addition, for all teachers:
- Pedagogical principles of the program.
- Five-year projection of the educational features and outcomes of the program.
- Possible collaborations among program and non-program teachers.
- What role can I play in the school or program?

In addition, for EE program teachers:
- How do language and culture mediate learning?
- How does second language proficiency develop?
- How does literacy develop in two languages?
- What instructional strategies promote language development?
- What strategies promote the learning of subject matter when students are not proficient in the language of instruction?
- How can we encourage student-mediated learning?
- How do I assess my students' progress?

Some Thoughts on Teacher Training

Based on an interview with Maritza Meyers
Director of Dual, ESL, Bilingual, and Title 1 Programs
Long Beach City School District
Long Beach, New York

The most important topic for training new monolingual English teachers who will be working in a dual language program is how to teach reading to limited English proficient (LEP) students. We have new teachers coming into the program every year since a new grade is added yearly, and even experienced teachers who may know how to teach monolingual English speaking children how to read are not prepared to teach bilingual children and to guide them into biliteracy. Teacher education colleges do not address the issue of learning to read in two languages adequately. English monolingual teachers do not know what it's like for a student to be learning through a second language. In our staff development, we have to cover even very basic teaching strategies such as using hands-on activities, using TPR to introduce vocabulary, etc. It would be nice if colleges of education in any urban area included a course on second language learners as part of any teacher's training.

For bilingual teachers, the focus of our training is on how to teach Spanish as a Second Language (SSL) through academic content areas. A few years ago, we got together teachers from the whole district and they wrote a scope and

sequence that specified the skills that children need to have by the end of the year. This serves as a valuable guide for SSL teachers. For both English and Spanish teachers, it is important to start with the theoretical basis, and move on to what the theory means for the classroom. In our initial staff development, we also cover the design of the program, assignment of languages to content areas, and time allotment for reading in the two languages.

For new teachers, we hold a three-day summer institute, and then we provide ongoing professional development during the year. During the year, we provide professional development in two ways. The first is through in-class support: the bilingual resource specialist *(see "Voices from the Field" by Wanda Toledo)* goes into the classroom and works with teachers, coaching them and giving them feedback. The second way is through workshops. It is very important to offer these workshops during the school day because they are simply not effective after school. Teachers are exhausted at the end of the day, and on Saturdays, they need to be with their families. Workshop days can also provide an opportunity to do something nice for the teachers: give them break-

fast, lunch, and let them enjoy it! These teachers need to be patted on the back. Some of them teach fifty children every day, and it takes a lot of preparation to teach content in a student's second language. We're lucky that we have Title 7 funding and other local funding that allows us to get substitutes and pay for workshop expenses.

In order to have a successful program, you must have a consistent staff development program that spans the whole year. The staff development must also span the entire staff in a school. All school personnel needs to know what dual language instruction is. Everyone must feel that they are involved in the education of these students. The cafeteria workers, the drivers, they all become the voices of the program. Sometimes a lack of understanding creates animosity. When we started our program, the superintendent didn't know enough about it and was not sure about the benefits of the program. Now that he is thoroughly familiar with the program, he has become one of its strongest advocates.

It is also very important to build flexibility into the program. At the end of the year, we all have to ask whether anything needs to be changed for the following year. Sometimes we make mistakes, but nothing is written in stone. We must look at the needs of every child and decide what is the best program for each child. Staff development also involves that process of questioning and making decisions.

How are students selected?

Programs differ in the way that they select students, both initially and in upper grades. Initially, in most programs, the first group of students start in pre-kindergarten to first grade and students are added as the program advances to higher grade levels. Thus, the first year of the program is restricted to kindergarten or first grade; in the second year, the following grade is added, and so on. In some programs that constitute a whole school, students are not selected as such, but rather, they participate in the program by virtue of being enrolled in that school. In most EE programs housed within a larger school, however, students participate by choice. In neighborhood schools where there is a restricted number of places to be filled and in magnet schools, some selection process occurs. In single language programs, such as developmental bilingual programs and immersion for language majority students, students are selected either on a first-come first-served basis or using a lottery system.

Programs that serve students from two language groups, such as dual language programs, often have to consider the proportion of students representing each group. Because it is highly desirable to maintain a balance between the two groups, quotas are often established. However, attrition over the years may be uneven, so that one language group becomes the majority at an upper grade level. To counter the effects of inevitable attrition that also contributes to lowered numbers of students enrolled in upper grade levels, some programs set up at least two classes at each of the earliest grade levels. That way, there is a better chance that enough students will be in the program in the upper grade levels to constitute a full class (Christian, 1994).

Some programs screen students for disabilities and other special education needs, but most do not. There is no reason for withholding special needs students from learning through two languages, and although no case has presented itself yet, it may be unconstitutional for schools to prevent special needs students from participating in an EE program. However, because of the rarity of bilingualism in the U.S., many parents of special needs children are reluctant to enroll them in a program that seems to have what they perceive as an additional learning load.

Programs also differ in their policy for admitting new students at upper grade levels. Some programs set an upper limit. For example, they do not allow new students to enter the program above the third grade unless they show grade level proficiency in both languages. This eliminates the possible gap in language proficiency levels between students who have had three or more years to develop bilingual proficiency and those who have not had an enriched language education. The gap between proficient and nonproficient users of the language of instruction becomes significant and increases after grade three. However, as more schools opt for enriched language and culture education programs, more students who possess the necessary language skills may be able to move into EE programs at upper grade levels. The following is a list of issues that staff must address regarding who will participate in the program (see Table 3.4).

Maintaining an EE Program

What role can parents play in an established EE program?

The support of parents whose children are in an EE program is key to the success of that program. Parents can be the best advocates for the EE program, both at its inception and when the program is going through difficult periods in its development. The dedication and perseverance of parents who demand a high-quality bilingual education for their

---

Table 3.4   Decisions to be Made Regarding Student Selection

- Will the EE program constitute the whole school and thus require all students to participate?

- Will students be recruited from among a select group?

- Will students be admitted initially on a first-come first-served basis or will a lottery be established?

- Will a quota be established to create a balance between speakers of the two language backgrounds?

- Will two classes be created at the lower grade levels so as to counter possible attrition in higher grades?

- Will potential participants be screened for special education needs, and what services will be provided to them?

- Will new students be admitted in the upper grade levels? If so, what provisions are made to help those whose bilingual skills are not up to par with their peers?

children constitute powerful forces that can change the attitudes of a community, a school superintendent, or a school board. Parents of participating students who have seen their children successfully on the road to bilingualism can convince other parents of the advantages of an enriched language and culture education and of the benefits of bilingualism and cross-cultural proficiency.

As important, parents whose children have been in an EE program can answer questions that novice parents typically have. Many parents may be afraid that their children's academic achievement will suffer as a result of receiving instruction in their non-native language. Parents who have seen their children gain bilingual proficiency without sacrificing academic achievement can convince other parents that they need not worry. Some parents are anxious because they are unable to help with homework and their belief that their child's performance in school will suffer. Veteran parents can reassure other parents that these fears are unfounded and that their own lack of proficiency in the other language need not impede their child's academic development. To provide some support with homework,

however, schools may establish a language network for helping both parents and children outside of school. Ways of providing support with homework will be suggested in a later section of the chapter.

Despite parents' possible lack of proficiency in their child's language of instruction, their support at home is essential. Parents can give their children valuable support at home in the native language. Some parents may have to be convinced of this; they have to be reassured that their support in the native language is valuable enough. Some parents have to be shown that by surrounding the child with a stimulating environment in the native language, they are in fact contributing to that child's cognitive growth and to learning in general. This is equally true for English-speaking parents and non-English-speaking parents.

Parents can also be a rich resource in the classroom or school library. Many programs take advantage of parents' willingness to volunteer in the classroom as instructional aides and cultural resources, or as storytellers and readers in the school library. Parents can also help administrators raise funds and organize events for the school (Montone & Silver, 1996).

Voices from the Field

Implications of Student Selection for EE Programs

Arlene C. Dannenberg
Director of Educational Equity
Salem Public Schools
Salem, Massachusetts

The selection of students for a two-way bilingual program is an important factor in the program's success. For parents to be supportive of the program and students to be enthusiastic, it is important that parents really know what they are choosing and to be sure that they want this kind of program. In Massachusetts, most urban districts assign students to elementary schools under "Controlled Choice Assignment Plans." With this kind of plan, all parents choose the school(s) they want their children to attend. The concept of "choice" of both building and program applies to all entering students. Choosing a two-way program fits a pattern used for all schools. Even so, we find that parents may not fully understand what their choices mean. Therefore, we must be very careful to describe our programs clearly and accurately, so that parents' and students' expectations can be met.

In Salem, we have a long established two-way program at one building and another emerging at a second building. Despite our best efforts to describe the program explicitly, we still find that some parents do not understand what they have chosen at the school with the newly evolving program. Each year, we learn to be more careful in explaining our program to assure that parents are making a choice they will want to stay with throughout their child's education. We look for parents who believe that learning a second language is valuable in and of itself and that learning in a diverse classroom is important for learning to live in a diverse world.

What competencies do teachers need?

Over and above the general qualifications expected of highly accomplished teachers, those who are involved in an enriched language and culture education program must meet the following criteria (National Board of Professional Teaching Standards, 1997):

1. *Knowledge of language and language development.* Teachers must be models of language proficiency in the language or languages in which they are expected to teach. All teachers in an EE program need not be bilingual, if they do not teach in both languages. Depending on the instructional setup of the program, it is possible that monolingual English-speaking teachers could teach the English components of the curriculum in partnership with bilingual teachers who would be primarily responsible for instruction in the other language. However, it is important that monolingual teachers make an investment in bilingualism and, ideally, begin to learn the other language of the school. Teachers who are not bilingual can either enroll in language classes that the school might offer to parents and teachers, or they can remain in class when that language is taught as a subject matter to their students. Many teachers find this intimidating at first, but once they have started learning alongside their students, they find it to be extremely beneficial and enjoy-

Voices from the Field

A Parent's Perspective

Deborah Short
Parent of two children in a two-way immersion program
Center for Applied Linguistics
Washington, D.C.

I was very excited when my first child was old enough to attend the two-way immersion program in our school district. He has continued with the program now into 7th grade and our second child is in the elementary school where the first began. As a family we have no regrets, only satisfaction, about choosing this educational option for our children and we anticipate sending our third child to the program when he is of school age.

Neither my husband nor I speak Spanish, although we both have knowledge of other foreign languages. We worried that the lack of Spanish might limit the assistance we could give our children when they reached the upper grades of elementary school but so far those fears have not been realized. When the homework comes out at night, we sit down with the children, as needed, to help. The elementary teachers are very considerate and provide instructions in both Spanish and English—so we know what needs to be accomplished. The middle school teachers do not rely on the parents for much homework help anyway. Our seventh grader, like his classmates, is proficient enough to understand the tasks and explains them to us in English if necessary. Using common sense, in fact, has helped more than we expected. If we still had questions though, we phoned another parent or had our children call a Spanish-speaking classmate. Sometimes we wrote a note to the teacher.

At the elementary school parents are encouraged to be involved with the day-to-day program. Because I work full-time and travel quite a bit, I am not able to participate as much as I would like. Nonetheless, I have looked for other opportunities to contribute. Apart from chaperoning a field trip (which I have only done a few times) and attending school functions like concerts, *fiestas*, and so forth, I found that I could serve on programmatic committees that met in the evenings. For two years I participated on the school-based committee that was part of a district-wide future planning process. This committee looked at the programs in the school, potential growth in number of students, available space, and school teaming. Another committee I served on designed the middle school program for the rising 6th graders. This committee looked at instructional options, scheduling, transportation, extracurricular activities, library resources, and more.

able. By going through the experience of learning a second language, monolingual teachers can begin to develop empathy for their students, and can also serve as models for their students. Exposure to a new language can enhance teachers' ability to understand the process by which their students acquire both their primary and second languages, to develop instructional strategies that promote language development, and to modify the curriculum to best accommodate the needs of bilingual learners.

2. *Knowledge of culture.* EE teachers must be knowledgeable about and sensitive to the dynamics of culture in general, and their students' cultures in particular. This enables teachers to understand their students and to structure a successful academic experience for them. Teachers must be able to draw on their knowledge of human development as mediated by language and culture. They must be able to draw on this knowledge to understand their students' backgrounds, skills, interests, aspirations and values.

3. *Knowledge of the subject matter.* Teachers must have a comprehensive command of the subject matter they are teaching and its relationship to the language of instruction to establish goals that make sense for the students. They must be thoroughly familiar with the breadth and depth of the concepts in the field of study, as well as the relationships among those concepts. They must also be up to date with the most current developments in the field.

4. *Delivery of instruction in a meaningful and varied way.* Teachers must feel comfortable with a variety of instructional approaches that allow students to explore and understand challenging concepts, topics, and issues in meaningful ways. They must provide multiple paths to help students develop language proficiency, learn new concepts in the various subject areas, and learn to function in a culturally diverse environment.

5. *Command of instructional resources.* EE teachers must be able to select, adapt, create, and use varied resources to help students reach their academic goals. This may be a special challenge for teachers of less commonly taught languages, such as Arabic and Korean.

6. *Assessment skills.* Teachers must be able to employ a variety of assessment methods to obtain useful information about student learning and development and to assist students in reflecting on their own progress. Teachers must also be able to use ongoing assessment results to modify their instruction, and to reflect on the quality of their practice.

7. *Maintaining linkages with families.* Teachers must create linkages with their students' families that enhance the educational experience of the students. They also must be willing to make connections with the community and understand the social context in which students live.

Regardless of the qualifications of staff, ample time must be devoted to professional development once the program has started. The following list of critical topics to address in seminars or workshops can help teachers generate an ongoing staff development plan (see Table 3.5).

Table 3.5   Ongoing Staff Development Plan: Critical Topics to Address

For parents and all staff:

- Spanish (or other language) as a second language: beginning level geared to social interaction within a school setting.
- How can I continue to help my child in the native language and in the other language?

In addition, for EE program teachers:

- Incorporating culture into the EE classroom.
- Establishing goals and designing instruction to facilitate student learning.
- Building on students' cultural, experiential background knowledge (see Glossary).
- Multiple paths to learning.
- Adapting and creating materials.
- Learning about students through a variety of assessment methods.
- Learning about our instruction through assessment.
- What to do about possible lagging achievement in the first two years.
- Creating and maintaining linkages with parents.
- Creating and maintaining linkages with the community.

How does the status of each language affect the success of the program?

The status of each language both within the school and the community at large must be taken into account in the design of an EE program. The more equal the status of the two languages involved, the more likely it is that students will develop high proficiency in both languages. Although EE programs strive to promote English and the non-English language in an egalitarian way, the two languages rarely have the same status in the larger society, and sometimes even within the school. With the exception of very few languages, many that are likely to be taught in EE programs are not held in high esteem by members of the dominant culture. English is the language of power, and it predominates in the society at large. Even in successful EE programs, English is often the language of choice among students when they are on the playground or in the lunchroom. Since English is so predominant, many programs choose to tilt the balance in favor of the non-English language by consciously elevating its status, at least within the boundaries of the school.

Voices from the Field

Supporting Teachers in Dual Language Programs

Wanda Toledo
Coordinator/Bilingual Resource Specialist
Long Beach City School District
Long Beach, New York

Professional development is of the utmost importance in ensuring the success of an enrichment language program. As a dual language program coordinator/bilingual resource specialist, I arrange ongoing staff development sessions and hire "experts" to give workshops to the teachers. Furthermore, I provide on-site training and support to teachers, administrators, parents, and students. The training and support consist of:

1. meeting with dual language team teachers on a regular basis to discuss issues regarding curriculum, instructional techniques, assessment, and student progress.

2. observing teachers and providing constructive feedback about method of delivery, lesson content, and classroom management.

3. providing demonstration lessons.

4. working with teachers in developing thematic units, selecting materials, and adapting texts.

5. conducting articulation meetings with dual language program teachers and other staff members who provide specialized services such as Title 1 reading and math teachers, and resource room teachers.

6. assisting teachers in employing multiple assessment tools.

7. being a program, teacher, and student advocate.

8. serving as an intermediary between teachers and principals, and between teachers and parents.

9. offering inservice courses to all district staff.

Hiring teachers who possess the seven competencies mentioned in this chapter represents the first step in ensuring a quality instructional program. In addition to these competencies, participating teachers need to fully comprehend the nature of a dual language program and truly take ownership of it. It is only when teachers wholeheartedly believe in the benefits of an enriched language program that students profit from teacher competencies. In addition to the seven competencies, teachers need to be sensitive and receptive to innovative teaching ideas.

An enriched language program can be demanding. Teachers need to be provided with on-site support and ongoing professional development. They also need common planning time built into their schedules so that they may meet and exchange ideas. Teachers who are new to a dual language program require pre-service training and a "buddy teacher" to provide additional on-site support. Continuous support and staff training are essential in refining the seven competencies.

Equality can be achieved by allocating significantly more instructional time to the non-English language. This is discussed at length in the section following this one. The high status of the non-English language also needs to be reflected in people's beliefs about the program and what it can achieve. There cannot be any disparity of expectations for the two languages. English-speaking students must be expected to attain the same level of proficiency in the non-English language as non-English-speaking students are expected to attain in English. Even when English-speaking students show early lags in their native language development, the temptation to cut back on instruction in the other language must be resisted. Culture learning must also be expected in the same manner and to the same extent for both groups of students. Even in cases where the EE program operates as a strand within a school, strategies can be used to help equalize the status of the two languages in the everyday functioning of the school. These strategies include conducting whole school activities in both languages, using the non-English language for announcements, or creating partnerships with sister schools in countries where the non-English language is spoken. These are some ways to send messages to the whole school community that the non-English language is valued (Howard & Christian, 1997). It is only in environments that promote linguistic and ethnic equality and that fosters positive cross-cultural attitudes that learning can be enriched.

What time allotments are made for English and the other language?

Two patterns of time allocation are popular in EE programs at the elementary level. In the first pattern, instructional time is divided equally between the two languages. Thus, students receive 50% of their instruction in English and 50% in the other language. This proportion is kept constant throughout the grade levels. In the second pattern, the "90/10" model, students receive roughly 90% of their instruction in the language other than English for the first two or three years. Instruction through English is gradually increased after second or third grade so that students receive 50% of their instruction in English by fifth or sixth grade. Thus, in this model, English-speaking students are immersed in the language other than English, and conversely, language minority students receive the bulk of their instruction, especially in the early grade levels, in their native language. Figure 3.1 depicts the allocation of time in the two models.

The 90/10 model seems to produce more effective results than the 50/50 model, precisely because of the imbalance in the time allocation between the two languages (Howard & Christian, 1997). First, as mentioned earlier in this chapter, by allocating more time to the language other than English, the status of the less powerful language is raised and the two languages can enjoy equal status. Second, research in second language education points to the need

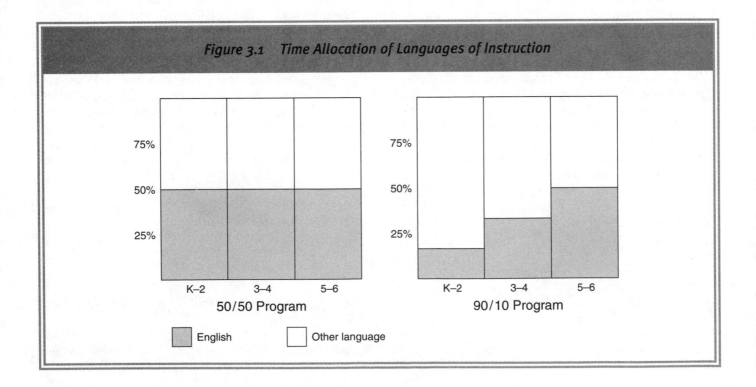

Figure 3.1   Time Allocation of Languages of Instruction

50/50 Program

90/10 Program

English   Other language

for minority students to strengthen their foundation in the native language in the early stages of learning (Collier, 1995). Conversely, the native language proficiency of English speakers does not suffer from early exposure to the other language. In fact, the only way for English speakers to become proficiently bilingual is to be immersed in the other language for the beginning few years of instruction.

Time allocation at the middle and secondary school levels varies. Since there are very few EE programs beyond the elementary grades, it is difficult to identify a single pattern. Time allocation in most secondary programs seems to be limited by constraints in scheduling and the availability of resources (Christian, 1994). As more EE programs become available at the secondary level, information regarding the most effective time allocation can be documented.

How are the two languages allocated for subject matter instruction?

Several models are possible for allocating the two languages for the instruction of different subject matter. Regardless of the model chosen, two principles are inviolable. The first is that the two languages must be kept separate at all times. This can be done either by having different teachers assigned to each language or by having distinctly different contexts for each language. Time, space, subject area, or even a marker of some sort (e.g., colored caps or ribbons) may delineate the contexts. Separating the two languages on the basis of time means that some programs use the two languages on alternate days or weeks. Others split that day so that part of the day is spent in English and the other part in the other language. Separating the two languages by space means that students receive instruction in each language in distinct locations within the school building. Additionally, each language should be allocated to the instruction of different subject matter. This would occur in addition to alternation by time or space. For example, in an 80/20 split, social studies and art may be taught in English in the afternoon, and the rest of the subjects in the other language in the morning. Some teachers even go as far as putting on a scarf of a specific color for "English time" and a scarf of another color for the other language. Regardless of the method used to separate the two languages, what is important is that they are not used interchangeably during instruction time. There is no indication that any one system of language separation is more effective than others, as long as the system makes developmental sense for the learners. Programs do not distinguish themselves as being more or less effective in achieving academic and linguistic goals on the basis of the language separation model they have chosen to apply. Rather, effective language separation is done in such a way as to allow for new concepts to be learned in the

most efficient way. Thus, it may not make much sense from the learners' perspective to alternate language of instruction for the same subject from day to day or week to week.

Complete adherence to the rule of language separation, however, is likely to be difficult. Children will answer the teacher in their native language even when the other language is being used for instruction. They will also use the common fluent language among themselves even during the time when the other language is being used by the teacher. Keeping in mind the importance of maintaining a nurturing environment, the teacher needs to encourage the students to use the less fluent language during the time when that language is being used for instruction. The teacher can acknowledge students' responses in the "inappropriate" language, but respond to them in the language of instruction, thus guiding the conversation into the realm of the "appropriate" language once again. Students in even the most successful EE classrooms seem to spend very little time using the language other than English (Lindholm, 1990); therefore, it is important that teachers offer as many opportunities as possible for students to use that language. As difficult as it is to avoid using the more fluent language that teachers and students share with one another, teachers must keep their own production of the two languages completely separate. They must make every effort to use the students' less fluent language when it is time for that language.

The second principle regarding the allocation of instructional time is that the two languages are taught explicitly either as a second language or as native language arts depending on the relationship of each language to the particular group of students. Regardless of the time allocation pattern chosen, each language is taught "as a second language" to students for whom that language is not native. Conversely, that language is taught as "language arts" to students for whom it is a native language. A question that arises regarding this aspect of EE programs is which language to start teaching reading in. Most programs prefer to begin instruction in literacy in the students' native language first despite research that indicates the native speakers of English can begin reading in their second language (Genesee, 1987). For English-speaking students in a 90/10 program, literacy instruction typically starts in kindergarten or first grade in English and it takes place within the 10% instructional time that is devoted to English language arts. This question is discussed in detail in Chapter Five.

What type of coordination is needed in EE programs?

It is important for staff in EE programs to closely coordinate with one another both horizontally, that is, across content areas, and vertically, that is, from grade to grade. Common

Making the Decision to Change From 50/50 to 80/20

*Janet Nolan, Office of Language and Cultural Education
Adela Coronado Greely
Co-founders of the Inter-American Magnet School
Chicago, Illinois*

Our first attempt in planning a dual language school in 1974 was based on our own experiences as parents. In our homes, one parent would use only English with the children while the other would use only Spanish—what would be called today a 50/50 model. So, the preschool program we designed began as a 50/50 model. Every day, children spent half the morning or afternoon in the Spanish room and the other half in the English room. It just seemed common sense to expect that the children would develop equal abilities in both languages, no matter which one was their mother tongue. We carried this model through—one grade at a time—from preschool to eighth grade.

Each year, however, we struggled with the dominance of English over Spanish. It seemed that all the fun things—special events, videos, the most attractive books, computer games, and gym class—were always in English. We tried placing signs at the school entrance declaring, "TODAY IS SPANISH DAY!"—but students and even teachers frequently lapsed into English before the end of the day.

It wasn't just laziness or lack of resources in Spanish. We let English overwhelm us. We let standardized testing scare us. The inevitable predominance of English in our 50/50 model sent a message to our students. By fourth grade, just about all our students were English dominant. By eighth grade, our English native speakers could read Spanish, but were not fluent. Our Spanish native speakers were losing their Spanish.

The catalyst for change came in the form of a working draft entitled, *Bilingual Immersion Education: A Program for the Year 2000 and Beyond*, developed by the Bilingual Education Office, California State Department of Education, in 1990. Study groups of teachers and parents were formed to reflect on this document, chapter by chapter. The result of this study was a community decision to change to an 80/20 model, beginning in preschool and continuing through third grade. Later, fourth grade was added to the 80/20 model, with grades five through eight using the 50/50 language model.

This decision was our "leap of faith." Would our students continue to do well academically? Would students learning English still be successful with so much immersion in Spanish? There was some panic in the beginning when English dominant children gradually began picking up reading in Spanish before they could read in English (the student's primary language has always been used to develop early literacy at the school). The "leap of faith" is critical. It means we had to suspend what we thought was common sense. We had to trust that young learners' strength in any language would serve as the bridge to their second language. The longer period of time permitted English speakers early on to become more fluent in Spanish. It gave Spanish speakers a longer, running start to develop academically in their first language while learning English with their English-speaking partners. The renewed commitment of the school community to bilingualism and deep multicultural appreciation sent a message that went far beyond the sign at the door announcing, "Today is Spanish Day." Commitment to an 80/20 model at the Inter-American Magnet serves as witness that the status of the Spanish language and the cultures of the Americas in the school have the place of honor with English and the multiculturalism of the United States.

The academic skills of students at the school are higher than ever. Spanish is freely used as the medium of instruction at all grade levels, because both English- and Spanish-speaking students are at home in either language. There is a positive difference. We are coming ever closer to the dream of creating a community of learners where two languages and strong cross cultural relationships are a reality.

time must be set aside for planning together. Common planning time is most effective when it happens frequently (about four times weekly), is of a significant duration (about 45 minutes), and has a predominant focus on improving instruction, curriculum, and assessment. This can be done through some of the following strategies (adapted from Massachusetts Department of Education, 1997):

- Organize the majority of district professional development time around sustained school-based initiatives.
- Release faculty from non-teaching duties (such as lunch and hall duty) and replace these assignments with common planning time.
- Pair teachers so that they are team teaching. In addition to the instructional advantages of such a setup, paired teachers can sometimes combine classes for selected whole-class activities, thereby allowing one teacher to attend planning meetings with other teachers.
- Pair classes for special events, thus freeing one of the teachers to attend planning meetings.
- Form a partnership with a teacher education program and increase the number of prospective teachers in the school who can teach classes and relieve teachers so they can attend planning meetings.
- Seek out grants and use funds to pay stipends to staff for team time after contracted hours.
- Schedule time in blocks so that classroom teachers can meet as grade-level or academic-subject teams on a regular basis.
- Create an electives block that is primarily staffed by community volunteers or tutors, while staff meet.
- Create a weekly community service learning block, staffed by an administrator, in which all students participate while staff meet in common planning time.
- Hire a long-term substitute to come in one day weekly to teach classes while staff meet in teams.

Vertical coordination, from grade to grade, is also very important for EE programs, especially those that include language minority students. Vertical coordination can be achieved only if a long-term plan is made for each incoming student. Since most EE programs begin at pre-kindergarten or first grade and students usually move from grade to grade as a cohort, such long-term planning is relatively easy. Individualized language and academic plans should specify how much would be taught in which language and for how long. The plan would cover the entire length of the student's participation in the program, and it would be revisited at the end of every year to be revised as needed. Such plans can also ensure that the transfer from one language to the other occurred in a way that makes developmental sense for the student. Parents should obviously be consulted regarding the goals that they have for their children. Those goals should be included in individualized language and academic plans.

These language and academic plans help teachers maintain a high level of awareness regarding individual students' transfer from one language to the other. Teachers need to plan for the transfer to occur as naturally and as efficiently as possible. Students will transfer what they are learning in one language to the other in idiosyncratic ways and at different times. Some students begin to write in their native language even if they have not received extensive instruction in it (Hudelson, 1986). This is more likely to happen when the two languages share an alphabet, as is the case with English and Spanish. Long-term plans for transfer of languages must also be made, which is why students need to be enrolled in EE programs for their entire elementary career in order to benefit from the enriched education model.

How are students grouped?

In most EE programs serving students from two language groups, such as dual language and some developmental bilingual programs, it is best if students are integrated with one another for the majority of the school day. That is, the most effective environment for language learning is one where students from the two language groups are separated as little as possible for instruction. In successful dual language programs, the only times that students receive instruction with similar language background peers is when the focus of instruction is explicitly on language; for example, when students receive native language and second language instruction. The rationale for integrating students as much as possible is that they benefit tremendously from naturally occurring interactions in the second language with peers who speak that language fluently and who come from a culture background that is different from their own. The benefits are linguistic as well as socio-cultural. Thus, English speakers benefit from solving a puzzle in Spanish with peers who are native speakers of Spanish by expanding the boundaries of their language and by learning to collaborate in culturally diverse ways. Conversely, Japanese-speaking children will make gains in their English language proficiency by completing a science project with English-speaking peers and might learn to negotiate with one another in ways that differ from their own.

For EE programs serving only English-speaking students, such as immersion programs, the need for authentic interactions with peers who speak the other language fluently is acute. In such programs, students rarely have the necessary amount of exposure to the language other than English in their everyday surroundings. It is crucial that teachers create opportunities for such interactions either through communication networks on the Internet, with peers in other countries, or through visits to communities where there are native speakers of that target language. Most schools in or near major urban centers have tremendous resources in all the ethnic communities that can be utilized for this purpose. Local guidebooks often list these neighborhoods and provide information about cultural resources within the communities. Parents can be encouraged to take their children to visit those neighborhoods and, alternatively, members of the local neighborhoods can be invited to come into the classroom to share their knowledge, craft, stories, and experiences with the students. Such local resources are often more valuable than exotic trips to countries where the target language is spoken because they expose students to the local varieties of the language they are learning. By becoming familiar with the local resources, students can also begin to build a repertoire of places and people where they can practice their newly acquired language.

For EE programs serving language minority students, there is an added socio-political reason for integrating them with native English-speaking peers. Because of the lower perceived status of minority populations and the minority language in the larger community, it is essential that EE programs be fully integrated into the larger mainstream school community. Not only are language minority students thus ensured access to all the privileges that the mainstream school or district has to offer, but they begin to be seen as equals to members of the majority community.

How are instructional materials located and adapted?

The availability of high-quality instructional and trade materials is key to the success of an EE program. Good instructional materials not only make learning much easier for students, but they also make teachers' lives much easier. As any teacher from a disadvantaged school district will confirm, it is extremely frustrating to teach without the appropriate materials: books, pictures, objects, videos, music, and the Internet. Unfortunately, good materials are extremely difficult to obtain for all but the most commonly taught languages in the US, such as Spanish, French, German, and Japanese. The difficulty is especially acute for academic content area materials. Sometimes, even when materials are readily available in languages other than English, they tend to be much less appealing than the materials available in English. They also tend to be more expensive, and sometimes too poorly constructed to withstand the wear and tear of everyday classroom use. The following are resources that may yield appropriate materials for EE programs:

1. *Other EE programs that teach the same language.* The guide published by the Center for Applied Linguistics can be helpful in locating a program near your school (Christian, 1994)(see Appendix D). Many schools have a wealth of materials, not just those that are available on the market, but also those that are teacher- and student-produced. While it is highly unlikely that you will find a whole unit that corresponds to an entire theme in your curriculum, you may find teacher-produced activities and student-authored stories that fit into units you are teaching. Recordings of students reading books on audio-tapes can be quite useful, especially as activities sent home over the holidays for children whose parents cannot read in that language. Teachers in other programs can also give you an evaluation of materials that you may be thinking of purchasing but are not familiar with yourself.

2. *Catalogs*. While catalogs offer the convenience of in-school "shopping", teachers are not able to actually view the material in order to make critical determinations about the appropriateness of the language and the conceptual level of the material. For this reason, it is wise to purchase material with a 30-day return preview period. Many catalogs are available through Internet web sites. Publishers that cater to ESL, bilingual, and foreign language education markets are listed in Appendix B.

3. *Conferences*. National, state, and regional conferences are excellent places to look for curriculum materials. While time consuming, conferences allow teachers to see the materials of many publishers at the same time, permitting comparisons among materials of the same type. Often discounts are given at conferences because publishers avoid shipping and handling costs by marketing their products to teachers directly.

4. *ERIC searches*. ERIC Clearinghouses are established around particular curricular domains, age-level concerns, or specific learner characteristics (rural/urban students, language minority students, gifted and talented students, and students with disabilities). By contacting the appropriate arm of the ERIC system or a central clearinghouse, teachers can conduct searches for materials in specific languages. (See Appendix C for contact information for the various ERIC Clearinghouses.)

5. *Ministries of education in countries where that language is spoken.* The consulates of some countries donate materials, although for the most part, the materials tend to be promotional and can serve only

as cursory language support visuals. If content area textbooks are needed, a personal contact needs to be made with an educator in that country. Again, the Internet may be a useful resource for making initial contacts.

Once materials in the language other than English are located, it may be necessary to adapt them so that they fit into the curriculum that currently exists for the rest of the school or district. The scope and sequence of the EE materials must align with the district curriculum. The EE materials must also be able to accomplish the linguistic, academic, and cultural goals and objectives of the program. More often than not, teachers find it necessary to supplement purchased materials with bits and pieces of books, video tapes, CD ROM, magazines, and newspaper articles in order to make it possible for students to develop their language proficiency and expand their cultural competence while learning new concepts in the academic content areas. When materials have been identified for possible use in the classroom, teachers may want to rate their appropriateness according to the criteria presented in the following checklist (adapted from Montgomery County Public Schools, 1989). This checklist can apply to both print and electronic computer materials (see Table 3.6).

What type of community outreach is necessary to maintain the program?

As children progress in their proficiency in the two languages, parents who are not proficient themselves in one of the languages of instruction may get frustrated at their inability to help their children with homework. This issue becomes especially accentuated after third grade, when the curriculum becomes demanding and abstract. It is helpful for these parents to have a well-functioning homework support network. A phone tree can be maintained so that children have easy access to assistance when they need it. Children and parents of different languages can be paired up, or children can get support from either peers or older students in the program. Parents of different languages can also be paired up with each other, not just for emotional support but for language learning.

Graduates of EE programs who are still living in or near the community can also provide support for the program, either by helping currently enrolled students and their parents or by serving as ambassadors for the program. They can help raise funds for the program from the community and convince administrators and parents of the benefits of an enriched language and culture education program (see for example, the video produced by Canadian Parents for French, 1995) (see Appendix D).

How can program effectiveness be ensured?

A good evaluation plan is needed to ensure program effectiveness during different phases of the program. It is important to identify all the people who might be interested in the evaluation results. Interested people include parents, teachers, school-level administrators, district-level administrators, community members, legislators, and the students themselves. Information needed to understand program effectiveness may vary from person to person. Thus, it is important to know not only the people with a special interest in the program but also their specific interest in the evaluation results. Keep in mind that these individuals may vary from school to school even within the same district. Because interest in evaluation information is likely to be different for different individuals, the type of information collected on program effectiveness will vary. The program effectiveness

Table 3.6
Selecting Instructional Materials

- How appropriate is the level of the language for the students?
- How appropriate is the cognitive demand of the content?
- Do the illustrations make the text clearer?
- Do the illustrations support the conceptual core of the lesson?
- How authentic are the illustrations?
- How attractive are the illustrations?
- How easy to follow is the format used to present new concepts?
- How accurate is the cultural information?
- How relevant is the cultural information to the local communities where that language is spoken?
- How well do the materials support curricular objectives?
- How accurate and up to date is the material?
- Do the materials contain enough guidance for teachers?
- How well is the cost justified?

Community Outreach for an Immersion Program

Jean Ramirez
San Francisco Unified School District
San Francisco, California

The San Francisco Unified School District's Alice Fong Yu Alternative School is a Chinese Immersion program for grades kindergarten through eight. Over the years, many siblings have joined their older brothers and sisters, and the "word of mouth" from current parents has encouraged new families to enroll their children. Although program and student success have helped in supporting continued community, interest and ongoing enrollment, the school continues to be proactive in its recruitment policies. In order to encourage student diversity, recruitment workshops are conducted at community centers and schools in the various communities throughout the city. Newspaper, television, and other publicity opportunities are encouraged and used to enhance recruitment. The school also utilizes the district's usual avenues for enrollment to advertise its program. The school's informational brochure is distributed through the district's Educational Placement Center and at preschool and children's centers, both public and private, throughout the city.

Principal Liana Szeto and staff realize that a recruitment effort can only be successful if the parents of current and perspective students have confidence in the instructional program. Parent education workshops and seminars on issues related to child development, immersion education, language, and language acquisition are conducted throughout the school year. Parent involvement is viewed as integral to successful student performance and parents are encouraged not only to observe instruction in action, but also to actively help out in the classrooms, to work on special events and field trips, to serve on the board of the parents' group, and to participate in fundraising activities. There is a strong sense of parent participation in creating the school community.

Although enrollment continues to grow and student performance continues to show success, parents of perspective students continue to ask one question: How will I know if my child is doing well and how can I help with homework if I don't know Chinese? This question is not unique to Alice Fong Yu, but is a concern common to immersion education. The administration, staff, students, and parent community at Alice Fong Yu have worked together to provide responses to this question. The immersion teachers are bilingual and make themselves available for classroom and telephone conferences to discuss student progress. It is the school's philosophy that parents can provide support and encouragement for homework without direct teaching, by ensuring that their children have a quiet place to study, with the necessary tools. Children are encouraged to phone each other for help on Chinese homework, a practice that promotes both independence and cooperation, as well as language proficiency. A roster containing the names of students and their parents, addresses, and telephone numbers is prepared annually and students and parents are encouraged to communicate with other students and parents for support and encouragement. Although most students come from families where only English is spoken, there is a small percentage of students and families whose primary language is Chinese. Students and parents in each of these linguistic groups are encouraged to serve as resources for the other. In addition to the immediate issue of homework assistance, this cross-language, cross-family connection has reaped an additional benefit, the empowerment and validation of parents and students who are recognized for the special linguistic knowledge they have to share. Before and After School Immersion Care, a private non-profit parent organization, also provides Chinese homework assistance. Although most students enter the program at the kindergarten level, additional enrollment occurs at the first grade. Special tutorial support is available for these students as needed.

The regular review and evaluation of the school's recruitment, instructional, and parent participation policies have supported the continuation and growth of Alice Fong Yu Alternative School.

question likely to be most important to each type of person involved in the program is listed in Table 3.7.

Once a consensus regarding these questions has been reached, assessments must be chosen to provide answers to the respective stakeholders. Any assessment conducted for purposes of gathering information on program effectiveness must match the objectives of the program and, once that is in place, who needs to be assessed, when, and how can be determined.

As a final check of whether an EE program is on the right track, it may be helpful to return to the critical features that are presented in Chapter 2. It is crucial that early in the inception of an EE program, the critical features of effective schooling be discussed explicitly and laid out for all to see. These features should form the foundation of the EE program and should be clearly understood by teachers, administrators, parents, and students. They are summarized in the form of a checklist (see Table 3.8) that can serve two

purposes. For programs that are in the early stages of development, the list can serve as a guide for discussions that need to take place among parents, teachers, and administrators as they design the program. For programs-in-the-making, the list can also serve as a reminder of all the issues that must be taken into account from the beginning when establishing a new program. Programs cannot be established in a vacuum, or worse, they cannot be dropped into an existing school without regard for the culture of that environment. It is essential that all stakeholders discuss the extent to which these characteristics of effective schooling are addressed in the design of the program. For EE programs that are already in place, the list can serve as a self-evaluation tool or as a guide for program improvement. Some statements in the checklist are characteristics of whole schools but can easily be applied to programs within a school.

Table 3.7   Questions Regarding Program Effectiveness of Relevance to Different Stakeholders

Parents:
- Is my child learning what he or she would have learned in a regular program?
- What is my child gaining in oral language and literacy by being in the EE program?
- Is the program too demanding or stressful?

Teachers:
- Are students learning what I am supposed to be teaching?
- How can I improve the learning environment for my students?
- Are the professional development opportunities allowing me to learn and to evolve as a teacher?

Program administrators:
- How do students in the EE program perform relative to other students in the school and district?
- What are the long-term benefits of this program to students, their parents, the rest of the district, and the community at large?

District administrators:
- Are there additional costs associated with this program?
- How do these costs compare to other programs in the district?

Students:
- What am I learning?
- What can I do to make my learning more efficient?
- How is this program helping me to expand my social skills?
- Will I have difficulty going on to high school or college or getting a job after this program?

Table 3.8   A Checklist of Criteria for Effective EE Programs

Check the extent to which each of the following applies to your program (1 = Strongly disagree; 2 = Disagree; 3 = Agree; 4 = Strongly agree):

Parent Involvement is an Integral Part of the Program

The school has positive, active, and ongoing relations with the students' parents.	1	2	3	4
The program has a well-conceived community outreach plan that genuinely responds to parents' goals for their children.	1	2	3	4

The Program Has High Standards

The program has clearly articulated and high standards in first and second language development, academic achievement, and culture.	1	2	3	4
Effective instruction and learning are the primary focus in the school.	1	2	3	4
The focus of instruction includes the same core curriculum that students in other programs experience.	1	2	3	4
Teachers and school personnel believe that all students can learn to high standards in academic domains while developing full proficiency in two languages.	1	2	3	4

Principals and Teachers Demonstrate Strong Leadership on Behalf of the Program

The principal is well informed of the critical features of EE and can use them to inform others about the program and to advocate on behalf of the program with parents, the community, and other educators.	1	2	3	4
Teachers and other educational support personnel in the school are knowledgeable about the critical features of EE and are prepared to discuss them with parents.	1	2	3	4

The Program is Developmental

The curriculum and instruction are developmentally appropriate (see Glossary) for all students.	1	2	3	4
The curriculum is organized to insure continuous development in language, academic domains, and culture.	1	2	3	4
The program provides bilingual instruction to participating students across all the elementary grades.	1	2	3	4
The program has a long-term plan with respect to curriculum, materials and professional development, space requirements, and other important resources.	1	2	3	4

Table 3.8 (continued)

Instruction is Student-Centered

Curriculum and instruction are student-centered and dynamic, changing to reflect the changing needs of students.	1	2	3	4
Assessment is geared to the special needs of students who are learning academic content through their second language.	1	2	3	4
Instruction and curriculum are culturally relevant *(see Glossary)* to the students' home backgrounds and communities.	1	2	3	4
Teachers are well informed of the backgrounds of all their students and know how to build such knowledge into lesson plans.	1	2	3	4

Language Instruction is Integrated with Challenging Academic Instruction

The curriculum is based on the premise that languages can be learned most efficiently while learning other challenging academic content.	1	2	3	4
Language that is comprehensible and interesting is used sufficiently to insure that students understand new academic content.	1	2	3	4
Students are provided ample opportunities for using language actively to insure oral and written language development.	1	2	3	4
The curriculum systematically plans for the development of language skills that are needed to master new academic content.	1	2	3	4
The non-English language is used for instruction a minimum of 50% of the time and English is used at least 10% of the time.	1	2	3	4

Instructional Personnel are Reflective

Teachers and administrators are engaged in ongoing learning and professional development.	1	2	3	4
Teachers understand and can use a variety of assessment methods creatively.	1	2	3	4
Assessment is tightly linked to instruction.	1	2	3	4
Teachers can conduct assessment in culturally sensitive ways.	1	2	3	4
The program for language minority students is flexible and provides a variety of instructional approaches.	1	2	3	4

EE Programs are Integrated with other School Programs and Schools

Student progress is monitored frequently and discussed by staff.	1	2	3	4
The program for language minority students is an integral part of the whole school.	1	2	3	4
Staff works closely together to plan instruction, both across grade levels and across content areas within the same grade.	1	2	3	4

Table 3.8   (continued)

The Program Aims for Additive Bilingualism

The school has a positive climate, where staff and students exhibit positive attitudes toward each other.	1	2	3	4
The school provides an emotionally and physically safe environment for students and teachers.	1	2	3	4
The program provides educational enrichment and is not remedial in orientation.	1	2	3	4
Staff shares the belief that bilingualism and cross-cultural competence are not only important individual and societal assets but also necessary skills for the future.	1	2	3	4
The program provides a learning environment in which all students have the opportunity to learn a second language in addition to their primary language.	1	2	3	4
The program for language minority students reflects the critical features of enriched education.	1	2	3	4

References

Canadian Parents for French. 1995. *Proud of Two Languages* (video). Ottawa, Ontario: CPF, 309 Cooper St., #210, Ottawa, Ontario, Canada K2P 0G5 (14:52).

Cazabon, M., Nicoladis, E. & Lambert, W. 1998. *Becoming Bilingual in the Amigos Two-Way Immersion Program*. Santa Cruz, CA: Center for Research on Education, Diversity & Excellence.

Christian, D. 1994. *Two-Way Bilingual Education: Students Learning Through Two Languages*. Santa Cruz, CA: National Center for Research on Cultural Diversity and Second Language Learning.

Collier, V. 1995. *Promoting Academic Success for ESL Students: Understanding Second Language Acquisition for School*. Elizabeth, NJ: New Jersey Teachers of English to Speakers of Other Languages-Bilingual Education.

Genesee, F. 1987. *Learning Through Two Languages: Studies of Immersion and Bilingual Education*. Rowley, MA: Newbury House.

Howard, E. & Christian, D. 1997. *The Development of Bilingualism and Biliteracy in Two-Way Immersion Students*. Paper presented at the 1997 Annual Meeting of the American Educational Research Association.

Hudelson, S. 1986. ESL Children's Writing: What We've Learned, What We're Learning. In P. Rigg & D.S. Enright (eds.), *Children and ESL: Integrating Perspectives*. Washington, D.C.: Teachers of English to Speakers of Other Languages. Pp. 23–54.

Lindholm, K. 1990. Bilingual Immersion Education: Criteria for Program Development. In A.M. Padilla, H.H. Fairchild & C.M. Valadez (eds.), *Bilingual Education: Issues and Strategies*. Newbury Park, CA: Sage.

Massachusetts Department of Education. 1997. *Common Chapters*. Boston, MA: Massachusetts Department of Education.

McLeod, B. 1996. *School Reform and Student Diversity: Exemplary Schooling for Language Minority Students*. Washington, D.C.: National Clearinghouse for Bilingual Education.

Montgomery County Public Schools. 1989. *Planning for Instruction in the Immersion Classroom*. Rockville, MD: Montgomery County Public Schools.

Montone, C. & Silver, J. 1996. *Learning Together: Two-Way Bilingual Immersion Programs*. Santa Cruz, CA: National Center for Research on Cultural Diversity and Second Language Learning.

Montone, C., Christian, D. & Whitcher, A. 1997. *Directory of Two-Way Bilingual Programs in the United States*. Washington, D.C.: Center for Applied Linguistics.

National Board of Professional Teaching Standards. 1997. *Standards for Teachers of English as a New Language*. Alexandria, VA: National Board of Professional Teaching Standards.

Part II
The Instructional Process

 **4** ORAL
LANGUAGE
DEVELOPMENT

In this chapter, we describe the contexts and the ways in which students' oral proficiency in both their native and second languages can be developed. We begin by asking questions regarding characteristics of successful second language learners and the stages of oral language development, and we discuss issues of transfer between the students' two languages. We then describe four contexts in which oral language skills can develop in an EE program: in native language arts classes, in second language classes, in content area classes, and in social interactions with others. This section is followed by questions regarding the coordination among different instructional components so as to build environments that are most conducive for oral language development. Finally, we suggest a way for checking the extent to which the oral language instruction plan meets the critical features of effective EE programs.

Predictors of Success in Learning a Second Language

One of the frustrations that teachers in EE programs often encounter is the uneven rate at which different students attain proficiency in their second language. This frustration, coupled with some commonly held misconceptions regarding second language learning, may lead some teachers to erroneously attribute the cause of the difficulty to cognitive or perceptual disorders. Others may move the child who is not a high academic achiever or whose languages are developing at a slower rate than his or her peers out of the EE program for fear that learning an additional language will pose an undue burden on that child. We must accept that not all students in the same classroom will attain the same level of proficiency in the second language. However, we can manipulate the learning environment so that it is most conducive to oral language development for all students. To understand the reason why a particular student may be having difficulties with second language learning, we need to explore the roles that individual characteristics and the type of environment play in the process of second language learning. Let us first explore learner characteristics.

What makes some students better second language learners?

Successful second language learners are likely to have certain characteristics in common. Despite a commonly held conception, verbal intelligence is not one of them. Verbal intelligence plays only a minor role in the attainment of proficiency in a second language and tends to be limited to the literacy component. This is important for schools to consider if they plan to limit enrollment in immersion programs to students who are high academic achievers on the grounds that only these types of students can be successful—research does not support this argument. More important than verbal intelligence are students' attitudes toward the language and its speakers, the level of motivation that a student has to learn the language, and how relaxed the student feels in the second language classroom context. Personality characteristics can also affect the attainment of second language proficiency. On the one hand, gregarious students may begin using the second language at a very early stage, not being bothered by mistakes in their utterances, and they may develop fluency in the interactive skills of the language. On the other hand, more reflective students may take longer to begin to use the second language but may develop a deeper understanding and a stronger grasp of the language. The specific learning strategies that learners have at their disposal can also contribute to efficient development of proficiency in the second language. A student who uses mnemonic devices and rehearsal strategies is more likely to retain new vocabulary and to apply grammar rules more fluently. The extent to which the student's learning style matches the teaching style can also affect how effectively the student advances in second language proficiency. Thus, if a student learns best by working in small groups, then it would be to that student's advantage if instruction were delivered primarily through cooperative grouping strategies.

Voices from the Field

Becoming Bilingual: A Perspective From Students

Leah Radinsky
Kindergarten teacher
Inter-American Magnet School
Chicago, Illinois

Emily, initially English dominant, Grade 6

When I first started at Inter-American (IA), it was really confusing. I wanted to know what everyone was saying 'cause when you're little, you want to know what the big kids are talking about. It was hard at first, but that really made me want to learn Spanish. It stopped being hard maybe around 3rd or 4th grade. I learned a lot from my friends and from my sister. Part of the fun stuff was learning about the Hispanic culture and the part that was the hardest was reading and writing in Spanish.

It's great to be bilingual. You can understand more people and you can make more friends and relate to more people if you know how to communicate with them. It makes me feel good to be able to talk to people who don't know English and

Larissa, initially Spanish dominant, Grade 6

The thing that helped me learn English when I first came here was the fact that my friends couldn't understand what I was saying, 'cause they didn't speak Spanish. Also, the support of my parents helped me a lot. The thing that was hard was the fact that some of my friends teased me because I didn't speak English. That made me feel like I didn't belong, so I just wanted to learn the language. Even when we were in a class that was all in Spanish, it felt like to speak Spanish was like being a dork or something. Some kids kept teasing me. Some of them didn't, and those were my friends.

I feel like I'm forgetting some of my Spanish because my friends only talk to me in English, and my father talks to me in English. He used to talk to me in Spanish when I

was little, but now that he knows that I can speak English, he only talks in English. But I'd like to stay bilingual, because it would help me with jobs and at school. My mother and grandmother talk to me in Spanish, and that really helps me.

William, initially English dominant, Grade 7

I started at IA when I was in preschool. I probably didn't speak a lot of Spanish, but I have a Mexican babysitter and probably learned something from her. I think learning Spanish came easier to me than other kids, because of my Mexican babysitter. I continue to talk to her in Spanish. Also, since the teachers here are so determined to teach the kids Spanish, they made it easier.

I think it's pretty cool to learn Spanish. It can help me a lot in the future, you know, if I go to Spanish speaking country and stuff like that. It's already happened. My parents are not at all bilingual, and I had to do all the talking when we went to Costa Rica, Mexico, and Puerto Rico!

Flor, initially Spanish dominant, Grade 7

I was in 2nd grade when I came to

(continued)

Voices from the Field (continued)

IA from Guatemala, and I didn't speak any English. At first, I didn't feel accepted because other people are talking English and you're not talking and you don't understand them. But it didn't take very long for me to start understanding English. I watched only English programs on TV, and that helped me. Also, I was taking ESL and my cousin was helping me. Some people were accepting, because they knew Spanish. It was only when they talked English that I was lost. And this was most of the time, because almost everybody spoke English most of the time. But what made it easy for me is that they speak Spanish in this school too. Spanish is still easy for me, reading and writing too. Writing English was hard because, you know, in Spanish the way you pronounce it is the way you write it. In English you have to use other letters; you don't write it the way you pronounce it.

It's great to be bilingual! You can be introduced to people, especially here, who only speak English, and if they need your help, you can help them.

Erica, initially English dominant, Grade 8

I started at IA in first grade. I believe I was young enough to catch on with Spanish. Also, my mom teaches here and that was a big help because I was getting some of the language at home and some at school. I think learning songs helped me a lot too. I do well with songs. It's more interesting than just learning a textbook word by word. I learned songs and eventually I learned what they meant and then I was even happier. I could understand if things were said slowly and gone over a couple of times and explained thoroughly, but in a way that I could still be interested in it. Spanish was taught to me in a way that I was interested and curious and I wanted to learn more. I made myself become able to learn more Spanish.

But it wasn't always easy. I have this memory of when we went to see The Day of the Dead exhibit at the Mexican Fine Arts museum when I was in first grade. I remember not being able to understand anything because the presentation was com-

pletely in Spanish. I remember the lady speaking so quickly. She could have been talking German! I also remember reading and writing being pretty hard. I didn't exactly know what I was setting out to do at the time. I was just taking it word by word and everyday I learned a little more. And now I feel very comfortable reading in Spanish. I have friends that I talk to in Spanish and English. By now, Spanish is so intertwined with the rest of my thoughts. Sometimes I don't even know when I'm speaking Spanish; it comes naturally. It just comes out of my mouth. Of course, I don't think I've dreamed in Spanish yet. So that's something I still have to do!

I love being bilingual. It's going to help me immensely because in the future I want to be able to travel and to get a job. It's something I accomplished in my life that I'm very proud of. Not many people, unfortunately, speak two languages, and I'm proud that I can understand people from a different culture, understand their point of view, and where they're coming from. I wouldn't have gone to any other school if I had a choice.

For language minority students, the single most important predictor of success in second language learning is their level of proficiency in their primary language. If a child comes to the second language learning situation with a shaky foundation in the primary language, that child is likely to have difficulty attaining full proficiency in the second language and acquiring new concepts through that language. A child's primary language may be less developed than expected for a number of reasons. Children may have had insufficient or inappropriate exposure to the language at home because they did not have sufficient opportunity to interact with adults in linguistically rich environments. Some children come from families where both parents work and have little time to devote to informal training that other children get before they enter school. Some parents may not be literate and may not be able to provide access to literacy to their children through storybook reading and other traditional printed material. Others, especially those who are sensitive to the low status their language may have in the larger society, may be under the misconception that they should speak English to their children, and thus they may be reluctant to speak the language in which they are fluent. When this happens, parents not only deprive their children of a rich linguistic environment, but they are likely to expose them to inadequate language models that lead to ambivalent or even negative attitudes toward their primary language.

Social factors may also contribute to shaky primary language development. Language minority children with a primary language that is not highly regarded in the larger society may have misgivings and low esteem for their primary language and culture. Even subtle messages of inferiority that are often found in the media regarding certain ethnic minorities can have a detrimental effect on children from those groups and on their language development. For these reasons, it is essential that children coming from minority backgrounds be given the opportunity to develop pride in their primary language and to develop their native language fully at the same time as they are learning English as a second language.

The availability of the target language outside of the classroom can also determine the rate with which students advance in that language. In analyzing whether students have optimal exposure to the second language, we should be careful to examine the quality of the language that the student encounters as well as its quantity. Students whose only exposure to the target language is through commercial television, for example, are not likely to benefit significantly from the experience. Besides, most commercial television programs at best provide only passive language exposure and, thus, are likely to have only slight benefits for students' language development. Public television provides students with a much better source of language since some of its programs are designed for children and have an educational value beyond language learning. Students who watch such programs may have a greater advantage in their attainment of second language proficiency.

Parental attitudes and the support parents give to their children in learning the second language are also important factors to consider. Positive attitudes toward the target language and providing support do not necessarily entail using that language at home. In fact, for minority children, especially those whose parents are not fluent in the target language, it is essential that parents surround the child with a rich linguistic environment in the primary language rather than attempting to use English inadequately. Even if parents

---

Table 4.1   A Checklist of Individual Characteristics that May Contribute to Difficulty in Learning a Second Language

Is the student motivated to learn the second language?

- What can I do to motivate the student more?

Does the student harbor any negative attitudes toward the second language and its speakers?

- What can I do to encourage more positive attitudes?

How relaxed does the student feel in the language learning context?

- What can I do to lower the anxiety level that this student may be experiencing?

Does the student have strategies that are useful for learning new vocabulary and for applying new grammar?

- What strategies does the child lack and how can I teach them?

Is the student's most comfortable learning style available in my classroom?

- How can I change my teaching style so that it matches more closely the learning style of the student?

Is the student's native language developed to its optimal level?

- If not, what can I do to strengthen the foundation in the native language?

Does the student have adequate access to the target language outside of the classroom?

- What can I suggest for the student to do at home or in the neighborhood?

Do the child's parents support the development of the primary language?

- What suggestions can I offer the parents?

show their support by encouraging the child and by lauding his or her every achievement.

As depicted in Figure 4.1, these individual and environmental factors are embedded within one another and are interrelated. They all play an important role in facilitating second language proficiency.

Students with different combinations of these characteristics and in varying home and societal contexts will advance in the second language at different rates and experience different levels of difficulty. The checklist in Table 4.1 may help in appraising the situation when a child seems to be having extraordinary difficulty with the second language.

The classroom environment and the strategies teachers use to teach the second language also influence how easily students attain proficiency in that language. The next section describes elements that are key to creating a classroom environment that is most conducive to second language learning.

How can I create the best classroom environment for developing oral proficiency in the second language?

Five factors must guide the way we design the environment for second language learning. The language with which we surround the learner must be meaningful and it must be relevant. It must also be just beyond the learner's current ability level in order to push language development forward. It also is important that the language is held in high esteem by both the learner and the larger society. Finally, a key to developing oral proficiency is the actual use of the second language. In the time dedicated to second language learning, teachers must insist that students use that language rather than resort to the more proficient language they have in common.

Structuring the classroom around concrete activities rather than paper and pencil tasks is the strategy that is most likely to result in authentic use of language among students. When second language lessons are centered

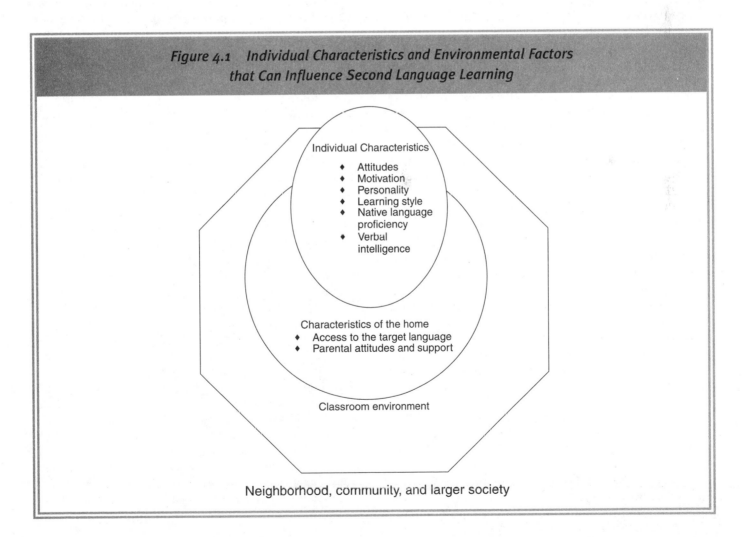

Figure 4.1   Individual Characteristics and Environmental Factors that Can Influence Second Language Learning

Individual Characteristics
- Attitudes
- Motivation
- Personality
- Learning style
- Native language proficiency
- Verbal intelligence

Characteristics of the home
- Access to the target language
- Parental attitudes and support

Classroom environment

Neighborhood, community, and larger society

around a theme or an activity, students are motivated to use language actively. The language that emanates from such activities drives learning and can serve as the context for language teaching. Two things make this situation extremely effective for language learning. First, when students are engaged in an activity or task that interests them, they learn language incidentally and naturally. Incidental learning is extremely effective for the development of language proficiency, in both first and second languages, when it take place in a structured classroom environment (Genesee, 1994; 1987). Second, if teachers take the language produced by students in specific activities as the discourse for teaching specific aspects of language, it is highly effective since it meets immediate communicative needs. The following are some suggestions on how to create such an environment.

Structure the use of oral language within a meaningful context. The best environment for developing oral proficiency in a second language is one in which significant portions of the new language are learned incidentally and in the context of doing something that is inherently meaningful. The best way to create such an environment is to center instruction around interesting and engaging activities, integrating the use of the target language into that activity. When the learner's attention is focused on the activity, language is internalized naturally. When concrete objects and interactive tasks are part of an activity, as they normally are, new language is meaningful even if it contains vocabulary and grammar that are unknown to the student. For example, students in a fourth grade Spanish as a second language class might undertake a project to analyze the waste paper generated in the school. Students can sort the paper according to categories (for example, according to color, or according to origin—such as from the math or science class) and then make art projects out of the waste paper. In the process, language that is meaningful because of its relevance to the activity will be used: "Put the colored paper in this pile," (pointing to the pile where the paper should go); "We need more water here," (pointing to the water); and "The biggest pile of paper is from the math class," (the pile is right in front of the student). Activities should be chosen that elicit language and encourage interaction among the students. Activities that require repetition of the same action or task, such as beating batter for a long time or perforating many pieces of paper may not sustain ongoing language use by the teacher or, more importantly, by the students.

Choose activities that are relevant to students. If, in addition to being concrete and meaningful, the activity revolves around an issue or topic that is relevant to students' daily lives, language learning becomes even more efficient because of the students' high level of interest in the activity. Relevant activities can be identified by choosing themes that reflect the students' backgrounds and past experiences or issues that students and their families are dealing with in their communities. Using the example above of analyzing waste paper, the project can be linked to recycling and waste management strategies used in the neighborhood or the city. If this is an issue that the larger community (or city) is dealing with, students can even take some sort of social action or suggest improvements on current practices. As an expansion activity, they may even explore the issue of waste management in countries where the target language is spoken and compare it to their country of residence.

Surround students with language that is just complex enough. The language that is used with students must be simple enough that they can understand it yet complex enough that they acquire new vocabulary and sentence patterns and they begin to understand the rules that govern the language. Most of us use this "one step ahead of the learner" approach naturally with young children acquiring their first language. We use sentences that are generally comprehensible (see "comprehensible input" in Glossary) to young children and insert a word or phrase that may be unfamiliar to them. When that occurs, the child will naturally ask: "What does (word) mean, mommy?" Teachers may need to consciously plan to create this type of linguistic environment with older students who already have other means of communication. Using activities with concrete objects helps make language more comprehensible for learners. Generally speaking, the teacher's task is to make sure that they are building on the language that the students possess at any given point in time. This requires constant informal monitoring of students' language skills. It also implies that teachers have a clear picture of students' current stage of language development. Ways of doing this are suggested in Chapters 7 and 8.

Equalize the status of the two languages. As mentioned in Chapter 3, it is crucial that the status of the non-English language be raised so that it gains importance within the culture of the school. If the non-English language plays a secondary role, students are less likely to pay the kind of attention to it that pushes language proficiency forward. The suggestions given earlier, such as using the non-English language for all public announcements, ensure a vital role for that language in the daily functioning of the entire school. In the classroom, teachers must take care not to revert to English when an urgent or important message needs to be conveyed to students during the time that the other language is scheduled for instruction. For example, when the teacher tells a student that her mother will be picking her up a little later than usual, or when a class rule is broken and the teacher discusses the issue with the students involved, the teacher should continue using the non-English language.

Encourage students to use the second language. A persistent challenge for teachers in the second language classroom is how to promote the use of the second language. Observations of EE programs (Lindholm & Gavlek, 1997) show that students produce very little oral language even in the best of classrooms and that students are reluctant to use the second language either among themselves or with the teacher. Since students in second language classrooms are grouped homogeneously and share a common native language, they tend to use their first language whenever possible. It is understandable why students prefer to communicate using their more proficient language rather than struggling to communicate with one another through a non-proficient language. Even adults learning a foreign or second language find it difficult to maintain its usage with others who speak their native language. Nonetheless, to promote language learning, the teacher must attempt to increase 1) the amount of oral language use by students in the classroom in general, and 2) the likelihood of students conversing with each other through the second language.

It is essential to plan for the specific language to be used during the activity so that the maximum amount of language learning occurs. If students are making paper, for example, the teacher could organize the activity so that students practice tag questions, for example, with each other: "Do you need more water, or don't you?" " Is there enough white paper, or isn't there?" If, in addition, one of the language objectives to be accomplished through this activity is the use of prepositions, the teacher can focus on prepositions used by students in the review that they present after they have completed the activity: "We put the water *in* the bowl." "We dried the paper *on* the screen." Many teachers are tempted to just do an activity with their students and to let language emerge in a completely impromptu way. This is not the most effective strategy. The list in Table 4.2 may help to ensure that the necessary preparations have been completed before engaging in an activity with students.

Table 4.2   Maximizing the Oral Language Development Potential of an Activity

Planning for the activity:
- ❑ Determine the specific aspects of language that you would like to teach, making sure that they fit into the curriculum objectives or the language plan created for the students.
- ❑ Choose an activity that lends itself to the specific aspects of language to be taught.
- ❑ List the main words that are central to completing the activity.
- ❑ Write informal dialogues that are likely to emerge around the activity.
- ❑ Prepare language props that you might need (such as word cards, labels, and sample dialogues for students to practice).
- ❑ Write an informal script for teacher talk that will accompany the activity.
- ❑ List different options for students in beginner, intermediate, and advanced levels.

Conducting the activity:
- ❑ Make sure that oral language accompanies all actions. The informal script you have prepared will help keep you on track.
- ❑ Familiarize students with new words through Total Physical Response strategies, if appropriate.
- ❑ Cue students to use the language that appears on your informal script.
- ❑ Allow students to informally practice the dialogues around the activity.
- ❑ Expand on students' language.
- ❑ Elicit oral summaries of the activity, or parts of it.
- ❑ Be ready to seize the opportunity at the spur of the moment to do a mini-lesson on a specific aspect of language when it happens to come up during the activity.

Expanding the activity into literacy:
- ❑ The oral language generated in the activities described above can be expanded into written text, and can be used to develop literacy (see Chapter 5).

Expectations for Oral Language Development

The stages of oral language development are essentially the same for students in EE programs as they are for children raised bilingually or children learning a second language in non-school settings subsequent to the development of their primary language. The stages appear quite regularly for both majority and minority children and in both the primary and the second language. However, the rate at which specific levels of proficiency are attained will vary among students, probably as a result of differences in the individual learner characteristics and the setting in which language learning takes place, as described earlier in this chapter.

What should we expect from students in their primary language?

In answering this question, we discuss language majority and language minority students separately. In the case of language majority students in EE programs, there may be delays in the initial stages of certain aspects of language development, specifically in reading and writing. However, their proficiency in all aspects of English should come close to or even exceed that of their monolingual counterparts by the time they reach fourth or fifth grade. Thus, it is extremely important to wait at least four of five years before EE students' scores on English academic achievement tests are compared to those of monolingual English-speaking students to ensure that test results early in the program are interpreted appropriately. In their fervor to test students and to examine student and school performance on the basis of standardized test scores, many school districts or states are unwilling to accommodate the special needs of EE programs. If EE students are required to take standardized district- or state-wide tests before their English proficiency has risen to age-appropriate levels, the program must ensure that their performance is interpreted within expectations that make sense for EE programs. As EE students begin to take standardized tests in English, say in third grade, a database can be started that in three or four years will provide a solid basis for establishing reasonable expectations of students in subsequent years.

The lag in initial literacy development in the primary language that English-speaking students in immersion often exhibit usually has far bigger implications for the school or the program within the larger educational system than it does for the learners. Misinterpretation of early test results could lead people to believe that the program is failing. Such misinterpretation could also lead administrators

to change the program, typically to increase the amount of instruction time in English. Although such a decision may boost proficiency in English immediately, it also will diminish the students' overall second language proficiency by the time they graduate from the program. Rather than make hasty decisions based on comparisons of results from EE students with those of their monolingual peers, administrators should interpret results in the context of expected development of EE students over the period of five to six years (see Chapter 6 for further suggestions).

The issue for language minority students is different. Many language minority students, especially those coming from low socioeconomic backgrounds, enter school with a shaky foundation in their primary language. Thus, they may be starting their formal education in the primary language with some preexisting gaps. In addition, because of the lower status of their primary language and because they have less access to it in the community, for example in the media, growth in that language may proceed at a slower rate than one would hope for. Again, it is crucial to begin building a database that would give teachers and administrators a sense of what the normal rate of development in their program might be and what long term goals to expect.

In addition to understanding the initial slower rate of primary language development for both majority and minority students, teachers in EE programs need to know what to expect students to do in their respective primary languages in the beginning and later years of the program. Standards developed for English language arts by the National Council of Teachers of English and the International Reading Association (1996) give teachers an idea of what students are expected to accomplish and to know as a result of instruction in native language arts (see Table 4.3). Because of their holistic and functional focus, the English language arts standards lend themselves to interpretation and transfer to other languages. However, teachers should also consult native language arts standards, objectives, or curricula developed in countries where the other language is spoken in order to address any language-specific components. For example, mastery of the social variations of oral language will have to be emphasized for children learning Japanese much more than in the standards listed in Table 4.3.

As can be seen in Table 4.3, many of the standards focus on literacy. However, it is important to remember that much of literacy is based on oral skills and, similarly, much of oral language is part of literacy. Let us take as an example the first standard. In order to be able to read a wide range of texts to build an understanding of texts, students need to have the oral language base that supports talking about and

Table 4.3   IRA/NCTE
Standards for English Language Arts

Students will:

1. Read a wide range of print and nonprint texts to build an understanding of texts, of themselves, and of the cultures of the United States and the world.
2. Read a wide range of literature from many periods in many genres to build an understanding of the many dimensions of human experience.
3. Apply a wide range of strategies to comprehend, interpret, evaluate, and appreciate texts.
4. Adjust their use of spoken, written, and visual language to communicate effectively with a variety of audiences and for different purposes.
5. Employ a wide range of strategies as they write and use different writing process elements appropriately to communicate with different audiences for a variety of purposes.
6. Apply knowledge of language structure, language conventions, media techniques, figurative language, and genre to create, critique, and discuss print and nonprint texts.
7. Conduct research on issues and interests by generating ideas and questions and by posing problems.
8. Use a variety of technological and informational resources to gather and synthesize information to create and communicate knowledge.
9. Develop an understanding and respect for diversity and language use, patterns, and dialects across cultures, ethnic groups, geographic regions, and social roles.
10. For students whose first language is not English, make use of their first language to develop competency in English language-arts and develop understanding across curriculum.
11. Participate as knowledgeable, reflective, creative, and critical members of a variety of literacy communities.
12. Use spoken, written, and visual language to accomplish their own purposes (learning, enjoyment, persuasion, and exchange of information).

Voices from the Field

Developing Primary Languages in a Dual Language Kindergarten

Leah Radinsky
Kindergarten teacher
Inter-American Magnet School
Chicago, Illinois

Many issues and concerns arise in the area of primary language development in a dual language program such as the one we have at Inter-American. Due to the powerful influence of English in our culture, we take very contrasting approaches to meeting these two language-learning needs.

For Spanish dominant students, we face the challenge of developing a strong base in the Spanish language, including literacy skills and a rich vocabulary. The pressure to

(continued)

Voices from the Field (continued)

learn and speak English is so prevalent and comes from so many sources in our society, that I am constantly struggling to validate the Spanish the students already have, and to create an atmosphere in which using and developing Spanish language is a natural part of learning. Most students, even those with a strong Spanish foundation, want to use English most of the time.

The issue for English-dominant children is different. Parents often begin the year excited that their child is learning Spanish, but they want to ensure that their child learn to read and write in English, and keep up with students in traditional English programs. They fear that the time spent learning Spanish will interfere with academic growth in English and other areas. However, with the exception of some students with greater primary language needs, the status of English, and the presence of English speakers in the student body lead most students to great success in English.

We have found the following practices to be the most successful for primary language development for both English-dominant and Spanish-dominant students.

- Using a thematic approach
- Language arts instruction in the primary language for both groups of students
- Spanish instruction across the curriculum for all students, which includes hands-on activities with opportunities for oral language use, and heterogeneous grouping

This is how these practices work together in my classroom and across the school. In January, all three kindergarten classrooms begin a new thematic unit, *Los Dinosaurios!* Throughout the day, we incorporate the theme of dinosaurs into activities across the curriculum. The one-hour long language arts period is where each group of students receives instruction in their primary language. During that period, children are divided by language group and they engage in literacy rich activities such as reading and responding to stories and poems, dictating and drawing pictures, practicing developmental writing skills, and developing vocabulary, all centered around the theme of dinosaurs. This structure is based on the idea that reading and writing are best learned in the primary language first. Once students learn to read, in first or second grade, they all receive language arts instruction in both languages.

After the language arts class, a crucial component to developing primary language skills, the class is brought together for the remainder of the day for activities such as measuring a tyrannosaurus footprint and comparing it to our own footprints, making fossils in clay, and painting dinosaur murals. During these activities, different goals are being met for the different language groups. When I say: "Vamos a hacer un volcan de arcilla," an English dominant student might ask a friend for clarification: "What's *arcilla*?" The Spanish dominant student usually explains the word to his friend. By serving as tutors for their English dominant peers, Spanish dominant students enjoy a position of power, which increases their self-esteem, and increases the status of their mastery of Spanish. Simultaneously, they are developing their own language skills and concepts.

The English dominant students, on the other hand, benefit from language-rich experiences in both languages, and they increase their abstract understanding of language. For example, a student might hear and use the word *"fosiles"* several times, and then exclaim, "Oh, *fosiles!* That's just like fossils!" Connections like these benefit both primary and secondary language development. In the meantime, the activity itself builds understanding of the concepts. I try to promote these kinds of learning experiences and natural interactions by grouping students in mixed language groups, and encouraging dialogue and oral language use whenever possible.

The development of the primary language is a fundamental building block for success in both languages. It is important that we think carefully how we are going to promote its development in both groups of students.

listening to different types of discourse. They need to be able to tell stories and to describe objects and to listen to stories being told. This tight relationship between oral and literacy skills can also be seen in the discussion and the suggestions given in Chapter 5.

What should we expect from students in their second language?

Second language development proceeds from an initial pre-production phase during which students respond nonverbally (with gestures or drawings) or with very limited single-word responses, to early production of short phrases, to intermediate fluency that gradually begins to resemble native-like proficiency. Both language minority and language majority students will go through these stages in second language development. Although Spanish-speaking students in a developmental bilingual program or a dual language program receive less instruction in English than English-speaking students do in Spanish in a dual language program or an immersion program, both groups of students will progress in their respective second languages at about the same rate. The reason for this incongruity lies in the differential status and function of the two languages in society at large. Being the language of power and the language of popular media, English is likely to develop at a more rapid rate than the other language even though students may have less exposure to it in school. Although the attainment of proficiency in the non-English language may seem labored, teachers must not reduce their expectations for the attainment of that language on the part of English-speaking students in the program. Lowered expectations are bound to lead to lower levels of second language proficiency.

In order to know what to expect from students as they develop proficiency in the second language, teachers can refer to two standards documents. The first includes the standards for English as a second language developed by Teachers of English to Speakers of Other Languages (TESOL, 1997) and the second consists of standards for foreign language learning (ACTFL, 1996) (see Table 4.4). The TESOL standards list expectations for everyday social interactions, for the use of language for academic purposes, and for the use of language in culturally appropriate ways. Although the document was developed for students learning English as a second language, the standards can apply generally to students learning any language as a second language in an EE setting. As was the case in the native language arts standards, the holistic and functional nature of the TESOL standards makes it possible to transfer them to languages other than English. However, as mentioned in the section on native language arts standards, the application of these standards for languages other than English may entail a greater emphasis on those aspects that are specific to a particular language. For example, in the specific progress indicators for using the language to participate in social interactions, students learning Spanish must learn the distinction between the use of *tu* and the use of *usted*. The ACTFL standards provide an additional resource for teachers, especially for languages other than English.

The Relation Between First and Second Language Development

For children growing up bilingually, that is, surrounded by two languages from birth, their two languages develop in parallel and in a similar fashion. Any mixing of the two languages that occurs very early in development disappears quickly and the young child learns that there are two distinct ways of saying something. In comparison, most students in EE programs are engaged in consecutive second language learning. In consecutive second language learning, the student's dominant primary language is bound to influence the learning and use of the less proficient second language. This often takes the form of transfer from the first (and presumably stronger) language to the second, newly developing, language. Students are likely to use aspects of their first language to produce and to understand the second language. In rare cases, transfer may occur from the second language to the primary one; for example, if a useful expression or word exists in the second language but not the primary language. Sometimes, transfer from one language to the other has positive results and will serve the student well. An example of positive transfer is when a student understands the meaning of cognate words—for example *gato* because of its similarity to "cat." Transfer can also be negative, when a rule or a word in one language is inappropriately applied to the other language. For example, a student may use the word *libreria*, borrowed from the English "library" to refer to a library when the appropriate word in Spanish is *biblioteca*. Even though transfer with negative results leads to errors in the second language, students should be encouraged to lean on their skills in the first language in developing their second. Finding connections between a proficient language and one that is in the process of developing is a useful strategy for EE students to use. A later section of this chapter tackles the question of what to do with errors in the second language, some of which may be due to transfer from the student's first language.

What about mixing of the two languages?

It is natural for EE students to sometimes mix aspects of the two languages they are learning. They will do so for

Table 4.4   Standards for English as a Second Language and for Foreign Languages

Second Language Standards for Pre-K–12 Students
(Adapted from TESOL, 1997)

Goal 1: To use the second language to communicate in social settings
Standard 1   Students will use the second language to participate in social interactions.

Standard 2   Students will interact in, through, and with spoken and written forms of the second language for personal expression and enjoyment.

Standard 3   Students will use learning strategies to extend their communicative competence.

Sample indicators for early second language development: to give and ask for permission, offer and respond to greetings, introductions, and farewells, and to ask information questions for personal reasons.

Goal 2: To use the second language to achieve academically in all content areas
Standard 1   Students will use the second language to interact in the classroom.

Standard 2   Students will use the second language to obtain, process, construct, and provide subject matter information in spoken and written form.

Standard 3   Students will use appropriate learning strategies to construct and apply academic knowledge.

Sample indicators for early second language development: to ask for assistance with a classroom task, compare and contrast information, and define, compare, and classify objects according to their physical characteristics.

Goal 3: To use the second language in socially and culturally appropriate ways
Standard 1   Students will use the appropriate language variety, register, and genre according to audience, purpose, and setting.

Standard 2   Students will use nonverbal communication appropriate to audience, purpose, and setting.

Standard 3   Students will use appropriate learning strategies to extend their communicative competence.

Sample indicators for early second language development: to make requests politely, demonstrate an understanding of ways to give and receive compliments, show gratitude, apologize, express anger or impatience, and use acceptable tone and intonation in various settings.

Standards for Foreign Language Learning
(ACTFL, 1996)

Communication: Communicate in languages other than English
Standard 1.1   Students engage in conversations, provide and obtain information, express feelings and emotions, and exchange opinions.

Standard 1.2   Students understand and interpret written and spoken language on a variety of topics.

Standard 1.3   Students present information, concepts, and ideas to an audience of listeners or readers on a variety of topics.

Cultures: Gain knowledge and understanding of other cultures
Standard 2.1   Students demonstrate an understanding of the relationship between the practices and perspectives of the culture studied.

(continued)

Table 4.4 *(continued)*	

Standard 2.2   Students demonstrate an understanding of the relationship between the products and perspectives of the culture studied.

Connections: Connect with other disciplines and acquire information

Standard 3.1   Students reinforce and further their knowledge of other disciplines through the foreign language.

Standard 3.2   Students acquire information and recognize the distinctive viewpoints that are only available through the foreign language and its cultures.

Comparisons: Develop insight into the nature of language and culture

Standard 4.1   Students demonstrate understanding of the nature of language through comparisons of the language studied and their own.

Standard 4.2   Students demonstrate understanding of the concept of culture through comparisons of the cultures studied and their own.

Communities: Participate in multilingual communities at home and around the world

Standard 5.1   Students use the language both within and beyond the school setting.

Standard 5.2   Students show evidence of becoming life-long learners by using the language for personal enjoyment and enrichment.

---

several reasons. In the beginning stages of second language learning, the stronger primary language may creep into the second language with little apparent control. Later, the student may mix the two languages out of necessity—when a word or phrase that the student cannot retrieve in one language is borrowed from the other language. At an even later stage, when proficiency has been attained in both languages, students may mix the two languages purposefully for social reasons; this is referred to as *code switching*. Since code switching is intentional and serves a variety of social functions, it will be discussed later in a separate section.

In the case of language borrowing, which typically happens after the student has attained some proficiency in the second language, a word or phrase is inserted from one language into the other in a given conversation or utterance. Borrowing occurs either because the speaker cannot retrieve a particular word or phrase from memory, or when a word or phrase is not readily available or does not even exist in the other language. An example of the latter might be the word "hobby" that does not have an easy equivalent in Spanish. Thus, one might say: "El *hobby* que tengo me da mucho placer." Both of these types of language mixing are

part of the natural development of bilingual proficiency and should only be a cause for worry if they persist longer than expected or are done inappropriately. Indeed, when second language learners borrow a word or phrase from the other language and adapt it to fit with the language they are using this as a creative strategy for keeping conversation going.

What should we do about code switching?

As already noted, when bilinguals deliberately alternate the use of two languages from sentence to sentence or even within one sentence, it is called code switching. The following are examples of code switching: "*Vamos* Gabriela, let's go," or "*Estuve dibujando muy despacio,* but this line went all over the page." Code switching may be misinterpreted as an incapacity to separate the two languages properly. This is rarely the case. Studies have shown that code switching by fluent bilinguals is rule-governed and is used in a highly controlled way. It is used to convey subtle meanings, to show identification with speakers of the other language, and to accommodate the listener. It is also used as an indicator of dual identity. Code switching is often

Voices from the Field

What to Do about Code Switching

Cheryl Urow
Third grade dual language teacher
Oak Terrace School
Highwood, Illinois

Overheard during science class in my third grade, dual language classroom:

"*Yo no puedo find mi lapiz,*" whines Brittany to her group.

"Watch out," Ricardo warns his partner, "*casi te come el dedo.*"

"*Mi turno! Mi turno!* I want to pick one up now," Larry says as he sticks his hand into the tank of crayfish.

"*Español!*" I shout from the other side of the room, proving to the students that I truly do have extra sensitive hearing, and can hear English spoken during Spanish time, and Spanish spoken during English time, from anywhere in the classroom.

Students in my classroom code switch—and it's most commonly the native English speakers using English during Spanish time—for a variety of reasons. Sometimes they just don't know or cannot produce the word they need, as in Brittany's comment above. Other times they are just so excited about the activity at hand that they don't focus on language, but simply on communication. Larry is perfectly aware that everyone in the room—students,

teacher, and aide—are bilingual, and any utterance in either language can be understood by all. "Spanish time" and "English time" are artificial constraints applied by the teacher. Knowing Larry and his oral language ability in both English and Spanish, I am sure he could have communicated all his ideas in Spanish if he had taken the time to think about it. But, he wanted to get his hand in the tank, and there was no real need to take the time to think it out in Spanish.

Once in a while, a student will actually use an English word or phrase intentionally during Spanish time, as in Ricardo's case. Ricardo was speaking to an English dominant child who was in danger of getting her finger pinched by an angry crayfish. Utmost in Ricardo's mind was getting Andrea to remove her finger from the crayfish's reach, so he used the English to warn her, and then switched back to Spanish to finish his thought.

But, regardless of their reasons, code switching is not allowed in my classroom. The students need to gain fluency in both languages; that is, they need to be able to say whatever it is they need to say, be it acad-

emic or social, in both English and Spanish. And, although it's not the case in our classroom, they have to be prepared to talk with others who speak only English or only Spanish. So, we establish rules at the beginning of the year: Spanish during Social Studies, Spanish Language Arts, Science, and Math (70% of the day) and English during English Language Arts, and all "specials" (30%). I tell the students that I have very sensitive ears and eyes in the back of my head, and I know when they are not speaking the target language. I give points to cooperative groups for using the target language, and even take points away from those groups that do not. I know; this creates an external reward, a pedagogical no-no. But, given that there is no authentic reason to be using one language or the other in my classroom, as we are all bilingual, and that external forces (the teacher) determine what language is to be spoken, I use the external rewards. Once the students are able to monitor themselves better, and become more fluent in both languages, the point system falls out of use.

And we talk a lot about strategies for not using the "other" language: use another word, a word you know, for the word you don't know; try making a cognate; ask someone in your group for help: the phrases, "*Cómo se dice…?*" and "How do you say…?" are posted prominently in my classroom.

Y…así luchamos against code switching.

evidence of linguistic creativity and sophistication, and it is no cause for alarm.

Although code switching is normal and can be used to great effect, it should be avoided in EE classrooms as much as possible for two reasons. First, it will be easier for students in the long term if the two languages they are learning are kept as separate as possible so that they have clear expectations of when and where the use of each language is appropriate. Second, since students' languages are still developing, it is likely that they are code switching because it is easier and not because they are controlling the two languages for social reasons and in a skilled way. Consequently, they will benefit from the "correct" model that the teacher provides them. Until proficiency levels in their two languages are balanced, students should be encouraged to hold a conversation in one language only, at least in instructional settings. The way most EE classrooms are set up, with the two languages being kept separate from one another for instruction, it is possible to implement this strategy easily. For example, without making students who tend to code switch feel bad about their language production, teachers can encourage students to stick to one language at a time. They can repeat what a student says in the single target language and expand on it. For example:

Student: *Ayer fuimos al cine,* and it was a great movie!

Teacher: Oh, yesterday you went to the theater and you saw a great movie? What was it all about?

Contexts for Developing Oral Language Proficiency

Within the school setting, students in EE programs develop oral proficiency in their two languages in the following contexts: the native language arts class, the second language class, academic subject area classes, and in social interactions with peers and adults who are fluent in that language. Students who have contact with speakers of their second language outside of school obviously develop proficiency in those contexts as well. Out-of-school contact with the target language is extremely important and must be taken into account in curriculum and instruction planning. However, the topic is outside the scope of this book and will not be addressed. In the section that follows, we consider the ways of developing oral language skills in different contexts.

The Native Language Arts Class

Students in most EE programs receive primary language arts instruction from the beginning of their education. One exception is the total immersion model in which majority students can receive their entire education for the first year or two in the non-native language. For those students, native language arts instruction may be introduced as late as the third or fourth grade. Minority language students in developmental bilingual programs, of course, begin native language arts instruction in kindergarten and continue to do so until they graduate from the program. Minority language students in most dual language programs have native language arts instruction as part of the 50% to 90% instructional day, and majority students receive native language arts in English during the 10% to 50% time that the program offers in English. In these programs, students in each language group are typically separated from one another for the native language arts period. With the exception of 50/50 dual language programs, English-speaking students have less exposure to their native language than their minority language peers, and this leads to some questions, discussed below. For language minority students, the main issues concern the establishment of a strong foundation on which to build the second language and the acquisition of academic content; questions regarding these issues are discussed below as well.

Will English-speaking students develop enough proficiency and skills in the primary language if they are not receiving all of their instruction in English?

Yes, eventually, they will. Studies show that English-speaking students' primary language development is not hampered by the fact that they typically receive less of their instruction through English than if they were in a traditional monolingual program (Genesee, 1987). To the contrary, despite the fact that they are acquiring a second language that may not be prevalent in the mainstream society and that they are spending a substantial portion of their school day in that language, the English language development of English-speaking students keeps pace with that of their monolingual peers. In many cases, because of the enriching nature of EE programs, English-speaking students outperform their monolingual peers in English. At the same time, it is important to remember that for many students, age appropriate levels of proficiency are not attained until the third or fourth grade. This delay should not be cause for alarm since research indicates clearly that immersion in the second language does not harm the native language development of English-speaking students in the long run.

What happens with English-speaking students who speak a nonstandard variety of English?

In some dual language programs, some English-speaking students come from families where a non-standard variety of English is spoken. African American students, for example, who speak Black Vernacular English (or Ebonics) encounter a different variety of their language in school. Thus, they need to learn the dialect used in school and textbooks (and typically, that of the larger society) while continuing to develop their own dialect. When these students are enrolled in EE programs, there is the added challenge of learning another language. These students will be immersed in another language for a large portion of the school day and, thus, may not be able to spend enough time on the development of their home dialect and the mainstream dialect. Like other language minority students, African American students who come from poor families may also arrive with lower than expected levels of proficiency in language in general. For all these reasons, some educators are concerned about the burden that language learning may pose for this group of students.

Research on bidialectal education in the U.S. is scant and is often tainted with political issues. The research on enriched bilingual education for students who speak a nonstandard dialect of English is even more meager. However, there are some indications that African American students in immersion programs fare just as well as their language majority counterparts (Holobow, Genesee & Lambert, 1987). They also usually fare much better than their African American counterparts in non-EE programs, since many African American students live in poor neighborhoods and go to poor schools, and consequently receive an inadequate education that is remedial rather than enriched.

EE programs with African American students must, nevertheless, pay special attention to the fact that these students must develop proficiency in two clearly different dialects in addition to a second language. The value and the role that the vernacular has in the students' home and school lives must be acknowledged, and a curriculum that is respectful and responsive to the students' cultural backgrounds must be offered. Such a curriculum must not only reflect the dialect spoken by the students but also their cultural norms, values, and customs. The role of the vernacular and the home culture in learning the standard dialect used at school and in textbooks must also be determined. Parents need to be informed of the language and dialect learning plan for their children and be given guidance as to how they can encourage the development of both dialects at the same time as proficiency in a language other than English is developing. Parents must be encouraged to use the vernacular at home, but also to read to their children in the standard written form of English. In other countries where EE programs are common and where children enter school with a dialect that is different from that of the school (for example, in Arabic-speaking countries), teachers use the vernacular dialect to expand the school and textbook dialect. It is also not uncommon in these countries for children to be learning a foreign language as well as the two dialects. In contrast, in the U.S., because of the low status of non-mainstream dialects, children who speak such dialects need to receive supplemental instruction in mainstream English in order for optimal levels of proficiency to develop in all three language forms (mainstream English, the vernacular, and the language other than English).

Are there any special considerations for language minority students in developing their primary language?

Because of the possibility that minority children come to school with a shaky foundation in their primary language, teachers must be aware of individual students' needs to develop basic concepts in that language and support that development. This is especially true of kindergarten and first grade students. The basic concepts that may be missing from children's native language may not be part of the regular kindergarten or first grade curriculum so that the support that teachers give has to be supplemental to regular school objectives. Enrichment curricula for young children who are considered at risk may be quite useful in laying or reinforcing the primary language foundation that some minority children are missing. A curriculum such as Headstart can provide teachers with activities that can be added to regular primary language arts instruction.

A second issue concerning the primary language development of language minority students concerns the status of their language in the larger society. Students must feel that their language is valued in the whole school, from the way it appears in the curriculum to the functions that it serves in the everyday life of the school. In addition to the strategies described in Chapter 3, and earlier in this chapter, whereby the language is used for whole-school activities and announcements, it is essential that bilingualism is valued by the monolingual English-speaking staff as well as the bilingual staff. It is advisable for monolingual teachers, administrators, and other school staff to enroll in second language classes for adults in the school community. If such classes are unavailable, adults in the school can learn the language other than English alongside the English-speaking children in the second language classroom or alongside the minority children in the native language arts class. This will not only send a strong message about the value of that language, but it will also make teachers more sensitive to normal difficulties and useful strategies in second language learning.

How can I ensure that students are meeting the standards that the district has set for native language arts?

In order to ensure that students in EE programs meet the native language standards set for their monolingual peers, it is essential to use the same curriculum and the same instructional materials that the rest of the school or district is using. It is also important that native language arts standards developed by the district or state guide the native language arts component of EE programs. Rather than reducing the objectives of the mainstream native language arts curriculum to fit the parameters of EE programs (for example, as a result of reduced instructional time in English), it is preferable to modify expectations regarding rate of learning, especially for English-speaking students. It is very useful to develop an expected timeline for the attainment of native language arts skills on an experimental basis and to monitor students' attainment of those skills over three or four years. This timeline can be modified, if necessary, and can guide teachers' instruction and assessment activities. This timeline can also serve as the basis for interpreting standardized test results of EE students. The English language arts standards described in an earlier section of this chapter can guide the development of such a timeline.

What can parents do to help the development of the students' primary language?

One of the most valuable things that parents can do to promote the development of the primary language is to use it at home as much as possible. This applies to minority as well as majority parents regardless of how much instruction the students are receiving in their native language. Any home event that an adult shares with a child is an opportunity to develop language. Parents can be given guidelines on how to sustain a "running commentary" while doing everyday chores: setting the table, making dinner, doing the laundry. Parents who are literate should read to their children and with their children, regardless of the extent to which the child has been taught to read in the primary language. Thus,

even if native English-speaking children have not had any instruction in English reading in the lower grades, they can still benefit from the experience of sharing a storybook with an adult. Parents who are not literate can be encouraged to "read" wordless books or to tell stories to their children. They should also encourage their children to read to them and to tell or retell stories to them. It can also be very useful to parents if the school has a media library with a good collection of video and audiotapes. The Public Broadcasting System is a good source of videos in English, and even a few in Spanish. Audiotapes or compact discs of children's songs are available in several languages.

Some English-speaking parents are upset when their children, who are not getting the majority of their instruction in English, mix their two languages and insert words from the other language in conversations, especially early on in the learning process. They need not worry. As discussed earlier, such mixing is normal, and, although it is highly unlikely, it should raise a red flag only if it persists beyond the second or third grade. Parents can use the occasion of their child using a word from the other language that the parent does not understand as an opportunity to ask the child to explain the word. If parents see their children code switching with one another, after they have developed proficiency in their second language, they need not worry either. It is perfectly normal for people who are bilingual to code switch when they are talking to another person who is also bilingual.

Parents of minority students may have to be convinced that despite the fact that their children are not receiving much instruction in English in the early years, they need to reinforce the native language at home rather than try to use English with their children. Many minority parents are not fluent in English themselves, and the linguistic environment that is created at home if a non-fluent language is used extensively is faulty at best. In addition, the affective dynamics of parent-child dialogues can be upset if parents attempt to use a language in which they lack fluency because their role as authority figures may be compromised. More importantly, even if parents are fluent in English, minority children need reinforcement in the minority language in order to counteract the force of English that surrounds them in the larger society.

The Second Language Class

In most EE programs, students receive formal instruction in their second language. Thus, minority students receive instruction in English as a second language, and majority students are given, for example, Spanish or Korean as a second language instruction. In dual language programs, students are usually separated for second language instruction.

Voices from the Field

What It Takes to Get Your Child to Develop Proficiency in Spanish

Josie Yanguas
Parent of a child raised bilingually

Diana is currently five years old and she is bilingual. One clear advantage for our family in this quest to develop her Spanish proficiency is that we live in a predominantly Latino neighborhood in Chicago. Whether we are walking down the block, cavorting at the local playground, swimming at the neighborhood pool, or shopping at the corner store, Diana is guaranteed to hear Spanish. Since the time she was born, about half of my conversation with her has been in Spanish. In contrast, my husband, who is not fluent in Spanish, has usually spoken to Diana in English, though he is extremely supportive of the efforts for our daughter to be bilingual.

Before she attended pre-school, all of Diana's major caregivers were Spanish speakers, including my parents who have taken care of Diana for several long stints over the years. My husband and I have purposely taken many vacations with the *abuelos* where they constantly speak with Diana in Spanish. We were also lucky these past two summers to have visited my relatives in Spain, prompting Diana to be concerned that her father would have to learn more Spanish in order to have a good time and get along.

When Diana was just barely six months, we participated for over a year in weekly music classes in a predominantly Mexican neighborhood, where Diana learned children's songs in Spanish. Even while driving her to school just recently, Diana began singing *"Pim-Pom es un muñeco, con manos de carton. Se lava la carita con agua y jabon..."*

Although books in English dominate Diana's book collection, she also has several books in Spanish. I have gotten some of these books at bilingual conferences, but the local Target also carries a number of books in Spanish, including translations of children's classics such as *Corduroy, Good Night Moon,* and *Rainbow Fish.* Disney, being keenly aware of the Spanish-speaking market, has also translated all of its major fairy tales including some of Diana's favorites *La Bella y la Bestia* as well as *Blanca Nieves y los Siete Enanos.* Likewise Disney has translated many of its most popular children's videos into Spanish available for purchase at local stores. Diana's latest holiday video acquisition was *La Dama y el Vagabundo (Lady and the Tramp).* Diana has recently started to enjoy playing interactive computer games, so our next challenge will be to try to find some in Spanish.

Since she was nearly two and a half, Diana has been attending a local pre-school called *Mi Casita* Montessori. Some of the 15 children started speaking only Spanish, others only in English, and others like Diana—with exposure to both languages. Both of the teachers at *Mi Casita* are bilingual—one is English dominant while the other is Spanish-dominant. Although Diana has been doing much of her formal reading and writing instruction at *Mi Casita* in English, she is still surrounded by Spanish. We have gone out of our way to emphasize to Diana's teachers that we want her to continue to be exposed to Spanish while at school. At a recent holiday show, Diana sang a lullaby in Spanish and also recited a few lines from the Bible, first in English and then in Spanish. Although in "rehearsing" for these lines, she complained that the Spanish was harder, we convinced her that all she needed to do was practice. By performance time, she was comfortable in both languages, and now happily repeats her lines whenever they are requested.

There is no doubt in my mind that Diana, in general, is more comfortable speaking in English, but she certainly can interact with others in Spanish. Sometimes when she and I are alone, I will speak to her in Spanish and Diana will reply in English. Other times, she will reply in Spanish. Sometimes she will demand that I speak to her only

(continued)

Voices from the Field (continued)

in English—and sometimes I will acquiesce to her wishes.

The next challenge my husband and I face is where she will go to public school in the fall—given the lottery system for magnet schools in

Chicago. Our first choice, a dual language school, is not readily close to our home nor are we eligible for bus transportation. There are a few nearby schools where Spanish is included as part of the school cur-

riculum and we are hoping that at the very least she will be admitted at one of those sites. Be that as it may, the continued development of Diana's Spanish will always remain as a goal.

Development in second language classes differs slightly for minority and majority students. These issues, as well as others that are common concerns for both minority and majority students, are considered in the next section.

What objectives should I set for my second language classes?

Generally speaking, two major kinds of objectives should guide instruction in the second language in EE programs:

1. The use of the second language for everyday social interactions.

2. The language necessary for learning academic knowledge and skills.

These two objectives are embedded in the cultural norms of the society in which the language is used. Hence, a third objective emerges:

3. The application of appropriate cultural norms in the use of the second language for social and academic purposes (see Figure 4.2).

The relative importance of these three objectives will vary depending on whether students are minority or majority language speakers. Since minority students in EE programs are usually immersed in their native language in the early grades,

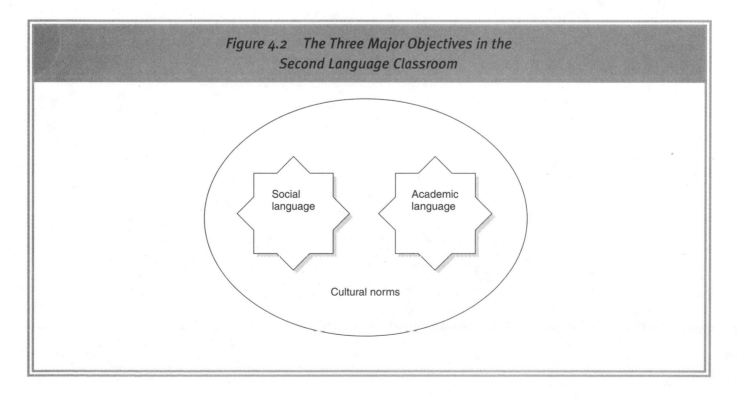

Figure 4.2   The Three Major Objectives in the Second Language Classroom

Social language

Academic language

Cultural norms

the ESL class might be their only exposure to English for the first two grades. Their most prominent need is to develop everyday social language in English in the early grades, and later, to learn new labels in English for content area concepts they have already learned in their primary language. Later, as the proportion of instruction through English increases, minority students need to develop more advanced skills in English for academic purposes in order to be able to learn new skills and concepts through that language. In contrast, majority students in EE programs are usually immersed in the second language for the first couple of years, and they spend most of their school day in that language. For these students, the second language class must prepare for, reinforce, and support content area lessons taught in the second language. Thus, the relative emphasis on each language objective will be determined by the particular needs of the students.

The relative emphasis on each language objective will also vary as a result of the stage of language development attained by students and the specific skills needed by individual learners. Table 4.5 shows examples of student behaviors at beginning, intermediate, and advanced stages of language development for each of the three objectives.

How do I organize instruction to help students attain the three language objectives?

Whether you are planning second language instruction for majority or minority students and regardless of the extent to which different language objectives are emphasized, instruction can best be organized and delivered around thematic units. Some themes lend themselves well to develop-

---

Table 4.5   Student Behaviors at Beginning, Intermediate, and Advanced Stages for Each Language Objective (adapted from TESOL, 1997)

Language for everyday social interaction

(Example from second grade)

Beginner	Intermediate	Advanced
Uses simple questions and appropriate gestures to ask the location of certain types of books.	Asks "wh" questions about types of books and story lines from peers.	Poses "what if" questions to peers and teachers about alternate endings to stories read.

Language for academic content knowledge acquisition

(Example from fifth grade)

Beginner	Intermediate	Advanced
Draws a sequence chart to illustrate the story line of a myth that was read and describes the chart orally.	Draws a sequence chart to illustrate the story line of a myth that was read and writes simple sentences describing the chart.	Develops a comparison chart to compare two nature myths with regard to characters, setting, and conflict resolution.

Application of appropriate cultural norms

(Example from seventh grade)

Beginner	Intermediate	Advanced
Identifies and explains idioms from the context of a simple dialogue written by classmates.	Writes dialogues that incorporate idioms expressing different emotions.	Generates a list of idiomatic expressions and matching non-idiomatic terms and talks about when they are appropriate to use.

ing everyday social interaction; for example, *My Home and Family*. Other themes are more amenable to teaching the language needed for academic content; for example, *The Weather*. Academic themes can be derived from the academic curriculum and will serve to not only develop general academic language, but will reinforce and support the acquisition of specific content area skills and knowledge. The whole collection of thematic units designed for each grade provides the context for second language instruction for that group of students. Each unit will, in turn, consist of one or more lessons, depending on the breadth of the topic and the depth with which the topic is to be dealt with (see Figure 4.3). When planning second language instruction, you need to consider the whole array of thematic units and lessons you have at your disposal, and modulate the time spent on each lesson depending on the specific skills that a group of students needs.

It is important to plan thematic units for the whole year so that they form a continuous curriculum that meets the language learning objectives for the students. In addition, you need to plan each unit in advance so that you attain consistency and coherence among the lessons. Each lesson, of course, also has to be planned in advance to ensure that the objectives set for the students are met. The questions in Table 4.6 can be used to check that instructional units and the lessons included in each unit are well planned (Gordon, 1997).

How can I optimize second language learning?

Language is best learned incidentally in the context of doing something that is meaningful and relevant. This is not to say that specific aspects of language should not be taught. To the contrary, the second language class in an EE program is the place for direct instruction of language. Once a meaningful context has been set, the focus of instruction can turn to language-specific issues. For this reason, the lessons that comprise a thematic unit should have a non-language focus. Sometimes this focus derives from everyday events and topics, such as riding the bus or current events. At other times, the focus is derived from the objectives of the academic subject areas that constitute the curriculum, such as plants or the Civil War. Thus, the second language class is the place where academic content and non-academic content meet.

Regardless of whether the focus of instruction is an everyday phenomenon or an academic subject area, the importance of meaningful content as a context for language instruction cannot be overemphasized. Otherwise, language teaching can be extremely inefficient for all but a very few students. Thus, lessons should focus primarily on non-language concepts that provide a context for instruction of language skills. Gordon (1997) has proposed a useful framework for lesson planning. The framework follows a sequence beginning with the students' own experiences and

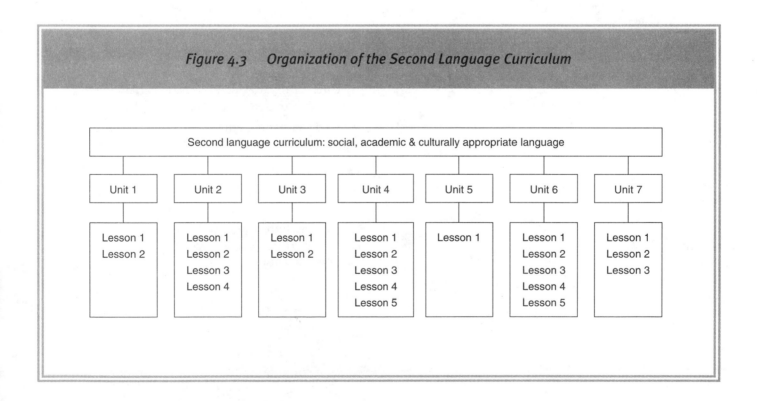

Figure 4.3   Organization of the Second Language Curriculum

Second language curriculum: social, academic & culturally appropriate language

Unit 1	Unit 2	Unit 3	Unit 4	Unit 5	Unit 6	Unit 7
Lesson 1	Lesson 1	Lesson 1	Lesson 1	Lesson 1	Lesson 1	Lesson 1
Lesson 2	Lesson 2	Lesson 2	Lesson 2		Lesson 2	Lesson 2
	Lesson 3		Lesson 3		Lesson 3	Lesson 3
	Lesson 4		Lesson 4		Lesson 4	
			Lesson 5		Lesson 5	

ending with the students taking some sort of action on their own environment. According to this framework, lessons consist of the phases shown in Table 4.7. In each phase, mini-lessons on different aspects of language can be introduced, using as text the language that emerged from the activities in that lesson (see the question on how to go from whole to part in the ensuing section).

Each of these phases can provide an opportunity for direct instruction of specific aspects of language or for highlighting special features of the language. Teachers can provide direct instruction in language by extracting mini-lessons on specific aspects of language from larger activities. The discourse that you use as a springboard for the language mini-lessons can be generated from activities that students engage in, a book that they have been reading, or a piece of writing that they have completed. For example, after students have read a book, you can focus on the past tense by having students count the number of verbs in the past tense in an excerpt and compare the different forms of the past tense they find in that excerpt. After learning a song about a character or an animal, students can sing the song from a first person perspective. The focus on skills can happen at the sentence level, at the word level, or at the sound or letter level. The following are examples of tasks at these different levels (Gordon, 1997).

Focus on sentence level skills:

- Identify examples of sentence or clause types.
- Take two or more sentences and identify how the author used sentence reduction techniques to combine the two ideas.
- Take separate sentences and use punctuation clues and logical reasoning to combine the sentences.

Focus on word level skills:

- Identify parts of speech in a familiar passage, taken either from a book or something that the students wrote.
- Categorize words from a selection according to given semantic or grammatical characteristics.
- Find connections among two or more words in a list of words selected from a text and explain rationale.

Focus on sounds and letters:

- Using comprehensible words from a selection, classify the words based on spelling patterns.
- Identify all the words in a text that share a given characteristic, such as beginning sound, number of syllables, tense.

Table 4.6   Creating Effective Instructional Units and Lessons

Planning instructional units:

- How many of the language objectives does this unit meet?
- How well is this unit aligned with the general school curriculum?
- How well is this unit aligned with state goals and standards?
- How important are the skills developed in this unit?
- How important are the thought processes and strategies developed in this unit?
- How relevant is this unit to the daily lives of the students?
- How appropriate is the unit theme for the age level and interest of the students?

Planning lessons:

- How timely is the introduction of content-specific language to help prepare students for learning in the content area classroom?
- How appropriate are the lesson activities for the students' age level and interests?
- How appropriate is the lesson for the students' stage of language proficiency?
- How important are the skills developed in this lesson?

Table 4.7   Phases of Second Language Lessons

Preview phase:

Purpose: To activate prior knowledge (see Glossary), create a common experiential base, and to generate interest. To prepare students for the most difficult concepts and principles of the lesson in ways that are not dependent on literacy.

Introduce the conceptual focus of the lesson through students' past or class-created experiences. Illustrate the conceptual focus of the lesson as concretely as possible. Present concepts through diverse modalities, such as visuals and hands-on activities. The emphasis is on developing conceptual readiness. The focus can be on content area concepts or language concepts depending on the needs of the students.

Focused learning phase:

Purpose: To give students additional opportunities to learn the conceptual and strategic focus of the lesson.

Provide practice in the use of the conceptual focus. Allow students to practice skills within a meaningful context and by using different modalities.

Expansion phase:

Purpose: To help students internalize learning by transferring and applying it to their own world and expanding it to other contexts. To encourage students to act on their learning in personally and socially relevant ways.

Help the students to create connections between what they have learned and the real world. Provide students with choices that best reflect the conceptual focus of the lesson. Provide students with different options that help them take actions that reflect the key concepts studied in the lesson.

(Adapted from *The Multidimensional Learning Web*, Gordon, 1997)

What activities can I use to expand oral proficiency at different stages of second language development?

Several teaching activities are suitable for expanding oral language proficiency. Some of these activities promote vocabulary development, others improve students' intonation in the second language. Some of the activities are more suitable for beginning level students, and others are more effective when students have attained more advanced levels of proficiency in the language. Most activities can be adapted to fit the students' proficiency level. The arts provide an excellent medium for oral language development, especially at beginning levels. At more advanced levels of oral proficiency, students can extend their language use to literacy. Table 4.8 lists some of these activities and provides brief descriptions of each.

What materials are available for teaching second languages?

There is a wealth of materials for teaching English as a second language as well as some of the most commonly taught foreign languages (see Appendix B for a list of publishers). However, it is rarely the case that a second language text or a specific series will suffice if the integrated and holistic approach suggested in this and subsequent chapters is followed. Ultimately, the best use of published materials is twofold:

1. As a resource that is made to fit into the general second language curriculum designed for a particular group of students.

2. As one set of materials to be supplemented by visuals, real objects, literature, and content area texts.

Second language textbooks should not be the sole source of instructional materials in EE programs (see Figure 4.4). Other published texts that should be part of the second language classroom include children's books, both fiction and non-fiction, and the content area texts that the students are using in their content area classes. Software programs, laser discs, audio- and videotapes can also contribute to the development of oral proficiency in the second language. In addition, it is essential for the second language teachers to have an extensive collection of pictures, toys, and real objects to aid in helping students understand language in which they are not fully proficient or to elicit language from students who are typically reluctant to speak.

Table 4.8   A Selection of Second Language Teaching Activities and Their Application at Different Levels of Proficiency

Strategy	Description	Application for beginning level	Application for intermediate/advanced	Primary aspects of language promoted
Total Physical Response (TPR)	Students follow directions given by teacher, pointing to, moving and placing objects, pictures, or words according to command.	Students model actions along with the teacher.	Students follow multi-step directions with several objects. They give directions to other students or the teacher.	Vocabulary
Shared Story Telling	Students listen to a story being told or read, with illustrations.	Students listen to a story told or read by the teacher, who illustrates the story with mimes, pictures, objects.	Students retell or tell a story with or without a script.	Integrated language
Songs	Students learn a song.	Students sing along with teacher or recording.	Students change words in the song.	Intonation Stock phrases
Dialogues	Students listen to and practice dialogues with one another.	Students learn the dialogues and repeat them word for word.	Students follow the format of the dialogue generally but change words and contexts.	Stock phrases
Role Play	Students are given roles to play in a structured context.	Students are given dialogues and vocabulary to make their role playing easier.	Students invent their own dialogues and respond to the other person spontaneously.	Stock phrases (beginners) Integrated language
Simulations	Simulations are an elaborate form of role playing, whereby a whole environment is created, typically in the classroom.	Students are given scripts to follow as they participate in different parts of the simulated environment.	Students participate freely and improvise as they go around the different parts of the simulation.	Integrated language
Language Experience Approach	Students do a project in class. Oral language is elicited around the activity.	Students follow directions to complete the activity.	Students summarize the activity or compose a story around it.	Vocabulary Grammar Integrated language

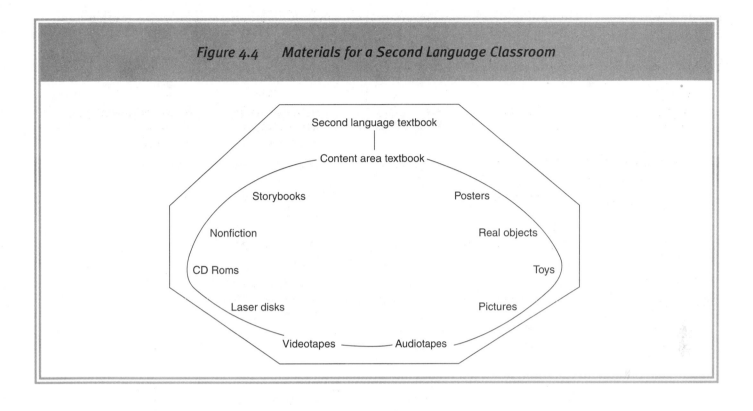

Figure 4.4   Materials for a Second Language Classroom

What do we do if students constantly use their native language in the second language class?

Despite the language-eliciting power of certain strategies, such as the Language Experience Approach, teachers are still often faced with students who do not use the second language, but rather, communicate with each other in their more proficient native language. Even in the best-planned activity-centered classroom, students may want to use their native language, especially when the bucket of glue spills or the big mound of wet paper scraps splatters on the teacher's desk! There is nothing you can do to force students to use a language in which they are not proficient, especially if they share a fluent native language. However, you must establish rules of classroom conduct and make it clear to students that you expect them to use the second language as much as they can. Although some teachers are able to increase students' second language production by means of incentives (such as points that a student or a group gains) or material rewards (such as coupons for pizza—usually sponsored by a local business), it is not recommended. Such external rewards for performance rarely work in the long term (Kohn, 1993) and, besides, it creates an artificial context for second language use that may discourage students from using it for authentic purposes in real-life situations. Rather than resorting to artificial incentives, it is advisable to create a learning environ-

ment that encourages students to talk to one another and to the teacher for real purposes. The teacher needs to encourage use of the second language by always using the second language her/himself and insisting that students do the same. It is important to apply this rule from the beginning of the program and to adhere to it until the student graduates.

Even though second language classes are intended for students who all speak the same native language, occasionally you may wish to bring in students who only speak the second language or who speak it very fluently. This is more likely in EE programs for a single-language population, such as developmental bilingual programs for minority students or foreign language immersion for majority students. In fact, it is an issue primarily for majority students who do not have access to the target language in their daily lives. For these students, teachers may want to create natural communication situations with peers who speak that language proficiently.

The following are suggestions for creating opportunities for authentic interaction with native speakers of the target language in single language immersion programs, when the target language is not represented in the school:

- Take the students on field trips to neighborhoods where the language is spoken. Most cities with large concentrations of minorities have vibrant communities that are rich with tradition. Almost any minority

---

Voices from the Field

Effective Strategies for Language Development

Frances Poy
Kindergarten teacher
Columbus Avenue School
Freeport, Long Island, NY

The Freeport School District has had a dual language program, under the direction of Sue Greca, for the past six years. The program, which began in the Columbus Avenue Early Childhood Center, has extended itself to four schools (Archer, Bayview, Giblyn, and Atkinson) throughout the district. The present fifth grade dual language class at Atkinson school is the original class, which began the program in kindergarten. The program added the pre-K component after its first year.

I am a bilingual kindergarten dual language teacher partnered with Cathy Harbulak at the Columbus Avenue School. For the past six years, I have found that theme songs, games, monthly newsletters, hands-on science and math lessons have been highly successful in developing oral language in our Native Language Arts (NLA) and Spanish as a Second Language (SSL) learners. Theme songs and games help students learn and review vocabulary in a warm relaxed manner which lends itself to first-time second language learners. Experience has shown me that parental involvement is synonymous with success and the newsletter serves that end. The monthly theme, vocabulary, songs, pronunciation guide, as well as homework activities are all included in the newsletter packet. Hands-on science and math mini-lessons also stimulate language production in both NLA and SSL learners. I encourage the use of cassettes, videos, books, radio, and TV programs to promote the exposure of the second language at home. The newsletter has also been very useful with my Hispanic parents as well as a communication means and as a guide in giving them the insights they need to help their children succeed in class.

The combination of these strategies and the involvement of parents are conducive to a successful learning environment for all second language learners in a dual language program.

---

community in an urban center is likely to have stores, restaurants, and community centers. As with any other activity, it is advisable to structure these trips so that they contribute to language development in addition to being fun cultural experiences.

- If there are no neighborhoods with speakers of the target language in your region, a trip to another region or country where that language is spoken is beneficial, although expensive.
- Establish a pen-pal, key-pal (on the Internet), or video-pal network with peers who speak the target language. If students are not comfortable writing, they may dictate what they want to say to someone who can write the language. A video-pal system could be done purely orally. Remember to join in the project yourself by holding a dialogue with the teacher of the students with whom your students are corresponding.

How and when should I correct students' errors?

The affective environment of the EE class is very important in promoting second language use. Students should feel completely at ease using their second language at all times, even if their usage is imperfect and fraught with errors. Errors in students' oral language use should not be singled out or highlighted at the expense of communication. However, this does not mean that errors should be ignored; nor does it mean that we can count on the students to pick

Voices from the Field

How I Get My Students to Use the Nonproficient Language

Marcela Moncloa
Spanish Immersion kindergarten teacher
East Orange School District
East Orange, New Jersey

Throughout the first two years of teaching in our program, I noticed how much Spanish the English dominant students were able to understand and express in my kindergarten classroom. However, whenever I asked older students simple conversational questions, I was always surprised that the majority of them couldn't respond to those questions or engage in a conversation in Spanish. So, I began to reflect on the strategies I was using in the classroom that seemed to support the children in their second language use. I knew that working with a group of kindergartners in Spanish would be like starting with fully primed language machines. There were only a handful of strategies that I needed to keep in mind to scaffold the natural language learning process which takes place in a child that age. I was also aware that for second language acquisition to take place, I had to not only make Spanish comprehensible for the children, but also make it so accessible to them that they would begin to use it for their personal communicative needs. I used several techniques in the classroom that supported this process. Repetition of chunks of language was very important. The

children heard these ready-made chunks of language in songs and literature with repetitive refrains. We also experienced them in everyday actions; for example, when someone sneezed, the children would have a script ready in their mind in response: "*Salud*". "*Gracias*". "*De nada*". For fun and reinforcement, we would dramatize these scenarios even when they weren't real at the moment. The children enjoyed these so much that they often initiated these dramatizations.

I used the repetitive value of songs to make language accessible to the children. So I would often make up songs on the spot to describe or comment on a situation. For example, after lunch we would sing: "Good afternoon, good afternoon, I already ate, I already ate. Very delicious, very delicious. Thank you, thank you," as the children patted and rubbed their full bellies and smacked their lips to show how delicious the food was. When the songs had become part of our class routine, I could easily take the chunks of language out of the context of the song and I found that the students could use it appropriately.

Children learned to use language naturally to tell someone not to hit them, and to ask them why

they hit them in the first place. They used language to tell which table of children had gone to drink water or taken a turn to use the bathroom. This process always started with me scaffolding the language for them. First I would give them the language. I would say, for example, "The red table already drank water." The students would repeat. After some days of this, I would ask, "Did the red table drink water, yes or no?" Afterwards, I would ask, "Which table already drank water?" By the end of the process, the students would give me information about who drank water without any solicitation from me. They were independently using language for their own needs. At this pace, I would get my first original complete thought in Spanish from an English dominant student around November. That was always a treasured milestone in the year for me.

Another strategy that fostered Spanish language use among English dominant students was thematic teaching. Using culturally driven themes like Guatemala, India, corn, or Carnival was invaluable in creating a language core that we used and which became part of our classroom culture. The children internalized the language that we used to interact with these themes for an extended period of time. They used the language in dramatizations, artwork and writing that they did as a group and much later, as their own chosen activities.

Dance was my favorite means of making language accessible to

(continued)

Voices from the Field (continued)

children and extending the idea of creating a classroom culture. My students could tell me *cumbia* was a dance from Colombia (they could show me Colombia on a map). They were able to articulate in Spanish that you need to move your feet like this and your hips like that. I chose the songs carefully. Although the music was rich, the words were simple enough for them to sing, understand, and enjoy. They also became part of our language repertoire when we used them outside of the context of the song. The dancing was sheer joy. All the children, no matter what their language development rate, thoroughly connected with the movements of the dances.

Finally, circle time was extremely important in promoting student language use. I would ask my students routine questions. They learned highly personalized language. At the beginning they would share in English. I would first respond to their news in Spanish, giving them the words they needed. I would ask the class to repeat some of those sentences and have the child repeat them. It was a painstaking process, but it yielded good results after the December holidays. At that time, children would start putting their own thoughts about what they did into Spanish.

Every June, I am proud of the children and myself for the way we took ownership and full participation in the language learning process. Every June, my beliefs are confirmed about the environment teachers need to create to make language learning and language use accessible to children.

up feedback about errors that is given implicitly by the teacher. Revising the student's responses by correcting their mistakes as recasts is a very common form of error correction, but relatively ineffective (Lyster, 1998). For example, if the student says: "Manuel, he go home he sick," it is not uncommon for teachers to recast that utterance by responding: "Oh, Manuel went home because he was sick?" By providing the student with the corrected form of her statement in this way, the feedback regarding the errors is too subtle and too implicit. The best way to counter students' errors is to focus the student's attention explicitly on the error and engage the students in finding the correction themselves. Thus, you need to gently point out an inconsistency or an error in the student's utterance and then ask the student what he or she thinks is wrong with it and how it should be changed. The teacher has to find the delicate balance between drawing attention to the meaning conveyed in students' utterances and focusing their attention to errors they have made. Many students, especially those who are older, actively seek explicit feedback, and will not be satisfied until the teacher formally corrects them. These students use error correction as a learning strategy. Four factors make error correction effective for the learner:

1. The focus of the conversation must remain on meaning; the teacher must show genuine interest in what the student is saying.

2. The student must explicitly be made aware of the error; the teacher must point the student's attention to the specific error.

3. The student must try to remediate the mistake him or herself; the teacher must encourage the student to guess at another word or grammatical form that would be correct.

4. The student should not be made to feel discouraged or embarrassed about making a mistake, but rather, must be praised for any attempt at communication.

Table 4.9 shows examples of more or less effective ways of responding to a student's erroneous language.

This type of error correction is most appropriate in natural conversational situations. In other cases, when the focus of the task is clearly on the form of language—for example, completing a grammar exercise—it is essential that errors be corrected systematically. In these cases, student errors can turn into a mini-lesson on the rules of language. Teachers can also track common errors that recur in

Table 4.9 Types of Error Correction

Teacher: What did you do last night, Adela?

Student: I go to movie.

Inappropriate response:

Oh, what did you see? *(Ignoring the error.)*

You went to the movies? What did you see? *(Providing the correct model, but without focusing the student's attention on the error, the student may not even notice the correction.)*

Appropriate response:

Good, Adela! *(Praising student's attempt at communi-* cation.) Now, we're talking about yesterday and you said "go." *(Focusing student's attention on an error.)* You need to say...what? *(Encouraging student to come up with a correction.)*

Student: Oh...I...went?

Teacher: Yes! Great! *(Praising the student's attempt at correction.)* You went to the movies; *(Providing the correct model.)* So, what did you see? (Showing interest in the meaning conveyed by student.)

students' spontaneous utterances and focus on those errors in mini-lessons during the second language class.

The Content Area Class

As we have emphasized, a great deal of language learning takes place in content area classes (see "content-based second language instruction" in Glossary). Of course, the role of language during content area instruction is much more of concern for majority students who typically receive content instruction through their second language, at least in the beginning. Because of the close relationship between content area and language learning in EE classes, it is essential that second language instruction and content area instruction are well coordinated with one another. When the same teacher teaches both, coordination is much easier. But in many EE programs, different teachers are responsible for each type of instruction. In those cases, it is imperative that the two teachers work together to develop joint curriculum and plan lessons. We address issues of language development during content instruction in the next sections.

How can I insure that students have the oral second language skills they need to learn new academic material?

Students should be introduced to language that they need for particular content area lessons *before* they are taught those lessons. To accomplish this, the teacher must first identify key vocabulary, grammatical structures, and discourse patterns that a discussion about a particular content area entails. As you will see in greater detail in Chapter 6, certain language skills are fundamental to certain content areas; these have been referred to as content-obligatory language. Other language skills simply line up well with the content area; those have been referred to as content-compatible language (Snow, Met & Genesee, 1989). Next, using strategies such as the Language Experience Approach, described in an earlier section of this chapter, content-obligatory and content-compatible language is introduced along with other key words and phrases. When the students become familiar with the words and the grammar structures that are both necessary and compatible with a particular content area lesson, then they are ready to be introduced to new concepts in that area in a subsequent lesson. Without such preparation, students may find it difficult to learn abstract concepts because they are not sufficiently proficient in the language.

Ideally, then, learning of language associated with content area learning precedes the content area lesson by at least a day and no more than a week or two. In real life, of course, such synchrony rarely happens. Teachers who are aware of the importance of timing of content and language instruction can systematically prepare students for the language demands of academic instruction. We discuss these issues in greater detail in Chapter 6.

How can I make it easier for students to understand?

Sheltered instruction (see Glossary) strategies are very useful for making content area instruction understandable and for pushing second language proficiency ahead. Effective sheltered instruction strategies include the following (adapted from Echeverria, Vogt, Short & Montone, 1998):

- Use a variety of question types that promote higher-order thinking skills.
- Pace the lesson appropriately to the students' ability level.
- Speak at a rate that is appropriate for the students' proficiency level.
- Use vocabulary that is appropriate to the students' proficiency level.
- Use short, simple sentences rather than complex ones.
- Avoid pausing before the end of sentences.
- Exaggerate intonation and gestures.
- Repeat sentences, without using too many different expressions and idioms.
- Emphasize key words.
- Provide frequent opportunities for interaction among students and between teacher and student.
- Provide sufficient wait time for student responses.

Chapter 6 provides further suggestions on how to plan and teach integrated language and content lessons.

Social Interactions with Peers and Adults

Any moment students are engaged in meaningful interaction in a language is an opportunity for them to develop their oral language skills. It follows, then, that every teacher and staff member of the school should think of themselves as language teachers or, at least, as facilitators of language development. Peers who speak the target language, and even those who are in the process of learning it can help others develop communicative proficiency in that language. Teaching as well as non-teaching staff with whom the students come into contact, such as the nurse, the librarian, and the lunchroom or cafeteria staff, have a role to play here. It is worthwhile, then, for an administrator or a teacher who is well versed in second language learning and instruction to give staff some training on issues of language development and how they can assist students in the process. It is also important to staff all functions of the school with personnel who speak the language other than

English and for them to use that language in everyday social interactions consistently with the students.

Why are social interactions so important for language development?

When students actively engage in authentic conversations with others who speak their second language fluently, language learning take place in the most natural and effective way. When learners and speakers are brought together, three types of interactive processes take place, and each of these is valuable in its own way to the learner (Wong-Fillmore, 1985):

1. *Social.* Learners assume that the language used is relevant to the immediate situation. They learn the rules that characterize the social convention of everyday language use. By interacting with peers who are fluent in the target language, students are exposed to models who exhibit appropriate behaviors.
2. *Linguistic.* Learners use what they already know about language to try to make sense out of the linguistic input they receive. Learners can practice what they know and can seek feedback, either directly and explicitly or indirectly and implicitly. This type of practice is extremely valuable because the learner is the one who typically controls and monitors it as he or she sees fit. In the classroom setting, it is most often the teacher who controls feedback and opportunities for practice.
3. *Cognitive.* Learners use strategies to figure out the relationships between what is happening and what is being said. Since most social interactions that learners get involved in are by choice, the motivation to get meaning is so strong that it prods the learner forward.

All three processes push the language development forward in a way that is different from direct formal instruction. For this reason, it is essential that you build opportunities for students to engage in authentic conversations with fluent speakers of the second language outside of the classroom.

How can we get students to use the second language with one another outside of the classroom?

In dual language programs, it is natural, especially during the first few months of school, for students of the same language background to congregate with one another in the lunchroom or on the playground. To increase the likelihood of students interacting with one another in their second language, at least once in a while, you can create situations or tasks

Thoughts from a Monolingual Teacher in a Dual Language Program

Judy Wilson
1st grade teacher
Anne Fox School
Schaumberg, Illinois

Four years ago, Anne Fox School decided to begin an enriched language program where Spanish language and culture was to be taught to all first graders. The program would then move up through the grades. This, then, is my fourth year of learning beginning first grade Spanish! I had never had the opportunity to learn a second language, so this opportunity was challenging, scary, and exciting. Most of the teachers in our school do not speak a second language fluently, so we all began preparing for change within our school and neighborhood. Although the first grade students were the only ones receiving the Spanish language curriculum that first year, we decided to expose the rest of the school to this experience by teaching shortened Spanish units to grades 2–6 and also by providing many school-wide cultural activities.

As an older, experienced, mono-lingual teacher, I was concerned. I have always been ready to try new ideas, and I do try to be flexible when working with others—but this was pushing me to new limits! Not only would I have 29 students in my class that year, but 12 of them would come from a Spanish bilingual kindergarten. My only Spanish was "Hola." I suppose that was a good beginning. I had many sleepless nights that summer before school was to begin. I did try to do as much reading and research as I could over the summer, but I was still extremely fearful. Somehow, I knew the children and I would "connect," but I also wanted a good rapport with the Hispanic parents. I decided and was given the time to join the children as they learned Spanish.

What a joy watching and participating with first graders in their language class! Their Spanish teacher is enthusiastic and places no pres-sure on the children. They are learning not only language but about the culture. The children (and I) think it is great fun. (I now have a Polish girl who is learning her third language, Spanish.) The children do so well with the second language; I wish I could say the same for their teacher (me)! They soak up the information and always get way ahead of me. I keep trying, but I am still insecure and embarrassed about my ability to learn and speak Spanish—although I am getting better at reading it. I wish that I had had the opportunity to learn at age six. My bilingual students and their families are very patient and supportive of me; however, I continue to do all my bilingual conferences with the help of the bilingual teacher.

Over the years I have learned so much from all my students. I have learned that young children absorb and retain so much information and are always eager for more. I have also learned to rely on and give more responsibility to the children. They are usually able to help each other in ways that hadn't occurred to me. They also choose their friends because of like interests, not language, color, or nationality.

where students of the two language backgrounds are mixed with one another. When small heterogeneous groups of students work toward the completion of an activity that engages their attention, they are compelled to use at least one group's second language at least part of the time. An example of such a situation might be the following. Groups of three or four students are created where at least one of the students is of a different native language than the rest of the group. Each group is given a task to complete over lunchtime, such as accumulating data on students' favorite cafeteria and home food. At the end of the semester, data from all the groups are compared and analyzed, and reports are prepared and presented to others. Cooperative grouping strategies are particularly effective for getting students to interact with one another in authentic dialogues and in ways that give each student an important role to play within the group.

Other ways that are useful for bilingual as well as monolingual immersion schools include the creation of language clubs and cross-age (or cross-language, in the case of bilingual schools) partnerships. In both cases, students need guidance regarding things to do. Language clubs might be encouraged to read and discuss books written by the same author, or to view and discuss different films dealing with a particular topic. Cross-age or cross-language partners can select a topic to research, preferably on an issue that is of interest to their daily lives; for example, the building of a shopping mall on the site of a playground.

A potential problem regarding peer interaction in dual language programs is the overuse of students as translators for one another. It is important to use students as models for one another, not as translators. Having students act as translators is especially pernicious when members of only one language group consistently translate for the other. In dual language programs, because the majority of instruction is delivered in the minority language, and because of the lower status of the minority language, the language minority students typically translate for the English-speaking students. In addition to the negative social outcomes of this imbalance, you must weigh the slight cognitive advantages of translating against the more significant disadvantages of not allowing the translator sufficient time to process the concepts being learned.

Will peer interaction encourage students to learn bad language?

Peer interaction among students who are not proficient in a language implies that much of the language used will be full of mistakes. However, that is not reason for worry. Using the language with one another creates the opportunity for students to develop even more communicative fluency. Besides, since students typically do not say much in most classrooms, they need all the opportunities they can get to talk to one another. Also, the non-proficient nature of peer language is only a minor factor in language learning. First, students' language is in flux; it is developing and progressing, and this means that it is highly unlikely that a specific error will persist for a very long time. Second, students are likely to be at different levels of proficiency even within the same classroom, and if someone makes a mistake, it is likely that at least one or two students will offer a correction. Rather than worry about students' mistakes preventing the development of good language habits among other students, we should worry about increasing peer interactions as much as possible.

Summary: Meeting the Critical Features for Effective EE Programs

Table 4.10 summarizes the critical features for effective EE programs and presents implications for oral language development.

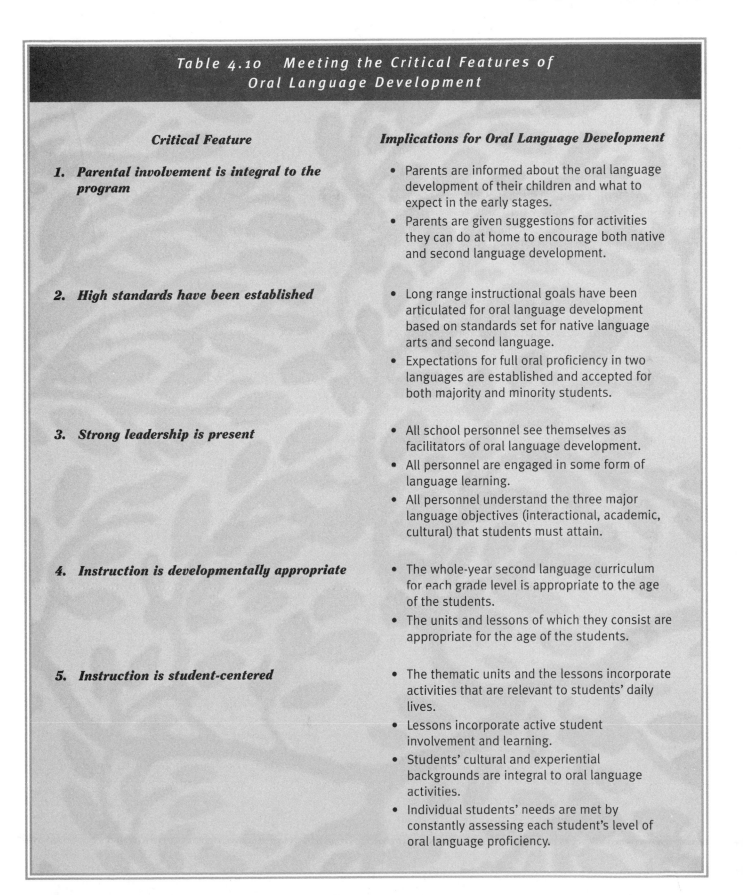

Table 4.10   Meeting the Critical Features of Oral Language Development

Critical Feature	Implications for Oral Language Development
1. Parental involvement is integral to the program	• Parents are informed about the oral language development of their children and what to expect in the early stages. • Parents are given suggestions for activities they can do at home to encourage both native and second language development.
2. High standards have been established	• Long range instructional goals have been articulated for oral language development based on standards set for native language arts and second language. • Expectations for full oral proficiency in two languages are established and accepted for both majority and minority students.
3. Strong leadership is present	• All school personnel see themselves as facilitators of oral language development. • All personnel are engaged in some form of language learning. • All personnel understand the three major language objectives (interactional, academic, cultural) that students must attain.
4. Instruction is developmentally appropriate	• The whole-year second language curriculum for each grade level is appropriate to the age of the students. • The units and lessons of which they consist are appropriate for the age of the students.
5. Instruction is student-centered	• The thematic units and the lessons incorporate activities that are relevant to students' daily lives. • Lessons incorporate active student involvement and learning. • Students' cultural and experiential backgrounds are integral to oral language activities. • Individual students' needs are met by constantly assessing each student's level of oral language proficiency.

Table 4.10   (continued)

Critical Feature	Implications for Oral Language Development
6. Oral language instruction is integrated with challenging academic instruction	• Challenging content area objectives are used as the context for oral language teaching and learning. • Native language arts are taught in a way that is interesting for students and develops a high level of cognitive processing. • Students are encouraged to develop an abstract understanding of language and bilingualism and the role that they play in their daily lives.
7. Teachers are reflective	• Teachers understand or ask questions about the process of bilingual development. • Teachers regularly monitor the effectiveness of their instruction for the development of oral language proficiency. • Teachers constantly assess their students' oral language proficiency and plan appropriate instruction. • Teachers reflect upon their own language and language development.
8. The program is integrated with other school programs	• EE students' bilingual proficiency is highlighted in the rest of the school. • Teachers meet frequently to discuss students' progress. • Teachers meet frequently to coordinate among the various instructional components offered to students.
9. The program aims for additive bilingualism	• All teachers understand and expect their students to be fully bilingual by the end of the program. • All staff is engaged in maintaining or developing proficiency in a language other than their own.

References

ACTFL. 1996. *Standards for Foreign Language Learning: Preparing for the 21st Century*. Yonkers, NY: American Council on the Teaching of Foreign Languages.

Echeverria, J., Vogt, M., Short, D. & Montone, C. 1998. *The Sheltered Instruction Observation Protocol*. Santa Cruz, CA: Center for Research on Excellence and Diversity in Education.

Genesee, F. 1994. Integrating Language and Content: Lessons From Immersion. *Educational Practice Report #11*. Santa Cruz, CA: The National Center for Research on Cultural Diversity and Second Language Learning.

Genesee, F. 1987. Learning Through Two Languages. Rowley, MA: Newbury House.

Gordon, J. 1997. The Multidimensional Learning Web. Des Plaines, IL: Illinois Resource Center.

Holobow, N., Genesee, F. & Lambert, W. 1987. *Summary of Kahnawake Test Results, Spring 1987*. Unpublished Report, McGill University, Montreal.

Kohn, A. 1993. *Punished by Rewards: The Trouble with Gold Stars, Incentive Plans, A's, Praise, and Other Bribes*. Boston: Houghton Mifflin.

Lindholm, K. & Gavlek, K. 1997. *Factors Associated with Teacher Satisfaction, Efficacy, Beliefs, and Practices in Two-Way Bilingual Immersion Programs*. Paper presented at the annual meeting of the American Educational Research Association, Chicago, Illinois.

Lyster, R. 1998. Focus on Form in Content-Based Instruction. In M. Met (ed.), *Critical Issues in Early Second Language Learning*. Glenview, IL: Scott Foresman-Addison Wesley.

NCTE and the International Reading Association. 1996. *Standards for the English Language Arts*. Urbana, IL: National Council of Teachers of English.

Snow, M.A., Met, M. & Genesee, F. 1989. A Conceptual Framework for the Integration of Language and Content in Second/Foreign Language Instruction. *TESOL Quarterly, 23 (2)*, 201–217.

TESOL, 1997. *ESL Standards for Pre-K–12 Students*. Alexandria, VA: Teachers of English to Speakers of Other Languages.

Wong-Fillmore, L. 1985. Second Language Learning in Children: A Proposed Model. In National Clearinghouse for Bilingual Education (Ed.), *Issues in English Language Development* (pp. 33–42). Rosslyn, VA: National Clearinghouse for Bilingual Education.

5 TEACHING LITERACY IN TWO LANGUAGES

This chapter is arranged around questions frequently asked by teachers when they design literacy instruction for first and second language learners. In the first part of the chapter, we share our beliefs about literacy and literacy development and answer foundational questions about developing students' literacy skills in two languages. In the second part of the chapter, we answer questions teachers ask about how to achieve their primary instructional objectives and how to teach their students in stage-appropriate ways. The third and final section of the chapter is dedicated to teachers' concerns related to students with atypical educational backgrounds or special educational needs. Later, in Chapter 6, we provide additional guidance on developing reading and writing skills during content area instruction.

Literacy Foundations

What is literacy?

In the narrowest sense, literacy refers to the ability to read and write. However, in line with current understandings of language development, we consider literacy to be an activity involving all interrelated aspects of language—listening, speaking, reading, and writing—with the purpose of constructing or conveying meaning. When readers interpret texts, they do so based on their prior experience and background knowledge, their cultural frame of reference (beliefs, values, norms), and their underlying language abilities. When they write, they draw upon these same sources to construct messages to communicate with others (See Holdaway, 1979, pp. 12–18, for a more complete discussion of important and essential features of literacy).

We understand literacy to be not simply a functional skill or a cognitive achievement, but a complex activity with social, linguistic, and psychological dimensions. We agree with Hudelson (1994, p. 130) that literacy has many functions—aesthetic as well as utilitarian, such as providing individuals a medium through which they can learn about the world and share their understandings with others, accomplish daily living tasks, connect with other people, reflect upon their life experience and current circumstances, act on problems, and experience and enjoy the richness of language (p. 130). We also recognize that literacy, as

defined above, is connected with other modes of symbolic representation, such as computer literacy, mathematical literacy, and scientific literacy. Those who construct comprehensive literacy development programs understand the interrelatedness of language, thought, and action and seek to develop biliteracy for all these purposes.

How does literacy develop?

Readers and writers go through predictable developmental stages. Each of these stages has characteristic behaviors that define the stage and cue teachers as to the types of activities that would be appropriate for their students. Later in this chapter, we present in more detail the following three-stage organizer that EE teachers can use to label student performance and guide their teaching efforts: 1) Preliteracy, 2) Early/Emergent Literacy, and 3) Late or Intermediate Literacy. These stages really define a continuum that demonstrates our view that literacy is not an end point, but rather an evolving process, with important milestones along the way. Understanding these milestones is essential if teachers are to achieve their goal of promoting high levels of literacy in two languages. We return to this point later in the chapter.

For additional information on the foundations of literacy development, the reader is referred to the sources suggested in Table 5.1.

Table 5.1 Additional References on Dual Literacy Development

Cummins, J. (1993). Empowerment Through Biliteracy. In J.V. Tinajero and A.F. Ada (Eds.) *The Power of Two Languages: Literacy and Biliteracy for Spanish-Speaking Students* (pp. 9–25). New York: Macmillan/McGraw-Hill School Publishing Company.

Ferdman, B.M., Weber, R. & Ramirez, A.G. (Eds.) (1994). *Literacy Across Languages and Cultures*. Albany, NY: State University of New York Press.

Holdaway, D. (1979). *The Foundations of Literacy*. Sydney: Ashton Scholastic.

Wells, G. (1990). Creating the Conditions to Encourage Literate Thinking. *Educational Leadership, 47* (6), 13–17.

Williams, J.D., & Snipper, G.C. (1990). *Literacy and Bilingualism*. White Plains, NY: Longman.

Foundations of Dual Literacy Development

What level of oral language proficiency is necessary to teach literacy?

Although reading specialists may disagree as to how early in the oral language development process second language literacy can be successfully introduced, there is widespread agreement regarding students' dependence upon oral language when performing reading/writing tasks for alphabetic and non-alphabetic languages alike (Chu-Chang, 1981). Because this is so, we recommend that literacy be developed taking into account students' current oral language abilities.

With younger students, we recommend that reading and writing instruction occur *after* some oral language and prerequisite cognitive skills are established (e.g. ability to establish relationships; actively attend; retain visual, auditory, and semantic information in short term memory). Because older students have more advanced cognitive skills and an expanded knowledge base, we recommend that the development of their literacy skills and oral language be done in an integrative manner. Regardless of the age or proficiency level of students, teachers must actively develop students' oral language to insure their overall comprehension of language and support their literacy activity.

In what order should literacy be introduced when two languages are being taught?

Studies of immigrant students learning ESL have shown that the introduction of literacy in a student's primary language is advantageous (National Research Council, 1998). But likewise, immersion studies have shown that it is possible to introduce literacy in a second language quite successfully to speakers of a majority language before providing instruction in their primary language. In determining the initial language for reading/writing instruction, teachers should consider the status of the students' language in the larger society. More specifically, we propose the following guidelines:

1. For speakers of a minority language, we recommend several years of uninterrupted reading and writing instruction in primary language. This should last from three to five years, depending on whether the program begins in Pre-K, K, or 1. Around the third grade, *formal* reading/writing instruction in the second language, English, can be introduced. However, reading/writing instruction should continue in the primary language in order to insure the attainment of high levels of competency. Throughout the program, there should be an emphasis on developing all of the language arts, exposure to authentic literature in the primary language, and the development of academic reading and writing skills through the students' primary language. *Informal* exposure to reading and writing in English can occur, as appropriate, beginning in grade 1.

2. For language majority students, we recommend that the second language be used as the initial language of general academic instruction and the language in which reading and writing are first developed. The percentage of instruction delivered in each language is determined by program organizers (see Chapter 3).

3. In dual language programs, we recommend that the above guidelines be followed; providing initial reading/writing instruction to both groups in the non-English language first. Alternatively, some dual language program organizers choose to provide formal literacy instruction to each group of students in their respective primary languages to capitalize on their existing oral language skills, while emphasizing the non-English language for instruction in other content areas.

When Does Second Language Literacy Instruction Begin in the Two-Way Program at Federal Street School?

Annie Homza
Resource Specialist
Federal Street Elementary School
Salem, Massachusetts

The Students

If we examine the kindergarten population of the Federal Street School (FSS), we see that the two groups of children that enter the program are, generally speaking, quite different not only in terms of their primary language (L1), but also in terms of their entering second language (L2) proficiency and beginning literacy skills. English speaking kindergarten students are typically monolingual, with little or no Spanish language background (although there are some exceptions). On the other hand, these students generally have fairly well-developed literacy skills in English. The L1/L2 literacy profile is somewhat reversed for the Spanish speakers in Kindergarten. Generally, these students have some English proficiency while, in many cases, their literacy skills in Spanish are limited.

Second Language Literacy Instruction

Based on the belief that literacy skills transfer easily from first to second language, the FSS Two-Way Program has emphasized literacy in

the first language first. Therefore, while kindergarten and grade one students are exposed to some L2 literacy activities, they receive formal reading and writing instruction almost exclusively in their first language. All teachers instruct students in integrated groups in the content areas so that typically by second grade, children begin to use both L1 and L2 literacy skills as they are learning content. In addition, second through fourth grade teachers have separate times to instruct students in L2, although these times have not been considered formal literacy instruction in the second language. Teachers approach these classes as times to build the second language and to refine literacy skills in the second language. Currently, by fifth grade, students spend all their time in integrated settings; there is no longer either separate L1 or L2 instructional time.

Current Issues

We, at FSS, are discussing how and when second language literacy is introduced within our Two-Way

model because we have noticed a trend for the L1 Spanish students to complete the program with more bilingualism than the L1 English students, while the L1 English students tend to have more literacy than do their L1 Spanish counterparts.

We believe it is important to ask questions about the access each group has to their first and second languages outside of school and their motivation to learn the second language. We know that our L1 Spanish students have more access to English than their L1 English counterparts have for Spanish, and that both groups are quite aware of the generally higher status of English in their world beyond the classroom. We also know that research shows that the full development of L1 literacy is very important to later L2 literacy development.

FSS is now examining ways we might respond to the achievement differences noted between our two groups of students and the differences in their socio-linguistic and socio-cultural realities while maintaining our commitment to developing each group's literacy in their native language first. This process is still unfolding in our school and it is fostering an important and challenging dialogue among our teachers.

As noted above, we recommend that teachers provide several years of uninterrupted, well-sequenced formal reading/writing instruction (two to three years) in one language prior to formal reading/writing instruction in the second. Real life illustrations of how different types of EE programs introduce literacy in the two languages can be found on pp. 89 and 91.

Why should literacy be taught in one language before beginning a second?

Although reading and writing instruction in two languages at the same time occurs quite successfully in other countries, we advise that EE teachers in the U.S. work in a sequential manner. We make this recommendation in part, because of the current socio-political context of schooling in the U.S. bilingualism and biliteracy are neither common goals of American education nor are they common occurrences in the population at large. As a result, there can be a fundamental lack of confidence in students' ability to become bilingual and biliterate or a generalized anxiety because English literacy is delayed. These fears and anxieties can undermine dual literacy development. There may be other risks as well.

First there is the risk that language minority students who are presented with literacy instruction in two languages simultaneously prior to establishing a threshold level of competence in their primary language will remain at low levels of literacy in both languages and lack feelings of competence so essential to future learning (Cummins, 1984). Second, there is the risk that so much instructional time will be dedicated to formal language and literacy instruction in two languages in the early grades that achievement in other academic subjects will be compromised. Third, students' reading fluency may be affected, especially in the early stages. More specifically, if students do not internalize the graphophonemic relationships of at least one of their languages well, they may labor to process text. They may hesitate when decoding individual clusters of letters when reading each of their languages. For example, students in Spanish/English programs might be uncertain about which sound is required when they see the letter "i" or "j" if reading is less than automatic. Students' reading rates, fluency, and comprehension can all be affected if both systems are weak. While it is certainly possible to teach students to read and write in two languages simultaneously, for all of the above reasons, we prefer a sequential plan for formal reading/writing instruction so that teachers can insure that their students have a firm foundation in reading/writing one language before beginning formal reading/writing instruction in the other.

What can teachers expect learners to transfer from the first language to the second?

In general, the following aspects can be expected to transfer from one language to another:

- *sensory-motor skills*—the eye-hand coordination, figure-ground awareness, visual memory, discrimination, and spatial and directional skills involved.
- *common writing system features*—identical elements or common features in the writing systems (alphabets, sound-symbol associations, punctuation rules)
- *comprehension strategies*—finding the main idea; inferring, predicting, getting important details, use of picture and context cues
- *study skills*—using reference materials; note-taking
- *habits & attitudes*—selective attention, feeling capable, persistence, and concentration

In general, the more similar the two languages, the more positive transfer will occur. However, even in the case of languages with non-roman alphabets or ideographic languages and English, positive transfer occurs in the more general skills categories listed above (Carson, et. al., 1990, 1994; Williams & Snipper, 1990).

Of course, differences among languages can "interfere" with a learner's performance as well. As noted earlier, learners may "miscue" when decoding languages with virtually the same alphabet because they may not be sure which phoneme to produce. This is to be expected and is highly predictable behavior if one analyzes the two languages in question.

Through contrastive analysis, teachers can identify those elements that will transfer readily from one language to the other (both general and specific skills) and those that are unique to each language to plan for a smooth transfer from one language to the other. Thonis (1983) has generated a careful summary of the elements that transfer between Spanish and English. This listing should prove highly useful to those supporting biliteracy development in these high frequency languages.

In this specific instance, some elements these two writing systems have in common are: the use of single consonants in initial, final, and medial positions, the use of word endings, prefixes and suffixes, and a good portion of the alphabet is similar. Some specific skills that must be developed in English are: contractions, possessives, vowel rules, consonant blends, and homonyms, to name a few. Skills unique to Spanish are: unique letter (ch, ll, rr), vowel rules, definite article and noun agreement rules, accent marks. For a useful contrastive analysis of approximately twenty

Strengthening Literacy in Both Languages in Grades 2–5

Kirstin Veeder
Second, Third, and Fourth Grade Teacher Specialist and
Jacey Tramutt
Fourthand Fifth Grade Bilingual Teacher
Barrick Elementary School
Houston, Texas

At Barrick Elementary School in Houston, 87 percent of the students are native Spanish speakers. Because of this, the school encourages continuous development of Spanish while students learn English. We focus on teaching primary language arts and academic subjects in Spanish in the early grades. At the same time, our students learn ESL and receive some instruction in English (e.g., art, music, and physical education) so that they can succeed in an English-based curriculum. Instruction in English increases progressively, so that children learn 50% of the curriculum in English and 50% in Spanish by grades 4 and 5.

Second and third grades are very important in the process of developing both languages. At Barrick, students coming to second grade know how to read in Spanish, but still need to develop their comprehension skills in that language. In the second grade, while we are working on that in the content areas, we are teaching ESL in a concrete way at the beginning of the year, which gives way to some reading and letter-sound instruction during the second half of the year. The teachers read to the students in English daily, assisting in their vocabulary and language enhancement. By the end of the year, the majority of the class is reading in English at a grade level below their native language level. According to the research, that is where they should be. In third grade, we use literature-based ESL units that are part of an integrated curriculum. One book is chosen for the unit and all content area instruction revolves around that theme.

In the fourth grade, while bilingual students still receive reading instruction in Spanish, at the same time, they are exposed to literacy in English in a variety of ways. English literature is taught as enrichment. Techniques used to teach English literature include, but by no means are limited to, discussing vocabulary words students will encounter in their reading ahead of time, and building background knowledge (that is, if they are reading a book on the environment, the teacher would first ask the students what they already know about the environment to raise their confidence). The teacher might also first read a paragraph and then have the students choral read to build fluency. English literacy is also being taught in social studies and science. By teaching English through the content areas, rather than in an isolated manner, the students are more successful and find reading in their second language more enjoyable. It's essential that they learn to read and write in their second language (English) through a meaningful context. The students also need to feel that they are in a safe environment and supported by the teacher as well as their classmates and we work to create this kind of literacy learning environment.

If students are struggling with English writing in the fourth grade this does not cause us great concern. It seems that writing is the most difficult skill for them to learn. However, because we have identified this as a need, we use direct teaching approaches in the upper grades to advance writing development in English. For example, one writing strategy we use is the Multisensory Grammar approach (MSG). In MSG, students learn different parts of speech (nouns, verbs, linking verbs, adjectives, adverbs, prepositions, etc.) by associating each part of speech with a different color. For example, nouns are color-coded yellow because like yellow yield signs, they give us very important information. Students write simple sentences comprised of nouns and verbs and eventually expand the complexity of their sentences by including adjectives, adverbs, and prepositions in their writing. By fifth grade we want our students' writing skills and confidence in English to improve.

languages or language groups and English, see *Learner English* by Michael Swan and Bernard Smith, 1987, Cambridge University Press. This book can help teachers identify linguistic features that may create difficulties for English language learners of various language backgrounds.

How can parents assist in their children's literacy development?

In general, it is helpful if parents and other family members serve as models for their children, *provided they are literate to the level required for effective modeling.* Parental influence can be maximized if we offer them encouragement and concrete suggestions as to how to get involved; for example, video storybooks, CD ROM "living storybooks," or audio-taped/recorded stories are useful resources for parents who are unable to read to their child due to lack of proficiency in the target language, low literacy levels, or time constraints. With the assistance of such media, children can be read to without placing excessive demands on parents. These resources also have the advantage of giving children a variety of reading voices and styles, and parents can enjoy being together with their child as they engage in active listening around the story presented in these formats. Having a take-home library of print and media-based materials is very beneficial to encouraging literacy outside of school.

All parents, regardless of their literacy level, can serve another important role—that of audience for their child. Parents can serve this role by expressing enjoyment and praising their children when they attempt to read and write, and by conveying to their children the importance of becoming biliterate.

Schools can support children's writing by sending home writing folders and attractive writing tools (colored pencils, pens, markers), and by giving parents ideas to encourage their children to practice writing and do creative writing. The *Reading is Fundamental* Project in Washington, D.C. has many useful brochures for parents on these topics (Reading Is Fundamental, 600 Maryland Ave., SW, Suite 600, Washington, D.C. 20024 or www.si.edu/rif/).

Finally, teachers can survey families to find out what forms of literacy occur in the home. In some families, children participate in writing family letters to friends and relatives who live at a distance. They may read and write in conjunction with religious education; or read documents for others such as leases, notices, announcements; they may write poems and stories for pleasure; or they may keep diaries to record important family events. Once these activities are

identified, parents can be encouraged to continue to support their children's participation in these naturally-occurring and culturally-authentic literacy events in the home.

In addition, often there are community resources that can be tapped to support children's literacy development. For example, libraries and clubs are two possible settings where children can practice their developing skills. Sometimes older neighborhood children welcome the opportunity to read with younger children. Some bookstores have special children's areas where children can explore the world of books. Parents can also participate in author visits at school or "storytime" in community libraries. All of these activities encourage children to become readers/writers and support parents' efforts.

It is important that teachers be sensitive to parents' interest in and availability for such activities so that they are better able to identify those which suit particular parents. Making the process comfortable and doable for parents guarantees success in promoting literacy at home. (See Macerra "Voices from the Field" essay in Chapter 6, pp. 124).

Teaching Objectives and Approaches

What are teachers' major tasks in developing students' literacy skills?

The five major tasks for teachers developing students' literacy skills are summarized in Figure 5.1.

Task 1: How do teachers select appropriate literacy materials?

Because it is so central to literacy development, teachers will want to provide their students with appropriate and plentiful experiences with print as well as create many outlets for written communication. Selecting appropriate materials or activities is perhaps the most important thing teachers do when they plan for their students' reading/writing instruction. For this reason it is at the center of Figure 5.1.

When choosing materials, we recommend that teachers consider: 1) the proficiency demands, 2) the contextual support provided, 3) the authenticity and naturalness of the language, 4) the target audience for which the material is intended, 5) the cultural relevance, and 6) the intellectual, aesthetic, and emotional satisfaction produced by the material (Barrs, et al., 1988). Table 5.2 on p. 93 provides a checklist of features that are relevant for selecting classroom materials.

Table 5.2   Checklist for Choosing Materials

Proficiency demands:

- ❏ The grammatical complexity and length of the text matches the student's stage of oral language proficiency.
- ❏ The core vocabulary is known by the student.
- ❏ The storyline will be easy to grasp and meaningful.
- ❏ The form of language used (British versus American English; Mexican versus Caribbean versus Castillian Spanish) matches the student's background.

Contextual support:

- ❏ Picture support is available at the level required by the student.
- ❏ Illustrations are interesting and complement the text well.
- ❏ The text is structured in a logical, cohesive way that the student will find easy to . follow.
- ❏ Text features (boldface, italics, dialogue bubbles) provide additional cues to readers.
- ❏ The size and layout of the print match the learner's age and ability.

Language authenticity:

- ❏ The language is natural and predictable.
- ❏ Texts are based on oral language and literary traditions of students.
- ❏ The level of formality of language is appropriate.

Intended audience:

- ❏ The text is appropriate for the reader's age group.
- ❏ The illustrations are inclusive (includes individuals of various ethnic, racial, and religious backgrounds, socioeconomic circumstances, life experiences, geographic. locales, etc.).
- ❏ The text is gender specific or gender fair, as appropriate.

Cultural features:

- ❏ The student possesses the background knowledge and life experience required to understand the text.
- ❏ Materials represent and honor the cultural groups present in the classroom/school.
- ❏ The norms and values inherent in the text are understood and appreciated by the reader.

Intellectual, aesthetic, and emotional satisfaction:

- ❏ The stories have powerful and imaginative content.
- ❏ The language is memorable—lively, rhythmical, humorous.
- ❏ The material has a clear purpose (pleasure, informational, commercial, educational).

Table 5.3   Classroom Materials Checklist

- ❏ Wordless picture books
- ❏ Big books (with corresponding student copies available for independent reading)
- ❏ Children's literature (stories, children's collections (poetry; prose), books organized by author for author study, etc.)
- ❏ Bilingual/multilingual books
- ❏ Folktales
- ❏ Sayings/famous quotes (in charts/posters)
- ❏ Graded readers (abridged novels, controlled stories, early readers)
- ❏ Chapter books and other books selected for "read alouds"
- ❏ Concept books (counting, alphabet, opposites)
- ❏ Interactive books (flip books, peek-a-boo books, hidden objects books)
- ❏ Advice books, personal development books
- ❏ Magazines (commercial, school-marketed, literary)
- ❏ Newspapers, newsletters (fan clubs, hobby clubs, special interest)
- ❏ Environmental print (instructions, cereal boxes, maps, manuals, kits)
- ❏ Comic, riddle, and joke books
- ❏ Non-fiction books (discovery books, text sets for thematic units)
- ❏ Picture dictionaries/word books
- ❏ Activity books
- ❏ Reference books (atlases, encyclopedias)
- ❏ Student-developed materials (books, chart stories, recordings, etc.)
- ❏ Recorded books (with records, audio/video cassette tapes)
- ❏ CD ROM/videodisks (interactive software, content-related materials, multimedia presentations)
- ❏ Computer software (writing to read, stories on disk)
- ❏ Internet sites

Teachers should have a wide range of materials available to entice students to read and write. Some of the types of materials EE teachers will want to have available in their classrooms are listed in Table 5.3.

A range of strategies for locating print and non-print materials in languages other than English was discussed in Chapter 3 (see pp. 42–43). Teachers will also want to consult on-line bookstores, like *Bilingual* (Spanish/English) *Books for Kids* (www.bilingualbooks.com/) or *Yahoo Bilingual Education Resources* (www.dir.yahoo.com/Education/ Bilingual/) to locate the latest materials available. To locate multicultural children's literature for your classroom, see the specialized reference books in Table 5.4.

Table 5.4   Reference Books to Help in Locating Multicultural Children's Literature for Your Classroom

Brown, D.S. (1994). *Books for a Small Planet.* Alexandria, VA: Teachers of English to Speakers of Other Languages.

De-Cou-Landberg, M. (1994). *The Global Classroom: A Thematic Multicultural Model for the K–6 and ESL Classroom (Volumes 1 & 2).* Reading, MA: Addison-Wesley Publishing Co.

Kezwer, P. (1995). *Worlds of Wonder: Resources for Multicultural Children's Literature.* Scarborough, Ontario: Pippin Publishing.

Nevarez, S., Mireles, R.C. & Ramirez, N. (1989). *Experiences with Literature: A Thematic Whole Language Model for the K–3 Bilingual Classroom.* Reading, MA: Addison-Wesley Publishing Co.

Smallwood, B.A. (1989). *The Literature Connection: A Read-Aloud Guide for Multicultural Classrooms.* Reading, MA: Addison-Wesley Publishing Co.

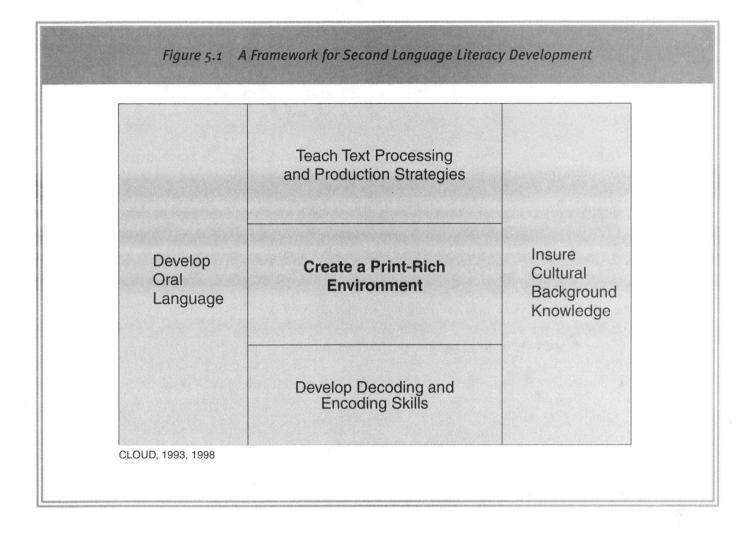

Figure 5.1   A Framework for Second Language Literacy Development

Teach Text Processing
and Production Strategies

Develop
Oral
Language

**Create a Print-Rich
Environment**

Insure
Cultural
Background
Knowledge

Develop Decoding and
Encoding Skills

CLOUD, 1993, 1998

Task 2: How can students' oral language skills be developed to support literacy development?

As mentioned previously in this chapter, there is a strong relationship between learners' oral language abilities and their literacy development. By developing students' oral language skills, teachers support their reading and writing performance in very significant ways. In Chapter 4, a variety of strategies were shared for developing oral language skills. Below are some specific oral language development activities that teachers can use during the prereading and prewriting phase of instruction to enhance learners' perfor-

mance (Table 5.5). An illustration of how this occurs in practice appears in the subsequent "Voices from the Field" essay.

Oral language can also be developed *during* reading and writing activities or as a *follow-up* to reading/writing tasks. For example, during reading, teachers can take time to ask students to explain key words in the text or to echo or choral read parts of predictable stories. During writing, teachers can suggest alternative terms that students can use, thereby expanding their vocabulary at the point of use; or they can teach them alternative phrasing or more native-like phrasing for ideas they have expressed in their writing. Because the language skills all interact, teachers should take advantage of

---

Table 5.5   Pre-Reading/Writing Activities

Prereading activities to develop oral language:
Scan the text to determine language features for preteaching; then:

- Preteach high frequency vocabulary and concepts using visuals, realia, actions or demonstrations.
- Involve students in the active use of new terms required for comprehension.
- Familiarize students with phrasing used in the material through songs, chants, pattern practice, or sentence strips.
- Practice new sight words with word cards, games, computer-based activities.
- Teach new meanings of multiple meaning words used in the text.
- Teach descriptive terms, figurative language, idioms as needed.

Prewriting activities to develop oral language:
Consider the writing task (theme, degree of difficulty); then:

- Brainstorm concepts related to the theme; list useful terms on the board (organize information in semantic webs, charts, and other graphic organizers (see Glossary) after it is collected).
- Provide students with a word bank of useful terms (especially words that are difficult to spell).
- Use techniques such as partner writes and dialogue journals (see Glossary) so that students can benefit from the modeling of more proficient students (emulate their phrasing, terminology).
- Employ Language Experience Approach or Read Aloud methodology to provide students with background knowledge and language related to the theme.
- Provide students with reference materials (dictionaries, pictionaries, spell checks, and especially a thesaurus) so they can expand and refine their language.
- Teach synonyms, antonyms, homonyms, prefixes, and suffixes.

---

the ways that reading and writing can advance oral language abilities and vice versa.

Task 3: How can teachers insure instruction is culturally appropriate?

Culturally relevant materials and pedagogy (see Glossary) are great supports for emergent readers and writers. When the content students are reading is familiar to them, they can comprehend the second language much more quickly because they are able to make accurate predictions about the text. Likewise, when writing about familiar themes, students can draw on their own ideas. When grouping structures and interactional styles are culturally familiar, students can concentrate on the task at hand because they are comfortable in the classroom. Choice is another powerful support. When students select materials and activities, it strengthens their motivation and level of investment. Two of these aspects will be used to illustrate the principle of culturally-appropriate teaching: learning-style based

instruction and use of culturally-relevant materials.

A lot has been written about culturally-determined learning style preferences of students and its relationship to student achievement (see Table 5.6). We now know that everyone has a unique learning style ("a natural, habitual and preferred way of absorbing, processing, and retaining new information and skills"—Kinsella, 1995). Based on research in this area, we also know that teachers can vary instructional dimensions (such as the amount of competition versus cooperation present in classroom tasks) to benefit learners according to their culturally-influenced preferences. Other areas such as the use of particular grouping structures and their compatibility with learners of various interactional style preferences, the amount of voluntary participation and talk (such as that expected in classroom discussions), or the need for feedback or direction from an adult are aspects that are culturally-influenced and define the classroom behavior of students. The more we understand about this area, the more we can construct culturally-responsive instructional conditions for

Voices from the Field

Strategies to Teach the Korean Language to English Speakers

Eun Mi Cho
Principal
Korean Language and Culture School
Sacramento, CA

I believe a successful language teacher knows the importance of creating a natural learning environment for acquiring a second language. Language learning has to be natural. By that, I mean that students need to be comfortable with the language learning atmosphere. To create this type of environment, as a Korean language teacher, I always make sure that students have an extensive and sufficient preparation period and include three major types of activities before I introduce reading and writing to children.

First, I invite students to become members of the Korean Club. Before I present any Korean words in print, students are first exposed to Korean culture by engaging in some authentic activities. These include playing Korean traditional games and play activities, such as *Kai-bal-bok* (Rock-Scissors-Paper), *Konggi Nori* (Jackstones), *Yut Nori* (Stick Game); singing Korean songs *Santokki* (Hill Rabbit), *Arirang*, *Oppa Saenggak* (My Brother), and *Toraji* (Beliflower); and making Korean traditional arts and crafts, such as folding paper Korean traditional costumes or making the national flag. The club activities take place at school and in the community. The games develop rhythm, quick observation, and visual skills. Taking students to Korean grocery stores and restaurants in the community are important activities, too.

Second, I organize a Korean Literature Day. I invite Korean American adults (parents, community helpers, pastors) to our classroom. They read or tell stories, riddles, and legends about Korea. These invited guests bring my students' attention to Korean literature and culture, not only by reading books, but they also expose students to our oral traditions and spoken language by talking about their community experiences as Korean Americans. How often do I have a Korean Literature Day? It depends on students' interest and the availability of community helpers. My favorite Korean American authors to include are Marie G. Lee and Sook Nyul Choi. These two authors have been actively writing stories for children and young adults about Korean and Korean American cultures for some time.

The third way I create a natural learning environment is by cooking traditional Korean foods. This is usually the most fun activity for students. After watching a videotape about Korean foods and discussing the similarities and differences between Korean and American food, I help the students to really cook. So far my students' favorite cooking menu is *Chapchae* (Long Rice Noodles with Vegetables), *Pulgogi* (Broiled Beef), and *Mandu* (Meat Dumplings).

By interacting with literature and authentic activities (cooking, field trips, songs, games, and art and crafts), the students become naturally attuned to the various styles and forms of the Korean language. I put much effort into these preparation activities so that students will be ready for the next step. Whenever the students feel comfortable with the spoken form of Korean, I can begin to introduce the written form of the language in lessons directed at developing reading and writing skills in Korean.

our learners. At the same time, we will want to develop their awareness of alternative cultural expectations and their ability to respond to these expectations so that they can function effectively in a variety of learning contexts. This is a very important part of the cross-cultural awareness and bicultural competence we seek to develop in *all of* our learners.

Use of authentic, multicultural children's literature is another powerful way to insure that students have essential background knowledge. When stories are taken from the culture of the students, the characters, their motives, the situations, and the settings all conform to students' beliefs, norms, and experiences. Students can identify with the stories being read and, in turn, the familiar stories can trigger personal expression and writing by students. As well, materials that affirm students' identities are likely to facilitate student engagement and learning.

In addition, students should be exposed to new experiences and world views. When students read or write about currently unfamiliar topics, it is useful to employ experience-based learning (e.g. Language Experience Approach, film and videotaped introductions, hands-on learning) so that students are given adequate exposure to these new experiences and topics prior to using them to promote reading/writing development.

An illustration of how one program is making instruction more culturally appropriate can be found in "Voices from the Field" on p. 99.

Table 5.6   Some References on Learning Styles and Language Teaching

Reid, J. (Ed). (1995). *Learning styles in the ESL/EFL classroom,* New York: Newbury House Teacher Development Series, Heinle & Heinle Publishers. (see the Preface, Chapters 1, 6, 15, and Appendix C)

Scarcella, R. (1990). *Teaching Language Minority Students in the Multicultural Classroom,* Englewood Cliffs, NJ: Prentice Hall Regents (see Chapter 6)

Scarcella, R. & Oxford, R. (1992). *The Tapestry of Language Learning: The Individual in the Communicative Classroom.* Boston: Heinle & Heinle Publishers.

Task 4: What are important decoding and encoding skills to teach?

Throughout the elementary grades, a variety of skills can be taught to students to assist them in *decoding* language: 1) phonetic analysis, 2) sight word recognition, 3) use of context analysis (through prior knowledge (see Glossary), previous information provided), 4) structural analysis (to use grammatical cues, semantic cues such as root words, prefixes, and suffixes), 5) use of visual cues such as word length or word shape, and 6) use of references (looking words up in the dictionary, requesting assistance).

A range of skills can be taught to students to assist them to *encode* language. Students can encode their messages by using: 1) known sound-letter relationships, 2) sight words, 3) models (looking at print in the environment; looking at messages written by others), or 4) requesting assistance.

First and second language readers need ways to decipher print. As noted, this might involve a phonetic approach, a sight word approach, or word analysis. The approach to decoding should be determined by: 1) the student's level of internalization of the language's phonemes/ graphemes, 2) the student's learning style, and 3) the features of the language.

In general, reading programs should de-emphasize graphophonics in the case of second language learners who do not know either the graphemes or the phonemes of their second language. Sight word and word analysis approaches are usually more beneficial in such cases. However, students' learning styles should also be considered. For example, phonetic or structural analysis might be easier for analytic/reflective learners than for learners who focus more globally on "chunks of language" or the entire text. In addition, teachers should select methods in relation to the language being learned. In the case of phonetic languages, of course phonics is a very sensible approach; whereas with ideographic languages this approach is not useful.

Task 5: What are important reading/ writing strategies to teach?

Text processing strategies vary by language, however, students can be taught to:

1. skim, scan, and use other previewing techniques.

2. use the title and illustrations to understand a passage.

3. use the surrounding context to decode an unknown word.

4. guess word meanings using lexical cues (phrasing, syntax).

Selecting Quality Literature for Enriched Education Programs

Ruth López
Director of Bilingual and Multicultural Education
Community School District Ten
Bronx, New York

Our district developed a set of literacy beliefs which underscore the importance of immersing students in meaningful print and providing access to a rich selection of books. These must include selections that are reflective of our student population and their cultural realities. While we provide good literature in all of our classrooms, our dual language and bilingual classes must also include books in Spanish written by Latinos at various reading levels.

The literacy period has been mandated to be a minimum of 90 minutes daily so that read aloud, shared reading, guided reading, independent reading, and writing workshop can be properly developed in all schools K–8. This restructuring of our literacy program revealed the need to acquaint our bilingual teachers with contemporary Latino/a authors so they could introduce their students to Latino/a writers and provide insights to them as people and to their life experiences. Toward this end, we provided copies of Frances Ann Day's *Latina and Latino Voices in Literature* as well as *Multicultural Voices in Contemporary Literature* (Heinemann) at our literacy workshops and summer institute. Discussions around authors' styles and backgrounds are on-going through teacher study and focus groups.

Read aloud and shared readings for young students often employ chants, poems, rhymes, and songs by Alma Flor Ada, Lulu Delacre, Jose Luis Orozco and others who use traditional material that can serve as a bridge connecting the generations as well as promoting literacy in the home. For older students, legends, myths, and folktales such as Delacre's *Golden Tales: Myths, Legends, and Folktales From Latin America* and short stories from Sandra Cisnero's *House on Mango Street* are favorites. Author studies centered around Nicholasa Mohr's books closely reflect experiences common to our students: living in two cultures and the experience of loss and separation. Prolific writers such as Alma Flor Ada, Pat Mora and Gary Soto are also excellent choices because their books are available in both English and Spanish and at various levels of difficulty making them ideal for heterogeneously grouped classes. They also represent good models of writing for students to emulate.

In the early grades, social studies themes are developed through topics such as the family and celebrations around the world. Many writers address topics such as the relationship between a child and a grandparent in various cultural contexts. Books such as Dorro's *Abuela* (set in New York City), Cameron's *El lugar más bonito del mundo* and Castañeda's *El tapíz de abuela* (both set in Guatemala) and Santiago Nadar's *Abuelita's paradise* (from Puerto Rico) explore these relationships. Upper grade students can use *Cuentos de mar y tierra* by Rivera Izcoa and *Encuentro* by Yolen to make connections between the past and their own experiences. The authenticity of the selections encourage our students to produce richer language, more effective communication, and to develop respect for themselves and their cultures.

Note: For children's books listed above, contact your local Spanish book distributor. For example, Mariuccia Iaconi Book Imports in San Francisco, or Chalco Educational Enterprises in the New York Metropolitan Area (Yorktown Heights, NY) can supply these and other titles.

5. back up and reread a word or phrase (regress).

6. match an unknown word to other words in the text (recognize rhyming words, words with the same root, words that begin/end the same).

7. use phonemic awareness of letters to phonetically recode words (sound words out).

8. request assistance (of a more competent peer, the teacher, another adult, use technological devices such as Franklin dictionaries, software programs, interactive CD ROMs).

In the important area of *reading comprehension,* we can teach students to identify the main idea and important details, predict outcomes/anticipate events, identify story sequence, and to recognize signal words and phrases, to summarize and paraphrase. We can also teach students *critical reading* skills, such as discriminating between fact and opinion, recognizing cause and effect, and making inferences. Related to *literature study,* we can teach students to recognize important feelings and motivations of characters, identify the conflict, or to identify literary devices. In writing, students can be taught a variety of *prewriting techniques* (brainstorming, identifying and generating a manageable topic, etc.); to proofread using known rules of punctuation, spelling and capitalization (*mechanics*); to recognize and produce the different parts of speech, or to use connectors (*language use*). In *paragraph development* and organization students can be taught how to write multi-paragraphed compositions, to support ideas with evidence, and how to revise their work. They can also be taught to *write for a variety of purposes*; such as to narrate, describe, explain, persuade, or complain. By teaching and modeling skills and strategies and questioning students about their use, teachers can advance students' skills in this important area.

For useful teacher resource books to help identify strategies and skills for teaching see *The Reading Teacher's Book of Lists* (1997), by Edward Bernard Fry, Jacqueline E. Kress and Dona Fountoukidis, and *The ESL Teacher's Book of Lists,* by Jacqueline E. Kress (1993), The Center for Applied Research in Education, West Nyack, NY. See also Table 6.2, p. 118 in the chapter which follows. A real life example of how one middle school program plans for and teaches essential language arts skills across the two languages can be found in "Voices from the Field" on p. 101.

What transfer effects can teachers anticipate?

As students acquire literacy in a second language, their reading and writing performance is often affected by knowledge they have gained about reading/writing in a first lan-

guage. When writing, we should expect cross-lingual inventive spellings and cross-lingual sentence construction. A Latino youngster in the emergent writing stage might write "¿Why he no go to escul?" A Chinese youngster might write "Then he have idea, very good one." These examples illustrate that the production of English will be affected by a student's native language phonology, syntax, and punctuation rules. This is natural and expected.

To further illustrate this point, Natheson-Mejia (1989) has documented six regular substitutions Spanish speakers make when encoding English sounds in writing. These include "es" for /s/ as in "estop"; "d" for /t/ or /th/ as in "de" or "broder"; "ch" for /sh/ as in "chort"; "J" for /h/ as in "jelper" and "g" for /w/ as in "sogen" [sewing]. There can also be regular, predictable vowel substitutions in the cross-lingual inventive spellings of Latino youngsters such as those noted in the example given in the previous paragraph.

Likewise, English-speaking majority group students might write "eye" for "hay," or "chaketa" for "chaqueta," relying on words and sounds they know in English to produce similar sounding words in their new language.

These behaviors usually disappear by themselves as students gain more proficiency in the target language, but teachers can actively assist students to resolve these intrusions by providing explicit feedback if they do not get resolved on their own. Such interlanguage forms are temporary markers that show the current working hypotheses the learner has about the language in question. If students are given continued exposure to the target language and/or provided explicit instruction, these behaviors will evolve until the learner acquires the conventional forms. For some learners, especially analytic learners, this process can be facilitated by selective teaching about important differences between the way the two writing systems operate. (As noted earlier, *Learner English* (Michael Swan and Bernard Smith, 1987, Cambridge University Press) can help teachers anticipate the natural developmental errors learners of various language backgrounds would make in their writing in English as well as explain why these errors occur.)

What does it mean to teach in stage-appropriate ways?

As noted earlier, it is widely accepted that children develop through a series of approximations, from novice to expert as they acquire literacy. We recommend that teachers construct lessons for students based on the following three stages of literacy development: 1) preliteracy, 2) early or emergent literacy, and 3) late or intermediate stage literacy.

In general, early in the literacy development process, teachers should move in the direction of "top down" focusing on general skills rather than specific skills. Later literacy

Planning Literature-Based Skills Instruction at the Upper Grades

Carlos Sánchez
Dual Language Intensive Language Experience (DILE) Program
Isaac E. Young Middle School
New Rochelle, New York

Our Dual Language Program operates within a middle school that is organized into three houses each made up of a 6th, 7th, and 8th grade cluster. Grade clusters consist of a social studies, math, science, language arts teacher and, in the case of the DILE program, also include a Spanish and ESL teacher. The cluster teachers have been supported with local funds and also external grants (such as one from the Mellon Foundation) to engage in curriculum development projects. The dual language program at our school has benefited from the school-wide philosophy of collaborative planning and is committed to mirroring in its curriculum, the curriculum offered to all students in the school—yet with the enrichment of developing two languages.

While I have taught in various roles over the years in our program, this year I am concentrating my efforts on the language development of our students, including their reading and writing skills in both languages. Our program includes Spanish speakers with average or better than average Spanish language skills. It also includes English speakers with average or better than average English language skills. Thus, our students' skills are at an intermediate literacy level. For this level of student, we believe that "reciprocal teaching' is very powerful teaching technique and use it throughout our program.

Collaborative teaching is essential to this approach. The Spanish language teacher and the English language arts teacher, as well as the ESL teacher and the English language arts teacher organize their units of instruction to parallel one another. As an example, at the sixth grade level, the Spanish language teacher works on characterization in literature prior to the students doing this skill with the English language arts teacher. This prepares our Latino students for advanced or more abstract English language arts skills development. Likewise, when the grammar point of possessive pronouns is to be taught in the Spanish language class, the English speakers are taught this in English prior to the lessons they will receive in Spanish so that they can truly understand how Spanish functions to support their independent writing and writing skills development. Essential language arts skills are taught and reinforced this way—across languages.

As a part of the seventh grade cluster, I am currently involved in a project to integrate the teaching of essential language skills (as mandated by the new standards) into our English reading program. We have selected ten short stories that are a part of students' 7th grade reading list to be taught across the English language arts and ESL classes. First, the English language arts teacher and I selected ten stories that address a wide range of cultural topics and issues present in American society. Next, we planned what essential skills we would develop in English across the stories. For example, when we read "Thank you Ma'am" by Langston Hughes, we will work on dialogue comparison, cause and effect, and external and internal conflict in stories. When we read "Say It With Flowers" by Toshi Mori, we will work on point of view, compound and complex sentences and the concept of sequels. By reading selected multicultural literature, we will engage students in a variety of reading and writing projects to build specific skills. Student exchange across classes will be frequent in teaching the units. Because we teach ESL and English Language Arts during the same period, we can combine our classes or team teach easily.

During instruction we divide our students into teams of two or three, with each team composed of at least one Spanish proficient and one English proficient student. We believe that peer support and interaction is critical to attaining our program's goals. That is why we favor the "reciprocal teaching" model which allows our students to learn from each other, value each other, and empathize with and support each other's second language learning process as writing partners, research partners, and team members.

instruction should "zoom in" on the specific skills, becoming more analytic in approach, and then zoom back out to how these elements operate in the context of the larger whole of the text. The combination of the two approaches, done thoughtfully and in an integrated manner over time, provides students with all the necessary skills to be successful.

What strategies are effective with preliterate students?

Instruction to students at the earliest stage of literacy development should focus on modeling of and experience with reading and writing, with an emphasis on relaxed enjoyment. Reading to students is beneficial. Encouraging students to express themselves through drawing and other forms of early symbolic communication (logos, pictographs) is also very beneficial. Students can engage in pretend reading and writing and have their messages written down by others. Older beginning readers who are beyond the "pretend" reading/writing stage can join in literacy activities—such as reading a repeated phrase or a line in a story or adding a picture or short message to another student's letter or note. Teachers should focus on high utility language—writing one's name, reading simple directions, or recognizing frequently occurring storylines. Students can produce labels, lists, and environmental print. They can play games that require limited reading; read familiar songs, chants and rhymes; and write their own verses (Eckes and Law, 1997). Responsive EE teachers provide students lots of positive feedback about their early attempts to read and write.

At this stage, teachers will want to choose texts that have a close relationship with student's oral language (i.e., "I can read" books) and those that are culturally-relevant. When teachers read to students, they should encourage them to construct their own meanings of texts, allow the sharing of tactics among students and, most of all, promote story enjoyment.

Peer support is particularly helpful. Second language learners find this tactic particularly beneficial because it lowers their anxiety, expands their strategic repertoire, provides a ready source of feedback, and often increases motivation and task persistence.

At this stage, several stories with the same theme might be selected so that skill integration occurs *across books*. During the first reading of a story, teachers should focus on story enjoyment. During subsequent readings, key strategies can be actively modeled by the teacher or peers and practiced by students. Finally, extension activities draw students into other enjoyable learning projects related to prominent story themes as well as allow the teacher to eval-

uate the success of the lesson. Some of the principal methods used with preliterate students are listed in Table 5.7.

What strategies are effective with early/emergent literacy students?

Teachers should expect learners at the early or emergent literacy stage to read and write simple text. Learners at this stage can receive and communicate messages, understand the gist of stories, and express their ideas. Emergent literacy students are most successful when reading simple stories with predictable structures (rhyme, repetition, expansion) or when writing in short phrases (answering simple questions, writing their thoughts in journals, writing simple notes and e-mail messages).

With regard to teaching methods, *Language Experience Approach (LEA)* is very useful because students use their existing oral language skills to create texts around experiences they have had. Once students have constructed texts, teachers can use them to develop a variety of skills—such as vocabulary, paragraph organization, mechanics, and decoding/encoding skills. Dialogue and buddy journals are also very useful because they provide students with ongoing feedback and encouragement. These techniques teach students

---

Table 5.7   Principal Methods for Preliterate Students

1. Shared literacy
2. Use of wordless picture books
3. Use of children's literature with repetitive, predictable, and cohesive text structure; literature which taps children's concerns and interests
4. Use of culturally relevant or traditional forms of literacy (proverbs, letter writing to relatives, songs)
5. Process writing approach (partner stories using pictures and wordless books as stimuli)
6. Use of environmental print
7. Use of simple recorded stories (on video/audiocassettes)
8. Illustrating stories, poems, stories

Voices from the Field

The Success of Our "Language to Literacy" Strategy

Alta Lucero, Dual Language Teacher and
Marvyn Luckett, Principal
Hacienda Heights Elementary Communications
Magnet School
El Paso, TX

At Hacienda Heights, the dual language teachers use a balanced literacy strategy which has been very effective with both Spanish and English dominant students in these classes, regardless of their learning styles. The "Language to Literacy" Approach is a five-part process. The first day's lesson begins with a book that is rich in vocabulary. Careful selection of the book is critical to the final results. The teacher selects homonyms, homophones, and new vocabulary from the book. The quantity of words selected depends upon the grade level. In first grade, for example, we start with three to five words. The number will increase throughout the year, and as students move up through the grade levels.

On Day 1, students predict what they believe the words mean. These predictions are recorded on chart paper by the teacher, who also notes in parenthesis the name of the contributing child. Following the word meaning predictions, the teacher reads the book aloud to the students, discussing it page by page.

On Day 2, students participate in "Observations." They share what they remember and feel is important or interesting to them from the story. Again, the teacher writes this on chart paper followed by the student's name. First graders begin the writing process on Day 2 by selecting a connected topic from one of the observations. An example might be a character trait, a feeling or emotion, or a summary of the story. For new writers, the teacher provides the opening statement and then the student adds to it, working in 5–30 minute segments depending on the amount of time necessary for the students to write one paragraph or more. Also, from the observations, the teacher pulls out the main idea and writes it on another chart paper.

On Day 3, the teacher has the students ask questions which were not answered in the story. Under "I wonder..." the teacher writes the unanswered questions on a new sheet of chart paper. The "I wonder..." contributions are then used as the basis for continued student writing, building upon what was written on the previous day.

On Day 4, students discuss the connections the story made with their own lives. By writing "This reminds me of..." on a sheet of chart paper, the teacher follows the same procedure as the previous days. The connections and personal experiences the children relate increase student comprehension of the story. It also provides additional context for them to use to further their writing.

On Day 5, students sit in the class's "author's chair" and read their compositions. Newspaper articles and focus poems can also be used in place of stories.

The results of this process have been significant. Visitors to our school from Texas and many other states are consistently amazed by the level of writing which first graders exhibit by the end of the first semester. This balanced literacy strategy has enabled children to write two- and three-page compositions on their own. Second grade teachers report that they see equal success with both the Spanish and English dominant children; although the English dominant students do exhibit more syntactical errors, but not ones which interfere with effective communication.

that reading and writing are done to communicate and that meaning is central. Teachers emphasize a range of skills with early/emergent learners. A representative list is given as Table 5.8 and illustrated in the "Voices from the Field" essay on p. 105.

What strategies are effective with late emergent and intermediate ability students?

With students at the late emergent or intermediate literacy stage, teachers shift their focus to promote use of conventional forms of language, such as embedded speech, as well as call their attention to other tactics they may want to emulate as writers, such as highly sensorial or descriptive language. Once students are writing whole paragraphs, they can attend to paragraph conventions, such as indenting, capitalization, and punctuation. Because students generally make fewer errors as time goes on, they can now edit their own work (using spell checks and grammar checks on the computer). This is not advisable at an earlier stage because of the high frequency of learner "errors" as well as diverting student attention away from their central purpose, that of communicating with others through print.

Direct instruction is effective at this stage. In general, teachers will want to *teach skills at their point of use* and provide plentiful opportunities for students to practice new skills. For example, when reading a story of interest, teachers could focus on skills such as the use of root words to aid in word recognition, recognizing an author's point of view, or paraphrasing and summarizing to monitor comprehension. When writing, teachers could focus on vocabulary development through synonym/antonym study, application of advanced spelling rules, paragraph organization and transition strategies, or construction of complex sentences with students.

Extended reading activities are beneficial at this stage; for example, the use of *author studies* (various books by one author) or *thematically-linked books* (books on the solar system). Reading and writing skill development can be linked through techniques like literature response journals in which students record their reactions to texts being read. Students may also want to keep writers' journals in which they note skills used by other writers which they would like to employ in their own writing.

Freewriting is a particularly useful method to advance writing skills at this stage. After a piece is written, peer and teacher-student conferences can be set up to go over points of difficulty, to revise the initial draft, and to provide direct instruction of skills at their point of use. Sentence combining and vocabulary replacement are two techniques teachers can use to advance intermediate writers' abilities In sum, a combination of expressive writing and direct skills teaching is recommended.

An illustration of how the above mentioned strategies are being used in the upper grades of an exemplary Two-Way Program in Boston can be found in "Voices from the Field" on p. 106.

In addition to the aforementioned strategies, a variety of media can be employed at this stage and students can create their own audiocassette, videocassette productions, and multimedia presentations. Computer Assisted Instruction (CAI) is very useful once students have basic reading/writing skills established. Students can research topics on the Internet, communicate with others via e-mail, get feedback about their writing from on-line help sites, and even maintain their own web-pages. They can publish their own poetry

---

Table 5.8   Instructional Emphases for Early/Emergent Learners

1. Vocabulary development (matching words and pictures, picture dictionaries, word banks, semantic organizers, word study (e.g. antonyms/synonyms)

2. Language pattern acquisition (songs and chants, writing parallel stories, sequencing, matching, and cloze activities)

3. Comprehension (dramatizations, illustrations, underlining true sentences, reacting orally and in writing, story retelling with flanelboards/magnetic way)

4. Decoding (finding words with same beginning/ending sounds, producing rhyming words, finding sight words)

5. Innovating (personalizing, reading other stories on the same theme, writing a new ending, creating stories or books on the computer, etc.)

6. Story mapping and use of visual organizers to represent the information gained from reading or as a prompt for writing

7. Technology usage (audiotaped and videotaped stories of increasing complexity as well as interactive books on CD ROM)

Voices from the Field

Literacy in the Early Grades

Catalina Villasuso
Early Grade Teacher (K–2)
Dr. John Howard Jr. Unique School of Excellence
East Orange, New Jersey;
CAZ Literature, Inc. Consultant, Eastampton, NJ

Literacy begins the minute the students walk through the classroom door. Students enter an environment which is challenging, encouraging, and vibrantly filled with learning. Launching an Immersion Program takes an extensive amount of planning and preparation. The center of this learning environment is where whole group instruction takes place. At this time, new vocabulary is introduced through the use of TPR activities, enhanced by flashcards, sight words, transparencies, and worksheets. All the necessary skills the students will need to apply at their learning stations will be modeled during the whole group instruction time.

Large group instruction is then broken down into the surrounding workstations. The students have the opportunity to choose which learning station they would like to participate in—mathematics, science, social studies, or language arts.

Each station includes language-oriented, hands-on, interactive activities. Station activities require each student to observe, analyze, compare, contrast, and document. For example, if the theme is "Living Things," at the science station, the students would measure and graph any plant growth, and document in writing and through drawings any changes that may have occurred. Students would hypothesize why they think such changes took place. In social studies, we would have activities involving how living things relate to a community or neighborhood. In mathematics, we would measure, graph, count, sequence, look at patterns, and solve word problems related to living things.

The largest learning station is that of language arts and it is divided into four stations: listening, reading, oral communications, and writing. The listening station includes a cassette player with headphones, where the students are able to listen to whatever book it is we are reading at the time. If a particular book doesn't include a cassette, one is recorded by me or one of the students. The reading station includes all the books we've read. It also has a special display for all the books related to our present theme. The writing station has activities including descriptive writing, narrative writing, creative writing, journal writing, letter writing, book making, skills activities, and folder games. The oral communication station is a place where students are able to read aloud to each other. A favorite activity is to record themselves speaking in the target language. They also perform skits or do puppet shows.

These workstations not only provide the students with limitless possibilities to develop their level of literacy, it also provides me with an abundance of opportunities to step back and watch what they can do on their own, with a partner or in groups. Workstations provide a lot of insight about how the students are progressing. What better way to assess informally yet so accurately!

and prose using desk top publishing resources (special formatting, clip art, type faces).

Various journals and websites are available to those wishing to use technology-based activities. Obviously, more plentiful resources exist in high incidence languages like English and Spanish. Representative journals and websites are: *CAELL Journal* (ISTE@oregon.uoregon.edu); *CALICO Journal* (CALICO@acpub.duke.edu); *Language Links* (polyglot.lss.wisc.edu/lss/lang/langlink.html); and for Spanish *Espacio Infantil*(www.ven.net/loscuentos/); or *Nueva Alejandria* (www.nale jandra.com/oo/amigos/htm). Another site, ESCUELA.NET, is a web-based magazine totally in Spanish for and by teachers around the globe. Its purpose is to share lesson plans and other resources and explore how teachers in different countries provide language instruction to their students in Spanish (www.escuela. nabe.net).

Voices from the Field

Improving Student Achievement in the Upper Grades

Mairead Nolan
Director of Instruction
Rafael Hernández Two-Way Bilingual School
Boston, MA

At the Rafael Hernández Two-Way Bilingual School, a Boston Public School, teachers recognized that too many students in grades four through eight were not sufficiently proficient readers and writers in either language. We have undertaken a literacy initiative in the upper grades to improve student achievement. The process began with a discussion of our purposes for literacy instruction. By answering the question, "*Why* do we teach reading and writing?" we hoped to illuminate the most effective methods and materials that would help us achieve our goals.

Clearly articulated purposes for literacy instruction enabled us to remain focused as we researched theory and practice. Our initiative for an effective literacy program is comprised of the following elements: silent reading, teachers reading aloud (yes, even in eighth grade!), instruction in word analysis, vocabulary development and instruction, explicit teacher modeling of reading comprehension strategies, and writer's workshop. At weekly school-based workshops we explore each component's research base, benefits, and implementation.

Many of these components allow teachers to provide direct instruction and to create both instructional level and heterogeneous groups. These two features are particularly vital for students becoming literate in two languages. Direct instruction is critical for students who do not have frequent exposure to the written aspects of their second language outside of school. Direct instruction eliminates the "guessing-game" and allows students to successfully learn skills. It also allows students to capitalize on their knowledge of their first language and to foster transfer of these skills. Recognizing that it takes four to seven years to learn a second language makes it more important to continue direct instruction beyond third grade.

Looking at one component highlights the importance of grouping students at their instructional level for some skills to provide direct instruction. Word analysis is the integrated study of spelling, phonics, and vocabulary that involves teaching students strategies for examining words. We are using an extremely teacher-friendly and comprehensive text by Donald Bear (Ed.) entitled, *Words Their Way: Word Study for Phonics, Vocabulary, and Spelling Instruction* (1995, Merrill Publishing Co.). After analyzing students' spelling, teachers group students according to their developmental spelling stage and then provide appropriate sequential instruction. Thus, a student in sixth grade who may be at a spelling stage usually associated with fourth grade can receive suitable instruction. This same student may be at a higher developmental stage in her home language. Small group instruction can meet all her needs. While teachers are providing direct instruction to a small group, other students are working independently and in heterogeneous groups that enable students to share their strengths and knowledge.

We are in our first year of this literacy initiative and our teachers are still learning new methods and research as well as grappling with implementing a comprehensive program that involves small- and whole-groups, direct instruction and independent learning. We hope that our homegrown initiative will more successfully meet the needs of our two-language learners. We are committed to reflectively critiquing and refining our instructional program as we work towards fostering literacy in our students.

As an additional resource for teachers, some key references follow (Table 5.9). These books are filled with teaching ideas for learners at different stages of literacy development. These references would be an important part of a professional library for classroom personnel.

Table 5.9 Books that Offer Teaching Ideas and Resources

Cox, C & Boyd-Batstone, P. (1997). *Crossroads: Literature and Language in Culturally and Linguistically Diverse Classrooms*. Upper Saddle River, NJ: Prentice-Hall, Inc.

Freeman, Y.S. & Freeman D.E. (1992). *Whole Language for Second Language Learners*. Portsmouth, NH: Heinemann.

Heald-Taylor, G. (1986). *Whole Language Strategies for ESL Students*. Carlsbad, CA: Dominie Press, Inc.

Igoa, C. (1995). *The Inner World of the Immigrant Child*. Mahwah, NJ: Lawrence Erlbaum Associates, Publishers.

Kotch, L. & Zackman, L. (1995). *The Author Studies Handbook: Helping Students Build Powerful Connections to Literature*. New York: Scholastic Professional Books.

Met, M. (1998). *Critical Issues in Early Second Language Learning: Building for our Children's Future*. Glenview, IL: Scott Foresman-Addison Wesley.

Peregoy, S.F. & Boyle, O.F. (1997). *Reading, Writing & Learning in ESL: A Resource Book for K–12 Teachers, Second Edition*. White Plains, NY: Longman.

Samway, K.D. & Whang, G. (1996). *Literature Study Circles in a Multicultural Classroom*. York, ME: Stenhouse Publishers.

Tinajero, J.V. & Ada, A.F. (Eds.) (1993). *The Power of Two Languages: Literacy and Biliteracy for Spanish-Speaking Students*. New York: Macmillan/McGraw-Hill School Publishing Co.

How can literacy be taught in multilevel classes?

Teachers in multilevel classes have a number of strategies available to support them. In this section we will highlight three: 1) Cooperative learning (see Glossary), 2) flexible instructional grouping, and 3) peer or cross-age tutoring. An excellent way for teachers to structure classroom activities to take maximum advantage of student heterogeneity is to use *Cooperative Learning* methodology. It offers concrete task structures (jigsaw, round robin, pairs check, think-pair-share, numbered heads together) for heterogeneous groupings of students of various sizes from pairs to small groups (Kagan, 1990). For example, in Jigsaw reading/writing activities, parts of a task are assigned to students based on their relative skill levels. Teachers can consider the length of the assignment as well as task complexity and difficulty level when making assignments to students. They can also assign roles to students according to what would be culturally appropriate. In linguistically mixed classrooms, this technique is very helpful because language minority and majority youngsters can receive assignments that are tailored to their respective language abilities and cultural characteristics.

The formation of homogeneous student groups according to skill level or language background is appropriate for teacher-delivered direct instruction, peer tutoring, or technology-based instruction. Grouping is justifiable when it is done for limited periods of time and for specific instructional purposes, such as teaching specific skills that a certain group of students need. By pairing students who are working on similar learning objectives, teachers can focus intensively on their needs. Students may be more willing to expose their current level of knowledge, ask questions, and participate more fully in homogeneous groupings than when mixed with students who are more advanced than they. Since assigning students permanently to ability groups has been documented to have negative consequences on achievement, self-esteem, and peer relations, it is important to use grouping flexibly, temporarily, and judiciously. Also, given the goals of dual language programs, teachers will most often want to place students in linguistically mixed, heterogeneous skill-level groupings to take advantage of the linguistic interactions and modeling that occur when students are encouraged to interact across languages and skill levels.

Multi-age and multilevel classes have advantages for teachers, yet, they require significant planning. Teachers must choose tasks with multiple entry points and roles. A wide range of resources must be available in the classroom, especially books written at various reading levels and spanning many subjects to meet the interests and abilities of all students. Computer software can also accommodate student diversity. For example, word processing packages are available that allow students to progress from rebus writing, to enlarged or primary-sized print, to conventionally-sized lettering.

Peer teaching and cross-age tutoring are compatible and beneficial methods for multilevel and multi-age classes (Thomas, 1993). Peer teaching should be used frequently in dual language classrooms to take advantage of native speakers. Clear directions must be given to peer tutors so that they understand their role and how to facilitate their partner's learning. Peer teaching and cross-age tutoring epitomize the principle of student-centered instruction first presented in Chapter 2.

A basic principle of instruction in multilevel groups is *thematic unity with task divergence*. This means that language majority and minority students work on the same topic or theme, yet each has their classwork and homework tailored to their individual needs. Teachers need to create several assignments related to the same lesson, varying in length, complexity, and amount of independence expected of the student. Once a range of activities has been created, teachers can periodically allow students to choose the activity they feel most confident completing. This will reveal students' level of self-confidence as well as their perception of their current ability levels. (See Sanchez, Villasuso & Nolan "Voices from the Field" essays in this chapter and Mieles and Ripley "Voices from the Field" essays, Chapter 6 for commentary related to this topic.)

What is the role of correction or feedback?

Early on, teachers' feedback to students about reading/writing "errors" is done indirectly by modeling and "embedding" corrections (where the correct form is embedded in the next comment of the listener who responds to the speaker's message by building on what the speaker has already said). Explicit corrections should be provided judiciously to aid in hypothesis formation or if requested by students. Students can be encouraged to revise and self-correct to the extent allowed by their existing skills. Using the computer and other electronic devices, students can record their performance and monitor it because it is stored and available for such purposes. If they don't like it, they can revise it relatively painlessly and only the final product is saved and shared.

Teachers' feedback about "errors" may become more explicit and direct with older students whose linguistic and cognitive abilities have developed to the point where they are able to make use of such direct metalinguistic feedback and not feel overwhelmed by it. Feedback needs to be provided in ways that contribute to student learning. It needs to be: 1) understandable, 2) focused, 3) offered at optimal learning opportunities (the "teachable moment"), and 4) offered with respect for the learner's efforts.

Students can be asked directly at fairly young ages what types of feedback and how much feedback they find most beneficial. This allows teachers to tailor their feedback to individual students. Students also have important preferences about how and when teachers should offer feedback to create conducive learning conditions for them.

Special Population Concerns

What do I do with students with limited formal schooling or special education needs?

Students with low levels of literacy development in their native languages and students with limited formal schooling are becoming more commonplace in our schools and classrooms. Helping these two groups of students gain functional literacy skills is critical because they need basic reading and writing skills to function in their daily lives and at school. All of the emergent literacy activities previously mentioned would apply to this group of students. Whole word approaches, such as the language experience approach, focus on the mechanics of reading and writing while insuring comprehension. Personalized approaches tend to be highly effective—such as reading stories on teenage life or reading about life in the U.S. Simplified, content-based readings are also very helpful. Teachers must select motivating texts, model skills for learners, and directly teach essential skills. Guided reading and writing activities are highly beneficial; such as the use of oral discussions to insure reading comprehension or the use of visual organizers to support writing. Teachers will want to select high interest themes, place students in supportive groups, encourage them, and point out their progress. For additional guidance on teaching students with special learning characteristics, readers can consult the references in Table 5.10.

What strategies are effective with special needs students?

Teachers can support special needs students by offering, as needed: 1) organizational support (organized work environments or use of a planner to make sure they take home needed materials and get assignments in on time),

Table 5.10   References for Working with Special Needs Learners

Cloud, N. (1994). Special Education Needs of Second Language Students. In F. Genesee (Ed.), *Educating Second Language Children: The Whole Child, the Whole Curriculum, the Whole Community* (pp. 243–277). New York: Cambridge University Press.

Cloud, N. (1990). Planning and Implementing an English as a Second Language Program. In A. Carrasquillo and R.E. Baecher (Eds.), *Teaching the Bilingual Special Education Student* (pp. 106–131). Norwood, NJ: Ablex Publishing Co.

Escamilla, K. and Andrade, A. (1992, February). Descubriendo La Lectura: An Application of Reading Recovery in Spanish. *Education and Urban Society, 24* (2), pp. 212–226.

Hamayan, E.V. (1994). Language Development of Low Literacy Students. In F. Genesee (Ed.) *Educating Second Language Children: The Whole Child, the Whole Curriculum, the Whole Community* (pp. 278–300). New York: Cambridge University Press.

Hayes, C.W. (Ed.) (1993). *Migrating Toward Literacy.* ERIC Document Reproduction Service Center Number ED 357 634.

Henderson, O.R. (1989). An ESL Communicative Curriculum Guide for the Preliterate High School Student. *Educational Issues of Language Minority Students, 3,* pp. 41–58.

Leverett, R.G. & Diefendorf, A.O. (1992, Summer). Students with Language Deficiencies: Suggestions for Frustrated Teachers. *Teaching Exceptional Children,* pp. 30–34.

Mace-Matluck, B.J., Alexander-Kasparik, R. & Queen, R.M. (1998). *Through the Golden Door: Educational Approaches for Immigrant Adolescents with Limited Formal Schooling.* McHenry, IL: Delta Systems Co.

Moran, C., Stobbe, J., Tinajero, A., & Tinajero, J.V. (1993). Strategies for Working with Overage Students. In J.V. Tinajero and A.F. Ada (Eds.). *The Power of Two Languages: Literacy and Biliteracy for Spanish Speaking Students* (pp. 117–131). New York, NY: Macmillan/McGraw Hill School Publishing Co.

Shifini, A. (1996, December 15). Reading Instruction for the Pre-literate and Struggling Older Student. *NABE News,* pp. 5–6, 20, 30.

Walter, B.J. (1992). *Supporting Struggling Readers.* Scarborough, Ontario: Pippin Publishing.

2) encouragement, 3) frequent feedback, 4) assistive technology (i.e. techniques such as enlarged print, closed captioning, use of note-takers or audiocassette recordings of class sessions, computer-assisted instruction), 5) social skills development, and 6) behavioral guidelines and support. Table 5.11 lists supportive teaching strategies for special needs students.

Summary

The main points from this chapter are summarized in Table 5.12 using the critical features from Chapter 2.

Table 5.11   Strategies for Special Needs Students

1. Use of carefully-selected materials (high interest, low readability) and assistive technology.
2. Use of peer tutoring; modeling and demonstration.
3. Use of cooperative learning groups; structured learning activities.
4. Provision of needed support and encouragement.
5. Provision of oral and written step-by-step directions (with models of expected products).
6. Provision of reading/writing guides; visual organizers.
7. Use of cued text (marginal gloss, underlining, highlighting, blackened out text where irrelevant details are given).
8. Establishing quiet, relaxing work spaces.

Table 5.12   Critical Features Summary

Critical Feature	Implications for Literacy Development
1. **Parental involvement is integral to the program**	**Support/encourage parental involvement** • Survey parents to understand literacy activity in the home • Provide materials for use at home
2. **High standards have been established**	**Work towards long range instructional goals as articulated in** • National standards set by professional associations for Reading/Language Arts, • State curriculum frameworks for the language arts • Local standards established by the district
3. **Strong leadership is present**	**Principals and lead teachers support the goal of biliteracy** • All personnel in leadership positions advocate for the goals of the program, understand the program's structure, and provide support to classroom teachers implementing the program
4. **Instruction is developmentally-appropriate**	**Teach in age/stage-appropriate ways** • Match instruction to the learner's current stage of literacy development • Match activities to the learner's age, conceptual development, ability, attention span • Plan introduction of each language

Table 5.12 *(continued)*

5. Instruction is student-centered

Monitor cultural appropriateness
- Select culturally-appropriate texts
- Create classroom routines and structures that are comfortable for learners.

Monitor linguistic appropriateness; insure that:
- Density of unknown vocabulary is low
- Sentence length and complexity match learner's proficiency
- Text features support fluent reading (rhyme, repetition, predictable structure)
- Organizational principles of the text are familiar (cause/effect, time ordering, cyclical structure)

Monitor individual appropriateness
- Respect grouping preference (individual, pair, small group, whole class)
- Utilize modality strengths (visual, auditory, tactile, kinesthetic)
- Honor cognitive style (active/doing, reflective/listening)
- Consider environmental needs (lighting, type of workspace, need for structure, quiet)
- Select reinforcers well

6. Literacy instruction is integrated with challenging academic instruction

Make certain learning activities are meaning-centered and purposeful
- Learners are actively engaged, participate at high levels
- Reading and writing contribute to student learning about other topics
- Reading and writing are developed across the curriculum

7. Teachers are reflective

Make assessment an integral part of instruction
- Regularly monitor teaching effectiveness
- Encourage student self-assessment, peer-assessment, invite parental feedback

8. The dual literacy program is coordinated with other school programs

Coordination among all language specialists and programs is strong
- Meet frequently; coordinate actively with other teachers

9. The program aims for additive bilingualism and biliteracy

Plan for Transfer
- Recognize that dispositions, knowledge and skills developed in one language can support literacy activity in a second language. Identify transferable elements
- Create affirming, empowering environments where both languages and cultures are valued and affirmed by all participants

References

Barrs, et al. (1988) *The Primary Language Record: Handbook for Teachers.* Portsmouth, NH: Heinemann Educational Books, Inc.

Carson, J., Carrell, P.L., Silberstein, S., Kroll, B., and Kuehn, P.A. (1990). Reading-Writing Relationships in First and Second Language. *TESOL Quarterly, 24* (2), 245–266.

Carson, J.E. and Kuehn, P.A. (1994). Evidence of Transfer and Loss in Developing Second-Language Writers. In A.H. Cumming (Ed.). *Bilingual Performance in Reading and Writing.* John Benjamins Publishing Co.

Chu-Chang, M. (1981). The Dependency Relation Between Oral Language and Reading in Bilingual Children. *Boston University Journal of Education, 163,* 30–55.

Cummins, J. (1984). *Bilingualism and Special Education: Issues in Assessment and Pedagogy.* San Diego, CA: College Hill Press.

Eckes, M. and Law, B. (1997). *Promoting Literacy Along the Emergent Continuum.* Presentation at the 31st annual TESOL Convention, Orlando, FL, March 13.

Holdaway, D. (1979). *The Foundations of Literacy.* Sydney: Ashton Scholastic.

Hudelson, S. (1994). Literacy Development of Second Language Children. In F. Genesee (Ed.) *Educating Second Language Children: The Whole Child, the Whole Curriculum , the Whole Community* (pp. 129–158). New York: Cambridge University Press.

Kagan, S. (1990, December/January). The Structural Approach to Cooperative Learning. *Educational Leadership,* 12–15.

Kinsella, K. (1995). Understanding and Empowering Diverse Learners in ESL Classrooms. In J. Reid (Ed.). *Learning Styles in the ESL/EFL Classroom* (pp. 170–194). New York: Newbury House Teacher Development Series, Heinle & Heinle Publishers.

Natheson-Mejia, S. (1989). Writing in a Second Language. *Language Arts, 66* (5), 516–526.

National Research Council. (1998). *Preventing Reading Difficulties in Young Children.* Washington, D.C.: National Academy Press.

Thomas, R.L. (1993). *ERIC Digest #D78: Cross-Age and Peer Tutoring.* Bloomington, IN: ERIC Clearinghouse on Reading and Communication Skills.

Thonis, E. (1983). *The English-Spanish Connection.* Northvale, NJ; Santillana Publishing Company.

Thonis, E. (1989, Spring). Language Minority Students and Reading. *The Reading Instruction Journal,* 58–62.

Williams, J.D., & Snipper, G.C. (1990). *Literacy and Bilingualism.* White Plains, NY: Longman.

 **6 TEACHING CONTENT**

This chapter is designed to answer EE teachers' questions about how to deliver quality content area instruction to language minority and/or language majority youngsters enrolled in their programs. Divided into three sections, we first outline the three major instructional goals of integrated language and content instruction. Next, we describe the planning process for creating effective integrated lessons. Finally, we present a range of useful teaching strategies and discuss key aspects of effective instruction. In Chapter 7 we will describe ways of assessing language and content learning. The reader is also referred to the appendices for listings of resources and references applicable to the teaching of content in English and other world languages.

The Goals of Integrated Instruction

In content area instruction, EE teachers must teach specialized subject matter as well as the specialized language skills associated with that subject matter. While content objectives are primary, the language objectives also feature prominently, especially when the content is taught through a second language. In addition, during content instruction, EE teachers develop their students' general learning skills so they can enhance their learning of all subjects (taking notes, observing carefully, working together with others to make decisions, etc.). Thus, there are three goals of content area instruction in EE classrooms as represented in Figure 6.1.

1. *Content goals.* The content goals include conceptual learning (knowledge, skills) as well as orientations and attitudes required by subject matter disciplines. As we note in Chapter 2, the techniques for teaching

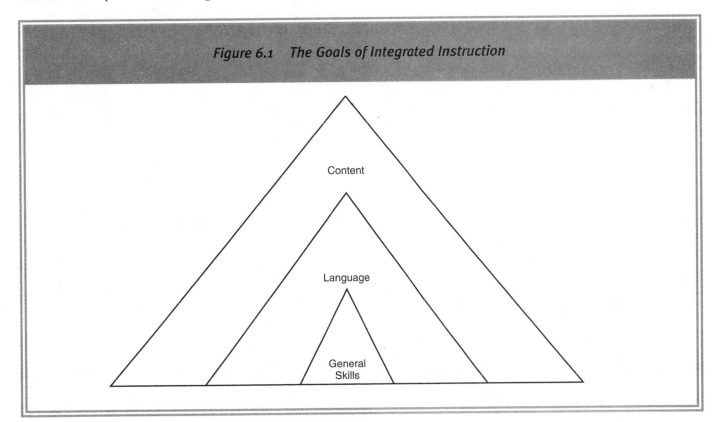

Figure 6.1 The Goals of Integrated Instruction

Content

Language

General
Skills

content are selected from among a range of alternative instructional strategies that are suitable for learners with diverse styles, characteristics, levels of language proficiency and experiential background knowledge in order to make instruction comprehensible. More detail about how to do this type of teaching is provided later in this chapter.

2. *Language goals*. These include both linguistic goals (learning the unique vocabulary words and sentence patterns needed to discuss particular content) and communicative goals (presenting findings to classmates, stating opinions, giving and following instructions). As we mentioned in Chapter 2, the specialized language or register (see Glossary) associated with each discipline includes vocabulary, sentence structures, and discourse patterns. EE teachers predict the language skills students will need to comprehend and learn new academic content. This language is then made a primary objective of upcoming content area instruction. In addition, teachers can teach needed vocabulary and language forms during second language and formal literacy instruction. In EE programs, strong linkages are carefully established between the oral language and literacy development programs and the content area classes to achieve the goals of the programs.

3. *General skills goals*. General skills goals include the acquisition and practice of study skills (knowledge and use of resource tools), research skills, learning strategies, and social skills that are needed in academic learning environments. These skills are highly correlated with academic success and can be taught directly. Therefore, EE teachers should identify the general learning goals that fit best with each academic course of study and systematically develop these skills in learners as they promote language and content learning.

Much has been written about integrated language and content instruction, particularly as it pertains to language minority students. Here the approach is sometimes referred to as "Sheltered English" (see Glossary) or "Specially Designed Academic Instruction in English (SDAIE)" (For more information about *Sheltered English/SDAIE* see Peregoy & Boyle, 1997, Chapter 3). Another well-known approach to integrated language and content instruction for language minority students is Chamot and O'Malley's *Cognitive Academic Language Learning Approach* (CALLA) (1994). As it pertains to language majority students, Curtain and Pesola (1994) also advocate integrated language and content instruction, as do Genesee (1994) and Met (1991).

(For more information on all of these approaches to integrated language and content instruction, see Table 6.1.) The approach we will describe in this chapter is informed by this professional literature and contributes to it. Our approach is constructed around the specific needs of teachers working in EE programs, with consideration of both language minority and language majority students.

One of the major challenges EE teachers face is how to accomplish all of their instructional goals in the time available in a typical school day, given that they are "adding" the additional instructional goal of teaching a second language. If teachers think of the second language as an additional subject to be taught, they will run out of instructional time or sacrifice other instructional goals. Rather than thinking of the teaching of the second language as "adding" one more subject, teachers must *integrate the teaching of language into the existing academic program*. This type of integrated teaching requires extensive planning and coordination. Because of this, we will focus next on planning well-integrated language and content lessons.

Planning Integrated Instruction

Because of the complexities involved, we recommend taking a step-by-step approach to the planning process. The approach we recommend involves: 1) setting content, language, and general learning objectives (both long range and unit-specific) 2) selecting or adapting materials to support those objectives 3) planning for evaluation. In this section, we guide teachers through these steps by answering teachers questions about each step. At the end of this chapter, we offer a sample instructional planning guide that accounts for all of the steps involved in the planning process. Teachers may wish to refer to this guide as they read this section to get an overall picture of the planning process (See Table 6.10, p. 134).

How do I identify the long range and short term content objectives?

Setting the Long Range Content Goals for a Subject
In setting long range instructional goals for each subject, EE teachers should consider *local, state, and national standards* established for the discipline. This is important to ensure that content area instruction conforms with local, state, and national expectations set for students in particular subjects. Teachers can consult with their professional associations, state departments of education, and local curriculum coordinators to determine expected cur-

Table 6.1   Resource Books on Integrated Language and Content Instruction

Brechtel, M. (1994). *Bringing the Whole Together: An Integrated, Whole Language Approach for the Multilingual Classroom*. San Diego, CA: Dominie Press, Inc.

Chamot, A.U. & O'Malley, J.M. (1994). *The CALLA Handbook: Implementing the Cognitive Academic Language Learning Approach*. Reading, MA: Addison-Wesley Publishing Company.

Crandall, J. (Ed.) (1987). *ESL Through Content-Area Instruction: Mathematics, Science, Social Studies*. Englewood Cliffs, NJ: Regents/Prentice Hall.

Curtain, H. & Pesola, C.A. (1994). *Languages and Children: Making the Match (Second Edition): Foreign Language Instruction for an Early Start Grades K–8*. White Plains, NY: Longman. (See especially Chapter 7, pp. 147–173)

Echevarria, J. & Graves, A. (1998). *Sheltered Content Instruction: Teaching English-Language Learners with Diverse Abilities*. Boston, MA: Allyn and Bacon.

Enright, D.S. & McCloskey, M.L. (1988). *Integrating English: Developing English Language and Literacy in the Multilingual Classroom*. Reading, MA: Addison-Wesley Publishing Co.

Fathman, A.K., Quinn, M.E., & Kessler, C. (1992). *Teaching Science to English Learners, Grades 4–8*. Washington, D.C.: National Clearinghouse for Bilingual Education. (Program Information Guide #11)

Genesee, F. (1994). *Integrating Language and Content: Lessons from Immersion*. Santa Cruz, CA: The National Center for Research on Cultural Diversity and Second Language Learning, University of California, Santa Cruz. (Educational Practice Report #11)

Met, M. (1991). Learning Language Through Content: Learning Content Through Language. *Foreign Language Annals*, 24 (4), 291–295.

Mohan, B. (1986). *Language and Content*. Reading, MA: Addison Wesley.

Peregoy, S.F. & Boyle, O.W. (1997). *Reading, Writing & Learning in ESL: A Resource Book for K–12 teachers. Second Edition*. New York: Longman. (See especially Chapter 3, pp. 59–97)

Short, D. (1991). *Integrating Language and Content Instruction: Strategies and Techniques*. Washington, D.C.: National Clearinghouse for Bilingual Education. (Program Information Guide #7)

Sutman, F.X., Allen, V.F. & Shoemaker, F. (1986). *Learning English Through Science: A Guide to Collaboration for Science Teachers, English Teachers and Teachers of English as a Second Language*. Washington, D.C.: National Science Teachers Association.

riculum sequences by grade level. The *content and performance standards* (see Glossary) established by these groups can help teachers determine *the focus* of their instructional efforts, *the content* to be addressed, and the *outcomes* learners must achieve in order for content area instruction to be considered successful at particular grade levels.

EE teachers will also want to *coordinate their work towards instructional standards across languages, settings, and grade levels* to ensure continuity of experience for learners. Coordination can best be achieved by actively working together with other teachers in the school who have responsibility for content area instruction. As noted in Chapter 3, this includes both vertical (from grade to grade) as well as horizontal (across classes at the same grade) articulation.

Selecting Appropriate Content Objectives for a Specific Unit

When planning content area units or lessons, teachers identify the specific orientations, concepts, facts, and skills students will acquire if the unit or lesson is successful. Because students in EE programs are held to the same challenging, high-level standards as all other students in the district or school, this step is identical to that taken by any content area teacher. Like other content area teachers, EE teachers consciously monitor the conceptual load being placed on students to make sure that it is at a cognitively-appropriate level, based on students' prior educational experience and abilities.

EE teachers tap students background knowledge by investigating their previous knowledge and experience on the topic of study. This can be done by giving students opportunities to talk about their former educational experiences and their life experience as it relates to the topic. Student beliefs and values should also be investigated because deeply held beliefs and values can greatly influence student understandings of topics (student beliefs about the causes of world events, evolution, reproductive technology, etc.). In short, teachers link new learning to students' prior learning and life experiences. Luis Moll has referred to the knowledge and experiences students bring to classrooms as their "funds of knowledge" (Moll & Diaz, 1992). All students have such "funds" that teachers can tap when initiating new learning. By actively questioning students, we can identify the appropriate starting place and cultural frame of reference within which to place our instructional units.

How do I identify the long range and short term language objectives?

Setting the Long Range Plans for Language Use in Content Area Classes

Students are most likely to develop age-appropriate levels of language proficiency if the target language is used systematically to deliver academic instruction. There are two important decisions EE teachers must make regarding language use: 1) the percentage of instructional time to be dedicated to each language from year to year in the program, and 2) how language will be used in teaching a particular subject from one year to the next.

In immersion programs, it has already been noted that it is quite common to select a principal instructional language, most often the students' second language, for the majority of instruction in the early grades. Up to 100% of instruction can be delivered through the medium of the second language. This would mean that teachers would be teaching all content area subjects exclusively through the medium of the second language on a daily basis. Later, when students have substantial proficiency developed in the second language, the other language would be used in the delivery of instruction.

In developmental bilingual classrooms, most subjects would be taught initially through the students' primary language. However, for student integration purposes, some special subjects (art, music, P.E.) might be taught from the beginning through the medium of the second language, English. Again, as students progress through the program, the two languages may be used more evenly in the delivery of academic instruction in the later years of the program.

In two-way classrooms, two arrangements for use of students' primary language are possible. In one arrangement—*consistent language use*—academic subjects are assigned particular instructional languages; for example, Social Studies might be taught in French and Science in English. In the second arrangement—*alternate language use*—both languages are used for a portion of the instructional time available. Here, each subject is taught alternatively, for example, in French one day and English the next day; or in French one week and English the next week. We prefer the first arrangement because we believe that it supports continuous development of language and content, creates less ambiguity for learners, and is less contrived. When teachers switch back and forth between languages in teaching the same content, they must teach the technical terms and discourse patterns in both languages. This "doubles" the language learning component of the course. There is also a possibility that students will not attend to instruction provided in their second language and will wait instead for the next instructional period when instruction is provided in their primary language. This could force teachers to provide reviews in both languages that slow overall course progress. In addition to recommending that each subject have a single instructional language, we also recommend that more instructional time be dedicated to the lower status language, because unlike the high status language, the low status language does not receive additional support outside of school. This would call for teaching more subjects through the low status language than through the high status language during the initial years of schooling. In the higher grades, the two languages might be used more evenly for the delivery of academic instruction.

Whatever language is selected, teachers must understand that *language development is very important;* as important as content learning in EE programs. Each day teachers are establishing important linguistic foundations for more complex content learning in future grades. Hence, there must be a strong emphasis on developing increasingly advanced skills in students' first and second languages. Teachers must avoid switching to students' native language to insure content learning. Instead, when working in the students' second language, they must use complex language and, using second language teaching techniques, insure that it is comprehended. They must also make certain that second language learners are developing ever more complex language to insure their success in the later grades of the program.

Selecting Appropriate Long and Short Term Language Objectives

In Chapter 4, we talked about the development of social language skills. In this chapter, we focus on the development of *academic language* skills—the language skills that are needed for, as well as developed through, content area instruction (Solomon & Rhodes, 1996). EE teachers have two primary language objectives during content area instruction: 1) the development of the language skills that are fundamental to the content area (or *content obligatory language*), and 2) the development of other related language skills (or *content compatible language*), selected because they are compatible with the content being taught and extend the students' language skills beyond the academic domain to that required in everyday communicative situations. "Content obligatory" language is required by all students to develop, master, and communicate about a topic. However, with second language learners, the teaching of "content compatible" language is also feasible, highly desirable, and moreover absolutely necessary in order to teach a second language successfully and still attain all the other educational goals set for students (Snow, Met and Genesee, 1989).

Selecting content obligatory language. When planning to teach a unit or lesson, teachers can identify the essential language skills by looking at textbooks and other instructional materials, thinking about the specific situations that will occur in the classroom during instruction, and drawing upon their prior experience with learners. Content obligatory language includes: 1) the technical vocabulary *(taxonomy, numerator)*, 2) special expressions *(least common multiple, common ancestral species)*, 3) multiple meanings of words *(mass, table)*, 4) syntactical features *(passive voice, embedded clauses)*, and 5) language functions which predominate in a particular content area lesson (informing, defining, analyzing, classifying, predicting, inferring, explaining, justifying, etc.). These language abilities are necessary for students to acquire concepts, ask questions, explain their understandings, demonstrate mastery, and prepare for future learning in the content area.

Knowing technical vocabulary is an obvious necessity if students are to communicate effectively in discipline-specific ways (the ability to communicate mathematically, for example). With respect to language functions, TESOL has provided useful guidance for teachers in its *ESL Standards for PreK–12 ESL Students* (1997) related to the development of academic language. One of their major goals for ESL instruction is for students to be able to use English to achieve academically in all content areas. They state that students must use English: 1) to interact in the classroom, 2) to obtain, process, construct, and provide subject matter information in spoken and written form, and 3) to construct and apply academic knowledge by use of appropriate learning strategies (p. 9). In describing the ESL standards related to the goal of learning academic English, they list the major language functions that go on in academic settings as "descriptors" (broad representative behaviors that students must acquire in their second language to perform successfully in academic settings). For example, they recognize that, in academic settings, students must follow oral and written directions, ask and answer questions, request information and assistance, elaborate and extend other people's ideas, compare and contrast information, select, connect, and explain information, and persuade others of or justify their positions (pp. 45, 49).

In content area classes, students are expected to learn concepts and facts through spoken and written language and to express their understandings orally and in print. As a result, students are provided opportunities to reinforce and extend, not only their oral language abilities, but also their reading and writing skills. They can be asked to capture the main ideas, to read for specific information, or to write about what they are learning. This type of purposeful reading and writing is very beneficial to language development. Instead of learning language for language's sake, here students are using language in meaningful contexts as they learn about other subjects.

The checklist in Table 6.2 presents some possible literacy objectives teachers can select when planning units or lessons. Choose those objectives that are relevant to the unit or lesson that you are teaching.

To summarize, because language is essential to content learning, teachers must identify the linguistic (vocabulary, language forms) and communicative objectives (language functions) for each instructional unit and actively plan for students' content-related oral and written language development.

Selecting content compatible language. In the case of students learning through the medium of a second language, teachers must also identify other language skills which can be taught during content area instruction; language that, while not required for content mastery, fits easily and naturally into a particular unit of study. For example, when teaching about length and measurement, it is easy to include comparatives and superlatives. When teaching map skills, it is easy to teach prepositions. Identifying content compatible language objectives in your lesson and unit plans is one way of insuring that needed language skills are systematically developed. Teachers can identify content compatible language objectives for each unit of study taught in the second language by: 1) reviewing the second language curriculum scope and sequence, 2) considering the learners

communicative needs in academic and social situations, and 3) reviewing content and language arts textbooks. In this manner students language skills can be systematically developed and extended.

How do I identify the long range and short term general learning objectives?

Selecting Learning Skills and Strategies as Objectives for Content Area Instruction

During content area instruction, plan to teach students to skim and scan, to summarize, to outline, and to take notes from assigned readings. Also, teach students how to study and how to conduct research in the library or on the Internet. Teach students to participate in academic discussions, produce written reports, and make oral presentations. Obviously, these general learning skills enhance their learning of all subjects, not just the one you are planning to teach.

Strategic behavior is also critical in language learning and learning in general. In recognition of this fact, TESOL in its *ESL Standards for PreK–12 Students* has placed emphasis on strategic learning in each of its major goals of ESL instruction and, as it relates to content instruction, stated that students should be able to use appropriate learning strategies to construct and apply academic knowledge (p. 9). Three types of learning strategies can be taught to learners: 1) metacognitive (planning, monitoring), 2) cognitive (use of background knowledge), and 3) social and affective strategies (use of self-talk, peer support) (O'Malley and Chamot, 1990, Oxford, 1990).

Sharing of strategies among students is particularly helpful. For example, teachers will want to provide time for students to tell one another how they achieve success in their content area classes (how they get organized and what they think, say, and do in order to be successful). This might involve determining and establishing the conditions that help one become an effective learner (when, where, how to study), actively connecting new information to information previously learned, evaluating one's own success in a completed learning task, imitating the behaviors of native English speakers to complete tasks successfully, knowing when to use native language resources (human and material) to promote understanding, and recognizing the need for and seeking assistance appropriately from others (teachers, peers, specialists, community members) (p. 91, *ESL Standards for Pre-K–12 Students*). Other important content area learning strategies might include: focusing attention on what is being said, listening for key words and ideas, keeping a notebook to write down new terms, creating an acronym to remember important steps in a process, surveying a chapter before reading it, asking questions while you

Table 6.2 Selecting Literacy Objectives for Content Area Units

Word recognition:
- context analysis
- sight words
- phonetic analysis
- structural analysis
- use of reference tools (dictionary) to discover meaning

Reading comprehension:
- predicting/extending
- locating
- organizing/sequencing
- remembering/recalling
- evaluating/critical reading

Writing skills:
- handwriting
- spelling
- organization
- language use
- mechanics (capitalization, punctuation, accent marks)

Writing forms/genres:
- formal/informal
- personal/academic
- narrative, descriptive, persuasive, and expository
- poetry and prose

On Teacher Collaboration and Joint Planning

Ximena Ripley
Spanish Language Content Teacher
Isaac E. Young Middle School
New Rochelle, NY

I am the Spanish language content-area teacher in our middle school program and am assigned to the sixth grade cluster. In our school, teacher collaboration is strong in all of the programs because of the cluster structure, however, in our case, it is absolutely essential. We have planning periods each day in addition to our preparation periods to coordinate our language and content instruction. We also communicate by phone and share materials among ourselves related to the units. I work with very experienced English-dominant content-area teachers. My partner teachers know their subjects, New York State's goals at each grade level, and effective methods for teaching their subjects. I respect their expertise and use it to guide my content goals.

Once I understand the content objectives and teaching methods to be used by my partner teachers, I investigate the background knowledge of the students, review materials, and plan the language learning experiences that I will integrate into the content-based lessons I will offer in Spanish. Because we also have language teachers (Spanish language and ESL) that work with the students, the task of pre-teaching the second language learners the vocabulary and expressions they will need for all of their subjects is assigned to them. In other words, they base their language instruction on the content learning that is planned by the content area teachers. My job as the DILE teacher is to plan coordinated content instruction in Spanish to complement the content instruction that will be provided in English.

For example, in mathematics instruction, if the students will be doing problem-solving with the cluster mathematics teacher in English, I plan related instruction in Spanish. To aid the second language learners, I would read the problem at a slower pace, ask more frequent questions to check on their comprehension, and provide them other types of support such as using actions, pictures, or drawings. Using a step-by-step approach, they review the question, go over strategies they will use to solve the problem, show their work, and state their answer. By using a step-by-step approach, English dominant students are able to fully participate in the sharing of problem solutions in Spanish be-cause they know what is being asked and get practice in communicating their problem-solving process. They also get opportunities to read, write, and speak in Spanish through problem-solving activities. The focus is on conceptual understanding, but they are practicing all four language skills through active class participation.

I also use grouping to support students. I place students into groups in which a Spanish dominant bilingual helper is present. I pair them this way in all activities for language learning purposes, but also to break down stereotypes and build students' self-confidence and self-esteem. In the groups, the Spanish dominant students take on a very important role by providing instructional support to their peers. Since I only use Spanish in the classroom, the bilingual students are the only ones who can provide L1 explanations to their English-dominant partners when needed to insure their comprehension. The benefits from this approach for the English and Spanish-dominant students are clear, yet different. For the English speakers, it is a chance to use Spanish and advance their proficiency. The Spanish speakers build their self-confidence and pride in their language.

Not only in the classroom, but throughout the program, we favor active learning approaches to support our personal, cross-cultural, language, and content learning goals. In addition, we often go on field trips and plan after-school activities that will get the kids to interact beyond what goes on in the classroom.

In our program, the cluster teachers are active collaborators and so are the students. We think this is the only way to work in a middle school where subject area instruction is provided by specialists in each content area. We use parallel programming across the two languages to accomplish our content goals and the second language teachers act as a bridge to our content area instruction.

read to make sure you comprehend, using visuals (charts, semantic maps) to represent new ideas, making outlines, and using a checklist to revise a piece of writing.

Teachers can: 1) inventory the strategies students are currently using and which they still need to learn, 2) identify the skills they consider to be most useful to learners according to their age, proficiency and learning styles, and 3) systematically introduce and practice these strategies in their content area classes. Chamot (1995) recommends that teachers follow the following 4-step process in teaching learning strategies to their students: 1) preview students prior knowledge about learning strategies, 2) present a selected learning strategy: Model it, name it, and explain when to use it, 3) practice learning strategies in each lesson and allow students to ask questions to clarify how to use the strategies, and 4) encourage students to assess how well different strategies are working for them and to build their own repertoire of effective learning strategies.

An example of how integrated instruction is planned and delivered in a middle school dual language program is provided in the "Voices from the Field" essay on p. 119. Readers will also want to refer to the other "Voices from the Field" essays provided in this chapter for additional examples of the planning and instructional delivery process.

How can I select materials and adapt curriculum for learners?

Choosing Varied and High-Quality Instructional Materials on the Topic

As noted in Chapter 2, teachers must have access to varied and high-quality curriculum materials that will be effective for diverse learners. *Varied* materials include books, workbooks, posters, charts, slides, overhead transparencies, models, audiocassette and videocassette tapes, computer software, CD ROMs and Laser Videodisks as available in the target language. The materials should be appropriate to the age level, grade level, and proficiency characteristics of learners. *High quality* means professionally produced, durable, attractive, motivating, and conceptually accurate materials. These criteria apply to both instructional languages.

When selecting materials for second language learners, several other aspects must be considered. Some of these are presented in Table 6.3.

If materials designed for native speakers are used with second language learners, modification is in order. Teachers can create visual and graphic representations of concepts to facilitate student learning. Teachers can also reduce the language and literacy demands through a variety of strategies. Suggestions for modifying instructional materials are provided in Table 6.4.

Table 6.3   Checklist for Selecting Materials for Second Language Learners

- Materials have an inviting layout.
- Materials have many useful illustrations and graphics to aid concept learning.
- Materials do not have an overwhelming amount of text.
- Materials are written in a logical and cohesive manner.
- Materials are written at a level that students can read independently.
- Materials are free of cultural bias; culturally inclusive examples and illustrations are present.
- Materials have a typeface that is easy to decipher and well-sized for the age group.

Table 6.4   Modifying Instructional Materials

1. Create a graphic depiction of the text (photographs, drawings, graphic organizers).
2. Outline the text/highlight main points
3. Rewrite the text to simplify the language (Control new vocabulary, simplify grammar, structure paragraphs carefully).
4. Shorten the amount of reading required.
5. Create audiotaped versions of the text.
6. Provide live demonstrations to bring texts to life.
7. Use alternate books (high-interest, low-vocabulary).

(Short, 1989)

When selecting materials in languages other than English, teachers must consider: 1) the readability of the text, and 2) the match to U.S. curriculum content. In the case of Spanish, teachers can apply readability formulas to determine the degree of reading difficulty (see Spaulding, S. (1956) or Vari-Cartier, P. (1981)). Teachers can also construct cloze tests to determine whether material is written at a frustration level, instructional level, or independent level (see National Assessment and Dissemination Center, (1980)). This can be done for a variety of non-English languages.

Finding materials in non-English languages that correlate well to local curricular content is sometimes a challenge. Having a scope and sequence chart to direct their search, teachers can begin to catalog their materials to find out which units are most in need of additional materials. Networking among programs and teachers can be a great aid in locating appropriate materials. Teachers must consider how well the topics and concepts developed in a particular text match the curricular objectives for the year. Teachers should also reference Internet web sites to their curriculum on a unit-by-unit basis. By downloading materials off the Internet or having students access resources via the Internet, teachers can expand their classroom resources considerably. The dynamic environment of the Internet also provides up-to-date resources as fields change and grow.

How can I plan for evaluation?

Because each lesson contains content, language, and general learning objectives, all must be actively monitored and evaluated. Teachers must plan to check frequently on students' understanding of the language being used and the concepts being taught during instruction. Such assessment might be done orally or through learning logs, for example. Also, plan to provide frequent feedback and encouragement related to students' conceptual understanding, task completion, and language usage. Plan for peer assessment and self-assessment of learning progress. Make sure that students understand how you will evaluate their learning when the lesson or unit is completed. Provide practice in the types of tasks you will use in any unit tests or assessments planned. Plan for how you will assess students, how you will record the results of your assessment and how you will report on student progress to the students themselves, to their parents, and to other interested teachers. More concrete guidance regarding assessment in EE classrooms is provided in Chapter 7.

Teaching Language and Content

Teaching Concepts with Recognition of How Students Learn

Concept acquisition is a developmental process that is facilitated if students are first introduced to a new concept, then provided practice so they can internalize the concept and finally, encouraged to apply the concept to real life situations. Consequently, we discuss content area teaching strategies according to these phases: 1) Preview, 2) Focused Learning, and 3) Extension (based on Gordon, J.M., © pending, *The Multidimensional Learning Web*, Illinois Resource Center). During the preview phase, you would investigate students' prior knowledge on the topic you are about to explore, determine their factual knowledge, interest in the topic, skills related to the topic, and questions they would like to explore. After collecting such information, you then plan your teaching activities for the preview (initial learning) and focused learning phases of instruction. During the extension phase you can aid students in transferring their newly acquired knowledge to other curricular areas, deepen their understandings of lesson concepts, and encourage learners' to apply their knowledge to real-life problem solving situations. The activities we recommend for each of these three major phases of instruction are summarized in Table 6.5 and discussed in the text which follows. All of the strategies to be described in this section are further elaborated in Chapter 8 (model lessons).

Preview Phase

In order to introduce new concepts to learners, teachers might employ any of the following techniques, alone or in combination with one another:

1. *Carefully-constructed demonstrations.* Step-by-step demonstrations conducted by teachers live in their classrooms or via instructional media are very helpful to students during concept acquisition phase. Such demonstrations can be repeated to insure comprehension by students. Teachers should match pace and redundancy of presentation to learner needs. Teachers can use real objects, models, or accurate visuals to demonstrate lesson concepts to students using the key vocabulary (see context embedded instruction in Glossary).

2. *Controlled reading material.* Many materials are available to learners today that have excellent visuals to support the text and which actively control the

---

Table 6.5   Planning Teaching Activities by Phase of Instruction

Preview Phase	*Focused Learning Phase*	*Extension Phase*
• Prior Knowledge Surveys • Carefully Constructed Demonstrations • Controlled Readings • Guided Experiences • Concept Charts, Tables, and Diagrams • Films, Videos, and Videodisks	• Learning Logs and Journals • Graphic Organizers • Games, Activities, Simulations, Role Plays • Student-Constructed Models/Texts • Field Trips, Guest Speakers	• Group Research Projects/Independent Investigations • Student Generated Problems • Bridging to Other Content Areas • Visual, Oral, Written Presentations • Home Study/Family Involvement

---

text presented to learners (vocabulary, sentence length, and complexity). Content-area photo books, such as those produced by *Capstone Press* and *Children's Book Press*, are especially recommended. The former has recently linked each book to other books on the topic and to several relevant web sites for easy integration of technology. (see Publishers List in Appendix B)

3. *Guided experiences* Students can work alone or in groups to have experiences or conduct experiments that help them grasp new concepts. Through direct experience they can come to understand things in a way that reading or teacher demonstration could never convey.

4. *Charts, tables, and diagrams* Key concepts can be reinforced or explained through charts, tables, and diagrams. These can be hierarchically or temporally organized as demanded by the concepts being learned. Use the charts or diagrams to clarify part-to-whole relationships; explain processes, and establish cause/effect relationships.

5. *Instructional films, videos, videodisks*. Visual learning is extremely important when students are learning a language. Complementary visuals that demonstrate a process or introduce concepts contribute positively to students' learning and make the new language comprehensible (see Glossary). Additionally, some learners are by nature highly visual, making the pairing of visual and verbal input

all the more desirable. Well-selected visuals can be used during the receptive phase of language learning, when the meanings of new terms are being established or during the productive phase of language learning as cues to elicit target language use in meaningful ways.

Focused Learning Phase

Once concepts are introduced, students need plentiful opportunities to confirm their understandings, correct misconceptions, and practice new skills. In order to do this, the following techniques are recommended:

1. *Learning logs and journals.* Learners can make information their own in learning logs (see Glossary) and journals. They can explain new concepts in their own terms, with accompanying visuals. They can review notes they have taken in class and reorganize or rewrite them to better represent what they have learned.

2. *Graphic organizers.* By reconstructing information in graphic form, students have a chance to internalize key concepts and review important ideas. This work can be done in pairs or small groups to enhance language use opportunities among students. Graphic organizers maintain cognitive complexity and accuracy while limiting the linguistic demands, hence their great utility in second language classrooms.

3. *Games, activities, simulations, and role plays.* Games and structured activities are a wonderful way to prac-

tice new facts or concepts. Board games, card games, team games, and activity sheets give learners the practice opportunities they need to internalize important information. Simulations and role plays allow students to practice target language in meaningful ways and often reveal their understandings of lesson concepts.

4. *Student constructed models/texts.* If students construct their own models or reading materials, they have an opportunity to demonstrate their understanding of lesson concepts. Models reduce the language and literacy demands placed on learners, while texts permit learners to simultaneously develop concepts and the language needed to express their conceptual understanding.

5. *Field trips and guest speakers.* The resources of the classroom are greatly expanded by taking students on field trips and inviting guest speakers. Students are often motivated by these novel experiences and they see that what takes place in the classroom is linked to the world outside of the classroom. They may also apply what they have learned and use more of the target language than in the traditional classroom setting. The expertise of guest speakers and specialists on-site can bolster the teacher's expertise and deepen students understanding of lesson concepts. What a marine biologist knows about marine mammals is certainly more extensive than what their teacher may know about the topic and enriches not only the students' but also the teacher's knowledge base.

Extension Phase

To complete any lesson or unit, students should be encouraged to apply and extend their learning. Problem solving exercises show students the value of the facts and skills they have acquired. Extension activities give students a chance to fully explore their interests and link their new learning to their existing repertoire of knowledge and skills. The following techniques are recommended:

1. *Group research projects/independent investigations.* As students are ready for further study on the same topic, they can expand their knowledge base through group or individual investigations. This can be done via further reading; instructional media, computer-assisted learning sequences, or via the Internet. Results can be shared through oral and written reports, teacher/student conferences, or visual displays. For example, when learning about the three branches of government, students can further their understanding of the executive branch of government by in-depth investigations of particular presidents.

2. *Student-generated problems.* Students can be problem-posers as well as consumers of information. Student-generated activities can be very motivating for other students and can also redirect the energies of teachers to aspects of a topic that are of great interest to students. Taking action around topics of interest to students can personalize the learning experience, increase motivation, and enrich the learning.

3. *Bridging to other content areas.* Interdisciplinary units deepen student understanding of topics under study. By unifying the learning experience thematically, learners can solidify their understanding of key concepts and core ideas. (see Kucer, et al., 1995)

4. *Visual, oral, or written presentations.* To culminate a lesson, students may prepare visual, oral, or written summaries of what they have learned. Presentations allow students to demonstrate their content and language learning and also have the added benefit of building self-confidence and peer relations.

5. *Home study/family involvement.* Sending instructional materials to be used at home allows interested family members to become involved in the learning process. Some publishers have produced materials for this purpose. For example, some publishers produce take-home materials as well as books for parents that describe ways they can become involved in their children's content area learning. These materials orient parents to the broad objectives in their child's science learning program and provide many activities and suggestions for home and community-based learning projects. Sending assignments to be completed at home is challenging when parents do not understand the language of the assignment. An example of how one program is responding to this challenge is provided in the "Voices from the Field" essay on p. 124.

Teaching Content: General Considerations

Preparing Yourself to Teach Content

Effective EE teachers possess both content area expertise as well as extensive proficiency in the language of instruction. They must fully understand the concepts they will impart to learners and have the technical terminology and content-specific language phrasing to do so.

Researchers have noted that teachers use more lengthy discourse when lacking technical, precise vocabulary to describe academic concepts. This undermines students' conceptual as well as linguistic development. Because of this,

Helping Parents to Support Their Children's Learning of Content through a Second Language

Monica G. Maccera
Third Grade Teacher
James F. Oyster Bilingual Elementary School
Washington, D.C.

The question of how to empower monolingual parents to best support their child's bilingual education is one we continually struggle with at Oyster. How to assist children with their homework seems to be most parents' biggest worry. The topic is brought up in casual discussion between parents in the hallways as well as in more formal settings such as PTA meetings. In the past, the subject has been dealt with by the individual teachers and the parents of their students; but this year we are trying to make a concerted school-wide effort to support parents.

Through the years, and through significant trial and error, my teaching partner and I have developed different strategies to include all parents in our classroom community. My first year of teaching, my students' parents just couldn't accept that if the child continually had trouble understanding homework, it was better for me to know about it than for them to spend hours coaxing the child to do a twenty minute assignment. I found it necessary to send a weekly homework calendar where I wrote instructions for all my Spanish homework in English. Needless to say, this was excessive and undermined the effort of the bilingual program to make all students truly *biliterate*.

In the past couple of years, we have made a lot of changes. We still send home a weekly homework calendar, but the instructions are directed to the students and are always in the language of the assignment. In addition, homework has been more carefully structured not to be a burden to the families. Students in third grade receive twenty minutes of mathematics homework every night, twenty minutes of language arts homework in *one* of the two languages and twenty minutes of Sustained Silent Reading. I know from speaking to parents that this organization is very helpful and greatly appreciated.

We have also developed a bilingual newsletter. The newsletter is sent home every two weeks in both languages. It is addressed to the parents and includes a brief sketch of the upcoming lessons in all subject areas as well as detailed ideas on how parents can best help their children master the objectives currently being taught. This gives parents a real sense of power over their child's education and allows them to accept that it is not always their role to make sure that their child understands the homework. I have found that these small changes, along with our care to ensure the homework is at the right level and

well-explained, have almost eliminated concerns about homework in our classroom. This is not the case in the school as a whole.

This year our organization of parents and teachers, the Oyster Community Council (OCC), has taken this issue very seriously. We hosted an evening of workshops designed to help parents help their children with their homework. Teachers gave workshops at different levels, with some teaching complicated linguistic theory and others leading discussions and brainstorming sessions. Although not much time has passed since this unique event, the feedback we have gotten indicates that parents found the practical sessions the most helpful. They were happy to hear about the different dictionaries that they could make available to their child, and learn how to use them most effectively. They were elated to receive a list of vocabulary commonly found on homework assignments that they could put on the refrigerator and refer to in the future. They have also requested that a school-wide program for language buddies be created. This program would give monolingual families the name and phone number of a bilingual family they could call for help. There has even been serious discussion about offering language classes to parents wanting to become bilingual. I hope that with this spirit of community involvement and cooperation we will make great strides towards achieving success for all our students.

EE teachers must be highly proficient—comfortable with the technical vocabulary and subject-specific discourse in the languages in which they teach. They must also understand any cross-cultural dimensions involved in the way students describe and understand concepts. For example, some researchers have found that if science instruction incorporates examples, analogies, and contexts that are culturally-relevant to students, it promotes greater science learning. Discourse patterns also differ across languages and cultures with some cultures viewing lengthy, repetitive explanations as appropriate and others viewing the same behavior as undesirable. As teachers plan instruction, they must consider these aspects, especially the vocabulary they use to teach concepts in a particular language (i.e., sink/float). This is because direct translation of terms may fail to produce the term or phrase that best represents a particular concept in a particular language (Lee, Fradd, & Sutman, 1995).

Effective EE teachers possess extensive familiarity with grade level curriculum sequences and have rich backgrounds in the subjects they teach. They have full command of the particular subject matter and its subject-specific pedagogy. Concerns about teachers-subject matter knowledge and their subject subject-specific pedagogical knowledge have been raised over the last decade beginning with educational reformers such as Shulman (1987) and Porter and Brophy (1988), and continuing in recent reports by the National Commission on Teaching and America's Future (1996). To address these concerns, teachers should make certain that they:

- have appropriate expectations for students related to the topic at hand according to their age/grade level.
- fully understand the concepts they will teach.
- understand the best ways to teach the new concepts to students (and have the tools and equipment necessary to effectively teach concepts).
- possess the technical vocabulary and subject-specific ways of communicating about the topics at hand.
- understand any culturally-specific or linguistically-specific ways of teaching that would facilitate concept learning (grouping arrangements or learning style favored; regional terms to use).

Making Lessons Comprehensible
When teaching in a second language, it is important to plan carefully the language demands you will place on learners (vocabulary and other linguistic features) to insure comprehensibility. Input and output demands placed on learners (what they are hearing; how they are required to respond) should be actively controlled by the teacher so they do not exceed students' abilities. When teaching content in students' second language, comprehensibility can be enhanced in the following ways:

- use cognates, controlled vocabulary, and shorter phrases.
- limit idiomatic speech during instruction for students at beginning stages.
- use natural redundancy in phrasing.
- repeat key vocabulary.
- reinforce key ideas.
- pace instruction appropriately.
- provide natural pauses between phrases to give students time to process language.
- give students the "wait time" they need to interpret questions and formulate a response.
- encourage interaction and provide opportunities to try out the new language and get feedback from those with more proficiency.
- check frequently on student understanding.

(See Chapter 7 in Echevarria and Graves, 1998 for more guidance on sheltering the discourse demands in classroom instruction).

Table 6.6 summarizes the kinds of language skills that can be expected of learners of different levels of language development. It provides guidelines for what you can expect of students at different stages of development. By referring to the table, teachers can plan learning activities that place appropriate demands on learners at different stages.

How can I plan stage-appropriate, student-centered teaching strategies?
EE teachers consider their students' language characteristics in order to plan effective instruction. They also make instruction interactive to promote language and conceptual development.

When students are instructed in their primary language, teachers do not have to actively manage their language interactions as with second language instruction. However, many techniques that are characteristic of good pedagogy when teaching new concepts to learners through the medium of their primary language are also beneficial to second language learners. Use of these techniques, in fact, is critical to establish understanding for second language learners who need concrete examples in order to comprehend instruction and learn new ideas. The following techniques are helpful:

1. demonstrations and modeling.
2. use of manipulatives and realia.
3. use of visuals and graphic aids.
4. film, video, or multimedia presentations.

Table 6.6   Task Demands Appropriate to Each Stage of Proficiency

STAGE I (pre-production):
- minimal comprehension
- no verbal production

listen	draw	underline
point	select	chart
move	choose	find
mime	act/act out	follow
match	circle	locate

STAGE II (early production):
- limited comprehension
- one/two word responses

name	list	identify
label	categorize	complete
group	tell/say	classify
respond	answer	produce
discriminate		

STAGE III (speech emergence):
- increased comprehension
- simple sentences
- some basic errors in production

recall	summarize	differentiate
retell	describe	record
define	role-play	recite
explain	restate	speak
compare	contrast	

STAGE IV (intermediate fluency):
- very good comprehension
- more complex sentences
- fewer errors in production

analyze	evaluate	formulate
create	justify	infer
defend	support	develop
debate	generate	expand
predict	hypothesize	modify
criticize	defend	propose
simplify	synthesize	systematize

(Sharon Weissbrot, NYC Second Language Workshop)

  5. acting things out or role plays

  6. active learning/engaging in a process

Because students are operating in their second language, verbal instruction must be amplified and clarified by learning that takes place through other modalities: visual, tactile, kinesthetic.

Multimodal Teaching

Plan lessons that combine visual, auditory, kinesthetic and tactile input to learners. Make certain that all channels of learning are being actively utilized. Do not require long listening periods where learning is completely dependent on understanding verbal input offered in a second language. Gestures, facial expressions, body language, props, graphs, and other graphic organizers, realia, overhead projections, media, posters, and other visuals can accompany verbal input and enhance comprehensibility for learners operating in their second language.

Teaching According to Learners' Stages of Development

How Do I Teach Content to Beginning Learners? Teachers must adapt their language to students' proficiency levels. For beginners, this means that teachers must make learning concrete by using demonstrations, modeling, visuals, and active participation. Teachers should use *caregiver speech*— language that is short in length, consistently uses the same vocabulary, is spoken at a comfortable rate, and with sufficient repetition (natural redundancy) for terms to become internalized. The teacher does most of the talking and uses videos, films, slides, pictures, and charts to amplify and clarify verbal instruction. Other important teaching considerations for beginning students are listed in Table 6.7. An illustration of this kind of instruction follows in the "Voices from the Field" essay provided by Daisy Chan, First Grade Teacher, in the West Portal Elementary School Chinese Immersion Program.

How Do I Teach Content to Intermediate Learners? In the case of intermediate students, teachers will want to extend and refine the students' language skills. This means that teachers will actively shape students' language, expanding their vocabulary through the use of synonyms, require more precision in the use of technical terms, and require more sophisticated and complex language. In contrast to beginning students, intermediate students should do most of the talking—explaining, describing, summarizing major concept in a lessons. They too can use models, manipulatives, and visuals, but in this case they will be the ones doing the talking, illustrating, and explaining as they discuss the visuals introduced by the teacher. They should also have greater reading and writing demands placed on them so they grow in their ability to use literacy for academic learning.

Table 6.7   Stage-Appropriate Teaching Strategies for Beginners

- Well-planned, controlled language use in instruction.
- Use of models and manipulatives when explaining lesson concepts.
- Amplification of verbal information with active demonstrations.
- Provision of many types of visuals to explain lesson concepts and display key information.
- Use of controlled reading and writing experiences.
- Allowing students to work with peers to check on their understanding; formulate answers to questions.

How Do I Teach Content to Advanced Learners? For advanced students, teachers will want to increase the language demands, requiring ever more sophisticated and complex language. As with intermediate students, advanced students should do most of the talking—explaining, describing, summarizing the major lesson concepts. Reading and writing should be emphasized as primary modes for promoting learning about subject matter. Students should make extended oral presentations in class, conduct research on topics, and write reports. They should be active consumers of information, questioning as well as comparing and contrasting their various available sources of information on each topic of inquiry. (For examples of content teaching to intermediate and advanced learners see the Mieles and Ripley "Voices from the Field" essays in this chapter.)

Teaching Heterogeneous Groups of Students

Grouping of students is very important in EE classrooms. When half of the class is proficient in the language of instruction and half is not, as in two-way bilingual programs, students should be grouped in ways that will place non-native speakers with native speakers in carefully planned interactions. Tasks must be planned so that each student has an appropriate role. For example, native speakers can be readers and recorders. Second language learners can create illustrations, label models, chart information.

Voices from the Field

Planning Content Area Instruction for Beginning Learners

Daisy Chan
First Grade Teacher
West Portal Elementary School
San Francisco, CA

The Chinese Immersion Program at West Portal Elementary School provides Chinese language learning for students from kindergarten to fifth grade and promotes cultural awareness and understanding for students of different ethnic backgrounds. The West Portal program was the first Chinese immersion program in the nation and has been recognized for its academic excellence and innovative curriculum. *Children in the program are taught in Cantonese, a major Chinese dialect and most commonly used dialect in the San Francisco Bay Area. West Portal is one of twelve San Francisco model schools* (SFUSD Language Academy Newsletter, 2 *(1), p. 1).*

I teach first grade Chinese Immersion students of varied ethnic backgrounds. Most of them are ABC (American Born Chinese) whose parents do not speak a word of Chinese. Others have fluent Chinese-speaking parents. A small portion of my students are African Americans, Vietnamese, and Hispanics.

After going through the kindergarten year, most of them can understand up to 80% of my instruction in Chinese. However, every year I do have students who are still struggling with the language. As a result, I need to use a lot of real objects and hands-on, minds-on activities to aid my teaching.

Take learning the concept of money as an example. I have to make sure that the students have a very clear concept of numbers before moving on to the abstract concept of money. The students need to be able to count from 1 to 100 (or at least 1 to 50). Then, I introduce counting by 2s, 5s, 10s, and 25s. I use methods like counting hands (5 fingers per hand), counting M&Ms, counting cereal pieces, and other real objects that interest children. After my students have all mastered these skills, they learn to do some simple addition with the numbers 2, 5, 10, and 25.

At this point I introduce common coins using visuals (pictures of both sides of common coins), along with their values and I provide students experience with each coin's actual size. I give them simple problems like how many coins to put together to make 7 cents or how many ways to make 11 cents. As they are trying to solve the problems, they have plastic replicas of coins to manipulate. Students who grasp these introductory problems with ease move on to more difficult problems or choose to help others.

Next, I set up a store in a corner of the classroom with things for the students to buy. I use chocolate, candy, crackers, fruit rolls, etc. The students price each item in the store together, assigning prices of from 1 to 20 cents. Then every student is allowed to pick up coins with a total of 50 cents in value. They take turns buying the things they want from the store. I am the storekeeper and give them change. I use a play cash register to store my coins. Things they buy are for them to keep. Students repeat this activity in small group time and they take turns being the storekeeper. Students are encouraged to go to the play store during the practice and review time.

Later, I ask them to cut pictures of things that they like from magazines. This time I give the price for each item. In this way, I can adjust the level of difficulty for each individual student. They have to draw the coins they need to use in order to buy that item. Advanced students can be asked to make change from an initial amount given to them.

The steps I have described apply to instruction in any target language. I try to use as many real objects as possible. I use peer helpers in small groups. I make sure the learning tasks are broken into smaller ones; small enough for them to master each step before moving on to insure their success.

Lessons can involve learning together and learning apart segments to better tailor instructional interactions to each subgroup's needs (see Ripley "Voices from the Field" essay earlier in this chapter and Mieles essay on p. 130). *Computer software and Internet sites* could also be selected with the different student groups in mind.

Another frequently used technique, *peer tutoring*, is beneficial because it gives native language learners an opportunity to communicate their understanding of a topic while providing second language learners access to native speakers with whom they can interact and attempt to communicate. Both have the opportunity to use the technical terminology they are learning in meaningful ways and both have the opportunity to check on their understanding of the concepts being taught in a non-threatening setting.

Cooperative learning is also beneficial because it offers well planned structures for heterogeneous groups of learners. *Dyad activities* (paired activities) are a key task structure that provide for high levels of student interaction. For example, in social studies instruction provided through a second language, students can be assigned A & B questions to investigate. They can then jointly complete an activity sheet each contributing the results of their individual investigations. How tasks are structured is critical to insuring active student learning. Collaborative interaction in which meaning is negotiated is known to promote oral and written language development (Ellis, 1985; Enright & McCloskey, 1988) and therefore is highly desirable when delivering integrated language and content teaching.

Providing options and choices to learners for classwork and homework is another way to accommodate the range of proficiency levels in the classroom. Second language learners might be given activities with controlled language demands while native speakers might complete assignments with more extensive reading and writing demands. Evaluation strategies would also accommodate differences between the two groups by providing ways for second language learners to demonstrate their achievement while limiting the language demands; native speakers would perform tasks with more demanding reading/writing expectations.

Making Instruction Interactive to Insure Concept Learning

As illustrated in the "Voices from the Field" essay which follows, EE teachers plan instruction in which their students will be *actively engaged* (Fern, Anstrom & Silcox, 1995) through *hands-on instruction*, not only to accommodate their linguistic needs, but more importantly, to insure their concept learning Interactive instruction leads students to construct knowledge for themselves and to fully understand lesson concepts because they experience them first-hand. When students are conducting experiments, applying skills

in real life problem-solving (planning nutritional meals, designing a house), interviewing one another or a third party, producing a learning log, critiquing a newspaper article or an instructional film, preparing a multi-media presentation or researching information on the Internet, they are more likely to be involved then when passively listening to lectures.

EE teachers frequently employ *discovery-oriented* teaching approaches where learners are responsible for discovering, constructing, and creating something new, and the teacher is in the role of facilitator. Students might construct theorems or formulas, write field observation notes that help them generate hypotheses for observed phenomena, or document history in the making. One approach is using the inquiry process (see Table 6.8).

Peer support increases the interaction among students, allowing non-native speakers to communicate with native speakers of the language. Peer support is invaluable in low-

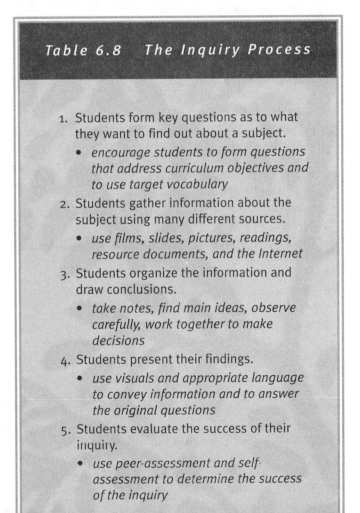

Table 6.8   The Inquiry Process

1. Students form key questions as to what they want to find out about a subject.
   * *encourage students to form questions that address curriculum objectives and to use target vocabulary*
2. Students gather information about the subject using many different sources.
   * *use films, slides, pictures, readings, resource documents, and the Internet*
3. Students organize the information and draw conclusions.
   * *take notes, find main ideas, observe carefully, work together to make decisions*
4. Students present their findings.
   * *use visuals and appropriate language to convey information and to answer the original questions*
5. Students evaluate the success of their inquiry.
   * *use peer-assessment and self-assessment to determine the success of the inquiry*

(Lorenz & Met, 1991)

Grouping Students to Maximize Learning

Dorothy Mieles
3rd Grade Teacher.
Lido Elementary School
Long Beach, NY

After teaching in a dual language program for six years, it is easy to see how this program benefits the language minority and the language majority students. You see the program truly come alive when both groups of students are together. The students are enriched with both languages through the content areas of math, science, and social studies.

My partner and I divide our native language homerooms into an A group and a B group. Both groups are then linguistically mixed; half native English speakers and half native Spanish speakers for instruction. We consider the content mandates from the district, state, and national levels. It is during these times that my partner and I need to plan meticulously to teach basic and more complex concepts in a comprehensible and interesting manner to a group of students who have varied linguistic levels. Careful planning is a key to the success of instruction in a dual language program.

Unless appropriate strategies are implemented, delivering math, science, and social studies instruction in Spanish can be an overwhelming task for the teacher who is providing the instruction and for the students who are learning the content. There is an abundance of instructional materials available in English but less so in Spanish, leaving the Spanish teacher the added

responsibility of translating a good portion of the materials used in content instruction. During the translation of the needed material, the linguistic levels of the students to be taught is kept in mind. The translation has to be appropriate for the native *and* the non-native speakers. Visuals may need to be added for reinforcement, especially for the Spanish Language Learners (SLLs).

Students can be easily motivated to learn in math and science because these two content areas lend themselves to hands-on experiments. Today, it has become very important to relate math to students' lives and promote higher order thinking skills instead of just teaching computation. Manipulatives are an essential component and provide an excellent way to get the language majority and minority students to learn together in a cooperative learning environment. Students work as buddies towards a common goal. They are encouraged to speak only in Spanish. The Spanish speakers serve as linguistic models, as does the teacher, for the SLLs. In terms of classroom management, the two groups of students sit next to one another in pairs so that peers can provide tutoring support. Many of the SLLs rely on the manipulatives to visually reinforce new vocabulary and concepts. The manipulatives also benefit visual and kinesthetic learners. This holds true in science which

involves use of many visuals and the use of hands-on experiments. Every student has a role in the activity so the responsibility is not restricted to the native speaker. Beyond the active learning, lessons have to be meaningful to the students' lives so they can form a connection.

In social studies, visuals and active learning experiences play an important role; such as the use of maps, pictures, objects, foods, music, videos, field trips, and so on. Students are immersed in opportunities to use language. Native speakers are given the tasks which use more complex oral and written language, while the SLLs are assigned language and writing tasks appropriate to their linguistic levels. Any concepts or vocabulary the SLLs may need prior to a pair activity are taught during the SSL (Spanish as a Second Language) period when all the SLLs are together. Concepts can be clarified so that the SLLs don't feel hindered when they are with their Spanish language counterparts. It is crucial to provide a comfortable working atmosphere for the SLLs so they will take the risks needed in Spanish language production. Native Spanish speakers are considerate and helpful to their buddies, who likewise help them when instruction is provided in English.

I have seen the multiple benefits of dual language instruction—students enriched with learning a second language and one another's cultures, while maintaining and strengthening their native languages and traditions.

ering anxiety during instruction, clarifying conceptual understanding, and encouraging communication in the second language about lesson concepts. Active discourse is beneficial for conceptual development and second language learning (Genesee, 1994). Small group learning and cooperative learning structures are helpful. Conducive *room arrangements* also foster interaction. Open learning areas that invite interaction are recommended. Individual desks isolate students and decrease interaction while joint spaces, such as tables and rugs, invite interaction. Favor all *learning styles*. When students' learning styles and interests are accommodated, they are more actively engaged. *Personalize* assignments and projects. Include student examples and experiences in lessons. Encourage students to personally respond and express opinions. If students' learning is related to their lives and to real world events, they will be more engaged. Make sure students know how the topics they are studying relate to other academic disciplines and to life outside of school. Show learners the functional relevance of what they are studying; make learning as purposeful as possible.

Table 6.9 summarizes the most important points in this section related to making instruction student-centered.

Teaching Special Needs Learners

Accommodations must extend beyond these basic considerations if learners have been identified as having special education needs. Teachers will want to consider the task demands in light of individual learner characteristics. For example, teachers may want to modify grouping arrangements, mode of presentation, activity length, or amount of feedback and support provided during task completion to make certain that learners with special needs are successful. Learners may need extended time to complete assignments, alternate testing arrangements, or the in-class support of an inclusion aide or special education teacher to succeed. Technology is another useful tool to help learners bypass barriers that might otherwise be in the way of their success (working on a computer instead of producing text manually). Special needs students can and should be included in EE programs with appropriate modifications to insure their success. (See Echevarria & Graves, 1998 for more information on this topic.)

Linking Instruction with the Home and the Community

There are many resources available to children in their homes and communities that can extend learning opportunities beyond the confines of the classroom. Museums, libraries, galleries, film archives, nature preserves, historical sites, and exploritoriums are all centers that offer learning experiences to children. Materials should be made available for home study in cases where parents, siblings, other relatives or family friends have an interest in working directly with a particular child. In addition, teachers can note television programs or rental videos that correspond to current units of study and provide encouragement for families to view particular programs together. Some parents have expertise related to units of study that they can share with their child or with the class. All of these resources send powerful positive messages to children and their families about their place in the learning process.

We also have opportunities to extend language majority students' exposure to the target language through content-related, community-based projects. These content-related projects can promote the natural use of language in the community and thus advance students' social and academic language.

Putting It All Together

Lesson planning in two-way bilingual classrooms is a complex process, distinguished by the conscious awareness of two primary groups of learners (native speakers and second language learners) whose needs must be accommodated simultaneously in the lesson. Because of this, having a split lesson planning guide that considers the needs of both groups simultaneously is very helpful. As it relates to the various aspects of lesson planning, there are some elements that are the same for both groups of learners, but frequently important distinctions must be made in how you are planning for proficient speakers of a language versus how you are planning for second language learners. To assist EE teachers who work in two-way bilingual programs

---

Table 6.9   Student-Centered Teaching Approaches

- Hands-on activities.
- Multi-modality learning.
- Varied grouping arrangements.
- Personally-relevant examples.
- Discovery-oriented teaching approaches.
- Varied opportunities to apply concepts to real life problem solving.
- Peer support.
- Student-to-student dialogue and sharing of experiences and strategies.

Voices from the Field

Extending Students' Exposure to the Target Language Through Community-Based Learning Projects

Yuderquis G. Santos
Dual Language Teacher
Public School 306
Bronx, New York

As a dual language teacher, I teach language through academic content. Recently I became aware that it is more common in dual language programs to design tasks for the Spanish language learners that are academically-oriented rather than tasks involving real-life situations.

I had to reconsider the purpose of acquiring a second language, particularly the short and long term goals for the English speakers acquiring Spanish. Ideally, I would like these students to become bilingual, biliterate adults who can function effectively in both English and Spanish. I would feel a sense of accomplishment if these students could leave my classroom speaking and reading English fluently, in addition to interacting with native Spanish-speakers in the community with fluidity and ease.

These goals are complex when one considers the English speakers' limited access to the second language. Languages are learned through immersion and through interaction with that language. These students are immersed in the second language approximately 15 hours a week and the Spanish language seems to be confined to the classroom. Although there is natural exposure to the Spanish language in the community, it is essential to bear in mind that the grocer, the waitress, the florist, all understand and more often than not, speak English. Because of this, an English-speaking customer will be served in English most times in our bilingual community. So although there is some exposure, that exposure too often is limited.

I was compelled to reflect on my teaching. How could I create a situation where children would be immersed in language in a more natural context? Most importantly, how could I create a risk-free environment that would equalize the Spanish language learners opportunities to use their second language as naturally exists for the English language learners?

I decided that the only way I could achieve my short term goal was to create an after-school program where the Spanish Language Learners (SLLs) would be given the opportunity to learn appropriate vocabulary for various real-life situations and then apply this knowledge in the community. I approached my supervisors, who not only understood my dilemma, but supported my decision.

I am in the process of designing this content-related, community-based unit. The teaching unit I will construct will comprise various naturally-occurring situations in the community to which the children learning Spanish will be exposed. They will include going to the *bodega* and asking for items and prices, visiting the local restaurant and ordering typical Latin American food, welcoming a Spanish-speaking parent and asking informational questions regarding his/her child (a fellow student), reporting malaise to the school nurse, giving directions to a passerby, translating information for someone else, and other community-based learning activities.

The SLLs will first learn the essential vocabulary through various activities. They will then engage in role play inside the classroom. The last part will consist of actually going outside of the school to the immediate community and practicing what is learned. As part of this, I will have the students reflect on their experiences. I am cognizant that I will have to arrange some situations. However, I have received so much enthusiasm from Spanish-speaking parents eager to help, that I can only perceive that my project will be successful.

I am eager to teach my students to be active participants in their community; to be able to engage in content-related dialogue confidently with native Spanish-speakers. Part of learning is practicing in authentic or almost authentic community-based situations. This is what I am now attempting to do for my Spanish Language Learners.

in planning content area lessons, we've designed the following lesson planning guide to bring all of the elements we've discussed in this chapter together in a single planning framework as provided in Table 6.10. Teachers who work in developmental bilingual programs that serve language minority students and teachers who work in immersion programs that serve language majority students would use that portion of the planning guide that pertains to their instructional situation—teaching content through the students' primary language or teaching content through the students' second language. Thus, the lesson planning guide presented in Table 6.10 should be useful to all EE teachers as they consider the needs of their learners and plan lessons accordingly.

Summary
To culminate this chapter, the main points are summarized using the critical features from Chapter 2 in Table 6.11.

Table 6.10   Instructional Planning Guide

THEME/TOPIC:

Planning

	STUDENTS LEARNING THROUGH L1	STUDENTS LEARNING THROUGH L2
A. BACKGROUND KNOWLEDGE OF LEARNERS		
B. SPECIFIC CONTENT OBJECTIVES		
• Knowledge, Concepts		
• Skills		
• Dispositions		
C. LANGUAGE OBJECTIVES		
• Content Obligatory		
• Content Compatible		
D. CLASSROOM DISCOURSE		
E. GENERAL SKILL OBJECTIVES		

Teaching

F. ACTIVITIES BY PHASE		
• *Preview Phase* (Experiential/Conceptual Review/Initial Learning)		
• *Focused Learning Phase*		
• *Extension Phase* (Transfer/Expansion; Learner Action)		
G. MATERIALS (Adapt as Necessary)		
H. GROUPING ARRANGEMENTS		
I. EVALUATION		
J. EXTENDING LEARNING THROUGH FAMILY AND COMMUNITY OUTREACH		

Table 6.11 Application of the Critical Features to Content Area Instruction

Critical Feature	Implications for Content Area Instruction
1. Parental involvement is integral to the program	**Support/encourage parental involvement** • Survey parents to understand their interest in becoming involved in particular units of instruction. • Provide materials for use at home such as take-home activities, books and videos, and monthly newsletters.
2. High standards have been established	**Work towards long range instructional goals as articulated in:** • National standards set by professional associations for each discipline • State curriculum frameworks • Local standards established by the district
3. Strong leadership is present	**Principals and lead teachers support high academic standards** • All personnel in leadership positions advocate for the provision of challenging instruction to all participants in the dual language program. • All leadership personnel understand that there are three major objectives in content area instruction: content learning, language learning, and general learning goals.
4. Instruction is developmentally-appropriate	**Teach in age/stage-appropriate ways** • Match activities to the learner's age, conceptual development, ability, attention span. • Account for the learner's cultural and experiential background.
5. Instruction is student-centered	**Model and provide guided practice opportunities** • Favor active learning strategies. • Personalize instruction. • Link learning to students' lives outside of the classroom.
6. Literacy instruction is integrated with challenging high academic instruction	**Make certain learning activities are meaning-centered, purposeful** • Engage learners actively; insure that they participate at levels • Insure that reading and writing contribute to student learning about other topics. • Make certain that reading and writing are systematically developed across the curriculum.

Table 6.11   (continued)

7. Teachers are reflective

Make assessment an integral part of instruction
- Make certain teachers fully understand the topics they will teach and possess all of the relevant terminology to teach about the topic with precision.
- Monitor teaching effectiveness regularly.
- Encourage student self-assessment and peer-assessment, and invite parental feedback.

8. The dual literacy program is coordinated with other school programs

Coordination among all teachers and programs is strong
- Meet frequently to actively coordinate each academic subject taught with other teachers.

9. The program aims for additive bilingualism and bilteracy

Understand the long range language use
- Plan for each subject
- Make sure all teachers understand how language will be used to teach each subject across the grades of the program.
- Create affirming, empowering environments where both languages and cultures are valued and affirmed by all participants.

References

Chamot, A. U. (1995). *Accelerating Achievement with Learning Strategies*. Glenview, IL: Scott Foresman. (pamphlet)

Echevarria, J. & Graves, A. (1998). *Sheltered Content Instruction: Teaching English-Language Learners with Diverse Abilities*. Boston: Allyn and Bacon.

Ellis, R. (1985). Teacher-Pupil Interaction in Second-Language Development. In S. Gass and C. Madden (Eds.), *Input in Second Language Acquisition* (pp. 69–85). Rowley, Mass: Newbury House.

Enright, D.S. & McCloskey, M.L. (1988). *Integrating English: Developing English Language and Literacy in the Multilingual Classroom*. Reading, MA: Addison-Wesley.

Fern, V., Anstrom, K., & Silcox, B. (1995). Active Learning and the Limited English Proficient Student. *Directions in Language Education*, 1 (2), p. 1–7.

Genesee, F. (1994). Integrating Language and Content: Lessons From Immersion. *Educational Practice Report: 11*. Santa Cruz, CA: The National Center for Research on Cultural Diversity and Second Language Learning.

Gordon, J.M. *The Multidimensional Learning Web*. Des Plaines, IL: The Illinois Resource Center.

Kucer, S.B., Silva, C. & Delgado-Larocco, E.L. (1995). *Curricular Conversations: Themes in Multilingual and Monolingual Classrooms* York, ME: Stenhouse Publishers.

Lee, O., Fradd, S.H. & Sutman, F.X. (1995). Science Knowledge and Cognitive Strategy Use Among Culturally and Linguistically Diverse Students. *Journal of Research in Science Teaching*, 32 (8), 797–816.

Lorenz, E.B. & Met, M. (1991). *Teaching Social Studies in the Immersion Classroom*. Rockville, MD: Board of Education of Montgomery County.

Moll, L. & Diaz, S. (1992). Funds of Knowledge for Teaching: Using a Qualitative Approach to Connect Homes and Classrooms. *Theory into Practice*, 31 (2), 132–141.

National Assessment and Dissemination Center, (1980). *The Initial Screening and Diagnostic Assessment of Students of Limited English Proficiency*. Los Angeles, CA: National Assessment and Dissemination Center.

National Commission on Teaching and America's Future, (1996). *What Matters Most: Teaching for America's Future*. (Online) Available: www.tc.columbia.edu/~teachcomm/fact2.htm.

O'Malley, J.M. & and Chamot, A.U. (1990). *Learning Strategies in Second Language Acquisition*. Cambridge, England: Cambridge University Press.

Oxford, R. (1990). *Language Learning Strategies: What Every Teacher Should Know*. New York: Newbury House.

Porter, A.C., & and Brophy, J. (1988). Synthesis of Research on Good Teaching: Insights from the Work of the Institute for Research on Teaching. *Educational Leadership*, 45 (8), 74–85.

Short, D. J. (1989, September). Adapting Materials for Content-Based Language Instruction. *ERIC/CLL News Bulletin, 13* (1), p. 1, 4–8.

Shulman, L.S. (1987). Knowledge and Teaching: Foundations of the New Reform. *Harvard Educational Review*, 57 (1), 1–22.

Snow, M.A., Met, M. & Genesee, F. (1989) A Conceptual Framework for the Integration of Language and Content in Second/Foreign Language Instruction. *TESOL Quarterly,* 23, 201–217.

Solomon, J. & Rhodes, N. (1996, Summer). Assessing Academic Language: Results of a Survey. *TESOL Journal,* 5 (4), 5–8.

Spaulding, S. (1956). A Spanish Readability Formula. *Modern Language Journal.* 40, 433–441.

Teachers of English to Speakers of Other Languages. (1997). *ESL Standards for Pre-K–12 Students.* Alexandria, VA: Author.

Vari-Cartier, P. (1981). Development and Validation of a New Instrument to Assess Readability of Spanish Prose. *Modern Language Journal.* 65 (2), 141–142.

 **7** ASSESSMENT

In this chapter, we discuss how assessment in EE classrooms can assist teachers to plan and deliver instruction that promotes student learning. Assessment is very broad in scope and we cannot discuss everything that teachers need to know about it. We provide a list of additional readings at the end of the chapter that compliment our discussion. The material in this chapter, like the additional readings we recommend, is not technical; it does not require specialized competence in statistics or psychometrics. Our focus is on classroom teachers and practical ways in which they can design assessment to guide instruction and improve learning. We do not consider assessment that is the primary responsibility of people outside the classroom—for example, testing conducted by district officials to place students in particular programs or by educational specialists who assess students with special needs.

Getting Started: Identifying Your Goals

Assessment in EE classrooms, as in all classrooms, can serve a variety of goals (see Table 7.1). It is important to start by carefully identifying your goals for assessment so that you can choose the most appropriate assessment activities for accomplishing your goals. In the section that follows, we discuss assessment goals one at a time. But, it is important to understand that an assessment activity can have more than one goal—for example, to demonstrate student accomplishments and to engage students in self-assessment. Certain assessment activities lend themselves to multiple goals better than others so it is important to have a repertoire of assessment activities that you can draw on.

A common and important goal of assessment is *to demonstrate to others that students are learning as expected*. This is more generally referred to as *accountability*. Teachers are accountable to parents about the progress their children are making in school and to administrators and other educators about EE students' achievement with respect to school or district standards or objectives. EE teachers are responsible for developing their students' skills and knowledge to the same high levels of achievement that are expected of all students. Assessment of student achievement is critical for demonstrating that this is, in fact, occurring. While accountability is important in all educational programs, it is especially important in EE programs because they are often viewed as special or out of the ordinary. Accountability on an ongoing basis is necessary to demonstrate to parents, other educators, and the community at large that student progress is on target.

Another very important goal of assessment is *to monitor student progress in order to plan appropriate instruction*. Effective teachers monitor student performance continuously even while they are teaching so that they can tailor their instruction on-line to promote student learning. Of course, teachers also conduct assessment at the end of major instructional units in order to plan follow-up instruction that will extend learning further. Effective teachers assess what incoming students know and can do at the

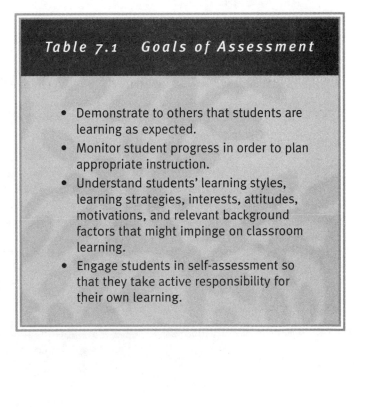

Table 7.1 Goals of Assessment

- Demonstrate to others that students are learning as expected.
- Monitor student progress in order to plan appropriate instruction.
- Understand students' learning styles, learning strategies, interests, attitudes, motivations, and relevant background factors that might impinge on classroom learning.
- Engage students in self-assessment so that they take active responsibility for their own learning.

How Is a Program Success Evaluated?

Mary Cazabon
Director of Bilingual Education
Cambridge Public Schools
Cambridge, Massachusetts

Having been involved in all programmatic aspects of bilingual education for the past 20 years, I have learned that collaboration and collective problem-solving with key school personnel are the only ways to ensure that all students are challenged to attain high standards. We have applied this philosophy to program development as well as evaluation. In Cambridge, we have taken program evaluation very seriously since the inception of *Amigos*, a Spanish/English (50/50) two-way program implemented during the 1986–87 school year. We have had the counsel of Dr. Wallace E. Lambert who has served as program evaluator since 1986 and has added a very important component of program evaluation, namely, field-initiated research projects that have yielded valuable information about our program. The three major goals of the *Amigos* program are:

1. students' high level academic and language development in English and in Spanish.
2. students' cultivation of cross-cultural friendships and increased knowledge about their own cultural distinctiveness.
3. involvement of parents in their children's education.

We have consistently found that students in the *Amigos* program are moving towards a state of balanced bilingualism in their oral language and academic development. Students also appear to be moving towards biculturality as well. Instruction in Spanish has not set them back in terms of their English academic attainment. We have also found an increase in parental involvement at the school level. (For a more complete report on the *Amigos* program evaluation, see Cazabon, Nicoladis & Lambert, 1998.) (see Table 9.1)

From my experience, I've developed some personal rules of thumb for program evaluation. First, it is critical to engage everyone in the discussion: parents, business community, staff, administration, school committee members, and university-based researchers. A steering committee of individuals involved in the program will emerge from the larger group representing this broad-based constituency. The steering committee's first duty will be to define program goals and how the goals can be measured. The outside evaluator is essential in setting up control groups for comparison purposes. We have felt that in order to do a comprehensive evaluation of the program, we need to gather information about various aspects of the school and from a variety of sources of information. Our evaluation is based on information obtained from standardized tests, writing samples, informal assessments, oral language interviews, attitudinal surveys, sociograms, parent questionnaires, classroom observations and videos, students' perceived competencies, and student interviews.

Once the evaluation plan is set, remember that the program and the evaluation design are evolving. We must be realistic and accept that the results of the evaluation might tell us what we do not necessarily want to hear. The process allows for tweaking and perfecting, so do not expect it to be easy. However, over time, longitudinal data will emerge that will enable important comparisons to be made about the attainment of program goals. Accept change as a natural consequence of the results of research and evaluation. Although we must discuss results honestly with colleagues, parents and community, we must do it in a non-adversarial way. Our findings will guide teaching and learning. The dissemination of program evaluation information must reach all those who have been involved in the process. Focus group discussions, school committee presentations, staff meetings, and comprehensible written information and Web site access are some of the ways to reach as many people as possible.

beginning of the school year, before instruction begins, so that they can take account of students' starting-level skills and knowledge when planning instruction for the coming year. Assessment at the end of the school year that is shared with teachers who will work with students so that they can plan appropriate instruction the following year is also important. To insure that there is adequate time for important assessment activities and for using assessment results to plan further instruction, it is essential that there be systematic planning. Without adequate planning, teachers run the risk of not using the results of their assessments to modify their instruction to ensure that it promotes student learning.

The goals of assessment we have discussed so far have focused on collecting and using information about student achievement in academic and language domains, both first and second. Another important goal of assessment that goes beyond collecting information about student achievement is *to understand students' learning styles and strategies, their interests, attitudes, motivation, and other relevant background factors, past or current, that might impinge on classroom learning.* You can be most effective if you understand your students as individual learners. While this is true for all classroom teachers, it is especially true for EE teachers working with students in developmental bilingual and two-way immersion programs since students in these programs often have widely diversified cultural and linguistic backgrounds that are associated with different learning styles, work habits, preferred interactional patterns, and response styles. Teachers who understand their students can be more effective. Collecting information about these aspects of your students is an integral part of assessment.

You might ask "How can this be assessment if we are not assessing student achievement?" We consider it part of assessment because we have a broad definition—we think of assessment as *a process of collecting information that assists in decision-making that promotes learning.* Using this definition, collecting information about student characteristics and their backgrounds is clearly an important component of assessment since such information supports effective instruction. In a related vein, we have talked about the importance of student-centered instruction—*collecting information about individual students as part of a comprehensive assessment plan is essential for individualizing instruction.*

Yet another goal of assessment that fits our broad definition is *to engage students in self-assessment so that they can take active responsibility for their own learning.* Traditional approaches to assessment treat students as objects of assessment, giving them no active role in assessing their own progress and accomplishments. In contrast, contemporary approaches treat *students as active agents* in assessing their own learning. Students who are active partners with teachers in assessment are more likely to take responsibility for and ownership of their own learning, to take pride in their accomplishments, and, as a result, to optimize their efforts. Actively involving students in self-assessment provides opportunities to inform students about instructional objectives and the criteria you use to determine success so they are aware of your objectives and the ways in which you assess achievement of those objectives; as a result, they can be more effective in directing their energies and time toward accomplishing those objectives.

Student self-assessment in the language domain can be particularly useful since it has the advantage of extending assessment beyond the classroom. Language minority students, for example, who are learning English as a second language need to use English outside the classroom. If they are familiar with self-assessment methods, they can provide valuable information about their out-of-school language needs and abilities to their teachers who can then plan instruction in the classroom that meets those needs. Or, language majority students in dual language immersion programs can monitor their ability to use their second language for social purposes, for example, when they are interacting with their peers who are native-speakers of the language, and report this information to their teacher who can then tailor instruction to meet their needs in these situations. Engaging students in assessment of one another's language skills—*peer-assessment,* can also serve many of the same goals.

Designing Effective Assessment
Effective assessment is:
- linked to instructional objectives and methods.
- designed to optimize student performance.
- developmentally-appropriate.
- based on performance criteria that are clearly defined and communicated to students.
- authentic.
- ongoing.
- planned.

Effective assessment in EE classrooms, like all classrooms, is closely *linked to instructional objectives and activities.* When this is done, assessment results can be interpreted with respect to targeted objectives and instructional plans

Voices from the Field

Assessment and Professional and Program Development

Dilsia Rivera-Martinez
Assistant Principal
The Edgar Allen Poe Literacy Development School
Bronx, NY

The Edgar Allan Poe Literacy Development School is in its first year of a two-year redesign plan. The main curricular focus of the school is literacy and critical thinking through five heterogeneously grouped literacy mini-schools, one of which is a Dual Language Literacy Program. As part of our redesign, we have adopted a balanced literacy program with an emphasis on the use of authentic literature and the inquiry approach to learning in order to meet the rigorous state standards. In doing so, the literacy program has been transformed from a skills and rote learning approach to one that encourages reading, writing, and problem solving through meaningful, interactive, thematically-driven experiences that support literacy development.

Our approach to literacy learning has demanded changes in the way we assess our students, including our dual language students. This year 100% of our teaching staff participated in staff development that focused on the use of authentic assessment to guide instruction. Across all schools, the Developmental Reading Assessment (DRA), published by Celebration Press Inc., and New York City's E-CLAS (Early Childhood Literacy Assessment System) serve as the frameworks for assessment. These tools for assessing English provide continuity of assessment from class to class, grade to grade, and school to school and fundamentally help guide instruction in a systematic and reflective way. The combination of sub-tests, such as the alphabet/ sound recognition, word lists (basic or advanced), as well as phonemic awareness sub-tests, provide our teachers with a foundation for assessing literacy skills.

Both assessment systems employ authentic literature books as benchmarks to determine student proficiency levels as well as provide insight about comprehension. Specifically, the running record and a combination of closed and open-ended questions provide the teacher with a realistic snapshot of the reading strategies employed by the students. The writing component allows teachers to see progress and plan instruction based on where individual students are functioning.

Additionally, our district provided our bilingual teachers with a week-long, intensive institute that clarified questions regarding authentic assessment for second language learners. A Spanish Language Assessment tool was developed locally to help the bilingual teachers assess literacy skills in Spanish—thus supporting the teachers' understanding of literacy development in that language.

Our school population is composed of over 60% second language learners and an additional 15–20% who may have been second language learners in the past. Therefore, assessing the needs of linguistically and culturally diverse learners is critical in our school. In addition to the English assessment required, Spanish language and literacy skills are also assessed. *"El instrumento de observacion"* (or *"El IDO"* as it is commonly referred to) allows the bilingual teachers to observe the students in Spanish (Escamilla, Andrade, Basurto, & Ruiz, 1996). Similar to the DRA and E-CLAS mentioned before, it facilitates the systematic collection of data and provides a baseline of the student's knowledge and use of the language. The instrument enables the teacher to determine Spanish language proficiency and tailor instruction according to students' individual needs. Our teachers are also encouraged to informally gather information from the home. Interviews with parents and students help the teacher elicit information about the student's prior experiences that are related to literacy in both languages.

can be modified to include follow-up activities that are tailored to students' developing abilities and needs. Instructional objectives are those specific skills, knowledge, or strategies you want students to acquire as a result of direct instruction (for example, writing a science report) or from classroom activities that provide students opportunities to learn by induction (for example, students engage in cooperative activities so that they acquire interpersonal communication skills). In any case, assessment is most effective when it is based on clearly articulated learning objectives. (Because standardized tests are not based on classroom-based learning objectives, they are generally not useful for assessing the effectiveness of instruction.) It is critically important that these objectives and the criteria for assessing their attainment be communicated clearly to students so they know what is required to succeed.

To be useful for instructional planning, assessment must also reflect the instructional methods or activities you have used in class to promote acquisition of your objectives. In other words, you should not assess student achievement using activities that are unfamiliar. At the same time, a characteristic of advanced levels of language proficiency is the ability to use language in situations that are somewhat novel although related to situations where language learning has occurred. Thus, assessment of language proficiency among students in the upper grades of EE programs need not be restricted to situations that are exactly the same as those they have encountered in class. However, there should always be some relationship between the learning situation and the assessment situation.

Effective assessment *optimizes student performance* so that you get evidence of the upper limits of learning. Performance is optimized when (a) students are mentally and physically prepared for the assessment activity, (b) your rapport with the students during assessment is supportive and your communication is clear and precise, and, of course, (c) assessment tasks are familiar, of appropriate difficulty, interesting, and culturally appropriate. When you optimize student performance, you get an accurate view of what students have learned and can do. Accuracy of assessment is particularly important when it comes to making so-called *high stakes decisions*. High stakes decisions are those decisions that have a significant and possibly long term impact on students—decisions about passing or failing, promotion to the next level, or placement in specific or special programs.

Effective assessment is *developmentally appropriate*. It sets cognitive, academic, and social demands that correspond to students' ages and grade levels, and it is based on activities that are interesting and meaningful to them. In the case of students being assessed in a second language, it is also culturally appropriate and does not make expectations or demand knowledge that are unreasonable, offensive, or beyond their experience. We discuss cultural factors in assessment in a later section (see also Table 7.3).

If assessment is to provide meaningful and useful feedback to teachers and students alike, it should be based on *performance criteria that are associated with successful performance that are clearly defined and communicated to students*. With clear performance criteria, teachers can design appropriate assessment and they can interpret assessment results in meaningful ways that lead to useful follow-up instruction. Likewise, students are better able to interpret their performance following assessment and to focus their attention in constructive ways if assessment criteria have been communicated clearly to them.

Effective assessment activities are *authentic*—they reflect good instructional practices and the kinds of skills and knowledge that students are expected to have in every day situations, in school and outside school. For example, students need specialized language skills in their science or mathematics classes. Systematically assessing students' proficiency in these skills is an example of authentic assessment (see Glossary) that permits EE teachers to identify language skills that students need. Authentic assessment also occurs when teachers in two-way immersion programs assess their English proficient students' use of the second language in informal settings with native speakers of the target language. Focusing on the English-proficient students' social language skills allows you to determine if they have acquired the interpersonal, social language skills they are called upon to use in the schoolyard or in other social settings. Results from your assessments that they have not learned these skills direct you to teach them. In a related vein, EE teachers are ever mindful of their students' future language needs so that they can create opportunities where those needs can be fulfilled before they become obstacles to learning.

Effective assessment is also *ongoing*:

- it occurs at the beginning of each school year, before instruction begins, in order to identify students' skills and academic knowledge as a basis for planning instruction for the year.

- it is part of day-to-day instruction so that teachers can modify instructional plans to work more effectively.

- it occurs at critical points during the year so that teachers can take stock of students' cumulative learning.

- it occurs at the end of the year and is shared with next year's teachers so that they can make use of it for planning their instruction.

General speaking, day-to-day assessment is relatively infor-mal and unobtrusive and is fully integrated with classroom activities so that teachers can monitor student performance without taking valuable time away from instruction. Assessment information at these times might be recorded using narrative or anecdotal records or a journal. Since these records are not going to be shared with others, they do not have to be as systematic as a report card. They are, nev-ertheless, very useful as a reminder to you of important observations about teaching and learning that you can refer to later. Assessment at the end of instructional units is more formal and systematic since it is often shared with parents and is used to make decisions about student advancement. Thus, it should be recorded in a systematic way that can be shared with others.

Assessment is *planned* along with instruction so that ample time is provided to design and conduct appropriate assessment and so that the results of assessment are used to plan follow-up instructional activities, as needed. Indeed, a number of activities, such as dialogue journals (see Glossary) and conferencing, have instructional value and, thus, can serve instructional as well as assessment goals at the same time. Assessment that is an after-thought is not likely to be carefully constructed and even less likely to lead to appropriate follow-up instruction.

Is assessment in EE classrooms different from assessment in other classrooms?

Assessment in EE classrooms is the same as assessment in all classrooms in some fundamentally important ways—it serves the same basic goals discussed earlier and it has the same essential qualities we have already discussed. There are a number of ways in which assessment in EE classrooms dif-fers. We have listed these differences in Table 7.2. Most of these differences are associated with the assessment of lan-guage proficiency. First of all, EE teachers must be able to distinguish between students' language proficiency and their competence in the subject matter being taught, at least during the early stages of second language acquisition. Native English-speaking students who are educated through the medium of English already have considerable profi-ciency in the language of instruction when they begin school, although even these students continue to develop their language skills for academic purposes in school. These students generally have sufficient proficiency in English to express what they are learning in their school subjects. In contrast, students who are learning through the medium of a second language, whether they are from language minor-ity or language majority backgrounds, initially lack even rudimentary language skills. As a result, they can be chal-lenged to express through language what they are learning in the content areas. This means that you must be able to

assess your students' academic achievement during the ini-tial stages of learning using methods that require only basic skills in the target language. We give examples of such tech-niques in a later section.

As students progress in EE programs, they become more proficient in language. In particular, they acquire spe-cialized language that is associated with specific academic subjects, such as science. When teaching advanced level EE students, it is important that you assess their proficiency in such specialized language skills in order to determine if they are acquiring the academic language skills that are a critical aspect of those subjects. While this would be inappropriate in the beginning stages, it is entirely appropriate in later stages of learning. In a related vein, you must also be able to assess your students' academic language skills *before* they need them so that you can identify which specific skills they are currently lacking and then plan activities that promote acquisition of those skills.

Second, whereas other teachers can assume that their students have already acquired or will acquire, without instruction, the social language skills they need to interact with other students and adults in and outside school, this is not necessarily the case for students learning through the medium of a second language. English language learners and English proficient students in two-way immersion pro-grams, for example, may lack even basic level social skills in their second language and, thus, they may have difficulty interacting with students from the other language group. Teachers in EE programs must monitor their students' pro-ficiency in the social uses of their second languages in order to identify those aspects of social discourse where students

---

Table 7.2   Distinctive Features of Assessment in EE Classrooms

1. EE assessment must distinguish between students' language proficiency and their academic achievement.
2. EE assessment must monitor students' proficiency in language for both academic and social purposes.
3. EE assessment must assess students' socio-cultural competence with respect to language use and social interaction in the target language.
4. EE assessment must be culturally appropriate.

need systematic instruction. Thus, in addition to monitoring and planning for their students' acquisition of academic language skills, EE teachers must also monitor their students' language skills in social situations so that they can plan for development in this domain of language use. Teachers in mainstream programs working with English proficient students need be much less concerned about these aspects of language assessment.

Third, whereas students who are educated through their primary language learn the socio-cultural norms associated with social interaction and language use, this is often not the case for students who are educated through the medium of a second language. A simple example is English proficient students in Spanish immersion programs. These students are usually unfamiliar with appropriate use of formal and familiar forms of address ("*Tu*" and "*usted*") since this distinction does not exist in English. English language learners in developmental bilingual programs may not know how and when to respond to English-speaking adults in school settings because they have had no or limited contact with English-speaking adults at home or in the community. You must be able to assess your students' socio-cultural competence with respect to language use and social interaction so that you can identify gaps in their socio-cultural competence and provide opportunities for learning relevant norms and customs.

A fourth aspect of assessment in EE classes that is different from many, although not all, other classrooms is that it be culturally appropriate. To the extent that students from diverse language and cultural backgrounds attend regular programs in urban schools, effective teachers in mainstream classrooms also need to know how to take account of cultural differences among students when planning and interpreting assessment. Assessment in EE classrooms should take into account the response styles and interactional patterns that students are most comfortable and familiar with in their own cultures. For example, students from some cultural groups are not accustomed to public, individual displays of what they have learned; instead, they prefer to respond in whole or small group formats along with their classmates. This may be particularly true for new students from minority backgrounds. In such cases, you might want to assess your students' academic knowledge or language skills using a small group format instead of individual testing. Table 7.3 summarizes some variables to think about when designing assessment for culturally diverse students. Research has shown that students from different cultural groups react differently to these aspects of assessment. Therefore, you should adapt your assessment methods to be suitable for students from different cultural backgrounds, particularly if assessment is done in their primary language. At the same time, it is important that students from cultural

Table 7.3 Cultural Variables in Assessment

- *Wait time:* Second language learners and students from some cultural groups require longer wait times than native-English speaking students from majority group backgrounds.

- *Individual or group response:* Students from some cultural backgrounds prefer to respond to teachers' questions or calls for displays of knowledge as part of the entire group; they are reluctant to give individual responses because they think it is inappropriate. Some students also prefer to work with their fellow students to formulate a response to a teacher's questions. This is frowned on by Anglo-American culture but is highly valued and preferred by many other cultural groups.

- *Feedback:* Whereas students from the majority English-speaking group like to receive individual and public praise from the teacher, students from some groups are deeply embarrassed by such praise; they do not expect public or explicit praise from the teacher.

- *Eye contact:* In contrast to students from the dominant Anglo-American culture who are taught to look directly at adults when being spoken to, children from many cultures are taught that direct eye contact with adults is inappropriate and is a sign of impertinence.

- *Guessing:* Some students will not give the answer to a question unless they are certain that they are accurate; language majority students are generally comfortable with guessing.

- *Question and answer format:* Be sure your students understand and have had prior experience with the question and/or answer format you are using. For example, do they understand what to do with multiple-choice questions that are presented with blank bubbles?

- *Volunteering:* Students from many cultural groups are very uncomfortable showing what they know by volunteering a response or initiating interaction with the teacher—such behavior is seen to be bragging and showing off. Chorale or group responding can be used to circumvent this cultural preference.

minority backgrounds become familiar and comfortable with response patterns that are associated with assessment in English. However, since an important goal of EE programs is bicultural sensitivity, you should teach language majority students to understand and be sensitive to these differences as well. In particular, it is important that language majority students in immersion and dual language programs learn the cultural norms that are relevant to assessment situations when their second language is being used. You can use assessment to illustrate important cultural differences to your students. Clearly, EE teachers need to know a variety of assessment methods and how to use them creatively to meet the diverse and changing assessment needs of their students.

What levels of achievement should be expected of EE students?

It is critical to establish achievement expectations for EE students to serve as benchmarks against which student learning is assessed and performance is interpreted. Of course, achievement expectations also provide the basis for curriculum and instructional planning and delivery. To establish expectations for learning, you should consider not only the level of competence or proficiency you expect of students but also the specific skills or knowledge you expect students to master at each grade level. The latter are sometimes referred to as *content standards* and the former as *performance standards*.

Generally speaking, the content standards, or expected learning outcomes for students, in EE programs should be the same as those for other students. Teachers can draw on at least three sources for identifying the specific skills and knowledge that can be expected of EE students. These are:

1. school, district, and regional curriculum documents.

2. district, state, and national content standards.

3. teachers' professional judgement of normal, age-appropriate learning based on their cumulative classroom experiences—less experienced teachers can confer with more experienced teachers if they lack confidence in their own judgements.

At the same time, teachers working in EE classrooms need to identify the social and cultural skills that characterize language use in the communities where the second language is used so that they can include these in their learning objectives along with related language and academic skills.

With respect to performance standards, or levels of expected proficiency, extensive research shows clearly that, over time, students in EE programs can and do attain the same levels of achievement in English and academic

domains (mathematics, science, social studies) as students in high quality English-medium classrooms (see Genesee, 1987; Lindholm, 1992; Christian, Montone, Lindholm & Carranza, 1997, for reviews of relevant research). In other words, there is no reason to expect or accept lower levels of English language development and academic achievement from EE students in comparison to comparable students in high-quality English-medium classrooms. At the same time, English-speaking students in EE programs can be expected to acquire advanced levels of functional proficiency in all aspects of the second language, and non-English-speaking students in EE programs can be expected to attain native-like and age-appropriate levels of development in all aspects of their primary language, provided they continue in the program to the end of elementary school. The attainment of grade-appropriate levels of achievement in English may be delayed in English-speaking and non-English-speaking EE students if they are initially taught reading and writing through the medium of another language. Generally, however, they demonstrate English language skills that are comparable to those of students educated entirely through English by grades 5 and 6, if they started the program in kindergarten or grade 1. As noted in Chapter 2, the beneficial outcomes of EE are cumulative and, therefore, native-like proficiency in English may not be achieved until students receive formal English language arts instruction. These high-level expectations should be reflected in formal statements of learning objectives as well as in teachers' instructional plans. Content and performance standards are important because they serve as benchmarks for planning instruction—in effective programs, there is a developmentally appropriate and coherent curriculum that articulates content and performance standards across grade levels. Content and performance standards are also critical in planning and interpreting assessment results—appropriate assessment reflects standards and the interpretation of assessment results is based on well articulated standards.

What are useful methods of language assessment?

In this section, we focus on *language* assessment since this is the feature of EE programs that sets them apart from other educational programs. However, most of the following suggestions also apply to the assessment of academic achievement. Earlier, we noted seven qualities of effective assessment. Four of these are important when identifying useful assessment activities, whether the focus is on language or academic achievement. The most useful assessment activities (1) are linked to instructional activities and objectives, (2) are authentic, (3) optimize student performance, and (4) are developmentally appropriate.

The place to start when identifying useful ways of assessing EE students' language proficiency is to carefully examine your instructional objective(s) that identify the skills you want students to acquire and the classroom activities that you use to promote acquisition of those skills. For example, imagine that you have been working on a unit to develop third grade students' literacy skills. Your primary objective is that students understand the main features of narrative text—notions about principal and supporting characters, plot, unresolved conflicts or problems as the core of plot development, resolution of the conflict, and lessons or morals of the story. An appropriate assessment activity could be to have students read a story and then ask them to identify or describe each of the features listed above in the stories they have read. If you had incorporated writing as an objective in this unit, you could assess the students' writing skills by asking them to write out their responses and read them to their classmates.

This is a useful assessment activity because it gets at reading skills the students are likely to encounter in their English language arts class or during leisure reading—these are authentic and developmentally appropriate skills. To ensure that it optimizes student performance, you would want to make sure that: students have sufficient time to read and re-read the text and sufficient time to think about and write their responses if writing is part of your objective. At this point, you have devised a way of soliciting a sample of the students' reading (and writing) performance. You still need to devise a way of evaluating their performance. There is a difference between soliciting language (or academic) performance and assessing it. You have a number of options open to you.

1. *Grades*. Grades are generally assigned according to the overall quality of student performance. When it comes to assessing language, we are generally concerned with the quality of students' language use. When it comes to assessing academic achievement in non-language domains, such as science, history, or social studies, we are also concerned with the accuracy or completeness of students' knowledge. For example, a student's written answer in response to a question about the life cycle of the butterfly could be graded high because the factual information given by the student is complete and accurate, whether or not the student used correct grammar, spelling, and punctuation to present the information. In contrast, a student's description of the life cycle of the butterfly could be linguistically correct, whether or not the factual information provided is accurate and complete. Teachers grade the quality of students' language performance and academic achievement all the time using internalized standards or norms they have developed over time. To be valid and useful indicators of performance, grades should reflect teachers' instructional objectives.

2. *Checklists*. Checklists are used to indicate whether student performance exhibits, or does not exhibit, certain features. For example, to assess students' ability to use the narrative form in writing, a checklist could be devised to indicate whether students' written stories include information or references to the setting of the story, the principle and supporting characters in the story, the situation that defines the relationship between the principle and secondary characters, the resolution of the conflict or problem that characterizes their relationship, etc. A checklist devised to assess a student's understanding of the life cycle of the butterfly would indicate whether the student had identified the main phases of its life cycle, whether main facts were presented accurately, and whether secondary facts were presented accurately. In this latter example, the checklist identifies what knowledge the student has acquired about a topic in science whereas the former example identifies what understanding the student has acquired about a genre of language use. Table 7.4 is a sample checklist that could be used with the example of the students who are learning about the main components of narratives. Checklists are not useful for assessing variations in the quality of students' language use or performance. This would call for rubrics (or rating scales).

Table 7.4   Sample Checklist for Assessing Students' Understanding of Narrative Texts

Place a check mark beside each of the features identified correctly by the student:

- ❑ *setting*
- ❑ *principal character*
- ❑ *secondary character(s)*
- ❑ *conflict/problem*
- ❑ *resolution*
- ❑ *moral/lesson*

COMMENTS:

3. *Rubrics (or rating scales):* Rubrics or rating scales are useful for describing variations in the quality of student performance along specific dimensions. Rubrics consist of descriptors that refer to specific aspects of performance. They can focus on the linguistic quality of students' performance or on the appropriateness or accuracy of the content of their answers. Rubrics that refer to the quality of language use can focus on discrete aspects of language use, such as organization, sentence formation, style, or mechanics; or on the overall quality of performance. The former is called an *analytic scale* and the latter a *holistic scale.* Table 7.5 is an example of an analytic scale for assessing writing skills. Analytic scales can be especially useful for planning instruction because they provide feedback about specific aspects of performance. Holistic scales usually lead to the assignment of single grades, as described earlier.

Let's take an example to illustrate the use of the rubric in Table 7.5. Imagine that you want to assess your fifth grade students' understanding that historical perspectives are relative and differ depending on whose point of view is taken. The students have just finished a history unit on early European settlement in the New World. They have read a chapter in their history book about John Smith's voyage to America and the settlement at Jamestown. They have also recently finished a unit in their language arts class in which they had to compare and contrast the points of view of two authors who had written about the immigrant experience in America. To assess their ability to take different perspectives, you ask each student to take the role of American Indians who were living in the area of Jamestown when John Smith landed, to describe an incident that might result in conflict or different reactions from the Indians in comparison to the colonists, and to describe their different points of view and explain why such differences might be expected. The students are asked to prepare their responses in the form of a written composition.

This is a useful assessment activity because it is linked to the objectives you covered in your history and literature units and the activities the students have previously encountered in class. Although the activity is not identical to what they have encountered, you believe that it is appropriate because these students are at an advanced level of schooling and they should be able to apply what they have learned in their literature class to critical thinking and perspective taking in a social studies context. This is also a good activity because the language, thinking, and performance skills the students are called on to demonstrate resemble skills they might need in their other school subjects and outside school. The task should optimize performance because it is developmentally appropriate and most students will probably find it highly motivating because they probably can relate to it. You decide to assess their compositions using a rubric made up of five components—like that presented in Table 7.5. It will probably be necessary to revise this set of rubrics to better conform to your purposes. Four or five descriptors that characterize different levels of performance accompany each component. The descriptors are presented in descending order of quality with the best performance described at the top. Performance that exceeds grade level (or average) expectations receives a 4 and performance that far exceeds grade level expectations is rated 5. Ratings of 1 and 2 are given to writing that falls short of grade expectations.

This example illustrates assessment based on a single instance. Educators are increasingly realizing the advantages of assessing student achievement using more than one test, one written report, or one oral presentation. Evaluations that are based on single instances of performance may not be reliable indicators of students' real abilities and, thus, they might provide invalid (inaccurate) assessments of what students can do. As an alternative to one-shot assessments, more and more teachers are using portfolios to collect a number of pieces of student work. *A portfolio is a purposeful collection of a student's work that documents their efforts, achievements, and progress over time in given areas of learning, either language or subject matter, or both (see Glossary).* Students can have different kinds of portfolios—portfolios of work in progress, completed work, or best work. With modern technology, it is possible to be creative in devising portfolios:

- Samples of speaking can be recorded on cassette tapes for later playback.
- Conversational skills can be recorded by video/audio-taping students interacting with one another.
- Samples of writing or talking can easily be transcribed using the capabilities of computers.

Portfolios can have a broad focus—samples of work from different areas of the curriculum, or a narrow focus—a portfolio of writing samples only. Portfolios with a narrow focus are desirable for assessment purposes because it is easier to assess work samples of a common sort. By themselves, portfolios are simply collections of student work. To be useful for assessment purposes, the work in the portfolio must be judged or assessed in some way. Rating scales or checklists of the sort we have already described can be used to assess each piece in a portfolio or can be used to assess the entire collec-

Table 7.5   Sample Analytic Rubric for Writing Assessment

Student Name: **Date:**

Class:

Organization:
5. Outstanding—very well organized, excellent use of opening and closing paragraphs, appropriate use of paragraphing, coherent, logical, and well developed arguments/story line
4. Above average—well organized, effective introduction and ending, good paragraphing, coherent
3. Average—includes opening and closing, main ideas/story line clear, good use of paragraphing
2. Below average—weak introduction and ending, somewhat incoherent, weak use of paragraphing
1. Needs work—no obvious organization, disconnected ideas

Sentence structure and variety:
5. Outstanding—effective and sophisticated use of varied sentence types, complex and accurate use of grammar, sentence structure, and variety appropriate for purpose of writing
4. Above average—good variation in sentence types, good use of simple and complex grammar
3. Average—some variation in sentence type, sentence grammar generally accurate and appropriate, use of some complex sentence grammar
2. Below average—mainly simple sentence types, some major errors in sentence grammar
1. Needs work—incomplete sentences, many errors in sentence grammar leading to incoherence

Content and originality:
5. Outstanding—highly original ideas, outstanding details
4. Above average—original ideas and interesting details
3. Average—good ideas, some supporting details
2. Below average—little originality or use of supporting details
1. Needs work—no originality or use of interesting details

Vocabulary:
5. Outstanding—appropriate use of varied, sophisticated, and colorful vocabulary
4. Above average—good use of varied, appropriate vocabulary
3. Average—appropriate use of vocabulary
2. Below average—use of simple, common vocabulary, little variation
1. Needs work—repetitious use of simple vocabulary

Mechanics:
4. Above average—consistent use of correct punctuation, capitalization, spelling
3. Average—generally correct use of punctuation, capitalization, spelling, some minor errors
2. Below average—inconsistent use of correct punctuation, capitalization, spelling
1. Needs work—frequent errors in capitalization, punctuation, spelling

Voices from the Field

Language and Literacy Assessment Rubric

Erminda Garcia
First Grade Teacher
Fairmount Elementary School
San Francisco, CA

The San Francisco Unified School District Language and Literacy Assessment Rubric (LALAR) was created and developed by Erminda Garcia and Jaime Sandoval. It supports teachers in documenting the language learning skills of their students. The rubric provides teachers with language use descriptors that are grouped together in beginning, intermediate, advanced, and fluent levels. It also allows a teacher to document a students first language and transitioning skills into second language levels. This format asks a teacher to document the language use in oral, reading, and writing contexts.

After listening and observing language use by their students, teachers identifying language descriptors on the LALAR, fill in appropriate bubbles and document the current language level of the student. The LALAR then provides the teacher with the next level of language level descriptors which can be used to inform instructional decisions around language learning.

The LALARs of individual students will support teachers in documenting the student's language growth in both languages. The LALAR rubrics of a class can be used to help teachers create specific language lessons for specific language student groups. The monitoring process that the LALAR reflects has become one of the major components of language review decisions.

Throughout the development of the LALAR, Language Art Standards and ELD standards for the district were consulted for both type and level of language descriptor. Within the LALAR teachers will begin to recognize the articulation and consistency of the LALAR, SFUSD Language Arts, and ELD Standards.

It is important to understand that the collection of artifacts, anecdotals, checklists, etc. are used to document language learning on the LALAR. These then become purposeful collections of language learning. Every year these portfolio collections place the LALAR as the centerpiece that gathers the instructional information shared from teacher to teacher.

(Note: See p. 151)

tion of work in a portfolio. If students are actively involved in assessing their own work using any of these techniques, portfolios become useful forms of student self-assessment. In fact, portfolios are particularly useful when they are managed and reviewed jointly by teachers and students.

Portfolio *conferences* (see Glossary) are another useful way for teachers and students to work together to assess the contents of portfolios. Portfolio conferences are semi-structured conversations between students and teachers about work in the students' portfolios—for example, a student describes to the teacher why a piece of work has been included, what its strengths and weaknesses are, how two pieces of work differ or show progress, how a piece of work could be improved, how the teacher could help the student make improvements, or any other issues that either partici-

pant feels is important. Table 7.6 suggests some other questions that teachers might use during a portfolio conference. In addition to providing useful assessment information and opportunities for student self-assessment, portfolios provide opportunities for students to practice their language skills in a one-on-one situation with their teacher about schoolwork. Portfolio conferences also give students the chance to develop meta-communication skills. These are skills that allow students to talk about their own communication skills and difficulties. If passed on to the students' next year teachers, portfolios also provide invaluable documentation of students' developing proficiencies to teachers in higher grades for instructional planning. They can also be shared with parents who might otherwise not know how well their children are progressing.

Language and Literacy Assessment Rubric, K–12

SFUSD LANGUAGE ACADEMY and other language programs

ORAL LANGUAGE
Upon completing this level, the student:

FLUENT L1 / TRANS. L2
- 23. **Engages/interacts effectively/productively in discussion.**
- 22. **Produces a full range of grade-appropriate grammatical structures/vocabulary in unfamiliar settings.**
- 21. Discusses abstract, academic content/concepts.
- 20. Understands/uses native-speaker cultural references.

ADVANCED
- 19. **Communicates ideas/information orally with increasing confidence/sophistication of audiences/purposes.**
- 18. Contributes to classroom discussions/responds to questions clearly/debates issues.
- 17. Uses age-appropriate vocabulary.
- 16. Demonstrates understanding of idiomatic expressions & colloquialisms in different registers.
- 15. **Communicates in new/unfamiliar settings.**
- 14. Critiques a movie/book orally.

INTERMEDIATE
- 13. **Speaks comfortably with peers/in small groups.**
- 12. Expresses responses in phrases/simple sentences.
- 11. Speaks in class on topic; may lack organization.
- 10. Identifies main topic/details of stories/lectures; retells sequence of events.
- 9. Asks for clarifications in different situations.
- 8. Expresses a range of personal needs/preferences.
- 7. Uses a variety of verbal/non-verbal strategies.

BEGINNING
- 6. **Begins to speak to peers/in some small group situations.**
- 5. Makes oral recitations/simple presentations.
- 4. **Responds appropriately/thoughtfully/actively to simple commands/questions, through actions or one/two-word phrases.**
- 3. Names principal locations/familiar objects.
- 2. Gives basic personal information; expresses personal/safety needs.
- 1. Dramatizes/gestures/draws pictures to show comprehension/needs.

COMMENTS

READING
Upon completing this level, the student:

FLUENT L1 / TRANS. L2
- 24. **Reads/comprehends grade-level text with complex language/vocabulary.**
- 23. **Reads independently from a wide range of materials while evaluating/analyzing text.**
- 22. Uses variety of reading strategies to construct/examine/extend the meaning of diverse materials.
- 21. Actively pursues own reading interests.
- 20. Makes predictions/inferences about readings on all topics including abstract ones.

ADVANCED
- 19. Reads with considerable fluency & comprehension; begins to comprehend highly decontextualized text/complex vocabulary.
- 18. Reads independently; chooses increasingly difficult texts; makes predictions/inferences about readings.
- 17. Expands vocabulary using (translation) dictionary/thesaurus.
- 16. Interacts with text by keeping a reading response journal.
- 15. **Reads across variety of genres; identifies features of different reading materials (e.g., theme, plot, characters, genre).**

INTERMEDIATE
- 14. **Constructs meaning from texts containing background knowledge relevant to student's experience.**
- 13. Locates/identifies specific facts in a text.
- 12. Chooses appropriate pleasure reading materials independently.
- 11. Uses dictionaries to define words (e.g., maintain a personal dictionary of important new words).
- 10. Recognizes main topic/supporting details of a reading selection; summarizes the selection.
- 9. Reads/follows simple written directions.
- 8. Responds to text in various modes such as drawing, mapping & diagramming.

BEGINNING
- 7. **Constructs meaning from text through illustrations and other non-print features.**
- 6. Enjoys being read to; demonstrates comprehension/sequencing.
- 5. Reads familiar words & phrases aloud.
- 4. Reads simple narratives of routine behaviors.
- 3. Identifies/associates written symbols; recognizes/identifies letters.
- 2. Demonstrates book sense: tracking/locating cover, author, title/matching pictures to words.
- 1. Follows along in text as story is read aloud.

COMMENTS

WRITING
Upon completing this level, the student:

FLUENT L1 / TRANS. L2
- 24. **Experiments with variety of writing styles/genres, including fact, fiction, persuasion, comparison.**
- 23. Writes expository text that is clear, consistent and organized.
- 22. Identifies a central idea and writes from an organizational plan.
- 21. Uses rich, expressive vocabulary.
- 20. **Writes with a strong understanding of conventions of written language.**
- 19. Uses writing to get and give information.
- 18. Writes on all topics normally required for grade level.

ADVANCED
- 17. **Writes from various points of view; with different purposes/audiences; develops fluency/style/voice.**
- 16. **Creates several connected paragraphs using appropriate conventions of print.**
- 15. Demonstrates variety of vocabulary choice, sentence types, and organization of written discourse.
- 14. Takes accurate notes on new/unfamiliar material.
- 13. **Applies the steps in the writing process to writing tasks.**
- 12. Uses graphics to present/describe data; writes about the data.

INTERMEDIATE
- 11. **Generates ideas for simple stories with awareness of sequence/detail.**
- 10. Creates original paragraphs using appropriate conventions of print.
- 9. Writes short answers to questions.
- 8. Uses variety of genres in writing.
- 7. Participates in revising/editing own work.

BEGINNING
- 6. **Uses some conventions of print including spacing between words, names and letters (e.g., mechanics explicit to language).**
- 5. Writes to describe a drawing or illustration.
- 4. Writes statements/questions on familiar topics/on visual prompt.
- 3. Writes primarily about experiences and retells stories written.
- 2. Copies simple text and or environmental print to communicate.
- 1. Uses invented spelling and familiar words or short phrases.

COMMENTS

TEACHER   STUDENT'S NAME

BOLD RED TYPE: Indicates alignment with SFUSD English/Language Arts Content & Performance Standards

Copyright © 1998. SFUSD Language Academy

Voices from the Field

Assessment in Two-Way Immersion Classrooms

Kathryn J. Lindholm
Professor of Child Development
College of Education, San Jose State University
San Jose, California

For the past 15 years, I have worked at the local, state, and national levels to help promote, implement, and evaluate two-way immersion programs. I have worked in different capacities—as a professor teaching about multicultural and bilingual education; as a consultant to the U.S. Department of Education, the California State Department of Education, and numerous school districts across the U.S. in evaluating and helping implement two-way immersion programs; with school boards, administrators and parents as a researcher in two-way immersion programs; and as a community person and parent in establishing two-way immersion programs in the school district in which I live. These different roles and contexts have provided me with a broad perspective on the importance of assessment and the various audiences to whom issues in assessment must be addressed.

In my roles as professor and evaluator of two-way immersion programs, I hear teachers' frustrations with standardized achievement tests that tend to underestimate the literacy and content knowledge of their students, particularly for language minority and lower socio-economic level ethnic minority students (African American or Hispanic students). At the same time, I hear par-

ents, principals, superintendents, school board members, legislators, and journalists ask the important question: Are students in two-way immersion programs developing the appropriate school-related skills? This question tends to permeate discussions at the state and national levels in this current era of increasing accountability for the education of all students. Added to the dialogue on school accountability in the U.S. is a political climate that is increasingly hostile to bilingual education—where the English-Only movement has made a significant headway.

In this politically charged climate, we must demonstrate that our programs work—not only for the middle class European American students, but for all student participants—language minority, ethnic minority, and low socio-economic-status. And we must demonstrate the two-way immersion program's effectiveness using, in large measure, tests (norm-based standardized achievement tests) that clearly favor middle class native English speakers over other students. How do we best go about balancing the various assessment needs—for accountability, for understanding what our students do know (and not only what they don't know), and for keeping assessment from becoming too resource intensive?

In some school districts I've worked with, teachers and administrators have carefully designed portfolios to provide a part of this balance. Such portfolios include: documentation of students' performance and growth which can be appropriated for any audience; rubrics that help teachers determine whether students are on-target in language development. What is really helpful about portfolios in two-way immersion programs is that school sites can tailor their portfolios to their own particular needs and the assessments can be developed for any language combinations. Some of the literacy portfolios included samples of student work, reading and writing rubrics, a student questionnaire on literacy, teacher ratings of students' oral language proficiency in the two languages, and a parent questionnaire regarding home literacy. We found that the portfolios provided important information that was instructive in understanding the oral language and literacy development of all students, including linguistically and culturally diverse students. Teachers had good samples of work and growth to show parents at parent-teacher conferences, and teachers had reliable evidence for particular problems students might be having.

While the portfolios were exciting and facilitated our understanding of students' development of oral language and literacy, we also found that too much documentation could prove cumbersome. For example, having teachers rate student

(continued)

writing samples four times a year was too time consuming, though twice a year was manageable. Rubrics tended to be easy to use and helped teachers gauge students' literacy development individually and in comparison to other students in the classroom. However, when teachers were not well trained in the rubrics, there were clear reliability problems: 1) Some teachers were much too liberal and others too conservative in their ratings; 2) Expectations for language minority and language majority students affected teacher ratings in ways that favored language majority students. Because people in the U.S. typically do not expect a native English speaker to talk in Spanish, the scores of these students tended to be higher in Spanish than the scores in English of the language minority students, who were expected to learn to speak English. Finally, we found that some teachers collected the portfolio data, but never used it. While it may seem obvious to some how to use portfolio data, training may be needed to assist teachers in using this rich source of information as an assessment tool.

Different assessment approaches are a must in programs which promote bilingualism and biliteracy—particularly if the program participants are diverse in language background, ethnicity, and social class. Regardless of the assessment approaches used, teachers must be trained in how to administer and utilize the assessment data.

When teachers and students collaborate in assessing the work in a portfolio, a number of positive effects can result:

- Student involvement in and ownership of their own learning is enhanced.
- Students take an active and responsible role in monitoring their own progress.
- Students take pride in their work and enjoy their successes.
- Students come to understand what is required to do good work in school.

How can I assess students' beginning language skills?

To answer this question, we distinguish between methods of eliciting language that require (1) closed-ended responses, (2) limited responses, or (3) open-ended responses. In *closed-ended response tasks,* students are provided alternative responses, or answers, and they simply select the one that is most appropriate or right. A common form of closed-ended response task is multiple-choice. For example, a kindergarten teacher who is interested in assessing her students' vocabulary skills might say a list of words *(cookie, horse, sandwich, shirt)* and then ask students to select the word that refers to an animal. Giving students response alternatives to choose from requires only beginning level language skills. Students only have to recognize the correct answers; they do not have to produce them. Because response alternatives are provided by the teacher, this format does not lend itself to assessing student-generated or discourse level skills.

Limited response tasks are like closed-ended formats except they allow students limited response choices; for example, the same kindergarten teacher might ask her stu-

Table 7.6   Teacher Questions to Guide Portfolio Conferences

- Why is this a good piece of work?
- What did you enjoy about doing this piece of work?
- What part of this work was the most difficult to do?
- What did you learn from doing this work?
- How is this work different/better than your earlier work?
- How can you make this work better?
- How can I help you make this work better?

dents to say words that refer to animals or family members, etc. A commonly used reading task with a limited-response format is the cloze test. An example of a written *closed-ended* format is a cloze test with individual words deleted and response alternatives presented after each deletion. If response alternatives are not provided and the student must fill in the missing word, then we have a *limited-response* task. With limited-response tasks, it is possible to elicit language skills that represent somewhat more advanced or complex levels of language production than a closed-ended task. By choosing the context carefully, teachers can focus on specific aspects of language; for example, teachers could assess students' knowledge of adjectives by selectively deleting all adjectives from a reading passage and asking students to fill the gaps with appropriate words. The shortcomings of this format are similar to those of closed-ended formats—they elicit very limited aspects of language production.

Open-ended response tasks, as the name indicates, elicit responses that are not highly specified, although some restriction on how students should respond is always involved in appropriate assessment. Writing an essay or a science report or giving an oral book report are all examples of assessment activities that call for open-ended responses. This response format resembles more closely the kinds of language skills that students are usually called on to use in their every day uses of language in and outside school. Open-ended assessment activities are often particularly suitable for assessing the proficiency of students who have attained relatively advanced levels of proficiency because they call for students to construct and organize responses, not to simply recognize the correct answer. There is clearly no absolute distinction between limited-response and open-ended response tasks; rather, tasks can vary from one extreme to the other.

Generally speaking, closed-ended and limited-response formats are most suitable for assessing students' language skills during the initial stages of acquisition. Closed-ended tasks assess reading and listening comprehension and limited-response tasks assess beginning level speaking and writing skills. There are several techniques that do not require verbal responses which can be used to assess beginning level comprehension skills:

- Students act out responses to questions—for example, students can respond nonverbally to verbal commands to move parts of their bodies or perform certain actions, like sit, stand, or turn around.

- Students can point out answers to questions—for example, to identify objects in the classroom that are different colors, shapes, or sizes or that are useful for standing on to reach high objects, for holding the door open, etc.

- Students can draw answers to questions—for example, "What are the planets in the solar system and what are their positions in the solar system?"

How can mastery of content be assessed when students have limited proficiency in the language of instruction?

There are a number of techniques that you can use that permit students to express what they know in academic subjects even though their proficiency in the second language is limited:

- Students can demonstrate knowledge or understanding of new material by drawing pictures that represent what they have learned. For example, they might draw pictures identifying the members of their family, the westward migration of early American settlers, or the phases of the water cycle.

- Students can demonstrate their understanding of categories, rank order, and other relational knowledge by manipulating objects that vary with respect to certain physical attributes that have been reviewed in a science unit. For example, students are given a set of objects that vary in weight, length, volume, etc., and are asked to cluster, order, or compare them.

- Students act out their knowledge. For example, they might express certain emotions or reactions to evocative verbal cues, or as a group they could represent the relationship of the planets in the solar system.

- Students can demonstrate knowledge by pointing to sets of pictures that go together. For example, foods taken from the oceans versus foods grown in soil; mammals and their habitats; historical events, peoples, and places that go together in some way.

- Teachers may permit students to demonstrate what they have learned using their primary language even though instruction has taken place in the second language. This strategy should be used very cautiously since, if it is overused, it can lead to an over-reliance on the primary language at the expense of second language use and acquisition. It is also important to keep in mind that this strategy does not always optimize student performance since students may not be able to express what they have learned using their primary language if learning has taken place in the second language.

As noted earlier, the longer students are in the program, the more important it becomes to assess their acquisition of content-specific language skills along with the content itself. Methods for doing this are the same as would be used to assess native speakers—they should be authentic, related to instruction, developmentally appropriate, and so on.

Are tests useful for assessment in EE classrooms?

To answer this question, we must first of all define what we mean by "tests." In fact, there is no single characteristic or set of characteristics that defines a test or distinguishes tests from other methods of eliciting performance. An essay, science report, oral presentation, or social studies project can all be tests depending on how they are presented to students, how they are assessed, and how they are used for decision-making. For example, if we accept a definition of a test as a method of eliciting performance from all students in a class in a standard or uniform fashion followed by the assignment of letter or number grades to be used in promotion decisions, then each of the above examples could be administered as a test.

There is one form of testing, however, that most people consider distinct—that is multiple-choice tests. Multiple-choice tests may be devised by classroom teachers or by commercial publishers. When developed by commercial publishers, tests are often standardized and include norms. Teacher-made tests of language or subject matter learning that use multiple-choice answer formats can be useful for assessment in EE classrooms if they are linked in a meaningful way to specific instructional objectives and classroom activities. Because they use a closed-ended response format, they are particularly useful for assessing what students know when their language skills are rudimentary and not sufficiently developed for them to express fully all they have learned. At the same time, closed-ended response formats have limitations—because students only have to recognize and choose a correct or appropriate response from the alternatives that are given, they do not have to actually produce or create a response. This means that when it comes to language assessment, they are limited to examining recognition or comprehension skills. They do not permit teachers to examine students' ability to generate a response. This rules out looking at how well students can organize ideas, speak or write creatively, or use language for interactive purposes. When it comes to assessing subject matter learning, multiple-choice tests do not permit teachers to examine students' breadth of learning or their ability to express what they have learned in creative, constructive ways. To the extent that there are actually few real world occasions that call for a multiple-choice type of response, they also generally lack authenticity. However, there are times when a multiple-choice type of response is authentic, for example, for filling out questionnaires and applications and other standardized forms for membership, etc.

Table 7.7 Resource Books for Classroom-Based Assessment
Brown, J.D. (1996). *Testing in Language Programs*. Upper Saddle River, NJ: Prentice Hall.
Brown, J.D., & Hudson, T. (1998). The Alternatives in Language Assessment. *TESOL Quarterly, 32*: 653–675.
Genesee, F., & Upshur, J. (1996). *Classroom-Based Evaluation in Second Language Education*. New York: Cambridge University Press.
Gonzalez, V., Brusca-Vega, R., & Yawkey, T. (1997). *Assessment and Instruction of Culturally and Linguistically Diverse Students with or At-Risk of Learning Problems*. Boston, MA: Allyn & Bacon.
Harp, B. (Ed.)(1991). *Assessment and Evaluation in Whole Language Programs*. Norwood, MA: Christopher-Gordon.
Hill. B.C., & Ruptic, C. (1994). *Practical Aspects of Authentic Assessment: Putting the Pieces Together*. Norwood, MA: Christopher-Gordon.
Law, B. & Eckes, M. (1995). *Assessment and ESL: A Handbook for K–12 Teachers*. Winnipeg: Peguis Publishers.
O'Malley, J.M., & Valdez-Pierce, L. (1996). *Authentic Assessment for English Language Learners*. Addison-Wesley.
Peyton, J.K., & Reed, L. (1990). *Dialogue Journal Writing with Non-Native English Speakers*. Alexandria, VA: TESOL.
Tierney, R.J., Carter, M.A., Desai, L.E. (1991). *Portfolio Assessment in the Reading-Writing Classroom*. Norwood, MA: Christopher-Gordon.

Commercially developed, standardized tests, in contrast, are much more limited in value because they generally do not reflect individual teacher's classroom objectives and activities and, therefore, they do not inform teachers about the effectiveness of their instruction. Nevertheless, to the extent that multiple-choice standardized tests are used systematically within a school district or region for accountability purposes, it is important that EE teachers prepare their students to take such tests. To ignore the importance of standardized testing in such cases runs the risk that students in EE programs will be ill-prepared for district testing and score poorly, thereby jeopardizing the viability of the program.

What are alternative sources of information for planning instruction and monitoring student performance?

So far we have talked a lot about assessing student learning or achievement. However, you will recall that earlier we said that an important alternative goal of assessment is *"to understand students' learning styles and strategies, their interests, attitudes, motivations, and other relevant background factors, past or current, that might impinge on classroom learning."* In this section, we discuss ways of collecting these other kinds of information. In addition, the reader is referred to the recommended readings shown in Table 7.7.

We have already discussed one source of additional information about students that can guide instruction and ultimately improve student learning; that is, portfolios and portfolio conferences. While the primary focus of portfolios is documenting and assessing student achievement, they are also a valuable source of information about students' preferences and attitudes about schoolwork, their learning styles and strategies, study habits, etc. This kind of information can be elicited from portfolios if teachers engage students in active discussion and reflection about the work in their portfolios. See Table 7.6 for some questions that can guide conversations about portfolio work.

Conferences need not be limited to portfolios. You can have a conference with your students about individual pieces of written work, about a book they have read, about solving math word problems, or any assignment they are working on. It is simply a matter of encouraging the student to talk about how they went about completing the work and what they think about what they accomplished. Table 7.8 suggests some questions that could be used during a reading conference.

Dialogue journals and *learning logs* are other sources of additional information about students. *Dialogue journals are written conversations between students and teachers.* They can be about anything students and/or teachers think is

appropriate—topics pertaining to schoolwork or out-of-school activities. Generally speaking, students use separate books for journal writing and they are given regular times in class, or sometimes at home, to write in them. The real benefits of journals occur when they are routinely and frequently shared with teachers; that is, when they take the form of a dialogue between students and teachers. In fact, if you are to learn more about your students from their journals, then you must take the time to read their journals and reply to students by writing responses or comments in their journals. When students write about their classroom experiences, you gain information that is useful for individualizing instruction. You also gain useful insights about your students' general likes/dislikes, hobbies, and lives when they write about out-of-school activities. Journals also provide teachers with samples of students' writing skills and the strategies they use when writing. Table 7.9 is a list of literacy skills that research indicates improve from journal writing.

Learning logs are like dialogue journals—they are written conversations between students and teachers; they differ from dialogue journals in that they focus exclusively on students' classroom learning experiences. Students can write about a single lesson, an assignment, a whole unit, or a whole subject, such as social studies. Students can make entries in their logs at the end of specific lessons, each day, or after and during particular instructional units. Like dialogue journals, learning logs are most useful for assessment purposes when they are shared with teachers so that teachers gain insights about what students like or enjoy, where they are progressing without difficulty, and, most importantly, where they are having difficulty and need more atten-

Table 7.8   Sample Questions for Use during a Reading Conference

- Why did you choose this story to read?
- What did you enjoy about this story?
- Are there any words you do not understand in this story?
- How could you figure out the meaning of these words?
- What was the most difficult part about this story?
- What did you learn from reading this story?
- How can you become a better reader?

Voices from the Field

Assessment in Immersion Classrooms

Eileen Lorenz
Assistant Principal
Flower Hill Elementary School
Gaithersburg, Maryland

My current role as Assistant Principal at Maryvale Elementary School gives me many opportunities to work with staff in both the English and French immersion program. In addition, my experiences as a French immersion teacher and as project specialist of several federally-funded projects on professional development for immersion teachers has taught me several important things about assessment in immersion classrooms.

Assessment in the immersion classroom serves a role similar to that in the non-immersion classroom. It is the vehicle that helps us know if adjustment is needed in the instructional process. Assessment is an integral part of the daily functioning of classroom instruction and impacts the pace and plans we use to attain objectives. A major difference between the immersion and non-immersion classroom is that immersion teachers must assess both content and language learning. Immersion teachers use a variety of instructional strategies to ensure that students are learning a second language at the same time as they are learning new concepts. The use of different types of manipulative materials, pictures, and gestures is critical to instruction and therefore must be an integral part of assessment. Assessment situations should provide students with materials and tasks similar to those used in instruction. For example, in grade 2 classrooms, as teachers introduce and reinforce the concept of fractional parts (two halves, three thirds, four fourths), they make sure students see and manipulate fractional parts of geometric shapes such as fruit, sandwiches, etc. Materials that allow students to manipulate and identify examples that are not fractional parts, such as unevenly divided pieces of an apple or a candy bar, are just as important.

In immersion classrooms, performance assessments are frequently used and very useful, especially in the earlier grades, because they offer students the option of demonstrating and/or talking about what they know. During a performance assessment about fractional parts, teachers can ask students to show halves, thirds, and fourths or to put fractional parts together to form a whole comprised of four equal parts. In addition to following a prepared "script" during a performance assessment, teachers can ask students open-ended question that allow students to share content and language knowledge.

Immersion teachers constantly assess the language learning component of classroom situations. Assessment of written and spoken responses offer teachers invaluable opportunities during which they can identify strengths and weaknesses in students' second language development. It is possible, for example, that a student might understand and be able to point correctly to fractional parts without using the second language. In such a case, a teacher would use this assessment feedback to examine factors that might be influencing student language learning. Is there adequate spoken language being modeled during instruction? Is the student focusing his/her attention on classroom activities during instruction? Has the student's hearing been checked?

Gathering information informally about what areas of written language need attention is also important. For example, a language rubric for a final draft of grade 1 writing sample could include items that reflected students' level of mastery with capitalization at the beginning of sentences and ending sentences with a period or question mark. A language rubric for a final draft of a grade 5 writing sample could include items that are more sophisticated based on a longer sequence in the immersion classroom, such as complete sentences with correct verb tenses, correct adjective form, and correct adverb form.

Informal assessment of students' daily use and understanding of social language in non-academic situations is critical. For example, grade 5 students who respond to French-speaking visitors using the

(continued)

Voices from the Field (continued)

formal *"vous"* form would elicit a teacher's approval and mental note that emphasis on different forms of address with different groups of people has been successful. On the other hand, lack of use of the formal *vous* should be a wake-up call to a teacher's use of the assessment-instructional cycle so that more emphasis and practice is devoted to this language objective.

Because district- and state-wide assessments have increased in prominence during the last ten years, immersion teachers must integrate not only the content but also the format of such assessments into daily classroom instruction. For example, Montgomery County Public Schools (Rockville, Maryland) administers Criteria Referenced Tests (CRT) in English to all students in grades 3 through 8 and Maryland State Performance Program (MSPAP) assessments to all students in grades 3 and 5. Students in immersion programs must have experience working collaboratively in groups to explore scientific data, organize the data, and write about logical conclusions from the data. Students must have prac-

tice following rubrics to determine what is expected as they write and/or research academic topics. Use of similar approaches in the immersion classroom is imperative if students are to perform well during local and state assessments. Of course, this requires additional work for immersion teachers as they must either translate practice materials offered by the district or state or develop their own materials using guidelines from materials in English.

tion. Learning logs are useful for obtaining feedback from students about their language needs in those classes where the second language is used but the teacher is not in attendance to observe directly where they are having difficulty.

Table 7.9   Literacy Skills Promoted by Dialogue Journals

- Topic initiation
- Topic variety
- Elaboration of topics
- Meta-communication about reading and writing
- Audience awareness
- Awareness and use of print
- Creativity and independence in writing
- Grammar
- Language functions

(from Staton *et al.*, 1987, and Peyton & Reed, 1990)

One final source of information about teaching and learning in the classroom that can guide instruction is something teachers do every minute of their school day—observation. Teachers continuously observe their students and classroom events and, based on what they observe, they redirect students and restructure activities to ensure optimal learning. That teachers make use of such observations in various ways to direct teaching and learning during day-to-day instruction is indisputable. The challenges facing teachers in using observation as a critical source of information for planning instruction and for assessing student performance are *how to organize observations in a systematic and manageable way* and *how to record their observations so that they are useful for decision making*. We want to suggest a number of ways that teachers can systematically observe their students and record their observations so they are useful for planning instruction and monitoring student performance. They are: *anecdotal records, narrative reports,* and *teachers' journals.*

Anecdotal records are brief notes about classroom events and student performance in class that teachers make based on their observations. They can be made on file cards, adhesive labels, or in a notebook that teachers can refer to later, when they have more time. While they can focus on anything the teacher wants, they can be particularly useful for recording observations about individual students—successes and difficulties they demonstrated in class, for example.

Recording impressions and observations about students in this way provides a useful and continuous record of student performance that teachers can refer to later when talking with parents, writing report cards, or planning instruction. Without such records, teachers' recollections of student performance in class can be forgotten or distorted because of memory overload or simply the passage of time. Anecdotal records ensure more accurate memory for salient details of student performance. A narrative report is simply a longer, more detailed description of a classroom event or of a student that the teacher wants to keep track of for later use.

Teachers may want to observe their students systematically while they are engaged in a planned activity—such as cooperative learning, to see how they are able to communicate with one another in the target language. In this case, assessment could consist of a checklist designed specifically to identify those aspects of communication you wish to focus on; for example, turn taking, forms of polite address, expressions of disagreement. Alternatively, you may wish to focus on the performance of an individual student. In this case, you might decide to write a narrative report of the student's performance immediately after the event has occurred. Important observations about individual lessons or whole units can be recorded in a journal kept separately for this purpose. Journal entries can be made at the end of the day, during breaks, or on weekends when there is more time to reflect on classroom events. You can refer to them later when you are revising your instructional plans—once again, these kinds of records ensure that you do not lose important information about the effectiveness of your instruction. Teachers' journals can be handwritten or kept on a computer files.

Should I involve my students in assessment and how?

There are benefits to involving students in assessment:

- Students can assess their language proficiency at times when it is difficult for you to assess—in subject matter classes taught by other teachers, in the school yard or cafeteria when students are socializing with one another, and even out of school. Through self-assessment, students can provide you with feedback about their proficiency in a variety of contexts where you cannot easily observe their performance.

- Students gain a greater sense of responsibility for and involvement in their own learning and become more motivated to learn.

- Students come to understand learning objectives and the criteria or standards for assessing performance. As a result, they can focus their time and efforts effectively in the pursuit of those objectives.

- Students learn to identify their learning strengths

and weaknesses and, thus, can better decide where and how to focus their energies.

- In learner-centered classrooms, self-assessment individualizes assessment and involves students in monitoring and planning their own learning.

There are a variety of ways of involving students in self-assessment:

- portfolio conferences with teachers and other students.

- portfolios with reflection questions that students respond to every time they add a piece of work to their portfolio. (Table 7.10 gives sample questions to guide student reflection.)

- conferences that focus on language or subject matter skills.

- dialogue journals and learning logs.

- student-developed rubrics to assess written products (see Campanario-Araica "Voices from the Field" essay on p. 160).

- peer-assessment during oral presentations or read aloud sessions.

Table 7.10   Questions to Guide Student Self-Reflection of Portfolio Work

- Why is this a good piece of work?
- What did I enjoy about doing this piece of work?
- What was the most difficult part of doing this work?
- What did I learn from doing this piece of work?
- How is this work different/better than my earlier work?
- What did I learn from doing this piece of work?
- How can I make this work better?
- Where do I need help to make this better?

Voices from the Field

Using Student-Generated Rubrics to Assess Writing

Maria Campanario-Araica
Teacher
Rafael Hernandez Two-Way Bilingual School
Boston, Massachusetts

I am a middle school teacher at the Rafael Hernandez Two-Way Bilingual School in Boston.

In working with students for many years I find that they often have an outstanding sense of what good work is, what they may lack is a way to quantify and or qualify the characteristics of that work. In order to help my students be able to discuss, critique, and produce quality pieces of work, I often have them produce a rubric.

At the very beginning of the year, I have a discussion with the class about excellent work. Together we decide what must always be present in student work to have it reach the level of being considered excellent. The list they generated this year includes: follow directions, plan (sketch), brainstorm, ask questions to help you understand, revise, label (heading, title), take your time, effort, neatness. This list is constantly referred to when creating rubrics.

We begin our conversation by defining the type of work we are looking at—a narrative, persuasive essay, expository essay, illustration, etc. (Of course there is discussion in class prior to the assignment about these styles and formats.) The students are asked to generate a list of what the elements of a good piece would be; once they have this list a decision is made about priorities. Which of the qualities are really most important, why, and so on. After we have done several rubrics as a class, students are then selected in smaller groups for various assignments. They go off by themselves and have to generate a rubric for the given assignment. When they have completed this rubric, they bring it back to the class, explain the rationale, and present it. Classmates then use the rubric.

How can I include parents in assessment?

When it comes to parents and assessment, EE teachers can:

- maintain communication with parents by sharing assessment results regularly.

- inform parents of their children's expected levels of performance in language and academic domains so parents know what to expect and are not unduly anxious if students are not performing like students in conventional programs.

- keep samples of student work over time so that they can show parents the progress of their children.

- include parents as active participants in some assessment activities—portfolios can be sent home with instructions about how parents and children can review the work in the portfolio together.

- describe assessment procedures and goals to parents so they understand how you are monitoring student progress.

As we noted in Chapter 2, parental involvement is critical to the development and ultimate success of EE programs. To ensure that parents stay committed and involved, it is important to let them know at the outset about what to expect from their children. In particular, it is common for the English language development of both language minority and language majority students in elementary school EE programs to lag behind that of native-English speakers in all-English programs in the beginning of the program when English is not used very much for instructional purposes. Failure to alert parents to this may result in their misinterpreting this initial lag as evidence of failure or something going wrong in the program.

It is important to maintain regular communication with parents throughout the duration of the program. In addition to conventional teacher-parent meetings, parents can stay in touch with the program by reviewing their children's portfolios with them on a regular basis at home, as noted above. Students' writing portfolios, for example, can be sent home to be reviewed by parents and children together—a kind of parent/child conference. It is useful to suggest questions that parents can use to help them engage their children in talking about schoolwork. Also, general guidance about how to conduct themselves during parent-student conferences is recommended. Table 7.11 provides some general guidelines and sample questions for parents to use when reviewing their children's portfolios. Parents will welcome these suggestions if they are reviewing work in a language they themselves do not know well. To ensure active parent involvement, ask parents to write their impressions of their child's work on a *Parents' Comment Form,* to be signed and included in the portfolio and then returned to the school.

Sharing students' portfolios or other school work, like science projects or writing assignments, with parents not only gives them opportunities to see what their children are doing in school, but also familiarizes them with the program's goals and approaches and reassures them of its strengths and benefits. It may be necessary to describe the assessment procedures you use in the program, how assessment guides your instruction and decision-making. This is particularly important when using assessment activities, like portfolios or dialogue journals, that may be unfamiliar to parents. Parents who are fully informed of the program and of their children's progress in the program can help pro-

mote learning by providing encouragement, guidance, or direct supervision at home. As well, informed parents can be strong advocates for the program and can assist schools in obtaining valuable resources from the district or community at large. Parents who speak the target language can also volunteer to participate in classroom activities, providing students with other native-speaking models.

Summary

Assessment is critical to planning and delivering effective instruction. Assessment in EE programs is the same as that in any classroom in fundamental ways; but, there are some important differences that we have reviewed in this chapter. Most of these differences arise from the fact that EE students are taught and learn academic skills and knowledge through the medium of a language that they are also learning. Thus, EE teachers must monitor their students' progress in language development for both academic and social purposes; they must assess their language proficiency at all times—in language classes, content classes, and outside of class when they are interacting with other students. Ongoing assessment of students' language proficiency informs EE teachers of their students' linguistic needs and, thus, provides critical information for instructional planning. EE teachers need a variety of assessment techniques that they can use creatively to provide them with this critical information.

When planning assessment, it is most important to identify your goals for assessment so that you can then identify the methods of assessment and when to conduct assessment to meet those goals. Assessment activities can involve students themselves as active agents in examining their own linguistic and academic progress. Parents are also important partners, and assessment results should be shared with them routinely and in ways that are comprehensible and timely. Parental support can be nurtured if they can see their children's progress in language and academic domains.

To summarize the material in this chapter, we have developed a checklist (Table 7.12) about effective and useful assessment in EE classes that is based on the nine Critical Features discussed in Chapter 2. These are only suggestions; the reader may want to add additional points.

Table 7.11 Guidelines for Parent-Student Conferences

General guidelines:
- Always be supportive and positive.
- Avoid negative judgments or statements.
- Focus on what students have done, not on what they have not done.
- Let students do most of the talking.
- Listen carefully and make comments that build on what students say.

Questions parents can use with their children to review portfolios:
- What is this piece of work about?
- What part do you like most? Why?
- What parts were difficult/easy to do?
- What would you do differently if you were to do it again?

Table 7.12   Assessment Checklist

1. **Parental involvement is integral to program success:**
   - Parents have been informed of expected student outcomes.
   - Parents review student's schoolwork on a regular basis.
   - Parents understand classroom assessment procedures and how they are used.
   - Assessment information is shared with and explained to parents on a regular basis.

2. **Effective programs have high standards:**
   - Assessment activities reflect high language and academic standards.
   - Assessment methods permit students to demonstrate high standards.
   - High standards are reflected in the use of authentic assessment tasks and activities.
   - Students are familiar with and understand expected standards of achievement and how they will be assessed.

3. **Strong leadership is critical for effective programs:**
   - The school principal and teachers emphasize high standards in assessment.
   - Assessment results are used to tailor instruction to insure the attainment of high standards.
   - Teachers have opportunities to develop skills that link assessment with instruction.
   - Teachers have professional development opportunities to develop assessment skills.

4. **Effective education is developmental:**
   - Assessment methods are appropriate for the age and grade level of students.
   - Assessment activities reflect developmental changes in achievement.
   - Assessment activities are culturally appropriate and varied.

5. **Effective instruction is student-centered:**
   - Students are actively involved in self-assessment.
   - Students understand instructional objectives and know how to use them in self-assessment.
   - Assessment results are used to tailor instruction to meet individual student needs.
   - Students' abilities are assessed at the beginning of the year in order to plan appropriate instruction throughout the year.
   - Assessment methods are culturally appropriate and sensitive to individual differences.
   - Relevant information about students, their families, and backgrounds is collected and used to plan instruction.
   - Assessment methods take into account cognitive and educational differences among learners.

6. **Language instruction is integrated with challenging academic instruction:**
   - Assessment activities are appropriate for beginning level language learners.
   - Assessment of content mastery by students with minimal levels of language proficiency minimizes the use of language.
   - Assessment of learners with advanced levels of language proficiency integrates content and appropriate language skills.
   - Language assessment includes skills that are linked to academic and social domains.
   - Teachers plan for language development by assessing language skills that students need for later academic learning.

Table 7.12 *(continued)*

7. *Teachers in effective programs are reflective:*
   - Teachers plan assessment along with instruction.
   - Teachers use assessment results to tailor instruction to students' needs.
   - Teachers use assessment results to understand their teaching effectiveness.
   - Teachers explore alternative forms of assessment to expand their repertoire of assessment techniques.

8. *Effective programs are integrated with other schools and school programs:*
   - Teachers use assessment standards that conform to district expectations and practices.
   - Teachers prepare EE students for district-wide assessment activities.
   - EE principals and teachers share assessment results with others in the district.

9. *Effective EE programs aim for additive bilingualism:*
   - Teachers have the same high standards for both languages.
   - Teachers use assessment to set advanced language learning standards among students.
   - Teachers use authentic activities for assessing student mastery of both languages.
   - Assessment activities reflect high standards for language learning.

References

Christian, D., Montone, C.L., Lindholm, K.J., & Carranza, I. *Profiles in Two-Way Immersion Education*. Washington, D.C.: Center for Applied Linguistics.

Cohen, A. (1994). *Assessing Language Ability in the Classroom*. Boston, MA: Heinle & Heinle.

Escamilla, K., Andrade, A.M., Basurto, A.G.M., & Ruiz, O. (1996). *Instrumento de observacion de los logros de la lecto-escritura inicial. (Spanish Reconstruction of an Observation Survey: A Bilingual Text)*. Portsmouth, NH: Heinemann.

Genesee, F. (1983). Bilingual Education of Majority-Language Children: The Immersion Experiments in Review. *Applied Psycholinguistics, 4*, 1–46.

Genesee, F., & Upsher, J. (1996). *Classroom-Based Evaluation in Second Language Education*. New York: Cambridge University Press.

Kreeft Peyton, J., & Reed, L.(1990). *Dialogue Journal Writing with Nonnative English Speakers: A Handbook for Teachers*. Alexandria, VA: TESOL.

Lindholm, K. (1992). Two-way Bilingual/Immersion Education: Theory, Conceptual Issues, and Pedagogical Implications. In R. Padilla & A. Benavides (Eds), *Critical Perspectives on Bilingual Education Research*. Tucson, AZ: Bilingual Review/Press.

O'Malley, J.M., & Valdez Pierce, L. (1996). *Authentic Assessment for English Language Learners*. Addison-Wesley.

Peyton, J.K., & Reed, L. (1990). *Dialogue Journal Writing with Non-Native English Speakers: A Handbook for Teachers*. Alexandria, VA: TESOL.

Staton, J., Shuy, R., Peyton, J.K., & Reed, L. (1987). *Dialogue Journal Communication: Classroom, Linguistic, Social, and Cognitive Views*. Norwood, NJ: Ablex.

Tierney, R.J., Carter, M.A., & Desai, L.E. (1991). *Portfolio Assessment in the Reading-Writing Classroom*. Norwood, MA: Christopher-Gordon.

Wajnryb, R. (1992). *Classroom Observation Tasks: A Resource Book for Language Teachers and Trainers*. New York: Cambridge University Press.

Weir, C. (1993). *Understanding & Developing Language Tests*. New York: Prentice Hall.

Part III
Applications and Resources

 **8** MODEL LESSONS
AND ASSESSMENT
PROCEDURES

UNIT ONE: ¿QUÉ COMES TÚ? (WHAT DO YOU EAT?)
A SAMPLE EARLY GRADE LITERATURE-BASED THEMATIC UNIT
FOR SECOND LANGUAGE LEARNERS OF SPANISH

Learning Context

This late first-grade/early second-grade unit is constructed around the eight-page, Spanish language book *¿Qué comes tú?*; a book designed for emergent readers (1996, *Celebration Press,* An Imprint of Addison-Wesley) (see Figure 8.1). The book concerns proper nutrition—things the main character eats to stay healthy. Ten other books on the same theme at various second language literacy levels are identified for independent reading time (see Figure 8.2). Books whose content is only appropriate for students in the lower grades are so noted, while those without notations could be used successfully with K–8 learners of any grade level.

Because the theme book (*¿Qué comes tú?*) is designed to invite participation by listeners, it is ideal for second language learning. Predictable language patterns support emergent literacy in a second language and the picture support is very helpful in insuring comprehension of basic food terms. The book also combines everyday and technical vocabulary related to food, major body systems, and nutrition to advance students' social and academic language related to key book concepts.

While the unit takes a piece of literature as its starting place and focuses on developing Spanish Language Arts (oral language, reading, and writing), it also integrates learning activities related to science, social studies, mathematics, music and creative arts. The entire unit might take up to three weeks to complete.

The unit relies on commercially published materials, nutrition education materials in Spanish/English available through the National Dairy Council, family math activities available through Project EQUALS of the Lawrence Hall of Science, U.C. Berkeley, commercially available children's songs and trade books, adapted pages from teacher activity books, teacher-developed activities, and authentic recipes (See Resources and Materials Section).

Content Objectives

- To understand the food pyramid and how to attain a balanced diet. (science)

- To understand the daily working life of farmers and their contributions to the rest of society. (social studies)

- To understand the concepts "producers" and "consumers." (social studies)

- To learn about types of graphs for recording information and their uses; and, where appropriate, weights and measures related to food items. (mathematics)

- To create and solve word problems with grocery store receipts. (mathematics; reading/writing)

- To construct a 3-D mobile related to the food pyramid and to use Mexican art prints of authentic family life scenes to stimulate sharing of experiences. (art; oral language development)

Language Objectives

- To develop students' oral language in Spanish related to food terms (bread, cheese, mangos, carrots, fish, beans, etc.), body systems (muscular, skeletal, etc.), and nutrition (vitamins and minerals, milk and dairy products, etc.). (language arts)

- To build comprehension skills by listening to and/or reading related stories at an emergent literacy level in Spanish.

- To acquire high frequency language patterns by reciting rhymes and singing traditional songs related to the theme of the unit.

- To advance students' reading and writing skills in Spanish by independent reading of books at appropriate literacy levels, filling in conceptual charts, and writing short paragraphs on personal themes. (language arts)

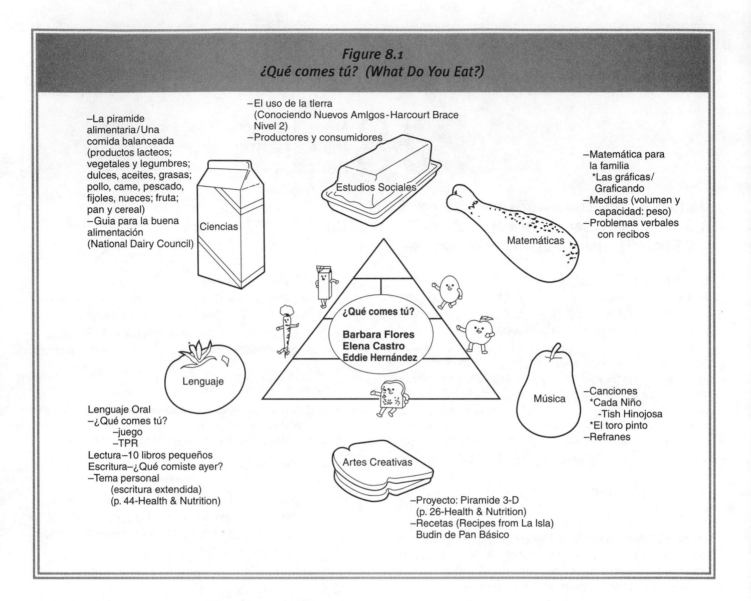

Figure 8.1
¿Qué comes tú? (What Do You Eat?)

Content Obligatory Language Objectives
Language required of students to develop key lesson concepts, master subject matter and communicate about a topic.

Vocabulary topics:	foods, nutrition, the food pyramid, producers and consumers, graphs
Adjectives:	saludable, mucho/a, sano/a, balanceado/a
Nouns:	cuerpo, huesos, dientes, músculos fuertes, comida, pan y cereal, productos lácteos, fruta, vegetales y legumbres, dulces, aceites y grasas, pollo, carne y pescado, frijoles y nueces, minerales, vitaminas; la pirámide alimentaria

tierra, granja, cosecha, siembra, campo, semilla, productos, productores, consumidores

información, la gráfica (realista, simbólica, ilustrada, de barras)

Prepositions:	que
Adverbs:	bien
Verbs:	dar, hallar, sembrar, cultivar, trabajar, comprar, comer, tener (que), hacer
Grammatical Structures:	-ar; -er verbs, Simple present tense, para + infinitive, gender agreement

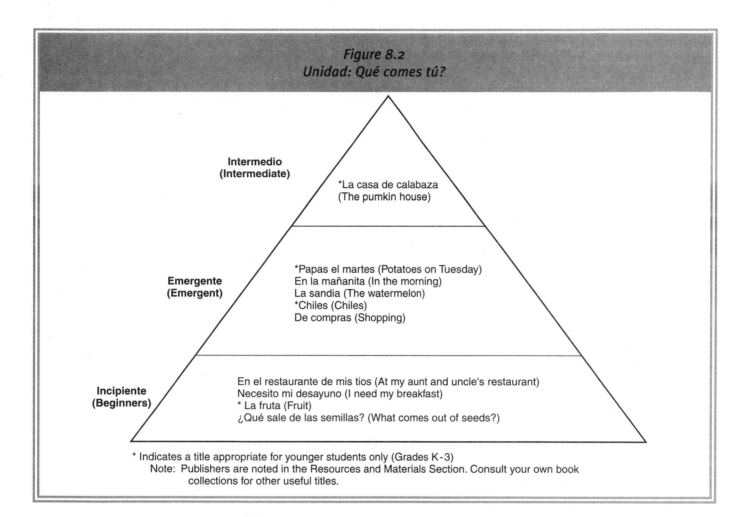

Figure 8.2
Unidad: Qué comes tú?

Intermedio (Intermediate)
*La casa de calabaza (The pumkin house)

Emergente (Emergent)
*Papas el martes (Potatoes on Tuesday)
En la mañanita (In the morning)
La sandia (The watermelon)
*Chiles (Chiles)
De compras (Shopping)

Incipiente (Beginners)
En el restaurante de mis tios (At my aunt and uncle's restaurant)
Necesito mi desayuno (I need my breakfast)
* La fruta (Fruit)
¿Qué sale de las semillas? (What comes out of seeds?)

* Indicates a title appropriate for younger students only (Grades K-3)
Note: Publishers are noted in the Resources and Materials Section. Consult your own book collections for other useful titles.

Content Compatible Language Objectives

Additional language that is possible and desirable, but not required for content mastery.

Vocabulary topics: common foods, dishes

Adjectives: frito/a, asado/a, delicioso/a

Nouns: queso, leche, nieve, plátanos, naranjas, manzanas, mangos, zanahorias, lechuga, calabazas, papas, brócoli, chícharo, col, pepino, cebolla, betabel, sandía, tomate, camote, ajo, manteca, trigo, harina, tortillas, etc.

platos tradicionales—burrito, taco, tostada, tamales, nachos, panaderita, (familia) bisabuelo/a, abuelo/a

Diminutives: -ito/ita

Verbs: decidir, organizar, interpretar, cantar, bailar

Expressions: ¡Qué rico/a!; Me gusta (el helado), ¿Qué puedes comprar por ($1.50)?

General Skills Objectives

- gathering and recording information via charts and graphics
- cutting and pasting skills (fine motor skills)
- categorization/classification skills
- problem solving skill development (i.e. creating a day's balanced meals)
- following directions
- working in small cooperative groups

Cross-Cultural Objectives

- To learn food-related songs and rhymes from around the Spanish language world. (oral language development, music, cross-cultural learning)

- To learn to make Puerto Rican bread pudding or other authentic Latin American dishes suggested in the National Dairy Council Publication: *Snack Stars* (in Spanish). (creative arts/cooking)

- To include families through homework activities, independent reading, music, art, cooking projects, and family math activities. To interact with native Spanish speakers as much as possible in conducting these activities.

Planning Checklist

- Prepare all visuals, objects, other realia, equipment and supplies needed to teach the unit (tape recorder/CD player; colored and lined paper; poster-board, food items for display, ingredients for recipe, clipboards for math investigations, etc.).

- Make copies of all activity sheets.

- Arrange *Reading Corner*. Place independent reading books in an attractive arrangement to invite students to browse and enjoy. Organize books into levels and mark them with a color code to assist students in making their selections.

- Place social studies textbooks in an accessible area, if they will be used.

- Set up writing station with attractive writing implements—colored markers, pens, colored pencils, glitter, glue, etc.

- Set up kitchen area in classroom for making bread pudding or bring in a toaster oven, bowl, ingredients, cake pan, and set up near the sink area.

Grouping Arrangements

During the independent reading time students will work alone. At all other times, students should be placed as much as possible into heterogeneous groups where more advanced students can act as supports to those who are less advanced.

Linguistic interactions should be structured according to individual student developmental needs, with students first listening to target language, pointing, matching, drawing, selecting, or locating items; then naming and labeling items, listing or categorizing information and answering simple questions; and finally by retelling, explaining or defining, comparing, summarizing, and offering personal information related to the major unit topics.

Sample Activities By Phase

Preview Phase

- To begin the unit, play *The Barnyard Dance/El Baile Vegetal*, on the bilingual CD, *Cada Niño/Every Child* by Tish Hinojosa (1996, Rounder Records Corp.). Let children enjoy and move to the catchy rhythm as they listen to the bilingual verses. Introduce the Spanish vegetable words in the song and, if desired, let the children wear vegetable signs and perform relevant actions to the vegetable dance.

- Bring in actual food items, models, and pictures of food items. Have students acquire the terms by actively identifying them, naming them, and classifying them into categories.

- Read the theme book to the class (*¿Qué comes tú?*). Follow the sequence recommended for shared reading, by previewing the book, reading the book a first time, and then reading the book several more times encouraging active participation on the part of the students.

- Using the last page of the theme book which shows the picture of a place setting and asks the question *"¿Qué comes tú?"*, and using small cut outs of food objects (taken from a nutrition activity book, for example), engage in a TPR activity in which students are directed to place certain objects on the plate according to what the activity leader says they eat. Once the *act-act* phase is complete, command students to place objects on the plate individually or in small groups in the *act-observe* phase to make certain they comprehend and acquire the key food item terms.

- Use visuals, such as the "Las cosechas" (crops) page from the ¡*Abrapálabra! Spanish Word Books*, from Hampton Brown Books to introduce and reinforce key vocabulary.

- If possible, visit a local farm. Use the key vocabulary (obligatory and compatible) while children tour the farm. Insure that students are hearing as well as using the target language.

Focused Learning Phase

- Introduce the food pyramid. Make sure students understand the six categories into which foods are divided. Demonstrate appropriate "portions" of various foods to insure understanding of the concept of "servings" and "portions."

- Group students into pairs. Have them interview their partner in Spanish using a food chart to name all the foods they can remember eating the previous day. Have them check off the types of foods they ate under the categories of fruits, vegetables, meat/protein, milk, breads or fats/sweets. Ask them when they are finished to make a judgment as to whether their partner had a good balance of foods for the day according to food pyramid guidelines. Writing demands for this activity are of the single word nature (names of foods eaten in column 1) and placing check marks under the 6 categories of foods represented in the food pyramid.

- Using a blank food pyramid, have students get into groups of three and plan one day of balanced meals for a man, woman, or child. Depending on body size, the day should add up to 6–11 grain servings, 2–4 servings of fruit, 3–5 servings of vegetables, 2–4 servings of milk products and 2–3 servings of protein, and limited fats and sweets. Make sure all work takes place in Spanish. Give students charts and picture cards to aid them in making suggestions for the day's meals in Spanish. (National Dairy Council visuals in Spanish will be very helpful for this purpose. Also, collect supermarket circulars in Spanish, picture menus from restaurants, and magazine pictures as visual aids for this activity.)

- Using pages 142–146 from *Matemática Para La Familia (Family Math)*, (1987, Project EQUALS, Lawrence Hall of Science, University of California, Berkeley) as a guide, have students develop picture and bar graphs to represent class responses to questions such as *¿Qué desayunaste?*

- Have students work in teams to create word problems with grocery store receipts. For example, students might ask: *¿Qué comida cuesta $1.29? ¿Qué puedes comprar por $5?* Trade the problems among the groups and have each team solve another's problems.

- Introduce the four-page social studies chapter: *"El uso de la tierra"* (How Land is Used) from the second grade book *Conociendo Nuevos Amigos* (Meeting New Friends) by Harcourt Brace. Determine whether students need a modified version of the chapter or can use the chapter as it is written. The visuals might be reordered to introduce the key concepts in an order that might be more helpful to second language learners, for example by first introducing the picture "Mi familia" (my family), then using one of the pictures to introduce the concepts of "tierra" (land), "granja" (farm), and "campo" (country) followed by

pictures that demonstrate the growing cycle from planting to harvest. Help students understand how food gets from producers to consumers.

Extension Phase

- Have students write a short narrative (one or two paragraphs) about the foods they eat regularly. Use a bordered writing page such as the Instructional Fair *Health and Nutrition* Whole Language Theme Unit Activity Guide, page 44 which has food pictures around the boarder of a one-page lined writing sheet.

- Giving oral directions in Spanish and modeling each step as you go, aid the students to construct the 3-D Food Pyramid suggested in the Instructional Fair *Health and Nutrition* Whole Language Theme Unit Activity Guide on page 26. Each side of the 3-D Pyramid will contain pictures drawn by or selected by the student. Decorate the room with the pyramids.

- To extend the previous activity and enhance cross-cultural understanding, read the book *Mis comidas favoritas* (My Favorite Foods) published by Celebration Press. This introduces favorite Latin American foods such as tostadas, enchiladas, tacos, tamales, and burritos. Students may want to see and try these foods. A field trip to a restaurant or an in-school food fair may provide the occasion for doing so. Make certain foods are authentically prepared. Read the book again and invite active participation.

- Make the recipe *Budín de pan básico* (Basic Bread Pudding) taken from the book *Recipes from La Isla!* (1995, Lowell House)

- Introduce rhymes such as *Tortillitas Para Mamá* (Tortillas for Mother) from the book of the same name (Henry Holt & Co., 1981). Teach children songs such as *Vamos a la Mar* (Let's Go to the Sea)(Guatemala) or *La Panaderita* (The Breadmaker) (Spain) (*El Toro Pinto and other songs in Spanish*) (The Colored Bull and Other Songs) (1995, Aladdin, Simon & Schuster). *Vamos a la Mar* has been recorded by Jose-Luis Orozco in his *De Colores* Album (1994, Arcoiris Records) and is also included in his book by the same title which contains gorgeous illustrations and rich borders by Elisa Kleven (1994, Dutton Children's Books).

- Have students use Mexican art prints of authentic family life scenes from the book *Family Pictures/Cuadros de familia* (1990, Children's Book Press) to stimulate sharing of family holiday food preparation experiences.

Discussion

Hudelson and Rigg (1994/95) recommend the use of "text sets" (Harste, Short, and Burke, 1988)—a group of books pulled together because they are alike somehow—same author, same story told differently, same genre, same topic. They believe that using multiple titles that are thematically related gives second language listeners and readers the opportunity to relate the books to each other and to their lives, thus increasing comprehension and facilitating the desired linguistic and conceptual growth by intensifying and deepening the experience.

By following the teaching cycle of preview, focused learning and extension, the teacher creates a predictable environment for students. Lesson activities maximize opportunities for language use because they encourage active participation and provide peer support. As in all immersion lessons, the teacher monitors and adapts his/her speech to students' proficiency levels and provides lots of contextual clues to support the linguistic input.

The lesson activities demonstrate the following principles: 1) there are plentiful concrete objects and visuals to support language and content learning, 2) communication motivates language use, 3) language is a tool of instruction and not an object of instruction, 4) content and language learning share importance, 5) oral language, reading, and writing are taught in an integrative manner, 6) cross-cultural learning is integral to the unit, 7) activities are student-centered and highly personalized.

Teachers use gestures, actions, props, and visuals to support the initial learning or preview phase. During the focused learning phase, teachers provide many hands-on experiences for students while encouraging oral and written language use. In this unit, the lesson begins and ends with a focus on advancing written language skills in the target language. Extension activities encourage students to express themselves artistically, participate more fully in the target culture, and develop more advanced oral and written expression.

Throughout the lesson, the teacher monitors student comprehension with frequent comprehension checks, actively observing student performance during all lesson tasks and by encouraging students to engage in self-assessment.

Application to Developmental Bilingual and Dual Language Classrooms

In dual language classrooms, 70% of instruction would take place in Spanish and 30% in English. It is suggested that language arts, science, social studies, music, and cooking take place in Spanish, while math and art could take place in English.

In DBE classrooms, formal English as a second language lesson activities could be added, paralleling those that are offered here for language majority students in Spanish.

For native Spanish speakers, whether in Dual Language or DBE classrooms, other independent reading books should be selected according to their reading levels. Stories should model more complex and expressive language. Literary quality should be high. Examples include:

- *El Sancocho del Sàbado* (Saturday's Stew), by Leyla Torres and Published by Farrar, Straus & Giroux, 1995 (ISBN 0-374319-979)

- *Granjas* (Farms), by Jason Cooper, The Rourke Book Company (ISBN 0-865932-379), part of the *¡Qué Maravilla!* Series available through Hampton-Brown Publishers.

- *Legend of Food Mountain/La montaña del alimento*, by Harriet Rohmer, Children's Book Press (ISBN 0-898239-022-0).

- *Una semilla nada más* (One Seed Nothing More), by Alma Flor Ada, *Rimas y Risas Cyles* Series, Hampton-Brown Publishers.

- *La tortillería* (The Tortilla Factory), by Gary Paulsen, 1998, Voyager Picture Book (ISBN 0-152107-143).

Grouping in Dual Language Classrooms should integrate native Spanish speaking students with second language learners of Spanish (linguistically mixed groupings). Independent reading would be individualized and, as the name suggests, engaged in independently.

During the *Preview Phase*, native speakers could be engaged in higher order thinking tasks (classifying, categorizing common foods) while non-native speakers learn the basic terms to communicate about lesson concepts. During the reading of the theme book, native speakers could be asked about their own experiences, likes and dislikes, and to draw relationships between the concept of balance in daily diet and the concept of balance in science, math, or art. While second language learners are engaged in initial TPR activity, native language learners could be creating collages of favorite meals on the same place setting page mentioned in the TPR activity and a shape book could be created with circles of lined paper for later writing activities. When not participating in common activities, each group of learners should be appropriately engaged and challenged in thematically related activities. If a farm is visited, native speakers should be encouraged to explore and investigate all aspects of life on a farm through verbal interactions with farm workers, while for non-native speakers basic terms and concepts would be reviewed in the natural context.

During the *Focused Learning Phase*, most activities could take place as planned (see this chapter, pp. 168–169). However, increased reading/writing demands could be placed on native Spanish speakers during partner and whole class activities. For example, native speakers could write down their partner's responses when inquiring about the foods they ate on the previous day and list the food pyramid category for each food eaten using the appropriate academic terms. Native speakers should be asked to read their social studies chapter in it's published version and to write short word problems around grocery store receipts, rather than do these tasks with modifications as is proposed for second language learners. Lesson visuals could be used as pictorial aids to support more extensive written verbal production.

During the *Extension Phase* (see p. 169 in this chapter), place more extensive literacy demands on native speakers. For example, have students read written directions for the art project and recipe or read along as traditional songs are sung. Allow native speakers to engage in the writing process (produce drafts, conference with peers, revise and produce a final draft) when writing their composition about regularly eaten foods. During art, cooking, and music activities, give native speakers a chance to lead the activities and to serve as models for their non-native Spanish-speaking peers. Encourage more extensive verbalizations during the sharing activities so that vocabulary is refined and expanded.

Assessment Strategies

As suggested in Chapter 7, various types of assessment are possible to evaluate the content, language, general skills, and cross-cultural objectives of the unit. A combination of observation, interview, self-assessment, peer-assessment, and product evaluation are recommended. Systematic teacher observation during all of the suggested activities is encouraged to assist in determining how well students are comprehending the target language and key concepts and to determine if the activity is working as intended. Students can evaluate their performance and that of their partners during any paired activities if rating tools are provided. Some ideas related to the language and content objective of the unit are presented in this section.

Assessment of Language Learning

Oral Language

At the end of the unit, rate students' overall stage of proficiency, using the following scale; based on your observation of their performance in class:

- ❑ 0 Preproduction—Minimal comprehension (follows along). No verbal production.

- ❑ 1 Early Production—Limited comprehension. One/two word responses.

Table 8.1 Sample Observational Checklist to Evaluate Language Comprehension and Use

Student Name: **Date:**

Target Language	Recognizes		Uses	
	Few → Many		Few → Many	
Common food terms	0 1 2 3 4 5		0 1 2 3 4 5	
Food pyramid categories	0 1 2 3 4 5		0 1 2 3 4 5	
Farming terms	0 1 2 3 4 5		0 1 2 3 4 5	
Graphing Terms	0 1 2 3 4 5		0 1 2 3 4 5	
Key concepts such as *cuerpo sano, dieta balanceada, sembrar la tierra, productores y consumidores, gráfica*	0 1 2 3 4 5		0 1 2 3 4 5	
Food-related expressions (*¡Qué rico!*, etc.)	0 1 2 3 4 5		0 1 2 3 4 5	

❏ 2 Speech Emergence—Increased comprehension. Simple sentences. Expected errors in speech.

❏ 3 Low Intermediate Fluency—Good comprehension. More complex sentences. Fewer errors in speech.

❏ 4 High Intermediate Fluency—Very good comprehension. Communicates basic messages well, but needs assistance in communicating ideas with precision and in enriching his/her vocabulary. Infrequent errors in speech.

Table 8.1, *Sample Observational Checklist to Evaluate Language Comprehension and Use* (page 171) could also be used.

Reading
Tape students as they read independently. Conduct a running record to analyze their performance. Ask simple comprehension questions. To learn how to take a running record, see *Instrumento de observación de los logros de la lecto-escritura inicial* (Escamilla, Andrade, Basurto and Ruiz, Heinemann, 1996) pages 42–56.

Writing
Evaluate students written production using a rating scale such as the one provided on pages 225–226 of *Languages and Children: Making the Match. Foreign Language Instruction for an Early Start Grades K-8* by Helena Curtain and Carol Ann Bjornstad Pesola (Longman, 1994; ISBN 0-8013-1140-3).

Assessment of Content Learning

Non-Verbal Response
Students can perform simple commands at the direction of the teacher. To demonstrate comprehension of key lesson concepts students could, for example, place the six categories of foods into the appropriate boxes on the food pyramid, or sequence pictures that demonstrate phases in the growing cycle on a farm from planting to harvest.

Labeling Tasks
Using any of the visuals introduced in the lesson, have students identify the key terms used in the lesson. If students are beyond simple recognition tasks, have them also verbalize or write responses to selected key concepts of the unit.

Matching Tasks
Have students match word or phrases (the stages in a growing cycle from planting to harvest) to pictures that represent each word or phase. Students could also match the six categories in the food pyramid to representative foods of each category.

True/False Quizzes
Using a simple answer sheet that uses happy/sad faces or the terms *Verdadero/Falso*, have students determine whether simple factual statements are true or false. For example, students could determine if the following statements are true or false:

—Para tener un cuerpo sano tienes que comer muchas grasas y dulces.   V   F

(To have a healthy body, you have to eat a lot of fats and sweets.)

—Pollo, carne, pescado, frijoles y nueces dan a tu cuerpo músculos fuertes   V   F

(Chicken, meat, fish, beans, and nuts will give your body strong muscles.)

Pictures and demonstrations could be added to the oral or written presentation of these statements to enhance comprehensibility.

Simple Explanations
Ask students to explain to you or to other students what they now know about the food pyramid. Ask students to explain what foods they enjoy and to categorize them according to the food pyramid categories. Use a checklist to assess performance. Items in the checklist should reflect the skills you were aiming for.

Unit Resources and Materials

Student Books for Independent Reading
Déjame Leer Series (1996, Good Year Books–An Imprint of Scott Foresman Publisher, 1900 East Lake Avenue, Glenview, IL 60025). Various titles recommended, including:

Papas el martes
and
La casa de calabaza (translated by Alma Flor Ada).

Pan y Canela (1995, Hampton-Brown Books, P.O. Box 369, Marina, CA 93933). Various titles of *Colección* A, including:

La fruta,
¿Qué sale de las semillas? (from Levels 2, 3)

and from *Colección* B:

Chiles,
En el restaurante de mis tíos,
De compras,
La sandía,
En la mañanita (from Levels 5, 6, 8)

Piñata (1995–97, Celebration Press (A Division of Addison-Wesley), 1900 East Lake Avenue, Glenview, IL 60025). Various titles of *Developing Readers* including:

Necesito mi desayuno,
¿Qué comes tú?,
Mis comidas favoritas

Other Materials for Activities Mentioned In the Unit

Boehm, R.G., Hoone, C., McGowan, T.M., McKinney-Browning, M.C., & Miramontes, O.B. (1997). *Conociendo nuevos amigos*. Orlando: Harcourt Brace & Co. (pp. 46–49).

EQUALS, (1987). *Matemática Para La Familia*. Berkeley, CA: Lawrence Hall of Science, University of California, Berkeley. (pp. 142–146).

Garza, C.L. (1990). *Family Pictures/Cuadros de familia*. San Francisco, CA: Children's Book Press (paperback ISBN 0-89239-108-1).

Hinojosa, T. (1996). The Barnyard Dance/El Baile Vegetal, *Cada Niño/Every Child*. Rounder Records Corp. (ISBN 0-11661-8032-2).

Koeppel, M.B. (1995). *Health and Nutrition* (Whole Language Theme Unit Activity Guide) Grand Rapids, MI: Instructional Fair (ISBN 1-56822-202-5).

National Dairy Council (1995). *Snack Stars* and *Snack Almanac* (Spanish Language Version). (Preschool/Elementary Curriculum Packages about Nutrition—Ordering Department, National Dairy Council, 10255 Higgins Rd., Suite 900, Rosemont, IL 60018).

Orozco, J.L. (1994). *De Colores*—Audiocassette Tape—Berkeley, CA: Arcoiris Records (ISBN 157417-015-5) and Book—New York: Dutton Children's Books (ISBN 0-525-45260-5).

Rockwell, A. (1995). *El toro pinto and Other Songs in Spanish* (1995). New York: Alladin, Simon & Schuster (ISBN 0-689-71880-2).

Rosado, R. & Healy Rosado, J. (1995). *Recipes from La Isla! New & Traditional Puerto Rican Cuisine*. Los Angeles: Lowell House. (ISBN 1-56565-339-4).

Tortillitas Para Mamá and Other Nursery Rhymes/Spanish and English (1981). New York: Henry Holt & Co. (ISBN 0-8050-0317-7).

Unit Two: The Weather

Jeanette Gordon, Illinois Resource Center

Learning Context

This fifth or sixth grade unit, with a content area topic as its primary focus, was developed by Jeanette Gordon from the Illinois Resource Center. It was prepared for students who are learning English as a second language but could also apply to students learning another language. The theme is *forces of nature*, and *weather* is one of the subthemes. This lesson is on weather forecasts, and normally, violent storms would follow. Since the primary focus of this lesson is a content area topic (weather), the language objectives take a secondary role. Literature is presented as a companion activity, rather than the main one, as was the case with the previous sample lesson, *¿Que comes tu?*

This lesson is presented within the framework of the Multidimensional Learning Web (Gordon, 1998) that goes through five steps of a learning cycle, beginning with the experiential phase, going to the conceptual preview phase, focused learning phase, the transfer and expansion phase, and ending with the learners' action phase. Assessment is woven into the lesson. An adapted version of this framework was presented in chapters four and six.

This lesson assumes that students have different levels of proficiency in English; therefore, many of the activities are completed in small groups, which allows for more individual attention. Students are allowed to complete the activities in different modalities (drawing or writing), and "challenge" activities are included for students who attain the objectives before others. Many of the activities use cooperative learning strategies (see Appendix A for a definition of terms which are identified in italic print).

Figure 8.3 shows how the unit can be expanded to different content areas.

Conceptual Focus Guide

Curricular Alignment (specify alignment with your state goals and standards)

Guiding Questions

1. What variables influence weather changes and what is the relationship among them?

2. How are weather data, collected, measured, communicated and used worldwide?

Key Principles (include a multicultural focus)

1. Weather is in constant change, and meteorologists around the world collaborate to make weather forecasts that help people plan activities and stay safe.

2. Meteorologists use instruments to collect data and observe weather patterns to predict weather.

3. Weather information is provided through different media, and many visuals are used to enhance communication.

4. Water in the air may be in a solid liquid or gaseous state and is affected by temperature.

5. There are causal relationships among temperature, density, air pressure, and wind.

6. The emphasis on weather forecasts is different in different countries and there are also informal cultural customs to predict and discuss weather.

7. The organizational pattern used to communicate or process any information affects understanding and retention.

Essential Concepts/Vocabulary

- meteorologist; evaporation; condensation; precipitation; thermometer; barometer; high/low air pressure; water vapor; molecules; cold/warm front; relative humidity; air mass; density; anemometer; wind

- cause and effect language

Strategic Teaching

Review

- web diagram
- sequence of events
- cycle, cause-effect diagram
- comparison matrix
- *Venn* diagram

Teach

- statement of a hypothesis for a scientific question

Preview

- scientific method/process

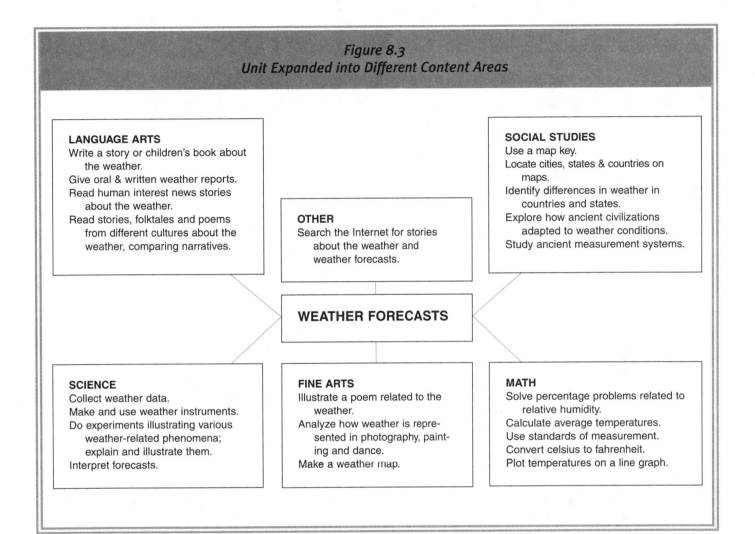

Figure 8.3
Unit Expanded into Different Content Areas

LANGUAGE ARTS
Write a story or children's book about the weather.
Give oral & written weather reports.
Read human interest news stories about the weather.
Read stories, folktales and poems from different cultures about the weather, comparing narratives.

OTHER
Search the Internet for stories about the weather and weather forecasts.

SOCIAL STUDIES
Use a map key.
Locate cities, states & countries on maps.
Identify differences in weather in countries and states.
Explore how ancient civilizations adapted to weather conditions.
Study ancient measurement systems.

WEATHER FORECASTS

SCIENCE
Collect weather data.
Make and use weather instruments.
Do experiments illustrating various weather-related phenomena; explain and illustrate them.
Interpret forecasts.

FINE ARTS
Illustrate a poem related to the weather.
Analyze how weather is represented in photography, painting and dance.
Make a weather map.

MATH
Solve percentage problems related to relative humidity.
Calculate average temperatures.
Use standards of measurement.
Convert celsius to fahrenheit.
Plot temperatures on a line graph.

Skill Focus

Review

- standards of measurement (math subtheme in this unit)
- units of measurement, accuracy in taking measurements
- comparison of measurement systems, measurement conversions
- use of charts and graphs to convey data
- use of Internet designated web sites and search engines
- skimming skills for using text materials

Teach

- measurement and collection of data related to weather

- progressive development in the use of graphic organizers
- designing a web diagram to meet a specified need
- predicting the organizational pattern of text material
- selecting the more appropriate organizer from two options
- statement of a hypothesis & identification of variables in weather experiments
- presentations using diverse modalities and cooperative structures for asking questions of an audience
- making predictions by analyzing experiences and information
- progressive development in applying scientific understanding
- use of "Ask Jeeves," a mega search engine that responds to specific questions (kid-safe version)

Preview
- recognizing intervening variables in experiments
- strategies for controlling or minimizing the effects of variables
- progressive development in identifying organizational patterns

Real-World Resources
- local meteorologist or weather station
- videotapes of weather forecasts
- any authentic weather instruments available
- parents and community members to share how weather impacts different careers and to provide information on weather forecasting practices in other countries
- newspapers
- school and public library
- Internet resources: weather channel www.weather.com search engines chosen by students, Ask Jeeves www.askjeeves.com, Ask Jeeves for Kids ajkids.com/, and scientists and other individuals on-line

Student Objectives
To demonstrate learning of all principles students will:
- Obtain weather forecasts from multiple sources. Interpret the information and share it with others using more than one communication mode. Analyze advantages and disadvantages of each resource.
- Share experiences related to weather variables and describe the characteristics of each. Discuss the complexities of measuring weather data.
- Collaborate with a team to do one of the following: 1) demonstrate one of the experiments designed to show scientific principles related to weather, or 2) use a search engine to answer weather questions and teach classmates the new search procedures.
- Predict the results of experiments by stating a hypothesis. Record, discuss, and apply the scientific principle demonstrated in the experiment.
- Use and read about weather instruments and discuss the principles that influence their designs.

- Compare and contrast instruments on a *Venn* diagram and Comparison Matrix. *On an exam, match weather instruments with the data collected.*
- Demonstrate understanding of essential weather concepts and related vocabulary. *On an exam, match key concepts with definitions.*
- Illustrate and explain the relationships among temperature, density, air pressure, and wind. *On an exam, illustrate and label the cause of wind. Given key vocabulary and sentence prompts, explain the illustration.*
- Illustrate and explain the water cycle and variables that affect evaporation, condensation and precipitation. *On an exam, draw and label the water cycle, write an essay explaining it and list variables that affect it.*
- Define and illustrate precipitation or type of cloud formation. Rank vocabulary from the best weather conditions to the worst.
- Sequence sentence strips describing the formation of a thunderstorm and illustrate or role-play the event.
- Use cause-effect diagrams and sentence variety to demonstrate the skill of explaining the reasons for cause-effect relationships. Identify sentences that explain the same relationship in different ways. *Demonstrate sentence variety when writing about cause-effect in exam essays.*
- Investigate a weather topic using original and secondary sources. Options include:
  - Collect weather data and graph information.
  - Research ways countries collaborate on weather forecasting.
  - Research historical development of weather instruments.
  - Collect biographical information about important inventors of weather instruments.
  - Research informal cultural customs of weather forecasting and weather sayings throughout the world.
  - Research weather careers.
  - Interview people whose jobs are heavily affected by weather.
- Using more than one modality, present independent or collaborative research results.
  - Write a letter to a meteorologist or a thank you letter to someone interviewed.

- Make a flannel board weather map and show weather report daily on a bulletin board.
- Make a weather instrument. Use to collect data.
- Collaborate to prepare a book about weather.
- Interact with someone on the Internet to get information on weather-related issue.

The Lesson Cycle
- Principles to be learned from the conceptual focus-guide: All

Experiential Phase (introduction of the conceptual focus through experiences)

1. Students use the *Three-Step Interview* to find out how their teammates' personal plans were affected by bad weather and share reasons for weather forecasts.

2. Students use *Think-Pair-Share* after they imagine themselves in a location doing a favorite activity. They watch a weather forecast to determine if the weather would have been appropriate that day for their activity or if the forecast even provided the information needed. Students contribute to the K (what we know) and the W (what we want to know) sections of a class *KWL chart* about weather forecasting. They will continue to add to the *KWL chart* throughout the lesson.

Conceptual Preview Phase (concrete illustration of the conceptual focus)

3. Students go to the weather channel on the Internet. They focus on visual symbols in different kinds of weather maps on the Internet and in the local newspaper. They discuss with a partner what they know about the information and copy the visuals onto a map of the United States. Students contribute to a class list of the visuals that are used in weather forecasting and discuss their effectiveness.

Focused Learning Phase (guidance in, use, and practice of the conceptual focus)

4. Given a Sunday newspaper, teams identify the broad categories that are included in the weather section and determine the kinds of information provided within each category. They record the categories on large post-it notes and the kinds of information within that category on smaller post-it notes of a different color. Students arrange their grouping into a large *web diagram (see semantic map)*. Teams share their diagrams and discuss similarities and differences in their organization of the information.

5. Individually, students use a prompt card from the *Q-Matrix Materials* to generate questions about the weather section of the newspaper.
   - Challenge: Students use the Q-Matrix dials to generate other questions. Teams exchange their questions with another team, answer those that can be answered from the weather section of the newspaper, discuss the higher-level questions and determine additional information needed to answer them.

Note: Return to the experiential and conceptual preview phases to prepare students through diverse modalities for the key principles related to collection of weather data, and the relationships among the variables that affect weather conditions.

Experiential Phase (introduction of the conceptual focus through experiences)

6. Review: Students use *Numbered Heads Together* to explain what happens to an ice cube on a hot sidewalk. They look at pictures of forms of precipitation and share prior knowledge about them. Later in the lesson they will learn about the variables influencing the water cycle and forms of precipitation. They will learn why the wind blows and understand how scientists measure variables influencing weather conditions.

7. Students go to an assigned learning center (or rotate to all of them) for activities designed to foster critical thought about key weather data and how scientists measure those data. Students draw or write about their experiences in their *learning logs*, record their findings and their predictions. They will continue to record information in their learning logs throughout the lesson.
   - Center one: Students observe a heat-activated rotating christmas/party decoration. (four candles are placed in a circle below four thin metal figures attached to a four-way balance suspended on a metal pole. When the candles are lit, the figures rotate, and a small metal rod hanging from each figure strikes four chimes that are suspended lower on the pole. Students predict what will happen when the candles are lit and discuss possible causes of the observed rotation.
   - Center two: Students try to measure how long it takes the wind from a hair dryer to reach a target. They blow hand-held pinwheels and discuss possible ways to measure the speed of the wind that turns them. They discuss possible ways scientists measure wind speed.

- Center three: Students follow directions to read thermometers to measure air temperature, water temperature, and body temperature. They compare and contrast the thermometers.

- Center four: Students put three drops of rubbing alcohol on their wrists and feel the temperature change as it evaporates. They compare evaporation rate and the temperature difference with three drops of water at room temperature. Students measure the evaporation rate and discuss variables. They discuss cooling effect of evaporation and possible applications.

- Center five: Students blow up balloons and release them. They compare the air pressure in the room with that in an inflated balloon and articulate air movement in terms of differences in air pressure when the balloon is released. They write about and illustrate the phenomenon.

- Center six: Students discuss and draw what happens on the outside of a cold glass of ice water on a hot day, to mirrors in the bathroom when they take a shower, or to windows in the kitchen when they boil water on a cool day. Students predict how many boiling teakettles it would take to make it "rain" in the kitchen. They discuss how water in the air might be measured.

Students share and discuss the learning center experiences.

Conceptual Preview Phase (concrete illustration of the conceptual focus)

8. Given a *web diagram,* the students record the most critical weather data needed to make weather forecasts: 1) temperature 2) air pressure 3) wind speed, and 4) humidity. Students copy the related principle on the diagram, "Meteorologists use weather instruments to collect critical weather data." (see Figure 8.4)

9. After the teacher models how to state a hypothesis for a science question/problem, students generate examples. Teams then use *Team Jigsaw* to present visual demonstrations of key concepts and experiments related to weather questions. Team one introduces prerequest key concepts. The remaining teams then each present an important weather question, ask classmates to state a related hypothesis, and do an experiment to answer the question and prove or disprove the hypothesis. The teams use *Think-Pair-Share* to state their hypotheses. Students draw each experiment (including illustrations of the movement of molecules and the formation of water vapor). They copy statements of the scientific principles that answer each question proving or disproving their

hypotheses. With preparatory assistance as needed, presenters explain the observations. Each team completes a large *cause-effect diagram* to explain the effects observed in their own experiment.

- Team one: Students observe and take notes as the first team explains two critical concepts: *Molecules* and *density* (prerequisite knowledge for understanding the relationships among weather data). Students observe sugar dissolved in water and listen to a comparison with air molecules in the atmosphere: too small to see, yet present. They observe the movement of oil and colored water in a closed container as it is inverted, define density and identify which liquid is denser. The team uses a metaphorical model to represent molecules and density. Students hypothesize movement of sand (representing dense molecules) and beans (representing less dense molecules) in a closed container if the container is inverted and shaken. They copy the principle, "molecules move from high density to low density."

- Team two: How does air move when heated? Effect: air rises when it is heated. Reason: heated molecules move farther apart and are less dense.

- Team three: Which is heavier, warm or cold air? Effect: cold air is heavier than warm air. Reason: cold air molecules are closer together and therefore denser than warm air.

- Team four: Which way does the wind blow– cold air to hot air, or hot to cold? Answer: the wind blows from cold to hot. Reason: as warm air rises, cold air with greater density moves in to fill the space the rising warm air leaves.

- Team five: Which holds more water vapor, warm or cold air? Answer: warm air holds more water vapor than cold air. Reason: because warm air is less dense, there is more room for the water vapor.

- Team six: When does water vapor condense and make clouds? Answer: water vapor condenses and makes clouds when air is cooled. Reason: when air is cooled and becomes denser, there is less room for the water vapor.

- Team seven: If the class has seven teams, the remaining team uses www.askjeeves.com to find answers to the key experiment questions. The team shares its findings and teaches the class how to use this search engine.

10. Students follow directions to use any other real weather instruments available and look at pictures of them. Students share what they know and orally compare and contrast the instruments.

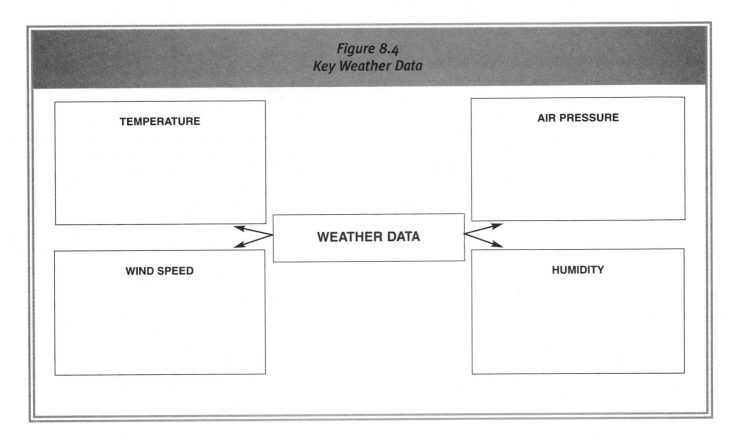

Figure 8.4
Key Weather Data

Focused Learning Phase (guidance in, use, and practice of the conceptual focus)

11. Given a list of words related to weather, students use *Think-Pair-Share* and the reading strategy of *Connect Two* to identify connections between any two words on the list. Challenge: connect more than two of the words. Students are told that after reading the chapter in the text, they will know all of the words on the list and identify additional connections among them. On a small *web diagram,* students predict the organizational structure of a chapter about weather forecasts in their textbooks. They skim the chapter to compare their predictions with that of the text and skim the introductory section to identify the purposes of weather forecasts and share skimming strategies.

12. Two team members (A partners) will collaborate to read a passage about thermometers. The other two team members (B partners) will read about barometers. They will answer key questions about their assigned weather instrument. If time permits, partners will read about another form of the same instrument. Then the students will pair with another team member (AB pairs) and they will use a *Venn diagram* to compare and contrast the two instruments.

13. Given key words for a passage that explains the cause-effect relationships among temperature, density, air pressure, and wind, students pair with a partner and use the reading strategy of *open word sort*. Challenge: students illustrate a high and a low, using small circles to represent molecules. Students use *Numbered Heads Together* to express the multiple effects of heat and cold on air molecules and to explain the cause of wind. Students use *sentence prompts* to demonstrate sentence variety when expressing cause-effect relationships. Using their original drawings of the party decoration, students check their predictions and elaborate on why the heat-activated decoration rotated.

14. With a partner, students use the reading strategy of *Say Something* to read a passage about an anemometer. The students review their earlier predictions about how wind is measured and determine whether any of their predictions reflect current scientific practices.

15. Following a lecture where transparencies with dots represent molecules and beans placed on them represent water vapor, students read a related passage. They then illustrate and explain relative humidity to a partner. They review the introductory experiments that helped them understand the concept. Students check the list of variables they had recorded when discussing evaporation of an ice cube as well as the

variables they listed that influence condensation and the number of boiling teakettles needed before it would "rain" in the kitchen. If not included on the earlier lists, they add relative humidity as an important variable.

16. After students recall the cooling effect of evaporation from their experiences with alcohol on their wrists, they *Pair Read* a passage about a psychrometer. Team members use *Numbered Heads Together* to explain to the class how the cooling effect of evaporation influenced the design of the weather instrument used to measure relative humidity.

17. Given a passage explaining the water cycle, partners use the reading strategy of *Sketch to Stretch* to illustrate and write about the water cycle. Partners edit the written descriptions of their team members and exchange them with another team for peer assessment.

18. Given sentence strips describing the sequence of events in the formation of a thunderstorm, each student pairs with a partner to predict the sequence. Students then read a related text passage to check the predicted sequence, and make any changes needed. Challenge: Draw and label the sequence of events. Students use *Numbered Heads Together* to define cold and warm air masses and cold, warm, and stationary fronts. They draw the symbols used by meteorologists to represent the fronts.

19. Partners use *Match Mine* to complete a weather map. Partners self-assess by checking whether the completed maps match.

20. Individuals or partners study a type of cloud formation or form of precipitation. The whole class discusses different ways to categorize the information. They demonstrate understanding of subtle differences by ranking the weather conditions from the most favorable to the least favorable.

21. Students review the cause-effect relationships in the lesson and practice related language.

    - Students work with their team to sort *sentence strips* that model different ways to express the cause-effect relationships among temperature, air molecules, density, air pressure, and wind.

    - Students work with a partner to select the appropriate causal vocabulary from a word bank provided to complete partial statements of cause-effect relationships among temperature, density, humidity, evaporation, and condensation.

22. Individual test:

    - Given key words, students illustrate and write an essay explaining the multiple effects of heat and cold on air molecules and the cause of wind. (rubric to assess content and writing development)

    - Students draw, illustrate and explain the water cycle. (rubric to assess content and writing development.) They list three variables that influence the speed of evaporation.

    - Students illustrate a "high" and a "low" and draw arrows to indicate direction of the wind.

    - Given a weather map, students use a key and apply content knowledge to answer related questions.

    - Students match key weather vocabulary with definitions.

    - Students match weather instruments with the weather data each collects.

    - Students answer multiple-choice questions about weather stations, weather data, the instruments used to collect the data, and relationships among weather variables.

Transfer and Expansion Phase (meaningful real-world connections with the conceptual focus)

23. Students interview a meteorologist in class or visit a weather station.

24. Students participate in one or more of the following research projects:

    - Collect weather data for a week and graph information.

    - Discover the ways that different countries collaborate on weather forecasting.

    - Describe the historical development of weather instruments.

    - Collect biographical information about important inventors of weather instruments.

    - Describe informal ways to forecast the weather in different cultures. Interview people from other countries.

    - Describe weather-related careers and careers that are affected by weather (include interviews with parents or community members).

Learners' Action Phase (action taken based on the conceptual focus)

25. Students choose at least one written and one visual or oral project:

    - Write a letter to a meteorologist or a thank you letter to someone interviewed.

    - Make a flannel board weather map and show weather report daily on a school bulletin board.

    - Give a weather report daily on the school public address system.

    - Make a weather instrument and use it to collect data.

    - Prepare a book about weather.

    - Make a poster to illustrate weather cause/effect relationships, inventors of weather instruments, cultural sayings related to informal weather-forecasting, or careers in weather forecasting.

    - Make a timeline of the development of weather instruments.

26. Students choose two examples of their work to include in their individual portfolio and give a rationale for their choice. Students evaluate the lesson and their own development on a self-assessment form. They identify personal strengths and state a specific goal for the next lesson.

Companion Literature Unit

This literature unit can be used as a companion to the previous weather unit. It is an abbreviated version of a lesson that could be presented in a much longer format if it were to stand by itself.

Conceptual Focus Guide

Key Principles (include a multicultural focus)

1. People against nature is a common conflict in many narratives.

2. Ancient civilizations made up stories to explain the unknown.

3. Ordinary people often perform heroic acts during extraordinary circumstances.

4. Complex sentences with adverb clauses help writers express clearly the relationships of cause and effect, sequential action, simultaneous action, and condition.

Essential Concepts/Vocabulary

narrative; myth; human-interest story; folktale; genre; comparative analysis; plot line; hero; conflict; climax or crisis; resolution; complex sentence; dependent clause; independent clause; adverb clause

Strategic Teaching

Review

- web diagram; sequence of events; cycle; comparison matrix; *Venn* diagram; cause and effect; metaphorical models; problem-resolution frame; story map

Teach

- plot line

Preview

- interaction frame

Skill Focus

Review

- language for expressing sequence of events or phases in a cycle

- Language for making comparisons

Teach

- vocabulary and sentence variety for making comparisons

- Forms and characteristics of narratives and news reporting/human interest stories

- Procedure for writing a comparative analysis of two narratives

Real-World Resources

- Parents and community members as storytellers and to share weather experiences.

- www.amazon.com as a resource for identifying books, synopses, reviews as well as an opportunity for students to publish their own comments about the books they read.

Student Objectives

Students will:

- Compare and contrast the plot, theme, and styles of two children's stories.

- Apply various reading strategies with others and individually to read diverse stories where humans against nature is the major conflict. Discuss the stories read and answer higher-level questions about them. Use library and Internet resources to select and read other stories related to the topic.

The Lesson Cycle

Experiential Phase (introduction of the conceptual focus through experiences)

1. Students discuss ways writers can also evoke weather images in the minds of readers.

2. Given a list of several words, teams employ the reading strategy of *story impression* to make up their own stories incorporating those words and the story elements on the guideline: main character, setting, conflict, complications in solving problem, and problem resolution. Teams each present their stories to the class. Students listen to an oral reading of the children's book, *The Wind Wagle* retold by Joyce Mcgreevy. (ISBN 1 56334-178-6, Hampton-Brown Books) students compare the story with their story impressions.

Conceptual Preview Phase (concrete illustration of the conceptual focus)

3. Review: students apply prior knowledge to predict the tribe represented in the visuals in *The Wind Eagle*. They examine visuals of the nashua people in *A River Ran Wild* (by Lynne Cherry ISBN 1-56334-737-7). They identify the similarities and differences between the tribes in the two books. Students discuss the importance of authentic illustrations, particularly when writing about groups that are often stereotyped.

4. Given a diagram of *Plot Line*, illustrating exposition, rising action (complications), climax (crisis), falling action, and resolution (denouement), students predict the meaning of the new terminology and how the events of *The Wind Eagle* would be recorded on the plot line. Following the teacher's explanation, teams check their predictions and individually copy the class example in their learning logs.

Focused Learning Phase (guidance in, use, and practice of the conceptual focus)

5. Given parts of cause-effect sentences (taken from a partial summary of *The Wind Eagle*) the students use punctuation clues to separate beginnings from endings. They then collaborate with a partner to combine beginnings with partner's endings and vise versa. They sequence the sentences in the order of the story. Given the partial summary of *The Wind Eagle,* students self-check. Challenge: partners collaborate to complete the cause-effect sentence prompts provided for them to summarize the rest of the story.

6. Students share prior knowledge of tall tales and other folktales that give a fantasy explanation of a natural phenomenon and discuss reasons people made up such stories.

7. Before reading *Bringing the Rain to Kapiti Plain* by Verna Aardema (ISBN 0-8037-089-2), students discuss the information provided at the end of the book that describes the origin of this narrative poem.

8. Students use the reading strategy of *Radio-Read* (also called spirit read and *Popcorn Read*) to pair read the book. They collaborate with their partners to complete a plot line of the story in the poem. Partners then use a *Venn diagram* to identify similarities and differences in the plot lines of *The Wind Eagle* and *Bringing the Rain to Kapiti Plain.*

9. Students review and expand on the language for making comparisons by interpreting the *Venn* diagram and talking about the comparisons.

10. Given a written sample of a *Comparative Analysis of the Plots and Themes* of the two books, students read the introduction and use *Numbered Heads Together* to identify the information included in the introductory paragraph. Students use the cooperative structure of *Roundrobin* to take turns to: # 1 read the paragraph, #2 identify how the plot lines were used to help organize the writing, #3 identify how the *Venn* diagram was used in preparation for the writing, #4 identify some strategies for vocabulary and sentence variety when making comparisons.

11. Review: students share examples of similes and personification found in the stories. Given the definition, students discuss the concept of theme. Students use *Think-Pair Share* to give examples of common themes in children's literature. They use *Roundtable* to generate examples of common characteristics in the style of children's stories.

12. Using the list of characteristics of children's stories, students identify those reflected in *The Wind Eagle* and *Bringing the Rain to Kapiti Plain*. Students make suggestions for a class *Venn diagram* to compare and contrast the style of the two stories. Given one aspect of comparison on the Venn diagram, students use the cooperative structure of *Team Jigsaw* to write sentences analyzing that aspect and share their writing with the class.

13. Given a word sort of vocabulary from *Bringing the Rain to Kapiti Plain,* students sort the words into groups of words that rhyme. They then combine some of those groups into larger ones by putting together the words where the underlined letters make the same sounds. Students record in the phonics section of their notebooks, some of their discoveries about conventions of spelling.

14. Given weather related vocabulary, students classify the words into two categories: nouns and adjectives. Students select words from one of the categories and put them in a continuum from the words reflecting the wettest to the driest conditions or rank the words that convey temperature from the coldest to the hottest. Given a list of action verbs, students match an action verb with an appropriate noun. Challenge: Students identify which noun-verb combinations reflect examples of personification and write them in a complete sentence.

15. Given weather-related vocabulary, groups select 20 words they need to learn to spell related to the theme. They discuss the words, write original sentences with each, and take a quiz before the conclusion of the entire lesson. Students add the words to the spelling section of their notebooks.

Transfer and Expansion Phase (meaningful real-world connections with the conceptual focus)

12. Students look up the two books on the Internet www.amazon.com web site. They do either a title search or search using the ISBN to obtain information about the books. Students then choose from one or more of the subjects provided to look for similar books or do another search (author, title, or subject and age) to identify a book of interest to them.

Students print out the information. They share their search results with each other and read the ordering information, as well as any other included for that title: synopsis, card catalog description, book reviews, publisher or author comments, and the comments or reviews of customers. Students check the school or local libraries to see if they can obtain a copy of the book. Some students may choose to purchase the book over the Internet with assistance and consent of a parent.

13. Students discuss the characteristics of a synopsis and collaborate with a partner to write a synopsis for a book they haven't looked up yet and compare their synopsis with that published on the Internet.

14. Students select one or more of the options:

- Collect weather-related art or pictures.
- Collect and read weather-related poems and songs.
- Collect particularly effective sentences describing weather conditions.
- Collect weather-related vocabulary and descriptions or definitions of the terms.

Learners' Action Phase (action taken based on the conceptual focus)

15. *Individual assessment: students will write and illustrate their own weather story or children's book. They will follow the steps in the "Guidelines for Writing a Story," to demonstrate the skills taught in the lesson. (students with limited language and/or literacy skills will follow only appropriate steps on the guideline and may modify a children's book.) The story will be evaluated with a narrative writing rubric.*

16. Students choose one or more of the following:

- Share with others the weather-related visuals and collected writing.
- Collaborate on a large comparison matrix to compare characteristics of narrative genre.
- Submit a review of a book to the www.amazon.com web site. Make a copy and share the site with parents and other classmates.

References

Curtain, H. & Bjornstad Pesola, C.A. (1994). *Languages and Children: Making the Match (Second Edition)*. White Plains, NY: Longman.

Escamilla, K., Andrade, A.M., Basurto, A.G.M., & Ruiz, O.A. (1996). *Instrumento de observación de los logros de la lecto-escritura inicial. Spanish Reconstruction of An Observation Survey: A Bilingual Text*. Portsmouth, NH: Heinemann.

Gordon, J. 1998. The Multidimensional Learning Web. Des Plaines, IL: Illinois Resource Center.

Harste, J., Short, K., & Burke, C. (1988). *Creating Classrooms for Authors*. Portsmouth, NH: Heinemann.

Hudelson, S. & Rigg, P. (1994/95, Winter). My Abuela Can Fly: Children's Books About Old People in English and Spanish, *TESOL Journal, 4* (2), 5–10.

9 ADVOCACY

You might well ask why a chapter on advocacy is in a book about enriched language and culture education—isn't advocacy about political activity and lobbying? The topic of advocacy is included in this book for those who want to start up a new program of enriched language and culture education of the type we have been discussing. It also contains suggestions for those who would like to develop a program with more enriched language and culture education than is currently offered in their school or district. The material in this chapter is also for those who already have an EE program but want to ensure that it is of the highest quality, in keeping with current research findings and theories. All of these cases are about changing education—starting a new program, transforming an existing program into an enriched model, or improving an existing program. Change in education, like change in any sphere of life, does not usually occur easily. Often people fail to see the need for or the merit in change; people often believe that the proposed changes threaten important aspects of the status quo; or they believe that change is only warranted if there is a serious problem to be fixed ("If it ain't broken, don't fix it.") and they do not see the need or reason for change otherwise; change often means compromise and even giving up something else and, thus, is difficult.

Advocacy is about demonstrating to others why changes you are proposing to make are desirable, feasible, affordable, and appropriate. Advocacy is about gaining the support of influential people or groups who have resources, power, or authority that is essential if you are to make the changes you have in mind. Sometimes the best way to garner support for your cause is to establish strategic networks with other advocates or groups who can assist you. For example, in Canada, the group *Canadian Parents for French* acts on behalf of parents and other groups to work with school districts to expand and improve the instruction of French as a second language. *Advocates for Language Learning* (see Appendix C for address information) is similarly constituted to assist in the establishment of effective second language programs for American students. Sometimes advocacy is about political action and lobbying—when the people you need to convince or the people whose support you wish to gain have access to resources and authority that are essential for the changes you want to make have political roles. Advocacy also means staying informed and up-to-date with respect to relevant research, experiments, and information about the program you are seeking to implement so that you can inform others of the educational, social, economic, and personal benefits of EE. A good way of staying informed is to attend and even participate in professional meetings where topics relevant to the program you are promoting is the subject of presentations, colloquia, and plenary speeches—a list of such professional associations is presented in Appendix C.

You can see that advocacy is not a single thing, such as lobbying, and it is not addressed to a single group of individuals, such as politicians. It is many things that promote change, and it can implicate a variety of very different types of people.

What is advocacy?

Advocacy is a process that includes a number of overlapping and interrelated components. In this section, we discuss each component briefly. Advocacy is:

- *To familiarize yourself thoroughly with the changes you are proposing and, especially, to understand the implications of the changes for other people and the existing educational system*—What are the implications of the proposed changes? What are the positive and potentially negative implications? What are the most important positive and potentially most negative implications? Clearly, effective advocacy requires that you have an in-depth and complete understanding of what you are proposing and how it will affect others so that you can plan your strategy for convincing others of your proposals. Without a clear understanding of such matters, you will have great

Voices from the Field

Establishing a Regional Support Network

John Hilliard,
Coordinator of the ENLACE Network
Illinois Resource Center
Des Plaines, Illinois

The ENLACE (Enriching Language And Culture Education) network is a support network for schools in Illinois that either are providing or interested in providing an enriched educational program to their students. The roots of the network extend back to the summer 1994 when the Illinois State Board of Education funded an institute to promote early foreign language education in Illinois. This gathering of diverse Illinois districts seemed to hold the potential for cooperation between foreign language and ESL/bilingual programs. The opportunity to make connections among diverse programs seemed very exciting to many of us that summer.

From that first gathering, five schools (four suburban, and one urban) emerged to take the lead in developing innovative language learning programs in Illinois. We all were convinced that enriched language and culture education programs held the potential to overcome the linguistic and cultural apartheid that have such negative academic and social effects on our students. As the network began to hold activities such as training and discussion sessions, we sought help from other schools with established programs (including the exemplary program at Inter-

American Magnet—see "Voices" in Chapters 3 and 4). These programs, in turn, began to use our fledgling network as a valuable resource for themselves. Thus, the summer institute that generated interest in five schools turned into a network, and the small group of people who began attending events devised the acronym ENLACE. We liked the way the acronym exemplified the intertwined cultural and linguistic mission of the network. From the initial five schools ENLACE has grown to include over 20 districts and seems to serve an important advocacy and support function in our region.

The following characteristics of the network contribute to its effectiveness:

- The network is open to schools or districts that are considering any form of innovative language learning. Although the majority of participants have dual language programs, the network does not turn away members with even the slightest interest in an enriched program.

- The events and programs offered by ENLACE come directly from the needs of the network. At an initial meeting, teachers hired for the new programs expressed their frustration at not being adequately

prepared by their ESL and bilingual training to meet the additional demands of a dual language classroom. And so the annual New Teacher Training Program was launched.

- Additional funding has been obtained to formalize and extend this "grass-roots" setup. The annual training for new teachers was the impetus for a Teacher and Personnel Grant from Title VII that would create a more comprehensive training program specifically for dual language educators.

- The network was supported by an existing resource center, the Illinois Resource Center (IRC) that provides help to schools in Illinois regarding ESL and bilingual education. Thus, under the auspices of the IRC, ENLACE continues to offer regular quarterly meetings where national experts in language and culture education come to talk to participants.

- A library of dual language materials, housed at the IRC, continues to expand with the needs of the network.

- A database of ENLACE participants is regularly published and keeps participants connected to one another.

- A collegial relationship was established among members from the very beginning. Administrators and teachers in the beginning stages of their programs established informal

(continued)

difficulty convincing others, especially detractors, of the merits of your proposals. An in-depth cost-benefits analysis can be helpful here.

- *To understand the general social, political, economic, and cultural climate in which you are proposing to make changes*—How can the changes you are proposing be seen or interpreted to be incompatible with the existing system or program, others' points of views, and current or future resources and plans in the district? Are there points of view or arguments that can and will be used to undermine support for the changes you are proposing? Understanding salient characteristics of the general context in which you are seeking to bring about change is invaluable in identifying specific pockets of resistance and support, specific issues that can be used for and against your proposal, and the scope of support and/or resistance to change. Understanding issues in the community at large is the starting point to developing a strategy for advocacy.

- *To know the stakeholders—those who will be affected by or are linked to the changes you are proposing* —Who are the stakeholders? Are there specific individuals with authority who will oppose your changes? Are there important stakeholders who will support you? Who are the most important stakeholders? Why are they important? What are their concerns? How can they benefit from the changes you are proposing? Once you identify key stakeholders and understand how they are implicated by changes, you can begin to consider ways of addressing the concerns of the resistors and ways of mar-

shaling the resources of your supporters. Knowing specific stakeholders and their points of view contributes to the refinement of a strategy to win over some of those who are resistant. Advocacy resources are always limited and, thus, it makes sense sometimes to identify people or issues that you choose *NOT* to address because you simply lack the resources you need to take them on. It is advisable to reduce your resource commitments to people or issues that you know to be totally beyond influence. Be strategic—commit resources to those issues and people whom you know to be important and likely to change.

- *To know and understand the stakeholders' attitudes, feelings, or predispositions with respect to the changes you are proposing*—Do they support the changes you are interested in? If not, why not? If yes, why? What do they stand to gain or lose by the changes you are proposing? Do they even know that you are proposing to make changes?

- *To identify information, evidence, and experiences that will counteract opposition to your proposals and reassure reluctant and resistant individuals and groups that the changes you seek are desirable, feasible, and affordable*—Is there some information of a research, theoretical, or common sense nature that will help convince resistors that you have a good idea? Are there experts or others who are familiar with the kinds of changes you are proposing who can speak to the concerns of the hesitant or resistant members of your community? Sometimes, information is less effective than having people see the kinds of changes you are proposing firsthand so that their fears are seen to be unfounded. Visits to successful programs in your region or viewing televised documentaries of successful programs of the type you are seeking to implement can be useful here (see Appendix D). The authority that comes from professional broadcasts as might be presented on television or presented in newspaper articles can be used to your advantage if made available to those whose support you are seeking. Networking with others who have sought to make changes of the sort you are seeking can be invaluable for sharing or developing effective change strategies, bolstering morale when it flags, and identifying ways of convincing others of your plans.

Some key references that will be useful to those advocating for EE programs are listed in Table 9.1.

Advocacy with whom and about what?

Although effective advocacy calls for tailoring your approach to the specific issues and individuals or groups in your community, there are three general issues that are relevant at all times:

1. the advantages of bilingualism and biculturalism for all students
2. the important role of public education in providing students with opportunities to become bilingual and bicultural
3. excellence in programs of enriched basic education

It is important to keep these issues uppermost in people's minds so that they do not get lost during discussions about the many details of EE programs.

Another set of advocacy issues that is very important and relevant to two-way immersion and bilingual education forms of EE concerns educational equity and excellence for language minority students. It is well documented that, generally speaking, language minority students are often not served well by traditional education—this is evidenced by the dramatic dropout and failure rates of such students. The same can be said for students of poverty. An especially

Table 9.1   Resource Books for Advocacy

Cazabon, M.T., Nicoladis, E., & Lambert, W.E. (1998). Becoming Bilingual in the *Amigos* Two-Way Immersion Program. *CREDE Research Report #3.* University of California at Santa Cruz, CA: Center for Education, Diversity and Excellence.

Christian, D., Montone, C.L., Lindholm, K.J., & Carranza, I. (1997). *Profiles in Two-Way Immersion Education.* Washington, D.C.: Center for Applied Linguistics.

Genesee, F. & Cloud, N. (1998). Multilingualism is Basic. *Educational Leadership, 55* (6), 62–65.

Genesee, F. (1983). Bilingual Education for Majority Language Children: The Immersion Experiments in Review. *Applied Psycholinguistics, 4:* 1–46.

Grosjean, F. (1982). *Life with Two Languages: An Introduction to Bilingualism.* Cambridge, MA: Harvard University Press.

Hakuta, K. (1986). *Mirror of Language: The Debate on Bilingualism.* New York: Basic Books.

Krashen, S. (1991). Bilingual Education: A Focus on Current Research. (*Focus: Occasional Papers in Bilingual Education,* Spring 1991). Washington, D.C.: National Clearinghouse for Bilingual Education.

McCargo, C., & Christian, D. (1998). *Two-Way Bilingual Immersion Programs in the U.S.: 1997–1998 Supplement.* University of California, Santa Cruz, CA: Center for Education, Diversity, and Excellence.

McLaughlin, B. (1992). Myths and Misconceptions About Second Language Learning: What Every Teacher Needs to Unlearn. *Educational Research Report: 5.* University of California, Santa Cruz, CA: The National Center for Research on Cultural Diversity and Second Language Learning.

Thomas, W.P. & Collier, V.P. (1997/1998). Two Languages are Better Than One. *Educational leadership, 55* (4), 23–26.

important reason why these forms of EE are appealing is because they promote equity and excellence in education for students from language minority or otherwise disadvantaged backgrounds. Educational equity and excellence for all students are concerns of parents, educational and community leaders, and politicians and, thus, constitute powerful arguments for implementing EE for language minority students. It is equally important to keep these concerns in mind in established bilingual or dual language programs since there is evidence that many of the educational disadvantages that are found in regular general education programs can also infiltrate EE programs for language minority students unless efforts are taken to counteract them. We have discussed how this can be done in previous chapters, for example, when we discussed ways in which both the minority language and English can be used in class and throughout the school to ensure equal status or when we suggested ways in which challenging academic instruction can be presented to language minority students.

Advocacy can implicate any of the following groups or types of individuals: students, parents, teachers, school principals and administrators, school board members, civic, business, or professional leaders, or policy-makers and legislators. We will discuss what advocacy for EE might entail with these different kinds of audiences shortly. Once you have identified possible stakeholders, it is useful to brainstorm possible reasons why each might (a) support your proposal, (b) resist your proposal, or (c) be undecided. Once you know the views of important stakeholders, you can begin to formulate responses to objections they might have, or identify ways that would convince the undecided to support you or, in the case of those who are already supportive, how they can help you garner support from others. It is important that you formulate specific responses that are appropriate for particular individuals or audiences and their concerns—for example, concerns that participation in a Chinese immersion program will diminish the English language abilities of native English-speaking students would be addressed quite differently if your audience is parents versus school principals or teachers—the latter would require, and appreciate, much more detailed technical information about language development that has emerged from research on immersion programs; whereas parents might simply need to be told that lots of other students have been in immersion programs and that research has shown repeatedly that they have done as well in English as students in the "regular" program. Table 9.2 presents some possible areas of concern for each of the groups identified earlier.

In fact, the individuals or groups you expect to be resistant may not be—it is critical to engage potential resistors in conversations to make sure you have a solid understanding of their concerns; unwarranted assumptions about who

will or will not be supportive can be costly. In any case, it is best to be prepared to address any and all possible concerns before they are raised so that you can present your proposal in a knowledgeable, confident, and reassuring way when and if concerns are raised. It is especially important that you be prepared to provide authoritative and detailed information to school administrators, teachers, board members and knowledgeable parents, stakeholders who are well informed about language and academic development. They will not be convinced of the merits of your proposal if you provide only generalities and platitudes. It is critical that you have a solid grasp of research, technical, and other professional material on the topic and be prepared to discuss it with stakeholders who are concerned about specific aspects of your proposal.

At the same time, be sure to identify individuals or groups who you know to be supporters and solicit their assistance in talking with others. Parents who have had children in bilingual or immersion programs can be very effective in reassuring first-time parents who are contemplating putting their child in an EE program that such programs are effective and have lots of advantages. Experienced parents can also advise new parents of areas of their child's schooling that might be unsettling because they initially exhibit developmental slow downs, but are eventually resolved successfully. For example, language minority students in 90/10 two-way immersion programs initially receive instruction in reading and writing in their native language and, as a result, may be behind similar students in all-English classes when it comes to reading and writing in English. However, both groups will perform at similar levels after English is introduced into the two-way program and, in fact, language minority students in two-way immersion programs often outperform students in all-English classes. These results are counterintuitive to many people, but parents who have seen these effects themselves can reassure other parents that they are real. Again, do not forget the power of direct experience with successful programs or of documentaries and other reports of successful programs.

Once you have identified key issues, sources of support and resistance or hesitancy, and gained some understanding of people's reasons for being resistant, you can formulate a plan to make best use of your resources to garner maximum support for your proposal.

Let us now talk briefly about advocacy with a number of the key groups we have referred to already to give some guidance on how to best reassure them of the merits of your proposal.

Advocacy with Parents

Seeking the active support of parents is critical to the development of new EE programs and to making innovations or

Table 9.2   Possible Areas of Concern for Different Stakeholders

Students:
- Will I do as well in my academic subjects in an EE program?
- Will my English language skills suffer?
- Will I have difficulty going to an all-English high school, college, or university?
- Will I be able to maintain my home language and culture?

Parents:
- Will my child learn English, especially reading and writing, as well as students in the all-English program?
- Will achievement in mathematics, science, and other school subjects be as good as in the regular program?
- Will my child have trouble in an all-English school after having been in an EE program?
- Is such a program suitable for children who struggle in school because of low general ability, poorly developed first language skills, or disadvantaged background?
- How can I help my child with schoolwork if I don't know the language?
- Is this program suitable for children who are shy and quiet?
- Will my child become isolated from other children in the regular program?
- For parents of minority language students: Will my child's self-esteem and sense of well-being be developed in this program?
- Will my child develop a strong sense of identify with his/her home culture? Will minority children learn about the cultural traditions and history of their parents?
- Will my child learn to read and write in the other language at grade-appropriate levels? And will he/she feel confident enough to use the language outside school with native speakers of the language?

Teachers:
- What will happen to my job?
- Will the students develop normal English language skills?
- Will this program strengthen the status of the minority language and members of the minority group in the community?
- Will they attain the same levels of academic achievement as students in the regular program?
- Are there adequate curriculum and instructional materials for the program?
- How will these students transition to an all-English high school or college?
- Will there be services for students who experience difficulty in the program?
- Will this program help language minority students progress successfully in school and integrate with students from the majority group?

Principals and school administrators:
- How much will this program cost?
- Where will I find adequately trained teachers? textbooks?
- Is such a program suitable for all students, even those who struggle in school?
- What about students with learning difficulties or language delays?
- Will the students in this EE program be able to do well on standardized district tests?
- Where can teachers get professional development to prepare them to teach in such a program?
- Will this program meet the needs of my language minority students?

Table 9.2 Possible Areas of Concern for Different Stakeholders

The community:

- How much will this program cost?
- What are the advantages of this program over the regular program?
- Will these students develop normally in language and academic areas?
- Will the students become segregated from students in the regular program?
- Is this program suitable for all students?
- Will this program promote positive inter-group relations and respect among the diverse language/culture groups that live in the community?

Professional and political leaders and policy makers:

- What are the advantages of this program that justify the expenditure of additional resources?
- How will students do on standardized tests?
- What are the additional costs of running this program?
- Where will we find qualified teachers?
- Where will we find suitable textbooks?
- Will this lead to segregated or elitist programs?
- Will this program promote respect and positive attitudes toward and among minority and majority group members?
- Will this program facilitate the academic development and integration of minority language students?

modifications to existing programs. In virtually all cases that have been documented, parents have been the single most important source of influence on school districts, policy makers, and school principals and teachers. Thus, it is imperative that there be good and regular channels of communication with parents.

Listen to parents concerns carefully and take them seriously. Be prepared to summarize and discuss research findings and theoretical aspects of EE programs thoroughly and authoritatively and in terms that parents can understand and accept. Bring in experts from university or other research institutes, parents from existing programs, and/or teachers and school officials from other programs to discuss their experiences and knowledge about the program with parents who are contemplating an EE program for their children. While acknowledging the special features of EE programs, be sure to point out that immersion and bilingual education programs have been in existence for over 30 years and that there is a wealth of experience, research, and knowledge about them. In other words, parents are not embarking on an entirely novel and untried "experiment" with their children.

Be sure to identify ways in which the education of EE students will differ from that of regular students as well as those areas that will be the same. Do not hide results from EE programs that reveal short-term differences or even deficits—be open and honest with parents so that they trust you and are prepared to consult with you if difficulties arise. In the case of language minority parents, discuss how bilingual education or dual language programs can help their children maintain their home language and culture, learn English and academic subjects effectively, and become fully integrated into the life of the school.

Here are some suggestions for communicating with parents about EE programs:

- If possible, arrange for new parents to visit programs in your district or in nearby school districts so that they have first hand experiences of what is being proposed. Sometimes, such experiences are far more effective than lengthy discussions (see Appendix D for directories of programs).

- Be sure to arrange for translators or others who are fluent in the minority language to assist parents who

Voices from the Field

In Praise of Bilingualism

Mimi Met
Montgomery County Public Schools
Rockville, Maryland

Relatively few students who pass through the U.S. educational system have the opportunity to acquire high levels of oral and literacy skills in both their native language and at least one additional language. As a result, the percentage of U.S. Americans who can understand, read, speak, and write two languages is low. Many U.S. Americans wistfully claim that they wish they were able to function in more than just one language. The success of EE programs, therefore, may be tied to the extraordinary results in language learning they can produce.

Parents who elect a special program option, such as EE, for their children are seeking something beyond that available in the typical school program. Certainly, the opportunity to leave school fully proficient in two languages is exceptional. EE programs can be successful to the degree that they deliver on the promises they make: high levels of academic achievement as well as competence in English and another language. Programs must set high standards of performance for all students in all areas of the curriculum including the two languages of instruction—and then they must ensure that all students attain those high standards, also in both languages.

Students' growing bilingualism needs to be lavishly praised and showcased both within and beyond the classroom. Many students in EE programs demonstrate an achievement—bilingualism—that is rare among their schoolmates, among school-wide faculty and staff, and even in the community at large (including their own parents!). Both students and their parents can take great pride in noting that 8- and 9-year olds are able to do things their own peers, parents, other relatives, and even most high government officials cannot do. We need to showcase what our students CAN do. It is also helpful that EE teachers be bilingual, especially those who teach in a non-English language. Students should understand that these staff members could teach in English but choose to use the other language because it is valued and important to them. Similarly, children should be encouraged to choose to use the non-English language to show off, to preen at their unusual competency, and to bask in the limelight of their ability to do what most people in contemporary U.S. society cannot do.

are not fluent in English during parent-teacher meetings or school visits. Also, ensure that all materials that are sent home are available in the parents' home language. It may be necessary to telephone parents who are not literate to provide important information to them in English or their home language.

- Identify a parent or parents to become the parent representative—this will give your initiative legitimacy in the eyes of other parents.

- Arrange for parents to view videotapes or televised broadcasts of successful programs (see Appendix D). If possible and appropriate, when working with language minority parents, locate material in the language that parents are most comfortable with or provide translation of materials for parents who do not speak or understand English fluently.

- Form study groups of parents, teachers, and others to discuss issues in the development of a new program or emerging issues in established programs. If parents are not fluent in English, arrange for discussions in their native language. Translators can also be useful as well. A useful source of professional information about alternative forms of education is ERIC (see Appendix C for relevant ERIC Clearinghouses' contact information).

- Inform parents of local, state, or national parent or professional associations devoted to enriched language and culture education—for example, Advocates for Language Learning or the Center for Applied

A Community Fights to Save Its Bilingual Program

Cathy Reilly
Nursery School Teacher and
Coordinator, Senior High Alliance of Principals, Presidents and Educators (SHAPPE)
Washington, D.C.

Do you want to find out how important bilingual education is in your community? Threaten to kill it. When I served as PTA co-president at Oyster Bilingual Elementary School in Washington D.C., the Superintendent placed it on a list of schools proposed for closure. The bilingual program costs more. Most of the children attending our school do not live within its geographical boundaries. When the system sought to reduce its inventory of buildings, Oyster was at risk. As word spread that the school's existence was in jeopardy, the sense of unity and perspective that emerged in our community created reservoirs of energy. It also forced us to articulate what was important to each of us about bilingual education.

The fight pitted schools against each other. It created a very difficult environment, because some schools had to close. We needed to make a powerful and persuasive case quickly that conveyed the enormous value of this education. We could educate our city about our program because we had built a strong sense of community within Oyster. The format of our Community Council meetings built the trust and the relationships we needed in this

fight. All Oyster families and staff are automatically members of our Community Council. The meetings started with a translated (sometimes from Spanish to English and sometimes from English to Spanish) introduction sharing general information and a principal's report. We then broke into two language groups to have a focused discussion on a specific topic. The uninterrupted flow of conversation in a smaller group facilitated involvement by more people. The discussions about everything from academic requirements to discipline codes and uniforms were passionate and animated. We then came back together and shared a summary of our discussion with each other. We learned a lot about both our common ground and our different perspectives. Instead of the groups becoming more separate we actually found more parents and teachers talking across the cultures, races, and class divisions. We offered pizza for a dollar a slice and childcare at every meeting. The attendance at our meetings increased substantially. It was like having a family dinner once a month.

This Community Council was able to take on the task of reaching

out to our alumni and to our neighborhood to marshall the willingness to work for the survival of our program. Oyster Bilingual Elementary School serves a broad cross-section of children from different economic and racial groups. This mix in a school of 300 with a committed teaching staff means we can demonstrate a high-performing academic program despite a significant number of children eligible for free and reduced lunch. We won; the city claims us as one of its jewels for now. Oyster is currently engaged in the process of building a new school building as part of a public/private partnership.

What an amazing gift this education conveyed to my family. My three children have lived an experience that has taught them an appreciation and respect for other cultures I could never teach. No matter how smart they are, they know what it feels like to not understand a word being spoken. They have felt the acute frustration of struggling to communicate. They have learned to read body language and look for clues in any situation where they are at a loss. This skill in navigating a sense of not knowing has been invaluable to them. They tolerated Shakespeare as something new to be deciphered and difficult classes in college as something to be mastered. I am a monolingual Midwesterner with bilingual children who crave a world of diversity and tolerance. They know what it is to live in a world of compassion, where no one is "other."

Linguistics and encourage them to become members and attend the meetings that such groups hold every year. See the list of additional resources in Appendix C for more suggestions.

- Prepare and distribute responses to parental concerns in the form of fact sheets. Be sure to provide such material in the language that parents can read fluently.

- Identify and make available to parents published material on EE that is of suitable depth and complexity. There is a wealth of published information about EE programs—review this material and select those articles that are suitable for parents. ERIC is a useful source of such information.

- Create a newsletter that covers important issues and current events in EE for distribution to parents; students can be contributors to such a publication. Be sure such material is available in languages that the language minority students and their parents use, as well as in English; in this way, you demonstrate that both languages will enjoy equal status and treatment.

Advocacy with Teachers

Teachers who work in the all-English program as well as teachers who are or will be directly involved in EE programs should be included in any plans for advocacy. This is important for a number of reasons. The support of teachers in the all-English program can make or break an EE program because they are in the majority and often have considerable influence on parents and/or other decision-makers. Moreover, close co-operation and collaboration among EE and other teachers is highly desirable in order to enhance the effectiveness and stability of EE programs. This means that even teachers not working in EE programs should be as well informed about the goals, organization, and workings of EE programs as EE teachers themselves. Ideally, teachers in the regular program should also be strong advocates for EE.

It is important to remember that many teachers, like other members of the community at large, will have many of the concerns and doubts about bilingualism, bilingual and immersion education, and learning through non-English languages. As a result, they will need to be convinced of the feasibility and advantages of EE as much as others. In general, teachers will require more detailed and complex information than parents because they have professional training in areas that are relevant to EE and, thus, will want and can understand more technical details about language, cognitive and academic development than the average parent who lacks such training. Most importantly, teachers must be knowledgeable about EE if they are to

make the sound educational decisions that are critical for its success. Thus, they require a solid working knowledge of many details of such programs.

Here are some ways of working with teachers:

- Solicit the assistance of teachers who are already supporters of and have had experience with EE programs.

- Hold meetings with teachers to address their concerns in a systematic and professional manner. Be sure to identify their concerns beforehand and be prepared with material that is relevant to their questions and concerns.

- Invite teachers from established programs to meet with new prospective EE and mainstream teachers to discuss issues of relevance to instructional personnel. (To locate programs in your area, obtain directories listed in Appendix D.)

- Partner new EE schools with established EE schools, using e-mail or conventional means of communication.

- Invite researchers and other experts familiar with EE to speak with teachers.

- Prepare information sheets about issues of concern to teachers. ERIC is a useful source of prepared information.

- Make relevant published materials on EE available to teachers.

- Establish study groups of teachers to discuss ongoing and new issues in the program.

- In the U.S., find out about *Advocates for Language Learning* and encourage EE teachers to attend their meetings. In Canada, *Canadian Association for Immersion Teachers* holds an annual conference devoted to the professional development of immersion teachers. (For contact information, see Appendix C.)

- Arrange for mainstream teachers who work in the all-English program to view and discuss video or other media presentations that document successful programs and approaches relevant to your proposal. (For list of informational videotapes, see Appendix D.)

- Where possible, reassure teachers in the regular program that their jobs are not at risk because of this new program.

Advocacy with School Principals and Administrators

School principals and administrators at the district or state level are likely to have many of the same questions and con-

Voices from the Field

Convincing Teachers that Two-Way Immersion Programs are a Good Idea

Esther Gaitan-Larocco
California State University
Chico, CA

Teacher's concerns about two-way immersion must be addressed early on in the process. Their concerns seem to vary depending on their exposure to bilingualism. In working with a district in northern California as it started a two-way immersion program, it became evident that the concerns of monolingual teachers differed from those of bilingual teachers. Furthermore, bilingual teachers' concerns also changed depending on the inclusion or exclusion of language minority students in the immersion program.

Monolingual teachers' concerns did not seem to distinguish between a foreign language immersion program for language majority students only and a two-way immersion program for both language majority and minority students. The main concern of the monolingual teachers was that the needs of the new immersion program would cast a shadow over the basic, neighborhood instructional program. Their concerns included unequal distribution of resources, increased demand for administrative support, possible curriculum changes, and to a lesser extent, the possible loss of the top students typically attending the neighborhood program. To address these concerns, monolin-

gual teachers were asked to participate in the steering committee and the various subcommittees when the two-way immersion program was being developed. This strategy was not implemented earlier, when the Spanish language immersion program was instituted in the district. This increase in the level of participation of monolingual teachers promoted a greater sense of ownership, kept them better informed, and provided a direct forum where questions could be answered and concerns assuaged.

One important question that needed to be addressed in the initial stages was why immersion in a second language was an effective instructional approach for language majority students and ineffective for language minority students.

A collaborative atmosphere was essential to ensure ongoing dialogues to facilitate understanding of the theoretical basis for the differences. For the most part, monolingual teachers needed to: (a) be informed, (b) participate in the process, and (c) share in the benefits of immersion for some of the school's children.

For the most part, bilingual teachers support the theoretical principles of immersion education.

However, many bilingual teachers in this district opposed the district's development of a Spanish language immersion program for language majority students in 1990. The opposition was rooted in the fact that it established a bilingual maintenance program promoting biliteracy in English and Spanish for language majority students, yet the same opportunity was denied for language minority students within the limitations of an early-exit transitional bilingual program. The issue was further exacerbated when the program was not established at any of the schools with existing bilingual programs. This decision was partially based on the notion that the majority parents would not participate in the Spanish language immersion program if it was housed in schools with a lower socio-economic population.

Four years later, in 1994, the bilingual teachers strongly supported the two-way immersion program to be housed at one of the district's schools with a bilingual program. Along with the overwhelming support came a few new concerns. Bilingual teachers, particularly non-native speakers of Spanish, were worried about the level of language proficiency two-way immersion would require of teachers. This was especially important to intermediate grade teachers, who had participated in the local transitional bilingual program for several years. As teachers in a program aimed at transitioning students into English-only instruction

(continued)

Voices from the Field (continued)

in the third or fourth grade, their use of Spanish for instruction had been very limited. Many felt they had lost the level of fluency they had when they entered the profession. Some of the non-native Spanish speaking teachers felt that a district-wide two-way immersion program would impede them from continuing to serve the language minority population, as intended when they started teaching. Therefore, there is a need for professional development opportunities for these teachers to further develop their proficiency in the target language of the two-way immersion program. These opportunities need to start prior to program implementation and continue after the program is implemented.

Another area of concern focuses on the percentage of time each language is to be used for instruction. A few teachers may question having initial reading instruction for English native speakers (ENSs) in their second language. They feel that ENSs need to be first taught to read in English. At times, there are questions about what may be the most effec-

tive percentage of language distribution. Should a 50/50 distribution start earlier than fifth grade so that students may be best prepared for English-only instruction at the junior high school level? Teachers must be informed about the various two-way immersion models and choose the model that best meets the needs of their student population in their community. There does not seem to be a clear understanding, particularly among monolingual administrators, that the language at risk for both groups of two-way immersion students is the target language and not English. This concern about increasing the percentage of English used for instruction seems to be gaining strength in this post-Proposition 227 era. Districts, maintaining two-way immersion programs through waivers, feel at risk of losing the two-way program unless their students continue to do well on English academic measures.

There is one final concern that until recently has not been raised—the equity of instructional strategies for both language groups. Teachers and administrators are becoming

aware of the importance of having professional development in the area of instructional strategies for both groups. Much of the impetus in this area is concerned with providing comprehensible input and conceptual development for the second language learner of the program's target language. However, are these same strategies meeting the needs of the native speakers in the program? How is their primary language developed? Are the same instructional activities aimed at second language learners in the initial stages of language acquisition challenging the native speakers? Future research needs to focus on classroom discourse, instructional strategies, and grouping practices at the lower grade levels of two-way programs. Two-way immersion programs have demonstrated positive academic outcomes for both groups of students. Now, it is necessary to ask some harder questions to fine-tune this effective bilingual program model. In this post-227 era, we cannot afford any missed opportunities to further improve the academic performance of language minority students.

---

cerns as parents and teachers. Thus, many of the sources of information and ways of working with these groups that we have already identified are also pertinent for principals and administrators. At the same time, principals and administrators will have questions and concerns about specific aspects of the administration of such programs (see Table 9.2 for some examples). It can be advantageous to invite other school principals and administrators who have had some experience with EE programs to meet with those being initiated to these programs. Administrators in nearby schools are an obvious source of support. If this is not possible, encourage principals and administrators to attend the meetings of

professional groups, like *ALL, TESOL*, or *ACTFL*, where they can meet with others who have had more experience than they have. (Organization contact information is listed in Appendix C; Program Directories in Appendix D.)

The single most important influence on principals and administrators is parents. Thus, it is important to arrange for meetings between supportive parents and the principal of the school which is likely to host the program. Schools with principals who are likely to support enriched language and culture education should be considered first as the site for new programs; getting the support of resistant principals and maintaining effective programs in schools without the full support of the principal is difficult at best. Thus, for both the initial and long term success of programs, supportive principals are extremely important.

Here are some suggestions for working with principals and administrators:

- Find out what principals' and administrators' attitudes are towards the kind of program or change you are proposing and then identify ways in which negative attitudes or fears can be addressed directly.

- Arrange for principals and administrators with experience in EE programs to meet with principals and administrators who are becoming familiar with EE programs.

- Familiarize principals and administrators with associations and other professional resources that they can draw on for information and support (see Appendices C and D).

- Identify to principals ways in which the new program will be good for the school, set them apart, and bring recognition to them.

- Present information that is relevant to the concerns of principals and administrators in succinct, clear ways so that they can grasp it quickly and easily— administrators are often overextended and do not have much time to spend acquiring new information.

- Make sure that principals and administrators are aware of the positive effects EE has on student achievement, especially when it comes to standardized tests for which they are held accountable.

- Recognize that principals and administrators often have to contend with the opposition of others, despite their own personal views, and need information and arguments that they can use to support innovation in their schools.

- Be prepared to serve as a resource for principals and administrators so that they are spared excessive additional work. In other words, make it easy for principals and administrators to support your program.

Advocacy in the Community

Important members of the community to consider are parents, school board members, and others with direct involvement with schools and educational decisions in the district. These individuals and groups should be given first consideration because, once convinced, they can be important allies who can convince others of the merits of your proposals. Local businesses and business leaders can also be important allies and sources of support if they are made aware of the professional and financial advantages of bilingualism and biculturalism. It is important to communicate early on in your advocacy efforts and regularly thereafter with individuals or groups who are in key decision-making positions or have public visibility so that they do not feel ignored or sidestepped. Key decision-makers want to be current on issues in their jurisdiction so that they can maintain their positions of authority. It is important to respect this.

When it comes to community advocacy, it is important to emphasize the long history of EE programs, the extensive record of research demonstrating their effectiveness, and most importantly, the enriched nature of EE programs. EE programs give parents and the community more value for their money because students acquire functional proficiency in a second language and familiarity with another culture at no expense to their primary language development, academic achievement, or home culture. The advantages that graduates of EE programs have in the local, national, and global job markets have been a primary motivation for communities to establish EE programs, and they are likely to be advantages in other communities that are contemplating starting one. These are all important points that need to be made to school boards who make critical decisions about program offerings in the district—be sure to establish extensive and solid relationships with members of the school board.

Here are some ways of working with the community to promote EE:

- Meet with important members of the community individually to seek their support. Once they are supportive, they can be invited to speak to others on behalf of EE.

- Reinforce the economic advantages to individual students and the community at large that result from knowing other languages and cultures. Link the goals of EE to the global economy, the international marketplace, and international travel and trade.

- Highlight the existence of successful bilingual forms of education in countries such as Spain, Japan, Hong Kong, Sweden, and so on so that community leaders realize that embarking on a program of enriched education will put their community at the forefront of other innovative communities around the world.

- Make sure that members of the school board are fully informed of your proposal and its merits. It can be useful to apprise them of the attitudes or policy statements of professional organizations, such as *Teachers of English to Speakers of Other Languages* (TESOL), *National Association for the Education of Young Children, National Council of Teachers of English* (NCTE) (see Appendix C), about the advantages of multilingualism and multiculturalism. School board mem-

Voices from the Field

School-Community Partnerships for Bilingualism

Alain Weber,
Head Master
The International School of Indiana
Indianapolis, IN

The International School of Indiana has an unusual start-up story. In 1991 a group of business, political, and educational leaders gathered as the International Issues Task Force to discuss Indiana in a changing world. These leaders focused their discussion on education, services, and transportation. In regard to education, their recommendation was simple: "If Indiana and its people are to thrive, the state must actively participate in the world community and especially its economy. To do so the state must attract more foreign corporations and make Indiana students more internationally competitive."

The Task Force recommended the establishment of an independent school in Indianapolis. Not just any school with some kind of global awareness component, but a school offering American and foreign students a program of academic excellence in which the development of fluency in more than one language is an integral part of the curriculum. The school was to function in French and offer an International Baccalaureate using the French *lycee* model and curriculum. The recommendations published, the saga was underway. A volunteer board emerged: some members came from the Task Force and others came as they saw the creation of such a school as urgent and vital.

The business community from Hitachi to Eli Lilly & Co. gave money, lent support and expertise to the leaders of the school. Not only did the support come at the onset from leaders but also from parents. It is interesting to note that the parents who came shared these visions:

They wanted their children to receive a better education; one in which bilingualism was important but so was the implementation of a rigorous and challenging curriculum based on European schooling. This was to be a truly "international school."

They also shared the ideal of bringing children of diverse national, ethnic, socioeconomic, and racial backgrounds together to learn and to appreciate each other's differences.

The other vital link has been the ability of the school to raise funds. Before the school doors were opened, $200,000 was received as well as in-kind donations. The donations came in large proportions from local, national, and international corporations.

Teachers were recruited in Spain, Mexico, France, and Indianapolis. They were not language specialists but trained elementary educators who are on leave from their respective Ministries of Education. They brought with them their methodologies, their pedagogies, and their cultures to enrich the programs.

We were ready to start on September 1, 1994. The School opened with 38 pioneer students: Pre K–Grade 2. In its fifth year of operation now, there are 264 students attending the International School of Indiana from a three-year-old program to Grade 7. From its beginning to its incredible growth, the emergence of the International School of Indiana is unusual.

bers see themselves as educational leaders in their community and, as such, they will be interested in the views and attitudes of other educational leaders about the innovation you are seeking.

- Make sure that members of the community are also

aware of the advantages of the program you are supporting. (Some of these advantages were discussed in Chapter 1.)

- Invite important and prominent members of the community to meetings of parents and educators who are supportive of EE so that they can become familiar with these programs and witness the level of support they enjoy in the community.

- Form an advisory committee of interested and important community members and publicize the workings of this group and their support.

- Arrange for important members of the community to visit established EE programs so that they have first hand experience of their success. (Directories of Programs are listed in Appendix D.)

- Share newspaper articles or other media coverage of successful programs elsewhere in the state or country with community leaders so that the successes of the programs in other communities are validated.

- Emphasize the educational advantages that result from EE—the quality of public education is an important issue to most community leaders and evidence of the academic success of EE can go a long way to soliciting their support.

- Point out the positive cross-cultural and inter-group outcomes of EE programs since these are issues that community leaders often deem very important.

- Invite media coverage of significant events connected to EE programs as they occur so that their successes and advantages remain fresh in people's minds and the programs are seen to be desirable and successful. As they say, "Nothing succeeds like success."

Advocacy with State and National Leaders

In the category "state and national leaders," we include (a) professional educational experts and leaders who can speak on behalf of EE and your efforts to institute an EE program in your district, (b) national associations with some professional connection to EE, such as *Advocates for Language Learning, Teachers of English to Speakers of Other Languages,* and *American Council on the Teaching of Foreign Languages (see Appendix C),* that can provide resources and support in your advocacy efforts, and (c) political individuals and groups with some influence in education. On the one hand, it is a matter of identifying state and national leaders who can provide support and resources in your efforts to institute an EE program and, on the other hand, it is a matter of convincing key state or national leaders of the value of your initiative in order to enlist their active support and, conversely, to minimize their active opposition. Open support from state or national leaders can be invaluable in giving your efforts credibility

and garnering support from others. As the adage "you can't be a prophet in your own land" suggests, sometimes *outsiders* have more credibility and influence in effecting change than *insiders*—take advantage of this tendency whenever possible. Local and district leaders can often be encouraged to support innovation if it has the stamp of approval of state and national leaders. At the same time, many state and national leaders, especially professional educators and educational associations, have resources that can be brought to bear to further your innovations. Inform yourself about these groups and what they have to offer. (Contact information for key organizations is provided in Appendix C.)

Here are some ways of involving state and national leaders in your advocacy efforts:

- Collect information and other material from state and national educational leaders and associations that are pertinent to your proposal to institute EE and prepare information packets for distribution; many organizations, such as *Teachers of English to Speakers of Other Languages, National Council of Teachers of English, National Education Association,* have prepared policy statements that highlight the importance of cross-cultural understanding, proficiency in other languages, and other outcomes that figure prominently in EE programs. (See Appendix C.)

- If possible, invite state or national leaders with expertise, experience, or an interest in EE to speak to local parent, educational, and community groups on behalf of your initiative—once again, the support of outsiders can sometimes be even more significant than that of insiders.

- Send copies of newspaper articles or other media coverage of your program to state and national leaders so that they are familiar with your efforts and can give a supporting hand, if the opportunity arises.

- Attend or make presentations at public meetings or conferences of state and national associations that will serve to publicize and give credibility to your efforts. Public attention to successful programs is invaluable in maintaining support and garnering new support.

- Inform yourself of the proceedings of state and national meetings or conferences pertinent to EE and disseminate relevant information coming out of these meetings to others in your community, once again, to draw attention to your efforts and give them credibility.

Summary

In this chapter, we discussed the role of advocacy in initiating new EE programs and ensuring excellence in established programs. We pointed out that advocacy entails a number of interrelated components:

- understanding the general socio-political climate within which you are working
- identifying key stakeholders
- understanding the attitudes and views of key stakeholders toward the innovation you are proposing
- formulating appropriate responses to their concerns so that they become supporters

Advocacy implicates a number of different kinds of individuals and groups, including parents, teachers, principals and administrators, the local community, and professional and political leaders at state or national levels. Advocacy at the local level can be strengthened if strategic alliances are formed with advocacy groups at the state or national level. Professional advocacy groups, such as National Association for Bilingual Education, can provide resources that are not readily available at the local level. Among the groups we have identified as stakeholders, there is no doubt that parents have the largest vested interest in EE, and experience in other communities that have instituted EE programs has taught us that parents can provide the advocacy that is required to create and maintain effective EE programs. No other group is likely to come forward to provide the level of sustained advocacy that is required. Moreover, no other group has the power to bring about the changes that will make EE a reality in local schools.

Additional Resources

DeGaetano, Y. Williams, L.R. & Volk, D. (1988). *Kaleidoscope: A Multicultural Approach for the Primary School Classroom.* Upper Saddle River, NJ: Merrill, Prentice-Hall (see Chapter 10: *Advocacy & Change: Strategies for Teachers*)

Teaching for Change, Network on Educators on the Americas, P.O. Box 73038, Washington, D.C. 20056-3038.

Rethinking Schools (Resource for Equity & Social Justice), 1001 E. Keefe Ave. Milwaukee, WI 53212 www.rethinkingschools.org

APPENDIX A:
A GLOSSARY OF TERMS
FOR EE TEACHERS

Academic language   Academic language is the language used in the learning of academic subject matter in formal schooling contexts. It involves aspects of language strongly associated with literacy and academic achievement, including specific academic terms or technical language, and speech registers related to each field of study. For example, there is vocabulary, special expressions, and discourse patterns that are particularly useful for talking and writing about scientific subjects.

Additive bilingualism   A process by which individuals develop proficiency in a second language subsequent to or simultaneous with the development of proficiency in the primary language, without loss of the primary language; where the first language and culture are not replaced or displaced.

Authentic assessment   The multiple forms of assessment that evaluate students' learning and their attitudes and approaches toward learning during instructionally-relevant activities; for example using a rubric to assess students' language use during a social studies lesson. Authentic assessment reflects good instructional practices and the kinds of skills and knowledge useful to students in performing daily life and school activities.

Bilingualism   The ability to understand and use two languages in particular contexts and for particular purposes. Bilinguals can have the same levels of proficiency in both languages (advanced in both) or different levels of proficiency (advanced in one and beginning or intermediate in the other). Bilinguals do not necessarily have the same level of proficiency in all aspects of both languages: speaking, listening, reading, and writing.

Biculturalism   Near native-like knowledge of two cultures; includes the ability to respond effectively to the different demands of the two cultures.

Cause-effect diagram   A graphic organizer which explains the causes and effects of particular phenomena. For example, a cause-effect diagram might demonstrate the situations leading up to the Civil War or factors contributing to global warming.

Cognitive demand of instruction (also referred to as "*cognitive load*")   In order to determine the degree of difficulty of instruction provided in a second language, teachers must consider the cognitive demand of instructional activities for the learner (Cummins, 1984). This can only be done in relation to individual learners and learning contexts. How cognitively demanding or undemanding instruction may be for particular learners will depend on factors, such as the extent of students' prior knowledge, the cognitive complexity inherent in the instructional task, student interest in the topic, effectiveness of the teacher, mode and pace of presentation, etc. The more active cognitive involvement required, the more demanding the instruction. When the cognitive demand exceeds learners' current capabilities, instruction will not be comprehensible or effective.

Comprehensible input   Comprehensible input is a construct developed to describe understandable and meaningful language directed at second language learners under optimal conditions. It is characterized as the language the learner already knows plus a range of new language that is made comprehensible by the use of certain planned strategies (the use of concrete referents). Providing linguistic (familiar language), paralinguistic (facial expressions, gestures), situational (in a laboratory) and contextual support (visuals, graphic organizers, background information in L1) to students to facilitate comprehension of information.

Communicative competence   The ability to recognize and to produce language correctly, idiomatically, fluently, and appropriately in a variety of communicative settings. The term includes grammatical competence, sociolinguistic competence, discourse competence, and strategic competence, both orally and in writing. (see also *language proficiency*)

Conferences   Semi-structured face-to-face conversations between a student or small groups of students and teachers about work that students have completed or are currently working on. A portfolio conference, for example, is a conversation about work in a student's portfolio—the student describes to the teacher why a piece of work has been included, what its strengths and weaknesses are, how two pieces of work differ or show progress, how a piece of work could be improved, how the teacher could help the student make improvements, or any other issues that either participant feels is important. Teachers can use information gathered during conferences to tailor instruction to meet the needs, expectations, and goals of individual students.

Connect-two   A reading strategy that can be used prior to, during, and after reading. Given a list of words, students try to identify connections between any two words on the list and explain the rationale. For example, they might explain the connections between "benefit" and "benefactor."

Content-based second language instruction (*Most commonly, Content-based ESL*)   Instruction designed to promote the acquisition of a second language using non-language content as the basis for teaching. A second language learning approach in which second language teachers use instructional materials, learning tasks, and classroom techniques from academic content areas (science, social studies, mathematics) as the vehicle for developing second language, content, cognitive, and study skills (Crandall, 1992). While content may be the focus of instruction, the primary objectives of instruction are to promote language learning. Content-based approaches can be used to teach ESL or other second or foreign languages.

Content standard   A statement that defines what students are expected to know and be able to do in a content area. Content standards specify the subject-specific knowledge, skills, processes, and other understandings that teachers are expected to teach and students are expected to learn. When applied to language learning, a content standard identifies the specific language skills that a student knows in the target language. (see *performance standard* as a complement to content standard)

Context reduced/embedded instruction   In context-embedded instruction, a wide range of cues to meaning (paralinguistic and situational) are provided to support the verbal input. In comparison, context-reduced communication lacks such contextual support, and, thus, relies heavily on linguistic elaborations (Cummins, 1984). Successful interpretation of the teacher's or textbook's message depends heavily on knowledge of the language itself. For example, when explaining a complex process such as osmosis for the first time, if the process is fully elaborated in the teacher's linguistic descriptions, without the aid of demonstrations or models—this is context-reduced instruction.

Cooperative learning   Cooperative learning is an approach to instruction in which students work together in pairs or small groups on tasks that require cooperation among group/team members. Tasks are structured to ensure that all students contribute to the group's learning and provide support and encouragement to one another.

Cultural/experiential background knowledge (also, prior knowledge)   Conceptual change research stresses the primary role of prior knowledge and personal experience in the learning of new academic concepts. Likewise cognitive development theorists stress the importance of considering prior knowledge in imparting new information to students (Piaget, Vygotsky). The role of prior knowledge may be particularly important for students from diverse cultural backgrounds since their experiences are different than those of mainstream students (Atwater, 1994; Lee, Fradd & Sutman, 1995).

Culturally-relevant curriculum and instruction   The selection of culturally-relevant content, examples, modes of pres- entation, grouping structures, learning activities, reinforcers, motivational devices, and the like, to promote understanding and learning. This requires that teachers understand the beliefs, norms, and values of their learners in relationship to concepts being studied so that instruction can be provided in a way that respects learners' deeply held belief systems.

Developmental appropriateness   Setting cognitive, academic, and social demands that correspond to students' ages and grade levels.

Developmental bilingual education   Programs that serve language minority students who come to school proficient in languages other than English and have no or limited proficiency in English. The program is designed to develop and maintain full proficiency in the students' home language while promoting full proficiency in all aspects of English. Also sometimes referred to as late-exit bilingual education.

Dialogue journals   Written or orally-recorded discussions between students and teachers about school-related or other topics of interest to students. When shared with teachers on a regular basis, the contents of students' journals can provide teachers with useful information for individualizing instruction—for example, information about students' interests, school-related or out-of-school activities, learning styles and preferences, accomplishments and challenges. Journals can be written or spoken (using tape-recorders). Written journals can provide useful assessment information about students' writing skills. Oral dialogue journals can provide useful information about students' oral language development.

Early exit bilingual education (also referred to as *transitional bilingual education*)   is a type of school program in the U.S. for language minority students who do not speak English or have limited proficiency in English when they start schooling. The students' primary language is used for some curriculum instruction for a limited number of years (usually two or three). This approach aims to promote the students' mastery of academic material while they are learning English as a second language. These programs are intended to facilitate language minority students' transition to instruction in English only. These programs aim for full proficiency in oral and written English, but do not aim to maintain or develop the students' primary language. They often lead to subtractive bilingualism.

English immersion   (also referred to as *"English-only"* or *"sink-or-swim"*). There is no generally accepted definition or set of criteria to define English immersion programs. They are recommended by some educators and policy-makers as programs for English language learners in the U.S. It can refer to regular programs for native English speaking students where English is the only language of instruction. They may or may not include special provisions for English language learners, such as ESL instruction. They aim for proficiency in oral and written English and full academic achievement; they do not aim to maintain or develop language minority students' primary language or culture.

English language learners   (sometimes referred to as *"limited English proficient," LEP,* or *language minority* students) are students who begin their schooling in the U.S. (or other English-speaking countries) with no or limited proficiency in English, the usual medium of academic instruction. These students must learn English as a second language for both academic and social purposes in order to benefit fully from instruction through English.

Enriched education   Educational programs that emphasize challenging standards in the core curriculum domains while enriching students' development in both their first and a second language. These programs aim for full proficiency in two languages, an understanding and appreciation of the cultures associated with those languages, and high levels of achievement in all core academic domains.

First (native/primary) language   The language which was learned and used first by students regardless of their later proficiency in that language.

Foreign language learning   The acquisition of a language that is not used routinely by the individual or others in the individual's day-to-day social environment. For example, German would be a foreign language for an individual living in a community where English is used for all communication. This contrasts with second language learning. (see *entry*)

Graphic organizers   Visual or pictorial representations of key concepts in a particular area of study. Graphic organizers are visually displayed in ways that help to explain the interrelationships among the main ideas. (see also *cause-effect diagram/Venn diagram*)

Immersion (foreign/second language immersion) programs   Programs which serve language majority students (native English-speaking students in North America), and which use a second or foreign language to teach at least 50% of the students' program of study during the elementary or secondary grades. Immersion programs vary with respect to the amount of the second language that is used for instruction and the grade levels during which immersion in the second language is offered.

KWL chart   An abbreviation for: *What I know, What I want to learn, What I learned*. An open-ended technique designed by Donna Ogle (1986) to help readers identify what they know and what they want to learn before reading an expository passage. After reading, they evaluate what they actually did learn.

Language majority students   In the U.S., refers to students who come from homes in which English is primarily spoken.

Language minority students   Individuals who come from a minority group and speak a minority language; non-native speakers of English. These students, who come from homes in which a language other than English is primarily spoken, may or may not be proficient in English.

Language proficiency   The ability to use language accurately and appropriately in its oral and written forms in a variety of settings. Proficiency varies as a function of the context, purpose, and content of communication.

Late exit bilingual education   (see *Developmental bilingual education*)

Learning logs Written records in which students reflect about their learning in a particular class or course of study. In their logs, students clarify their thoughts, connect with what they already know, record different ways of doing things, and reflect on their understandings. Information from students' learning logs provides teachers insights about their students' learning experiences in content classes that can help the teachers tailor language instruction to meet the students' language needs in their other classes. Information from logs can also reveal content strengths and weaknesses. This is information that the teacher can then use to plan follow-up instruction.

Learning strategies Learning strategies are mental activities or actions that assist in enhancing learning outcomes. They may include metacognitive strategies (planning for learning, monitoring one's own comprehension and production, evaluating one's performance), cognitive strategies (mental or physical manipulation of the material), or social/affective strategies (interacting with another person to assist learning, using self-talk to persist at a difficult task until resolution). Active engagement and high performance appear to be positively related to the use of cognitive strategies (Oxford, 1990).

Learning style A broad descriptive term which refers to the characteristic ways in which an individual learns. It includes modality or perceptual preferences (visual vs. auditory), cognitive style (analytic/reflective vs. global/intuitive), social/emotional characteristics (individual vs. group learning, peer vs. adult feedback), and physical needs during learning (need to recline, eat, be near a natural light source, etc.).

Match Mine A cooperative structure where students work with a partner and strive to have the partner complete a task identical to his/her own. One type of match mine involves the collaboration of two partners with partial information. They share the unique information (orally or in writing) to complete a task. Another variation is for a student to give oral or written directions to another student to complete a visual task identical to his/her own. No peeking is allowed!

Numbered Heads Together In order to check on group members' subject mastery following instruction, the students break into groups and the teacher assigns numbers to each student (1, 2, 3, 4). Then the teacher asks questions requiring that team members consult with one another to make sure everyone knows the answer to the question. The teacher then calls one number and the student(s) assigned that number is(are) called upon to answer. There are 4 steps: 1) students break into groups and each group numbers off, 2) teacher asks a question, 3) students put their heads together and make sure they all can answer the question, and 4) the teacher calls a number and that student answers.

Open Word Sort A pre-, during, and post-reading strategy. Student pairs are given words written on individual strips of paper. They collaborate to categorize the words by identifying and explaining relationships among them. Students then read and reorganize the words in a way that would be effective for teaching key information to others. Following the reading they use the resorted words to explain the reading or answer questions.

Pair Read *(Also called Partner Read.)* Refers to various strategies for having students read with a partner. Radio-Read *(also called Popcorn Reading)* is one such strategy. Students take turns reading, but the reader decides when to stop (always at the end of a sentence). Since the exact stopping point is not predetermined, the partner must follow along closely.

Performance standards Also, sometimes referred to as *"performance criteria."* Statements that refer to the degree to which students have met a particular content standard. Performance standards specify how students will demonstrate their knowledge and skills as well as at what level they must perform in order to be considered as meeting the standard.

Phonological awareness Awareness of the acoustic or individual sound elements that make up a word and the ability to manipulate those elements independent of the word of which they are a part. Children's awareness that words are made up of individual speech sounds—the word *"cat"* consists of three sounds: *[c], [a],* and *[t]*. With such knowledge, children can then learn to associate the written letters of a language, such as English, with the sounds they represent.

Plot Line A visual representation of the action or events in a story. It has five parts: exposition, rising action, climax, falling action, and resolution. Students record the events from a story that represent each part on a plot line provided or they draw the line themselves and label it.

Portfolio assessment A portfolio is a purposeful collection of a student's work that documents their efforts, achievements, and progress over time in given areas of learning, either language or subject matter, or both.

Primary language   The language or languages that children acquire naturally, without instruction, during the preschool years from parents, siblings, and others in their social environment. A child can have more than one primary language if he or she acquires more than one language during the period of primary language development. Learning two languages at the same time is also sometimes referred to as simultaneous bilingual acquisition.

Q-Matrix Materials   Consist of Q-Dice, Q-Spinners, Q-Strips, Q-Chips and Quadrant Cards. Question prompts are selected by spinning, rolling, or reading strips or cards. Based on the prompt, students generate questions to ask of fellow students (Why...?; What...?). Q-Matrix, Q-Materials and Q-Structure are ways to review information.

Radio Read   (see *Pair Read*)

Register   Specific features of discourse (talk or text) that is associated with specific academic subjects, such as math or science. Register involves the unique terms and expressions, meanings, and sentence structures that occur in talking or writing about a particular discipline.

Roundrobin/Roundtable   The teacher asks a question with many possible answers. Each student shares an idea with his or her teammates orally (roundrobin) or in writing (roundtable; paper goes around the table with each students contributing in turn). With simultaneous roundtable more than one pencil and paper are passed around the group at the same time.

Say Something   Children are invited to take turns saying something at intervals during the reading of a story; to respond personally to an engaging piece of literature. The focus is on reading to say something rather than reading to decode individual words.

Second language   Refers to a language learned by an individual after another language has already been acquired. In contrast to foreign languages, second languages are languages that are used in the larger community and, thus, have some functional value outside school. (see *second language learning*)

Second language learning   The acquisition of a language that is used by at least some members of the community in which the individual lives. For example, French is a second language for native-English speaking students living in Quebec; but, it is a foreign language for students living in Ames, Iowa.

Semantic map   (*Also referred to as "web diagram."*) A method for visually demonstrating the relationships among key components of stories or information about topics of study. Webs should include a central main concept, supporting details organized into categories, and connecting lines which show the relationships among the strands.

Sheltered Instruction   (*Also referred to as Sheltered English Instruction*).   Sheltered instruction is an approach in which students develop knowledge in specific subject areas through the medium of their second language. Teachers modify their use of English to teach core subjects (math, science) in order to ensure that the material is comprehensible to learners and that it promotes their second language development. They adjust the language demands of the lesson in many ways, such as by modifying speech rate and tone, simplifying vocabulary and grammar, repeating key words, phrases, or concepts, using context clues and models extensively, relating instruction to students' background knowledge and experience, and using certain methods familiar to language teachers (demonstrations, visuals, graphic organizers, or cooperative work) to make academic instruction understandable to students of different second language proficiency levels.

Sketch to Stretch   A reading strategy that helps students learn to visualize what they read. Individually, with a partner or team, students draw and share the mental images conveyed in a reading. They may also sketch the personal meaning of a reading.

Story Impression   A reading strategy that prompts students to creatively predict the plot of a story based on approximately seven words. The words should convey the main character, the setting, and the problem in the story. Students then read the story and compare their versions with the original.

Submersion (sink or swim education) programs
Programs which encourage students from language minority backgrounds to learn English as quickly as possible and give up their existing linguistic skills as well as assimilate to the dominant American culture as quickly as possible. English is used exclusively as the medium of instruction in these programs and there may or may not be any specialized support for English language learners. (*see English Immersion*)

Subtractive bilingualism A process in which individuals lose their primary language (and possibly culture) as they acquire a new language and culture. This occurs frequently in the case of language minority students who attend schools where no provision is made to maintain and develop their primary language.

Team Jigsaw (Also called "Jigsaw" when referring to individuals as experts; rather than teams). Each team becomes an "expert" on one aspect of a topic of study by working together. They then spread out to share their knowledge with others in the class; and all students are later assessed on the entire learning unit.

Think-Pair-Share First, students think to themselves on a topic provided by the teacher. Then, they pair up with another student to discuss it. Last, they share their thoughts with the class.

Three-Step Interview An activity designed to allow classmates to share information or experiences they have acquired about a topic of study. For steps one and two, students interview each other in pairs. First, one is the interviewer and one the respondent, and then they switch roles. During step three, students share with the group the information they learned by interviewing each other. For example, when studying the westward movement in the U.S., students might interview one another about their personal experiences moving and the hardships they faced.

Transitional bilingual education (see *early exit bilingual education*)

Two-way immersion (dual language immersion) A program which serves both language minority and language majority students in the same classrooms. These programs use each group of students' first language for academic instruction at certain points during they program. They aim for bilingualism and biculturalism for both groups of students. A combination of the Developmental Bilingual and Immersion program models.

Venn diagram A graphic organizer which shows how concepts are interrelated as well as how they are discrete. For example Venn diagrams might analyze two books to show how they are alike and how they are different in plot, characters, setting.

References

Atwater, M.M. (1994). Research on Cultural Diversity in the Classroom. In D.L. Gabel (Ed.). *Handbook of Research on Science Teaching and Learning* (pp. 558–576). New York: Macmillan.

Cummins, J. (1984). *Bilingualism and Special Education: Issues in Assessment and Pedagogy*. San Diego: College-Hill.

Crandall, J. (1992). Content-centered learning in the United States. *Annual Review of Applied Linguistics, 13*, 111–126.

Kagan, S. (1994). *Cooperative Learning*. San Clemente, CA: Kagan Cooperative Learning

Lambert, W. and Tucker, G. (1972). *Bilingual Education of Children: The St. Lambert Experiment*. Rowley, MA: Newbury House.

Lee, O., Fradd, S. & Sutman, F.X. (1995). Science Knowledge and Cognitive Strategy Use Among Culturally and Linguistically Diverse Students. *Journal of Research in Science Teaching, 32*, (8), 797–816.

Ogle, D. (1986). A Teaching Model that Develops Active Reading of Expository Text. *The Reading Teacher, 39*, 564–570.

Oxford, R. (1990). *Language Learning Strategies: What Every Teacher Should Know*. New York: Newbury House.

While the selection of materials has already been discussed in Chapter 3, we present a list of publishers of curriculum materials to aid EE teachers in their search for texts to use with students. We have concentrated on Spanish/English bilingual materials since this is the highest frequency language and due to its greater availability.

Publishers of Curriculum Materials Suitable for EE Programs

Asia Kids, 4480 Lake Forest Drive, Suite 302, Cincinnati, OH 45242-3726; 1-800-888-9681; www.afk.com

Capstone Press, P.O. Box 5669, Mankato, MN 56002-0669; 1-800-747-4992; www.capstone-press.com

Celebration Press, 1900 East Lake Avenue, Glenview, IL 60025; 1-800-552-2259; www.celebrationpress.com

Children's Book Press, 246 First Street. Suite 101, San Francisco, CA 94105; (415) 995-2200

Dominie Press, Inc., 1949 Kellogg Avenue, Carlsbad, CA 92008, 1-800-232-4570; www.dominie.com

Flame Co., 62 Water Street, Ossining-on-Hudson, NY 10562; 1-800-535-2632; fax (914) 769-4145

Franklin Electronic Publishers, One Franklin Plaza, Burlington, NJ 08016; 1-800-266-5626; www.franklin.com

Hampton-Brown Books, P.O. Box 369, Marina, CA 93933; 1-800-333-3510; www.hampton-brown.com

Haitiana Publications, 170-08 Hillside Ave., Jamaica, NY 11432, (718) 523-0175

Harcourt Brace/Holt, Rinehart and Winston, 6277 Sea Harbor Drive, Orlando, FL 32887; 1-800-225-5425; www.harcourtbrace.com

Heinle & Heinle, 20 Park Plaza, Boston MA 02116; 1-800-354-9706; www.heinle.com

Houghton Mifflin, (D.C. Heath) 222 Berkeley Street, Boston, MA 02116; 1-800-733-2828; www.eduplace.com/main.html

JACP, Inc., 414 East 3rd Avenue, P.O. Box 367, San Mateo, CA 94401 (Asian; Southeast Asian Languages)

Kagan Cooperative Learning, P.O. Box 72008, San Clemente, CA 92674-9208; 1-800-WEE CO-OP; www.kagancooplearn.com

The Learning Connection, P.O. Box 518, 19 Devane Street, Frostproof, FL 33843; 1-800-338-2282

Lectorum, 111 Eighth Avenue, Suite 804, New York, NY 10011; 1-800-345-5946; www.lectorum.com

McGraw Hill, 220 East Danieldale Road, Desoto, TX 75115 (Merrill/McMillan); 1-800-442-9685; www.mmh-school.com/products/bil3.html

Modern Curriculum Press, 4350 Equity Drive, Columbus, OH 43216; 1-800-321-3106; www.mcschool.com

Niños, P.O. Box 1603, Seacaucus, NJ 07096; 1-800-634-3304; www.ninos@genesisdirect.com

Perma-Bound, 617 Esat Vandalia Road, Jacksonville, IL 62650; 1-800-637-6581; www.perma-bound.com

Santillana, 2105 N.W. 86th Avenue, Miami, FL 33122; 1-800-245-8584; www.insite-network.com/santillana

Scholastic, 2931 East McCarty Street, Jefferson City, MO 65101; 1-800-325-6149; www.scholastic.com

Scott Foresman/Addison Wesley, 1900 East Lake Avenue, Glenview, IL 60025; 1-800-552-2259; www.sf.aw.com

Silver Burdett & Ginn, 4350 Equity Drive, P.O. Box 2649, Columbus, OH 43216; 1-800-848-9500; www.sbgschool.com

Steck-Vaughn Company, P.O. Box 26015, Austin, TX 78755; 1-800-531-5015; www.steck-vaughn.com

Shortland Publications, (Storyteller/Sra. Sabiduria Book Collections), 50 South Steele, Suite 755, Denver, CO 80209; 1-800-775-9995; www.shortland.com

APPENDIX C:
USEFUL ORGANIZATIONS, RESOURCE CENTERS,
PROFESSIONAL PERIODICALS AND JOURNALS

Useful Organizations and Resource Centers

Advocates for Language Learning, P.O. Box 4962, Culver City, CA 90231; (310) 313-3333

American Council on the Teaching of Foreign Languages, 6 Executive Plaza, Yonkers, NY 10701-6801; (914) 963-8830; www.actfl.org

Association for Supervision and Curriculum Development, 1703 North Beauregard Street, Alexandria, VA 22311-1714; 1-800-933-ASCD; www.ascd.org

Canadian Association of Immersion Teachers, (Association canadienne des professeurs d'immersion), 176 rue Gloucester, Suite 310, Ottawa, ON, Canada K2P 0A6; (613) 567-2223

Canadian Parents for French, 176 rue Gloucester, Suite 310, Ottawa, ON, Canada K2P 0A6; (613) 567-2223

Center for Applied Linguistics, 4646 40th Street, N.W., Washington, D.C. 20016-1859; (202) 362-0700; www.cal.org

Center for Research on Education, Diversity & Excellence, University of California, College Eight, Room 201, 1156 High Street, Santa Cruz, CA 95064; (831) 459-3500; www.crede.ucsc.edu or www.cal.org/crede

Council for Exceptional Children, 1920 Association Drive, Reston, VA 20191-1589, 1-888-CEC-SPED, www.cec.sped. org; also houses the ***ERIC Clearinghouse on Disabilities and Gifted Education***, 1-800-328-0272

ERIC Clearinghouse on Assessment and Evaluation, The Catholic University of America, 210 O'Boyle Hall, Washington, D.C. 20064, 1-800-464-3742; ericae.net

ERIC Clearinghouse on Languages and Linguistics, Center for Applied Linguistics; 4646 40th Street, N.W., Washington, D.C. 20016-1859; 1-800-276-9834; eric.syr.edu/ericll

ERIC Clearinghouse on Science, Mathematics, and Environmental Education, The Ohio State University, 1929 Kenny Road, Columbus, OH 43210; 1-800-276-0462; www.ericse.ohio-state.edu

ERIC Clearinghouse on Social Studies/Social Science Education, Indiana University, Social Studies Development Center, 2805 East 10th Street, Suite 120, Bloomington, IN 47408; 1-800-266-3815; www.indiana.edu/~ssdc/eric-chess.html

ERIC Clearinghouse on Rural Education and Small Schools, 1031 Quarrier Street, Charleston, WV 25325; 1-800-624-9120; www.ael.org/~eric/eric.html

ERIC Clearinghouse on Urban Education, Box 40, Teachers College, Columbia University, New York, NY 10027; 1-800-601-4868; eric-web.tc.columbia.edu

International Reading Association, 800 Barksdale Road, P.O. Box 8139, Newark, DE 19714-8139; (302) 731-1600; www.ira.org

National Association for Bilingual Education, 1220 L Street, N.W., Suite 605, Washington; D.C. 20005-4018, (202) 898-1829; www.nabe.org

National Association for the Education of Young Children, 1509 16th Street, N.W., Washington, D.C. 20036-1426; (202) 232-8777; www.naeyc.org

National Board for Professional Teaching Standards, 1730 Rhode Island Avenue, Suite 909, Washington, D.C. 20036; 1-800-22-TEACH; www.nbpts.org

National Clearinghouse for Bilingual Education, The George Washington University, Center for the Study of Language and Education, 2011 Eye Street, N.W., Suite 200, Washington, D.C. 20006; 1-800-321-NCBE; www.ncbe.gwu.edu

National Council of Teachers of English, 1111 West Kenyon Road, Urbana, IL 61801; 1-800-369-6283; www.ncte.org

National Education Association, 1201 16th Street, N.W., Washington, D.C. 20036; (202) 833-4000; www.nea.org

National Foreign Language Center, 1619 Massachusetts Avenue, N.W., Washington D.C. 20036; (202) 667-8100

National K–12 Foreign Language Resource Center, Iowa State University, Ames, IA 50011; nflrc@iastate.edu

National Network for Early Language Learning (NNELL), c/o The Center for Applied Linguistics, 4646 40th Street, N.W., Washington, D.C. 20016-1859; (202) 429-9292; www.cal.org

Teachers of English to Speakers of Other Languages, 700 South Washington Street, Suite 200, Alexandria, VA, 22314; (703) 836-0774; www.tesol.edu

Professional Periodicals and Journals

Applied Linguistics

Applied Psycholinguistics

Bilingual Research Journal

Canadian Modern Language Review

Educational Leadership

International Journal of Bilingualism

Foreign Language Annals

Language Learning

Modern Language Journal

TESOL Journal

TESOL Quarterly

Informational Videotapes

Proud of Two Languages, 1995, Canadian Parents for French, 309 Cooper Street, Ottawa, Canada K2P 0G5

Learning Together: Two-Way Bilingual Immersion Programs (VS6) and Profile of Effective Two-Way Bilingual Teaching: Sixth Grade (VS5), Bilingual Research Center, UCSC, Social Science II, 1156 High Street, Santa Cruz, CA 95064

Teaching in the Immersion Classroom (Series), 1990, Montgomery County Public Schools, Office of Instruction and Program Development, Division of Academic Skills, 850 Hungerford Drive, Rockville, MD, 20850-1747

Two-Way Bilingual Programs of Excellence, Fall, 1998, New York State Education Department, Office of Bilingual Education, 89 Washington Avenue, Room 367 EBA, Albany, NY, 12234

Directories of Programs

Directory of Total and Partial Immersion Language Programs in U.S. Schools, 1997, Compiled by Nancy Rhodes and Toya Lynch, Center for Applied Linguistics, 4646 40th Street, N.W., Washington, D.C. 20016-1859; www.cal.org/crede (under databases/directories on home-page)

Directory of Two-Way Immersion Programs in the U.S. (and yearly Supplements), Center for Applied Linguistics, 4646 40th Street, N.W., Washington D.C. 20016-1859; www.cal.org/crede

APPENDIX E:
INDEX TO TABLES
AND FIGURES

 **INDEX**